Histories of the Irish Future

Histories of the Irish Future

BRYAN FANNING

Bloomsbury Academic
An imprint of Bloomsbury Publishing Plc

B L O O M S B U R Y
LONDON · NEW DELHI · NEW YORK · SYDNEY

Bloomsbury Academic

An imprint of Bloomsbury Publishing Plc

50 Bedford Square	1385 Broadway
London	New York
WC1B 3DP	NY 10018
UK	USA

www.bloomsbury.com

BLOOMSBURY and the Diana logo are trademarks of Bloomsbury Publishing Plc

First published 2015

© Bryan Fanning, 2015

British Library Cataloguing-in-Publication Data
A catalogue record for this book is available from the British Library.

ISBN:	HB:	978-1-4725-2645-8
	PB:	978-1-4725-3295-4
	ePDF:	978-1-4725-2898-8
	ePub:	978-1-4725-2372-3

Library of Congress Cataloging-in-Publication Data
A catalog record for this book is available from the Library of Congress.

Typeset by RefineCatch Limited, Bungay, Suffolk
Printed and bound in Great Britain

CONTENTS

ACKNOWLEDGEMENTS

This book is the product of many conversations mostly with friends and colleagues at University College Dublin. It was born out of the opportunities that UCD gave me to be part of an intellectual community of scholars, one that exists on no organisational chart or website or in any managerial map of what multi-disciplinary synergies might look like. It was conceived in an out-of-hours invisible college of shared manuscripts, debate and conviviality. I wish to thank in particular Professor Andrew Carpenter, Professor Gerald Casey, Professor John Coakley, Professor Tony Fahey, Professor Tom Garvin, Dr Andreas Hess, Dr Kevin Howard, Professor Tom Inglis, Professor Michael Laffan, Dr Ivar McGrath and Professor Geraldine Meaney. Thanks also to Joan Maher and Neil Fanning who gave me a room of my own.

CHAPTER ONE

Modest proposals and Irish futures

This is a book about shifting understandings of the predicaments facing Irish society from the seventeenth to the early twenty-first centuries. Histories of the Irish future, like the science fictions of yesteryear, can be mined for insights into the hopes and fears of the times when these were written. Twelve interpretations of the forces shaping Ireland and related efforts to influence its future are presented as a series of documentaries on Irish intellectual history. The bigger picture that I address is a history of understandings of the crises that the Irish, however defined, have faced. Over the course of almost four centuries intellectual, ideological, ethnic and religious vantage points inevitably shift. What is meant by Ireland changes over time. The crises facing Ireland as understood by eighteenth-century Protestant patriots inevitably differed from those perceived by subsequent Catholic nationalists. The intellectual vantage points through which Irish crises were defined and contested also shifted over time. The very taxonomies that might be used to classify the writings of the twelve protagonists that I examine were also in flux.

Some of these are widely acknowledged as major intellectual figures outside Ireland. William Petty is regarded as one of the founders of political economy and economics as well as an important figure in Irish history. Edmund Burke, Thomas Malthus and Friedrich Engels were internationally influential thinkers who wrote insightfully about crises affecting Ireland. Each placed Irish dilemmas in wider contexts. It would be implausible to write John Mitchel, James Connolly or Conor Cruise O'Brien out of the history of debates about Ireland's future. Cases are made for the inclusion of William Molyneux, Richard Whately and Jerimiah Newman as key figures in the history of the ideas and debates that shaped Ireland. Of these Molyneux was arguably the most influential. He became a totemic influence on the Protestant patriots of the Irish Ascendency. Whately and Newman respectively articulated anxieties about the decline of Protestant power during the nineteenth century and about the decline of Catholic power a century later. Both left extensive bodies of writing about the dilemmas, as they understood them, arising from the waning power and influence of the churches they represented.

The subjects of this book have been for the most part politically engaged intellectuals who left significant bodies of writings on predicaments facing Irish society. For much of Irish history women were mostly invisible within public intellectual life for the same reasons that they were also marginalised in other domains. Writing was integral to Hanna Sheehy Skeffington's activism more so than for other iconic early twentieth-century feminists and Republican women. For this reason she has been selected for inclusion here. In addition to decades of journalism and some pamphlets she left an extensive personal archive. The choice of which living writer to include on Ireland's most recent crisis was not difficult. More so and better than any of his contemporaries, Fintan O'Toole has written about the shortcomings of Irish public morality that precipitated Ireland's near economic collapse.

With a few exceptions I was not drawn to ideologues that became dogmatically fixed on some political position or set of beliefs and thereafter ignored other perspectives or changing circumstances. Like politicians who are always 'on message' such figures reveal little of their personal understanding of wider dilemmas or of their own inner complexities. Cardinal Paul Cullen, the nineteenth-century architect of Catholic power fits this profile, but his nemesis Whately, who presided over the decline of the Established Church, does not. Bishop Jeremiah Newman exemplified twentieth-century Catholic orthodoxy but continually engaged with social change. Patrick Pearse, for all his importance as a cultural nationalist intellectual and revolutionary, falls into this camp but Connolly, who struggled to reconcile socialism and ethnic nationalism, does not.[1] Many of their efforts to influence the future ended in apparent failure. They made history but not necessarily in ways or at times of their own choosing. For example, it proved difficult to advance universal ideals such as socialism, republicanism or feminism (as the cases of Connolly and Sheehy Skeffington reveal) in an Ireland divided along religious and ethnic lines.

In making sense of their writings I locate the twelve within or in opposition to three traditions or sets of thought about politics and society. Viewed from the twenty-first century it is useful, I argue, to categorise Irish thought within conservative, liberal and republican traditions as these have developed, warped and shifted over time. For example, Edmund Burke, since regarded as a conservative philosopher, was in his time a Whig opponent of absolute monarchism, not a Tory. The nineteenth-century Liberal Party that grew out of the Whigs came to be intertwined with Catholic nationalism yet late-nineteenth and twentieth-century cultural nationalists were often explicitly opposed to liberalism. Hopes for a universalist Irish Republicanism were stymied by sectarianism. While republicans archetypically stood for a secular state republicanism in the Irish case was often a byword for Catholic ethnic nationalism, particularly in Northern Ireland. And any given time these traditions often intermingled like sets on a Venn diagram.

Ireland drew many of its intellectual ideas and debates from other countries, most notably republicanism from France and America, liberalism and conservatism from Britain and Catholic conservatism and the nationalisms within which all these ideas might be packaged from continental Europe. However, Irish experiences of colonialism, penal laws, famine or sectarian conflict have lent Irish writers some distinct vantage points. For many nationalist and Catholic intellectuals the new science of Francis Bacon came to be implicated in post-Elizabethan colonialism. Jonathan Swift lampooned, with serious intent, the scientific Royal Dublin Society positivism of Petty and Molyneux, the subjects of the next two chapters. Nineteenth-century critics of colonialism such as Mitchel influentially opposed liberal political economy ideas of progress. After independence some isolationist nationalists saw Ireland as locked into an existential conflict between culture and economy.

The efforts of various Irish intellectuals to conjure a nation state into existence followed the playbook of nationalists elsewhere. Shared national identities were made possible by mass literacy and the promotion of national literatures. As elsewhere intellectuals projected the Irish nation back into history, depicting it as a primordial entity, one now to be recovered, as a nation once again when in fact what was being proposed was something new. Thomas Davis's Young Irelander movement was inspired by Giuseppe Manzzini's Young Italy. The romantic nationalism that fuelled the 1916 Rising had been a European-wide phenomenon. Gaelic revivalism coincided with ideals of a Catholic restoration that would somehow undo the Reformation and the Enlightenment. Irish utopias were not so much built on belief in progress as on hopes for religious and cultural restorations that might somehow turn back the clock on the influence of the Reformation and the Enlightenment.

In the decades before and after independence the presiding genius of Irish poetry who channelled the *Geist* of Irish nationalism was W. B. Yeats, an anti-modernist who professed to despise the filthy modern tide. Yeats appears in a number of chapters, whether for a poem that conjures up the spirit of Mitchel, as an object of obsession for Conor Cruise O'Brien or, in the concluding chapter, as an intellectual force in his own right. O'Brien like Yeats played the role of iconoclast to the hilt but, in his obsessions with nationalism and its discontents, swam in the main current of twentieth-century Irish intellectual life.

Irish nationalisms cannot be really understood without considering the influence of a range of conservatisms. Some figures examined in this book might be categorised as conservatives but what they stood for and against was by no means homogenous. Burke feared the destructive influence of the French Revolution. He advocated progressive constitutional politics of the kind subsequently realised by Daniel O'Connell as the means to Catholic emancipation. In no sense did Burke call for the restoration of some bucolic past state of affairs. Mitchel from the mid-nineteenth century depicted the emergence of liberal political economy as the last conquest of Ireland. Its enemies were his friends. He was a reactionary conservative who championed slavery in America and the social order defended by the Confederacy. A century later, Jeremiah Newman, the then-leading Catholic conservative intellectual, was preoccupied with the decline of Church power.

From Petty's time onwards advocacy of 'progress' in Ireland has most prominently been defined in economic terms. From the 1950s onward an economic nation-building project began to explicitly supplant an earlier Irish-Ireland cultural one. Such Irish developmental goals of promoting economic growth and improving individuals through education can be traced back to the early nineteenth century. A number of chapters focus on some advocates (Malthus and Whately) and opponents (Mitchel, Engels and Connolly) of a liberal political economy. Modern Ireland came to be as defined by economic liberalism as much as it had been by Catholicism. Long before Margaret Thatcher did so, Irish Catholic clerics cited Friedrich Hayek in their arguments against the welfare state. For much of the twentieth century Catholic social thought was actively promoted in Irish universities and the trade union movement in order to undermine the potential influence of socialism.[2] Irish economists and politicians for their part sometimes cited papal encyclicals. A long ideological consensus between Irish liberalism and Catholicism in favour of a minimalist state worked against the influence of republicanism, the third intellectual tradition that this book addresses through chapters on Connolly, Sheehy Skeffington and O'Toole.

The structure of this book is chronological. The next three chapters deal respectively with seventeenth-century visions of what a successfully colonised Ireland might have looked like, with political visions of an autonomous Protestant Irish nation and with late-eighteenth century premonitions that Henry Grattan's Ascendancy Parliament held out no viable future for Irish Protestants vastly outnumbered by Catholics. Petty, the subject of Chapter Two, helped organise the Cromwellian plantation of Ireland and in doing so invented the science of political economy. In the preface to his *Political Anatomy of Ireland* written about 1672 he described Ireland as scarcely twenty years old. The future he advocated, an Ireland forcibly emptied of its Catholic peasantry, never quite came to pass. Political economy, as he understood it in the Irish context, was the science of understanding the social and economic consequences of a Catholic majority for the politically dominant Protestant minority. Molyneux (Chapter Three) was the intellectual architect of Henry Grattan's Protestant parliament that lasted from 1780 to the Act of Union in 1801. In declaring it Grattan invoked the spirit of Molyneux. Molyneux's 1698 pamphlet *The Case of Ireland's being Bound by Acts of Parliament in England, Stated* was the earliest political invocation of natural rights as depicted by his friend John

Locke. But it expressly denied Catholics rights to representative government. The future that Burke (Chapter Four) feared in his writings on Ireland was one where the Protestant Ascendancy's unwillingness to cede such rights to Catholics ended in catastrophe. He argued that the Catholic emancipation could only come about if the veto of the Ascendency parliament was abolished. Between them, Petty, Molyneux and Burke charted the rise of aspirations for and the political implausibility of a Protestant Irish nation. No longer could the Irish question be addressed intellectually or politically without taking into account the material circumstances of Ireland's large Catholic majority.

Chapters Five and Six address nineteenth-century premonitions about respectively the dilemmas facing this Catholic majority and those facing the Protestant minority. Malthus (Chapter Five), the most influential political economist of his day, came to be preoccupied with how the Penal Laws impeded the improvement of the rapidly expanding Catholic population. Whately (Chapter Six), another political economist, was appointed Archbishop of Dublin in the Established Church in 1832. This was in the immediate aftermath of Catholic emancipation. His brief as he understood it was to adjust Irish Protestants to the end of their Ascendancy. Political economy, the social science of nineteenth-century liberalism, became a language for thinking about Ireland's future but also one for thinking about how Ireland might be ruled.

Engels (Chapter Seven), though virulently opposed to the ideals of liberal political economy, saw the predicament of the Catholic Irish in somewhat similar terms to Malthus. Unless the unruly Irish could somehow be improved they would not survive the nineteenth century, let alone be useful to the cause of socialism. Engels took much of his understanding of Irish character from the conservative critic of industrial capitalism Thomas Carlyle. Mitchel (Chapter Eight) took all of his critique of Britain's liberal political economy from the same source and influentially, amongst Irish nationalists, blamed liberalism for the Famine. He railed against the economic system that displaced survivors of the Famine from the countryside and threatened to turn Ireland into the great ranch envisaged by Petty. Malthus, Whately, Engels and Mitchel were Protestants. Only Mitchel was Irish. Like Engels, he identified explicitly with the Catholic Irish. Malthus had only a slight connection with Ireland but is included because of the scale of his intellectual influence at a time when the Irish question came to be understood as a population question.

Chapters Nine and Ten address efforts to envisage Republican futures which offered alternatives to the meld of Catholic conservatism, cultural nationalism and economic liberalism that came to define the Irish Free State. Connolly (Chapter Nine) was considerably influenced by Mitchel's critique of colonialism. Connolly's hopes for a fusion between Irish nationalism and international socialism were dashed some time before his death after the 1916 Rising. If anything the circumstances of his death exemplified the triumph of Catholic conservatism. Post-independence Ireland hardly represented the kinds of future envisaged or wanted by Engels, Mitchel or Connolly, let alone Petty, Molyneux or Whately. Its conservative project was the propagation of the Irish language and the defence of Catholicism. It romanticised the seventeenth-century, mostly-Catholic society that Petty (and three catastrophic wars) helped destroy. Burke, the great theorist of conservatism, might have welcomed its staid stability. Malthus might have applauded the improved standards of living that followed the post-Famine crash in population but would not have seen such depopulation as necessary for social and economic improvement. Mitchel might have been cheered by the apparent rejection of liberal economics and utilitarianism that had taken hold of post-colonial nationalism. Engels, as a life-long student of Irish affairs, would not have been surprised by the still-birth of Irish socialism but would have been disappointed that Ireland's rebellion had not helped bring down English capitalism. Connolly, for all that he had helped proclaim a Republic that aspired to treat all of its children equally, had to some extent set socialism aside for the comradeship of relatively conservative Catholic cultural nationalists.

At the beginning of the century Irish suffragists sought the right to vote for women in Ireland. In doing so they were opposed by the Irish Parliamentary Party that sought Home Rule for Ireland. Throughout her life as an activist and journalist Sheehy Skeffington (Chapter Ten) contested what she saw as the betrayal of Irish women by, in turn, the Home Rule movement, the Free State victors of the civil war and the Fianna Fáil government led by Eamon de Valera. Her feminism intertwined with a republican idealism inspired by James Connolly. She was also a republican in the sense that the term has been usually used in Ireland: a nationalist opposed to the partition of the island.

The intellectual mission of Reverend, later Bishop, Jeremiah Newman (Chapter Eleven) was the rearguard defence of Catholic power in the face of growing expectations of its collapse, just as Whately, more than a century earlier, envisaged the disestablishment of his Church. Conor Cruise O'Brien (Chapter Twelve) nicknamed Newman the Mullah of Limerick, for articulating a religious neo-conservatism of the kind that still flourishes in the United States. In later life Cruise O'Brien came to inhabit the secular wing of political neo-Conservatism, having previously staked out ground as a Catholic intellectual, been a civil servant working for the cause of a united Ireland, a post-colonial left-liberal and an authoritarian scourge of republican nationalism. His final political persona, that of a Southern Irish unionist, was in a long tradition of imagining Irish futures that took the point of view of the other side of the sectarian divide. Burke, of course, but also Mitchel and Whately, in this were his intellectual antecedents. Ireland's present uncertain future is represented by Fintan O'Toole (Chapter Thirteen). His concerns about the ability of the Irish to govern themselves – and to what purpose – can be traced back to the preoccupations of Jonathan Swift.

Irish intellectual politics have been long characterised by ambivalence towards progress for all that Irish society has modernised. The main Irish intellectual conflicts of the last century have involved post-colonial and revisionist efforts to define and redefine the Irish past. For its own part *Histories of the Irish Future* is necessarily sceptical of teleological narratives that portray events as leading inevitably to where we supposedly are now. The idea for the book came from thinking about Swift's anxieties about the Irish future, about the schemes of improvement he proposed in earnest, about his satires on such earnestness and, even, about the very idea of progress. Swift's writings about Ireland have already been the subject of a huge literature and he looms as a presence in much that has been written since his death on the condition of Ireland. It has certainly influenced this book. But for all his brilliance the crises that Swift wrote about might be explained without him. Petty, Molyneux and Burke were, by contrast, pivotal figures who addressed key moments in the rise and decline of Protestant Ireland. Like many other figures that I examine they were preoccupied with endgames.

My unwritten chapter – the template for those in this book – might have been called 'Jonathan Swift and the Corruption of Ireland'. It would have focused on the 1720s when he was most engaged with dilemmas facing Ireland and, fairly understandably, those of Protestant Irishmen of his particular social class. Towards the end of this decade in 1729 Swift published *A Modest Proposal for preventing the Children of poor People from being a Burthen to their Parents or the Country, and for making them Beneficial to the Public.* The modest proposal was to rear the babies of the impoverished poor, a vast proportion of the population as a whole, 'destined to turn thieves for want of work, or leave their dear native country to fight for the Pretender in Spain, or to sell themselves to the Barbados as a luxury dish for the tables of persons of quality or fortune'. Swift computed the gaps between the rich and poor that made his modest proposal financially feasible. He assessed the charge of nursing a beggar's child (he included all labourers and four-fifths of farmers in this category) to be about two shillings per annum. A gentleman would, he assured, pay ten shillings for the carcass of a good fat child, leaving the mother with eight shillings net profit and fit for work until she produced her next baby.[3] Swift's satire on poverty was specifically one about the treatment of the Irish Catholic poor by their landlords who 'as they seem to have devoured most of the parents, seem to have best title to the children'. His modest proposal offered the collateral advantage of lessening the numerical superiority of Papists, the preoccupation of William Petty whose un-ironic final solution to Ireland's problems and whose marshalling of statistics, weights and measures to explain the condition of Ireland is the subject of the chapter following this.

During the 1720s, in pamphlet after earnest pamphlet, Swift lamented the condition of Ireland, detailed the specific causes of its woes and complained that these had fallen on deaf ears. He lambasted what he saw as the trite efforts by others to propose schemes for improvement that did not take adequate account of the profound disabilities under which Ireland laboured. To say that he mistrusted belief in progress would be an understatement. He was acutely preoccupied with decay.[4] He believed that the world was charged with pervasive degeneration. Paper rotted, bodies decayed, grand schemes of improvement unravelled and the promise of science and progress held out by Royal Society men, like Petty and Molyneux, could only be mocked.[5]

In 1720 Swift published his first major essay on the condition of Ireland. The subtitle of *A proposal for the Universal Use of Irish Manufacture* made no bones about the need for economic patriotism: 'Utterly Rejecting and renouncing Everything Wearable That Comes From Ireland'.[6] In his assessment Ireland's then economic crisis was the symptom of an underlying moral crisis. Prudence dictated that industrious cultivation was encouraged by law in England but in Ireland this was impeded 'everywhere by *penal clauses*'. The result was that it was cheaper to import corn from England than to grow it in Ireland. Swift lambasted country landlords (and landed clerics by implication) who (heed *his* original italics) 'by unmeasurable *screwing* and *racking* their tenants all over the kingdom have already reduced a miserable *people* to a *worse condition* than *peasants* in France, or the *vassals* in Germany and Poland; so that the whole *species* of what we call *substantial farmers*, will in a very few years be utterly at an end'. In *A proposal to the ladies of Ireland* (1729) he wondered 'how we Irish wretches came by that fashionable thing a national debt'. This stood at £250,000, about £50,000 more than all the cash circulating in the country at the time.[7] Ireland, he argued, was hardly in a position to pay the interest on this ('not the principal, for this is allowed impossible') for the want of trade and industry. For the want of a viable economy the country appeared to be lost.

Unlike so many who have written so badly about economics, he was exercised by human psychology and behaviour. There was more than a little self-awareness here. Swift railed against what he saw as unnecessary imports but purchased his own shirts from the Continent. He lambasted Irish provincials in thrall to the latest imported novelties from London. But he saw himself as an exile from the metropolis. He satirised English complaints about the rents and tithed incomes that could be commanded in Ireland, when he became a cleric himself to secure a living from the Established Church. He was very much, in the present day usage, embedded in the system he criticised. Different issues placed him at various degrees of separation from the Irish masses he depicted as enslaved to the Interests of England. The Irish for Swift were both a 'them' and an 'us', evincing both disgust and self-disgust.

Swift was revered by what came to be called the Ascendancy along with Molyneux because of his Protestant Irish patriotism. He also came to be revered by Catholic nationalists because his patriotism had focused upon the economic exploitation of Ireland and on the destructive irrationality of injustices perpetrated upon Catholics. Something of the despondency found in Swift emerges in several of the histories of the Irish future set out in the chapters that follow. Some of the best and most influential writing about Ireland's future over the last few centuries has been the product of despair and an unwillingness to surrender to it.

CHAPTER TWO

William Petty's final solution

William Petty (1627–87) was the inventive steward of the great transplantation that reduced the proportion of Irish lands held by Catholics from three-fifths to one-fifth. He proposed to James II that most of the Irish, one million persons in all, be transplanted to England, leaving Ireland as a thinly-populated agricultural 'factory'. Petty's final solution to the Irish question, commended to the King months before his own death in 1687, was never taken seriously and was soon overtaken by events. England's last Catholic monarch was soon to fight and lose a war in Ireland against William of Orange. Yet Petty's story and that of his prescriptions cast light on the tumultuous history of post-1641 Ireland, one where colonialism and ideas of progress went hand in glove, where science was the handmaiden of politics and of the pursuit of wealth. Petty's lasting intellectual reputation is as the father of what he variously called political economy or political arithmetic. Ireland was his laboratory.

Petty went to sea as an apprentice to a ship's captain. When he was fifteen years old he broke his leg and was set ashore in France. His apparent precocity and very forward nature gained him entry to the Jesuit University in Caen. From the Jesuits he acquired an abiding interest in educational formation. In a letter to a cousin he described himself being known as 'le Petit Matelot Anglais qui parle Latin et Grec'. In Caen he studied 'the whole body of common arithmetic', geometry, astronomy, Latin, Greek and French, all of which recommended him to the King's navy where he served until the age of twenty. By then he had saved £60 and claimed to know 'as much mathematics as any of my age was known to have had'.[1]

After the outbreak of the Civil War Petty retreated to the Continent. He frequented the schools at Utrecht, Leiden and Amsterdam and lived for some time in Paris where he found employment as Thomas Hobbes's personal secretary.[2] Acquaintance with fellow scientifically minded expatriates gained him entry to Oxford where at the age of twenty-three he returned to study medicine. In Oxford he was welcomed into the circle of mathematicians, scientists and physicians, the self-styled 'invisible college' that became established there during the Civil War. Through their friendship and patronage he quickly rose from being a fellow at Brasenose College to vice-principal and Professor of Anatomy. Petty was particularly influenced by the writings of Francis Bacon. The new science flourished under the Commonwealth. Like Petty, many practitioners of the new science were men on the make who placed it at the disposal of men in authority.[3] Just as they found a protector in Cromwell they also benefited from the patronage of Charles II after the Restoration.

Petty first came to public prominence in 1650 when he revived Ann Green, an Oxfordshire servant girl who had been hanged for trying to conceal an abortion. She had miscarried an illegitimate pregnancy. Comprehensive efforts to ensure that she had been properly executed were made. She was lifted up several times and jerked down again to ensure her neck had broken. She was stamped on by her friends as she lay in her coffin to make sure that she was dead. Petty, then a Deputy Professor of Anatomy, had provided the coffin so that she could be brought to his dissecting room. There he discovered that she was somehow still alive, restored her to health, petitioned on her behalf to an astonished world, reputedly raising a collection for her from other Oxford scholars that provided her with a small dowry. In doing so Petty became a celebrity doctor.[4]

But it was his first published work, *Advice of Mr W.P. to Mr. Hartlib for the advancement of some particular parts of learning* that showcased the abilities that equipped him for his first post in Ireland. Hartlib was one of the best-connected intellectual figures of the Commonwealth era. Petty's *Advice to Mr Hartlib* set out many ideas for educational reform including the curriculum for literary workhouses which all children above the age of seven would attend in order to learn trades and to read and write. It also included proposals for the organisation of a model teaching hospital, run for the benefit of the scientific practitioner as well as the patient. He emphasised the need to record accurate patient case histories.[5] The publicity over Ann Green along with his contacts in Oxford helped him secure the post of physician to the Commonwealth Army in Ireland.

When Petty arrived in Ireland on 10 October 1653 the country, according to one of his biographers, was helpless and almost lifeless at the mercy of its conquerors, like Ann Green's body in the dissecting room, and badly in need of competent administrators.[6] Petty streamlined the provision of medicines, saving the army, in his own estimation, £500 per annum. His organisational ability impressed Henry Cromwell whereas that of the then-Chief Surveyor Benjamin Worsley did not. Petty won the contract to survey the forfeited lands upon which the Commonwealth's plantation of Ireland would depend. In 1642 some 2,500,000 acres of Ireland land had been pledged to the 1,043 investors who adventured money needed to pay an army to put down the rebellion in Ireland.[7] Much of this money was never spent as originally intended because the English Civil War had broken out shortly after. Ireland was retaken a decade later by the New Model Army whose 35,000 or so members now also had to be paid off with Irish lands. A third category of creditors rewarded with estates in Ireland included those who had loaned money to the Commonwealth or those like Petty who were owed fees for their services.[8]

Managing such claims required a detailed assessment of all landholdings. There were, to say the least, administrative complexities in disbursing Irish spoils to those who invested in or fought for English victory. By May 1657 the transplantation of Catholics to 'Hell or to Connaught', as it passed into folklore, was deemed to be complete. Yet many former Catholic landowners remained *in situ* as leaseholders and many Catholic tenants merely changed landlords.[9] On the basis of Petty's work some 8,400,000 acres of forfeited land were finally allocated to new and mostly Protestant owners.[10] Petty as an architect of this settlement came to be blamed for its inadequacies by aggrieved parties including the hapless Worsley and the Anabaptists who were less favoured by Henry Cromwell than the Old Protestants he increasingly turned to for support.[11] Those who lost out in wealth and influence could not help but notice Petty's growing personal fortune.

For the Down Survey, which employed more than 1,000 men, Petty received a payment of £18,552. He managed to keep one half as profit. Within four years of arriving in Ireland with £480 he was worth £13,000.[12] He used some of his capital to buy up debentures (promises of land) from demobilised soldiers; 32,149 such debentures had been issued but just 11,804 were translated into land grants. The remainder were sold on for cash.[13] Petty grasped such opportunities to build up his estates and by 1661 had acquired some 50,000 acres. He complained that he had lost 'a great deal of these' in 1663 when the Court of the Innocents restored a portion of the forfeited lands in Ireland to loyal Catholics. Yet, by 1668 he had amassed 150,000 acres in Kerry as well as other lands throughout Ireland.[14]

In 1659 Petty had been subpoenaed to appear before the House of Commons to answer charges put by Worsley and other rivals that he 'hath received great bribes, that he had purchased a vast number of debentures illegally', and that he had conspired with other officials to deny 'to others the security which of right belongs to them'. Petty rebutted these charges in a long speech to the House of Commons and never had to formally answer to them again. In 1660 the political landscape shifted abruptly with the restoration of the monarchy. Petty fared well in the ensuing political scramble and found favour with the new King along with other members of the Royal Society of which Charles II was an active patron.[15]

The survey data he compiled was published towards the end of his life in 1685 as the *Hiberniae Delineatio*. It was the first comprehensive atlas of Ireland. Many of the writings that gained him a reputation as a founder of the science of political economy were published posthumously. The preface to Petty's *The Political Anatomy of Ireland*, written around 1672, began by announcing the birth of a new social science out of this experience of counting, weighting and measuring Irish lands, wealth and population:

> Sir Francis Bacon, in his Advancement of Learning, hath made a judicious Parallel in many particulars, between the Body Natural, and Body Politick, and between the Arts of preserving both in Health and Strength: And it is as reasonable, that as Anatomy is the best foundation of one, so also of the other; and that to practice upon the Politick, without knowing the Symmetry, Fabrick, and proportion of it, is as casual as the practice of Old-women and Empyricks.[16]

It was not enough, Bacon had argued, to conduct mechanical experiments like the Renaissance technicians and alchemists – the 'empyricks' Petty referred to – or to seek to reason principles of natural law as the scholastics attempted to do. A true philosophy would fuse both reason and material facts and thereby seek to elaborate upon understandings of the world. Political arithmetic as a branch of this new science would take account of that which could be counted or measured and leave deliberations that depended 'upon the mutable Minds, Opinions, Appetites and Passions of particular Men, to the Consideration of others'. Political arithmetic, Petty maintained, could be applied to all matters: 'Unless They bee Mystical, Spirituall, eternal.'[17] It would address what Hobbes called *logica sive computatio*, in effect the logic of quantities.[18]

Petty first coined the term 'political arithmetic' in 1672 to refer to the statistical analysis of social phenomena. Near the end of his life he wrote to a friend that algebra had been brought to Spain from Arabia by the Moors and 'W.P.', as he referred to himself in the third person, then applied it to other than purely mathematical matters, 'viz: to policy by the name of Political Arithmetick by reducing many termes of matter to termes of number, weight and measure, in order to be handled mathematically'.[19]

Petty, who trained as an anatomist, also used the term political anatomy to draw analogies between the science of medicine and attempts to understand the workings of interdependent elements of society. Wise doctors, he argued, knew the limits of their understanding and 'tamper not excessively with their Patients, rather observing and complying with the motions of nature, then contradicting it with vehement Administrations of their own; so in Politcs and Oconomicks, the same must be used'.[20] As explained in *The Political Anatomy of Ireland*, just as students of anatomy practised their inquiries on animals he had chosen Ireland 'as such a political animal'.[21]

Ireland was a metaphorical body on Petty's laboratory table – like Anne Green bruised but not dead – to be diagnosed and revived by the medicine of political arithmetic. But what Petty called Ireland in 1672 was just two decades old. He defined the Irish question strictly in terms of the predicaments of those who had come to own much of the country twenty years earlier. Petty's diagnosis, mostly set out in papers that were not published until after his death, proposed a radical surgery, one described by a nineteenth-century editor of these as a 'final solution' to the Irish question.[22]

The political arithmetic of transplantation

Petty's final solution was most comprehensively set out in his 1687 *Treatise on Ireland: An Essay in Political Arithmetick* that he submitted to King James II. In summary, it propounded 'a perpetual Settlement of Ireland, with a Natural Improvement and Union of England and Ireland by Transplanting a Million People out of Ireland into England, leaving in Ireland only enough hands to manage as many cattle as that country would feed'. Much of the Treatise addressed likely objections to the financial practicality and feasibility of the proposed scheme which Petty argued was neither impracticable nor utopian.

In *The Treatise on Ireland* Petty calculated that Ireland in 1687 had a population of 1.3 million, an underestimate according to modern historians who put the then population at about 1.9 million.[23] Based upon his own estimates Petty argued that it would take the removal of a million Catholics to settle the Irish question. Drastic surgery was needed. Petty proposed to:

> cut up the Roots of those Evils in Ireland, which by differences of Births, Extractions, Manners, Languages, Customs and Religions, have continually wasted the Blood and Treasure of Both Nations for about 500 years; and have made Ireland, for the most Part, a Dimunation and a Burthen, not an Advantage, to England.[24]

The problem was that there were about eight Roman Catholics in Ireland for every one Protestant: 145,000 non-Catholics of all sorts and 1,155,000 Catholics. Petty argued that it would take the transplantation of the majority of these Catholics to stabilise Ireland in perpetuity whilst even the arrival of a million Catholics in England, dispersed throughout its larger mostly non-Catholic population, would be manageable. His 1687 *Treatise on Ireland* proposed that the population of Ireland should consist solely of 267,000 Catholics and 33,000 non-Catholics. England's population would rise by 1 million to 8.1 million of which 913,000, a sufficiently small minority to be religiously and culturally assimilated, would be transplanted Catholics.

The resultant land clearance would, he claimed, bring considerable economic benefits. Ireland, he calculated, could breed and feed six million beeves of three years old. He calculated that 300,000 herdsmen and dairy women would be sufficient to manage said cattle at a cost per person of £5 per head per annum. He calculated that this cattle trade would be worth about six million pounds and with efficiencies that might be achieved through streamlined ranching or, as Petty put it, when the cattle trade was rendered simple, easy and constant in the breeding, feeding and vending, seven million pounds in all. The depopulated country could be secured by 4,000 men at sea, 2,000 horse and 15,000 foot at land. The diminished population could be ministered to for £20,000 which would allow £100,000 in surplus tithes to be expropriated to the Established Church in England. The inhabitants of England who owned Irish lands would receive one and a half million pounds out of Ireland per annum. This was, Petty claimed, more than England gained by foreign trade with all the rest of the world. The costs of 'Civil Government in Ireland, under the Paucity and Simplicity of the People above-mentioned being but a Kind of Factory' would be cheaper, not least because the immense litigation that characterised Irish affairs in the decades since the 1652 Act of Settlement would almost be abolished.[25]

Petty argued that a rise in the population of England engineered by large-scale transplantation from Ireland and Scotland would increase the wealth of England and the revenues available to the King. Much of Petty's argument turned on his methods of calculating wealth. He measured this in terms of consumption per head and land values. In the case of the latter he repeatedly emphasised how the post-1641 war in Ireland depressed the value of lands so that wealth diminished. According to his political arithmetic it would be better for impoverished Catholics to be transplanted to England where individual earnings and consumption per annum were higher. In this context he argued that the million who were to be transplanted would after seven years in England become worth about £30 per head more than at present, in all £30 million. In arriving at this figure he considered earnings, estimated the effects of a million additional people on rents and supposed that in time the earnings of transplanted persons would rise to the level of the indigenous tenant population.

Petty had proposed an earlier transplantation scheme in *The Political Anatomy of Ireland*, a pamphlet written in 1672 that had yet to be published when he made his 1687 submission to James II. However, it is likely that Petty pondered the political arithmetic of the Irish question from his earliest days in Ireland. Early biographers of Petty argued that he had co-authored a 1655 pamphlet that was extremely critical of the human cost of the transplantation of Catholics to Connaught. The grounds for so believing included the similarity between the style of opening sections of *The Great Case of Transplantation Discussed* and Chapter Four of Petty's *Political Anatomy of Ireland*.[26] Both employed similar analogies between the human body and the State. But such analogies were hardly unique to Petty. The second edition, published soon after the first, identified Vincent Gookin as sole author. Gookin was a friend and political ally of Petty and a fellow rival of Benjamin Worsley whom he supplanted as Surveyor General in 1657. Both found common cause in defending their land and political interests against overlapping rivals and opponents.[27] Both served together on the six person commission that adjudicated land claims following the Down Survey. Gookin was Petty's neighbour and Member of Parliament. He worked to get Petty elected as a fellow MP in 1659 in order that Petty could defend himself against Worsley's charges in the House of Commons. In Parliament Gookin was regarded as the leading spokesman for Protestant landowners in Ireland and, alongside Petty, a leading expert on the Irish land question.[28] Gookin's pamphlet offered a similar account of Ireland's political anatomy even if their diagnoses differed:

> The Irish numbers (now abated by Famin, Pestilence, the Sword, and Forein Transportations) are not like to overgrow the English as formerly, and so no fear of their being obnoxious to them hereafter: but being mixed with, they are likelyer to be swallowed up by the English, and incorporated into them; so that a few Centuries will know no difference present, fear none to come, and scarce believe what were pas'd. The chiefest and eminentest of the Nobility, and many of the Gentry, have taken Conditions from the King of Spain, and have transported at several times. 40,000 of the most active spirited men, most acquainted with danger and discipline of War, and inured to hardness; the Priests are all banished; the remaining part of the whole Nation are scarce the sixth part of what were at the beginning of the War, so great a devastation has God and Man brought upon that Land, and so far are they from those formidable numbers they are (by those that are strangers to Ireland) conceived to be; and that handfull of Natives left, are poor laborious usefull simple Creatures, whose design is onely to live, and their Families, the manner of which is so low, that it is design rather to be pitied, than by any body feared, envyed, or hindered.

For all that Gookin was optimistic that the seeds for successful Anglicisation had been sown – a conclusion disputed by Petty's subsequent political arithmetic – both similarly understood the issues at stake. *The Great Case of Transplantation Discussed* addressed 'the many great inconveniences in the transplanting the Natives of Ireland generally out of the Provinces of Leinster, Ulster and Munster'.[29] 'The unsettlement of a nation', Gookin wrote, 'is easy work; the settling is not'. He argued that the transplantation of Catholic landowners to Connaught could only result in the permanent mutual antagonisms between Catholics and Protestants. The injustice of the policy had driven the people of the country into madness and had fostered lawlessness. It had, Gookin emphasised, turned the Irish into Tories, a word derived from the Gaelic *toruighe*, meaning, in its general seventeenth-century usage, a robber or plunderer.[30] The original Tories were Irish Catholics who had become dispossessed from their lands and then become outlaws. From about 1680 the term came to be applied to supporters of James II, who was then the Duke of York. After 1689 it was applied to the political faction that eventually became the Conservative Party. Gookin argued that rigorous transplantation to Connaught would create many Tories.

For all that Gookin lamented its human costs he inferred that the Commonwealth plantation had left unfinished business. There would not be peace or order 'until the whole land be otherwise planted'. For the 1652 Act of Settlement was by no means as comprehensive as the earlier plantation of Ulster which had imported not just settlers but their ways of life, housing, farming and skills. The Commonwealth settlement amounted to a transfer of wealth and power from Catholics to Protestants. What it created was not a Protestant society but a Protestant upper class now struggling to realise the value of their lands and, with Ireland's history of rebellions in mind, anxious to solve the Irish question in perpetuity.[31]

Gookin set out some of his analysis in the form of a dialogue where he responded to objections he imagined his readers would have. Against the objection 'that the English may degenerate, and turn Irish, unless a separation by transplanting the one from the other be observed' Gookin argued that the balance of power had shifted sufficiently in Ireland to remove the factors that had led to the assimilation of previous waves of English settlers into Irish ways of life, language and religion:

> When England was reformed from Popery, no care was took, nor endeavours used to spread the reformation in Ireland; by which means the English Colonies there continued still Papists, and so in Religion were alienated from the English, and fastened to the Irish: But now it being most probable that most of the Irish will embrace the Protestant Profession, it is upon the same grounds most probable that they will embrace the English Manners.
>
> Former Conquests of Ireland were either the undertakings of some private persons, or so managed by publick persons, that the power and profitable advantages of the Land remained in the hands of the Irish: But as in the present Conquest the Nation of England is engaged, so is the power and advantage of the Land in the hands of the English. For instance:
>
> 1. The Irish were the Body of the People, and too potent for the English (especially at such times as the troubles of England caused the Armies to be called thence, which Historians observe to have been the times of degeneration, as a means to self-preservation.
>
> 2. The Irish were the general Proprietors of Land, and an English Planter must be their Tenant; and the temptation of this relation and dependence is very prevelant (at least) to bring the Posterity to a complyance, and that to a likeness, and that to a sameness.
>
> 3. The Irish were the chiefly estated, and the inter-marriages with them were accompanied with greater Friends and Fortunes than with the English, who were not only Strangers, but for the most part (till of late years) comparatively poor.
>
> 4. The Lawyers were Irish, the Jurors Irish, most of the Judges Irish, and the major part of their Parliament Irish; and in all Disputes between Irish and English, the Irish were sure of the favour.

But now the condition of Ireland is (through God's goodness) so altered, that all these Arguments are much more forcibly persuasive, that the Irish will turn English.

English, Gookin argued in 1655, would now replace Irish as the main language of commerce and the population would now, by necessity, become Anglicised. But the physical displacement of the Catholic Irish would, he argued, undermine such assimilation: 'If they be transplanted into Connaught, the distinction of the English and Irish tongue will not only be continued, but also the Irish left without means of learning English'. In the years that followed most of the Irish population remained *in situ*. Those Catholic landlords who forfeited their estates took just some of their retainers to Connaught. The remaining Irish had not become particularly Anglicised.

Gookin wondered if the 1652 Act of Settlement had gone too far. Petty in his *Political Anatomy of Ireland* (1672) was emphatic that it had not gone far enough. There could be no satisfactory solution to the Irish question that did not involve diminishing the numerical superiority of Catholics. Petty's prescriptions focused on the transportation of Irish women to England and their substitution by English women. A large proportion of Irish of marriageable age were to be distributed between the parishes of England and these were to be replaced by English women who would civilise, educate and Anglicise the impoverished Irish families they married into:

There are among the 600,000 above-mentioned of the poor Irish, not above 20,000 of unmarried marriageable women; Nor would above two thousand *Per Ann.* Grow and become such. Wherefore if, ½ the said Women were in one year, and ½ in the next transported into England, and disposed of one to each Parish, and as many English brought back and married to the Irish, as would improve their Dwelling but to a House and Garden of £3 value, the whole Work of natural Transmutation would in 4 or 5 years be accomplished.

The charge of making the exchange would not be £20,000 per Ann. Which is about 6 weeks pay of the present or late Armies in Ireland.

The aim, as identified by Gookin in 1655, was that 'the language of the children would be English as would be the economy of family life in terms of diet and dress'. How such English brides would be selected from amongst those sufficiently skilled in domestic science to move into the brutish, nasty cabins of the wretched Irish poor that he depicted a few paragraphs earlier in his *Political Anatomy of Ireland* was not specified. More feasible than Petty's proposed mass bride swap, perhaps, was his plan for the regulation of Catholic clergy:

If the Irish must have Priests, let the number of them, which is now between 2 and 3 thousand Secular and Regulars, be reduced to a competent number of 1000 which is 800 Souls to the pastorage of each Priest; which let be known persons, and Englishmen, if it may be. So as that when the Priests, who govern the Conscience, and the Women, who influence other powerful Appitites, shall be English, both of whom being in the Bosom of the Men, it must be, that no massacring of English, as heretofore can happen again.[32]

Petty also insisted that such social transmutation should be accompanied by a political union that placed Ireland and England under the same laws and parliament. He considered it absurd that Englishmen in Ireland were treated as aliens and had to pay import and export duties upon commerce with England.[33] In various pamphlets Petty combined demographic and economic data for both countries, presenting them as one economic unity and polity.

By 1672 Petty believed that the Catholic Irish were incapable of any further uprising. *The Political Anatomy of Ireland* expressed his assessment of the extent to which the Irish had been already reduced by poverty and forfeiture and quantified Protestant economic and military superiority:

That the British Protestants and Church have 3/4 of all the Lands, 5/6 of all the Housing, 9/10 of all the Housing in wall'd Towns, and Places of Strength, 2/3 of the Foreign Trade. That 6 of Eight of all the Irish live in a brutish nasty Condition, as in Cabins, with neither Chimney, Door, Stairs nor Window; feed chiefly upon Milk and Potatoes, whereby their Spirits are not dispos'd for War. And that although there be in Ireland 8 Papists for 3 others; yet there are far more Soldiers and Soldier-like Men of this latter as lesser Number, than of the former.

That his majesty, who formally could do nothing for, and upon Ireland, but by the help of England, hath now a Revenue upon the Place, to maintain, if he pleases, 7000 Men at Arms, besides a Protestant Militia of 25,000 more, the most whereof are expert in War.

That the Protestants have Housing Enough within Places of Strength within 5 miles of the Sea-side, to receive and protect, and harbour every Man, Woman and Child belonging to them, and have also places of strength of their own properly, to situate in all parts of Ireland, to which they can easily travel the shortest day of the year.

That a few Ships of War, whereof the Irish have none, nor no Skill or Practice of Navagation, can hinder their relief from all Foreign Help.[34]

Lastly, he added, let the Irish know that there were and always would be 'sufficient men discontented with their present conditions in England ready to exploit any changed state of affairs in Ireland and make their fortunes from quelling any insurrection'.

Like Gookin, Petty believed that Protestant military and economic power was sufficient to quell any future Catholic rebellion. However, the linguistic and religious Anglicisation predicted by Gookin was hardly in evidence. In this context, Petty made the case for mass transplantation of Irish Catholics.

His 1687 final solution outlined in the *Treatise on Ireland* evolved from earlier versions that set out various alternatives whereby large numbers of Irish could be transplanted or English settlers introduced so as to reduce the ratio of Catholics to Protestants. He calculated that forty small vessels of about 60 tons each would be enough to transplant a million Irish people over a five-year period. The freight per head need not exceed two shillings. An additional twenty shillings per head would serve, with good method and order, to bear the travelling charges of men, women and children from the middle of Ireland to the middle of England; being about 120 miles by land.

Petty gave some thought to how transplantation on this scale might be administered. Initially, there should be every effort to coax the Irish population to comply. It would, after all, be in their best material interests to do so:

> Nor do we insist upon an Act of Parliament in Ireland, to force a Million of People to Remove out of their Native Countrey; or an Act of Parliament in England to force them hither: Which may be interpreted, in a Case between Catholicks and others, to be a Breach of the Liberty of Conscience lately granted by his Majestie. Wherefore, we shall shew, That it will be the Profit, Pleasure and Security of both Nations and Religions to Agree herin.[35]

Once it was established that his scheme would be in the greater good, because it would address the root cause of 500 years of war and disturbance, because the King would increase his wealth, as would the Established Church, he supposed 'that particular Men will not long persist in their Perverseness and Humor; Or (if they do) that a Parliament of England, may cure this Evil, in both Kingdoms, as kind Parents may correct the Children whom they love'. As with previous plantations and transplantations, this would be achieved through legislation:

> And when such a Law is made, it is possible within Six Months to give a List of all Tenants in Ireland, who are to be removed, and of the lands they hold; with the Yearly Value thereof. And within Six Months more, to make a Particular of the Lands in England, by the Names, Quantity, Situations, and Values, correspondent to the said Tenures and Occupancies in Ireland, if men shall humourlessless refuse to agree otherwise.

The driver of transplantation, as during the 1650s, would be the change of ownership of Irish lands. Instead of beginning with forfeitures, Petty recommended that scheme whereby Irish lands would be purchased by the King at market rates. Move the landowners to England, designate areas where these would be resettled – east of the Irish Sea rather than west of the Shannon – and their million Catholic tenants would follow. Except, however, most Catholic tenants did not follow their Catholic masters to Connaught during the 1650s when the pragmatism of Protestant landlords like Gookin had won out over ideological visions of mass transplantation.

As during the 1650s administrative systems to establish title of lands and assess their values would be needed. Most landowners were now Protestants but since the Restoration some lands had been restored to loyal Catholics. To deal with Protestant landowners Petty proposed that an elected assembly of 500 be chosen by 15,000 electors who each represented one of Ireland's 15,000 parishes having been elected by presumably non-Catholic males over twenty-one years of age. This assembly would adjudicate matters relating to the Protestant estates of Ireland.[36] Catholic claims to land would be addressed by a different process. Here, the purpose was to examine whether the claims of restorees were founded or not before the lands were then sold as a prelude to mass transportation of tenants. To this end Petty proposed that a Court be erected by an Act of Parliament, consisting of 'five of the most Ancient, Substantial, Upright and Experience'd Catholic Gentlemen of Ireland'. No lands would be sold until this court had determined what every restoree or removee was to have.[37]

In effect, Petty claimed that the quantitative techniques of the Down Survey and along with the kinds of law and administrative measures that made earlier forfeitures and transplantations feasible, would enable the transplantation of a million Irish to England. Nowhere in his *Treatise on Ireland* did he specify how these would be settled into England. In 1672 he had teased through the practicalities of sending one Irish woman to each of the 20,000 English parishes. How a million Catholics might be settled in England was not addressed in his 1687 proposal to the King.

Prescriptions and endgames

In his writings on Ireland Petty emphasised a recurring history of failure to settle the question of English settlement in Ireland since the time of Henry II. The premise of *The Political Anatomy of Ireland* was that the forfeiture of Catholic lands during the 1650s had not resolved the ills of the political anatomy of Ireland as understood by Protestant settlers. Since the time of Henry II no political settlement had removed the threat of English ruling minorities in Ireland becoming assimilated. Gookin maintained that the 1652 Act of Settlement tipped the balance, ensuring that Protestant economic and legal power was now sufficient to Anglicise the Catholic Irish. When Petty set out his first prescription for the future of Ireland in 1672 he concluded that such superiority made any further Catholic revolution unlikely. Yet, the simple political arithmetic of Catholic numerical superiority meant that such Anglicisation was unlikely.

For all his advocacy of political arithmetic Petty was hardly dispassionate in his analysis of Irish affairs. *The Treatise on Ireland* chided the King for overt generosity towards Catholics. Petty complained that the Catholic innocents – those guilty of no treason or disloyalty in the years after 1641 – got a better Restoration settlement than they deserved. Whether at the Court of Claims in Athlone or at the Court of Innocents in Dublin in 1663 ('we may think that the said innocents got by foul play also much more than what was their own in 1641'), the return of lands to Catholics was a sore topic. Not least, of course, because Petty's own landholdings were affected. His *Political Anatomy of Ireland* proposed the mass transplantation of Catholics as an alternative endgame to the genocide wished for by some Protestants:

> Some furious spirits have willed, that the Irish would rebel again, that might be put to the Sword. But I declare, that motion to be not only impious and inhumane, but withal frivolous and pernicious even to them who have rashly wish'd for those occasions.[38]

Mass transportation with its promise of economic benefits was preferable to hundreds of thousands of deaths as had occurred in the decade after 1641. Most of these deaths, Petty emphasised, were of the native Irish. For all that Petty placed his political arithmetic at the service of Protestant colonisation he also challenged prevailing accounts of the scale of the massacre of Protestants that had so inflamed English public opinion after 1641:

> And some say, to Blacken the Irish, that they caused the Death of above 150,000 English and Scotch Protestants in the first Year of their Commotions. And others, to extenuate the Causes of Forfeiture, do shrink that Number to 400. But you have started a most soft and Candid Question, by Asking onely, without Rancour, How many of the King's Subjects were fewer in Ireland, when the War ended in Anno 1653, than they might have been, if there had been no war at all. That is to say, Whether they perished by Murders and Massacres committed by Private Hands, or by Hunger and Cold, or being frightened out of the kingdom; or Whether they were slain as Soldiers on both Sides; or Whether they perished by the Plague, which reigned very fiercely Ann. 1650; or by Famine and Desolation, which was great about the End of the War. Or whether this Number was Lessen'd, by Hindering the Ordinary Course of Generation. For it is all one, by what Means they were Lessen'd, as to the Account we are now stating, of the Damages which accru'd from the Rebellion.[39]

But for Petty these claims simply did not add up even if such claims had their political uses. An unknown number had been killed and others had fled to England but these formed just a small proportion of the overall loss of life and property. Petty estimated that the people of Ireland were fewer in 1653 than they might have been by about 600,000 souls; by reason of the sword, famine, plague, banishment and desolations which had occurred since 1641. Modern historians put the death toll somewhere between 300,000 and 600,000 or between 20 per cent and 40 per cent of the population. This compared with death rates of just 3.7 per cent in England and 6 per cent in Scotland resulting from the contemporaneous civil wars.[40]

In 1686, one year before his death, Petty set out yet another transplantation scheme. *Of Reconciling the English and Irish and Reforming Both Nations* was a hybrid of the two-way transplantation he had proposed in 1672 and the plan for clearing most Catholics out of Ireland that he advocated in his 1687 *Treatise on Ireland*.[41] It proposed the transplantation of 10,000 Irish Catholic families to England along with 40,000 unmarried women. The first such scheme aimed to transmute the Irish into English by importing English wives to govern their hearts and hearths. An equivalent number of Irish women would be settled in England. Transmutation was a recurring term in Petty's writings, one with alchemical undertones. The political arithmetic solution to the ills of Irish political anatomy involved altering the ratios of Protestants to Catholics of Ireland. But the ultimate aim of transmutation or Anglicisation necessitated mixing both elements within households and families.[42] In the *Treatise on Ireland* submitted to James II in 1687 the mass transplantation of Catholics to England was not to be balanced by any corresponding plantation of English settlers. In the last months of his life Petty came to the conclusion that the Irish question was otherwise insolvable.

Petty's blithe use of numbers, weights and measures to demonstrate how a million Catholics could be taken out of the equation stood in contrast to the innate messiness of Irish land politics that Petty knew all too well. The post-forfeiture land settlement had been administered in an 'atmosphere of political conniving, delays and endless referrals between committees and councils'.[43] English policies on Irish affairs were inevitably shaped by wider political considerations. Petty had what one biographer described as 'curious and ill-founded hopes' in the government of James II. His hopes for influence were entirely based on the intellectual strength of his arguments – as distinct from efforts to address the actual politics of policymaking – and the King's personal liking for him, which was strong enough to result in frequent personal meetings.[44] But the problems of the political anatomy of Ireland that Petty could heal on paper with his political arithmetic were beyond the King's ability to contain, let along control.

For all that Petty's final solution was to turn Ireland into a ranch, Petty was no rancher. The historian Toby Barnard described him with some irony as the Kerry Ironmaster for his protracted efforts to promote the extraction of ore and smelting on his estates. Much of the land he owned in Kerry was unsuitable for farming. Only a small proportion of his lands were used as pasture for cattle. He built furnaces in various places where water flowing into the ocean could be harnessed. He founded the town of Kenmare as a

Protestant colony. He found himself in competition with more efficient iron works elsewhere, bedevilled by poor quality workmanship and logistical difficulties in profitably transporting his product. He also faced ongoing difficulties in attracting skilled Protestant workers and competent managers to Kerry.[45] Petty was no great success as a planter. His industries turned a modest profit compared to rents from his estates and he struggled to create the simple rural industries already successfully established by Protestant colonists elsewhere in Ireland. His Kenmare operation was an isolated plantation. There is little evidence to suggest that Petty sought to Anglicise the local population.[46] In later life Petty spent most of his time in London.

In March 1687 news arrived in London that Perry's colony in Kerry had been attacked by the native Irish. The colonists, some forty-two families, retreated to Killown House near the coast at Kenmare, which had been fortified along the lines Petty advocated in *The Political Anatomy of Ireland*. The surrounding population 'plundered haggard, barn and granary'. The Protestants of Kenmare escaped in two ships to Bristol, arriving in so miserable a condition that the mayor ordered collections for their relief. Some died from the effects of cold and exposure. The survivors went to London and were hospitably entertained by Lady Petty.[47]

Edmond Fitzmaurice's 1895 biography described these events and the general worsening of conditions in Ireland as 'an almost intolerable blow' to Petty: 'It seemed as if his life-work had been destroyed. When he died in December 1687 a handwritten paper was found in his room containing a forecast of the tumultuous events to come.' In essence, Petty predicted that 'When the Establishment of Popery in England is found to be impracticable' James II would be displaced by William of Orange. The Catholic Irish 'Irish officers, with their 8,000 soldiers, will make a convention of the forfeiting Irish and a militia of 15,000 men' would rally behind James and would ally with France. This would precipitate a wider war. 'The Hollanders and all the Northerne States would will oppose France in having Ireland.' Protestant refugees would flood into England. These fugitive English and the Scots would rally behind William of Orange. The British under William would beat the French and Irish and in the aftermath, Petty's final solution to the Irish problem would, he came to believe, come to pass. Furious spirits would prevail over the rational calculus of arithmetic but Ireland would be made into a place of pasturage.[48]

In June 1688 James II fathered an heir and the spectre of a Catholic dynasty prompted a rally behind his son-in-law William of Orange. Within months of Petty's death the precarious reign of James II had collapsed. Protestants in Ireland were deeply hostile to the King's Catholicism. Irish Catholics felt he had sold them short when it came to the restoration of their lands. James fled to France and subsequently landed in Kerry in March 1689 at the head of a French army. By 1691 the Catholic Irish lost their third war of the seventeenth century and a new Protestant settlement was imposed upon Ireland. By 1688 about 1,300 Catholics had come to own 22 per cent of the profitable land in Ireland. By 1702, when William III died, the Catholic share had fallen to 14 per cent because of further forfeitures. However, the introduction of Penal Laws from 1695 worked to reduce this proportion over time so that by the 1770s Catholics owned just 5 per cent of Irish lands. By 1841 the country's mostly Catholic population had risen to 8.2 million. Only after the nineteenth-century Famine did Ireland experience the kind of state-sponsored emigration advocated by Petty. By the time a million Irish had emigrated such numbers were far too few to alter the underlying political arithmetic.

CHAPTER THREE

William Molyneux and the case for Ireland

William Molyneux (1656–98) was a man of many parts assembled to fit the seventeenth-century father-of-the-Enlightenment archetype. He was a natural philosopher who engaged in scientific experimentation and contributed to philosophical debates. He had inherited wealth and status that enabled him to do so. His grandfather, Sir Thomas Molyneux, arrived in Ireland in 1576 and was appointed by Queen Elizabeth as Ireland's Chancellor of the Exchequer. In the winter of 1679 William translated Descartes' *Meditationes de prima philosophia* into English; it was published the following year. In 1683, at the age of twenty-five, he became a founding member of the Dublin Philosophical Society, established upon the empirical principles of the Royal Society. His studies of optics were highly regarded by Robert Boyle amongst others. By profession he was a lawyer and a surveyor. He held a number of posts on government commissions. Before the war between William of Orange and King James II he was the surveyor-general of fortifications and buildings. He was literally an architect of Dublin castle. After the war he sat on a commission that assessed wartime losses to government property. He inherited estates in Armagh, Limerick and Kildare. From 1692 he became one of the two Dublin university representatives in the Irish Parliament. He retained his seat in 1695.[1]

He owed two claims to posterity to John Locke. Firstly, the Molyneux question, as it came to be known amongst philosophers, addressed the role of sensory perceptions (as distinct from innate knowledge, which both rejected) upon human understanding and personality. Suppose, he wrote to John Locke in 1693, a man, blind from birth, had learned to distinguish between a cube and a ball by touch alone. If somehow his sight was restored could he tell them apart without touching them first? Molyneux was responding to Locke's account of the human mind as a blank slate shaped by what was empirically perceived through the five senses as set out in

Locke's *Essay Concerning Human Understanding* (1689). Locke cited Molyneux in the second edition of his *Essay*.[2] Lebniz, Voltaire, Diderot and, closer to home, Berkley pondered Molyneux's question.

The focus of this chapter is on Molyneux's use of Locke's political philosophy in his 1698 pamphlet *The Case of Ireland's being Bound by Acts of Parliament in England, Stated* and upon the afterlife of these arguments.[3] Decades after his death he came to be cast as something of a John the Baptist to Henry Grattan's Irish saviour (by Grattan himself) at the inauguration of what came to be known as Grattan's Parliament. On the 16th of April 1782, Grattan reputedly declared to the assembled Irish House of Commons: 'I found Ireland on her knees; I watched over her with an eternal solicitude; I have traced her progress from injuries to arms, and from arms to liberty. Spirit of Swift! spirit of Molyneux!, your genius has prevailed! Ireland is now a nation! In that new character I hail her!' These invocations were added later to the published version of his declaration.[4]

The essence of Molyneux's argument in *The Case of Ireland* was that England and Ireland were two distinct kingdoms under one king, each with their respective Parliamentary tradition and there could be, by the precepts of natural law as depicted by Locke, no subordination on either side. Each ought not to interfere with the jurisdiction of the other. Molyneux's defence of Irish parliamentary autonomy applied Locke's concept of natural rights to the old English in Ireland. This was one of the earliest applications of Locke's *Second Treatise of Government* (1690) which otherwise did not properly enter the political bloodstream on either side of the Atlantic until the 1770s. In his 1698 pamphlet Molyneux pointed readers who desired 'a more full disquisition' of the matter to Chapter Sixteen of *The Second Treatise*, said to be written by his excellent friend John Locke Esquire: 'Whether it be so or not, I know not', wrote Molyneux, 'this I am sure, whoever is the Author, the greatest Genius in Christendom need not disown it'.

Locke had published his *Two Treatises on Government* anonymously; until named by Molyneux without permission, he had never publicly admitted to being its author.[5] *The Case for Ireland* offended English sensibilities. An inquiry at the London House of Commons declared it 'to be of dangerous consequence to the Crown and People of England'. By the 1720s, when its reputation had begun to rise in Ireland, the myth that *The Case for Ireland* had been condemned by parliament to be burnt by the public hangman entered circulation. In reality, Molyneux had influential friends and escaped censure. In any case, *The Case of Ireland* did not find an immediate audience. Molyneux's reputation as an Irish political prophet peaked three-quarters of a century later by which time his pamphlet had been reprinted many times.

Molyneux wrote his pamphlet late in his short life in the aftermath of the 1689–91 Williamite war. He had fled with his family to Chester in England and returned to Dublin after the Battle of the Boyne. Many other Protestant

Irish with the means to do so did likewise. As described in *The Case of Ireland*:

> In the Year 1689, when most of the Protestant Nobility, Gentry, and Clergy of Ireland were driven out of that Kingdom by the Insolencies and Barbarities of the Irish Papists, who were then in Arms throughout the Kingdom, and in all Places of Authority under King James, newly returned to them out of France; the only Refuge we had to fly to was in England, where Multitudes continued for many Months, destitute of all Manner of Relief, but such as the Charity of England afforded, which indeed was very munificent, and never to be-forgotten.

The Williamite war instilled a heightened sense of insecurity amongst Protestants in Ireland. Had William of Orange lost Ireland to James II, they would have lost their ascendancy, their property and perhaps even their lives. Later Whig histories of the seventeenth century, such as David Hume's, placed huge emphasis on the massacre of Protestants by Catholics in 1641. Protestant insecurities also extended to relations with England. *The Case of Ireland* coincided with other efforts by Irish Protestants to consolidate their battered Ascendancy.[6] Real political power rested with officials appointed by the Crown and with the Government in Westminster. Protestant political activism in the 1692 sitting of the Dublin Parliament focused on wresting back some control of Irish affairs.

Molyneux and Locke

Molyneux had written in praise of the first edition of Locke's *Essay Concerning Human Understanding*. In 1692 Locke instigated a correspondence and asked Molyneux's 'advise and assistance' about a proposed second edition of the *Essay*. Their ongoing correspondence features prominently in a 1708 volume *Some Familiar Letters Between Mr Locke and Several of his Friends*.[7] Locke repeatedly encouraged criticism with the aim of improving the second edition of his *Essay*. Their correspondence focused more on their shared interest in natural philosophy than on political philosophy but sometimes alluded to the latter. The focus of the *Essay on Human Understanding* was epistemology and Molyneux subscribed to Locke's theories of human knowledge. In their correspondence on what became Molyneux's question in the second edition of the *Essay*, both agreed that empirical experience was necessary for a blind person to be able to distinguish one shape from another by sight alone. Against this, for example, Leibniz argued that such a person could identify a shape by sight by applying rational principles to the sensory knowledge he had already acquired by touch.[8] These epistemological questions – whether a person was born a blank slate and shaped by empirical experiences (Locke's view) or born in possession of innate ideas and understandings (Leibniz's view) have had considerable ramifications for social questions.

In a letter dated 20 January 1693 Molyneux professed to agree with Locke's epistemology (essentially the notion of individual human identity as a blank slate informed by what it continuously perceives from birth through the five senses[9]) but strongly challenged his writings on children; Locke's prescriptions for forming the minds of children were more authoritarian than those of Molyneux. In effect, Molyneux argued that their development would benefit from a greater degree of autonomy, especially in being allowed diversion and recreation, than Locke seemed to sanction. He vehemently disagreed with Locke's statement that 'a child should never be suffered to have what he craves, so much as speaks for, much less as he cries for it' and another that 'in all wants of fancy and affection, they should never, if once declared, be hearkened to, or complied with'.

He argued that what was 'delightful to the child' were 'diversions of his own choice'. Locke replied that the natural wants of children included recreation as much as their need for food but their development did not benefit from over-indulgence of these. Molyneux explained how he educated his young son – Molyneux's wife had committed suicide in 1691 when their child was two years of age ('He is come from a tender and sickly mother') – using methods proposed by Locke. Molyneux used flashcards (numbers, syllables and words printed in hand on the face of a pack of cards) in games aimed at teaching the child to read and count at the same time. Locke, who had no children, described how, in the house where he lived, the only son of a very tender mother was almost destroyed by a too tender keeping. Though Molyneux subscribed to Locke's theories of human understanding he disagreed on the practical implications of these. So too, when it came to Locke's political philosophy, Molyneux could at once faithfully subscribe to Locke's theories yet impose his own interpretations upon these.

The topic of Chapter Sixteen of *The Second Treatise of Government* was conquest. It addressed how the Norman conquest of England gave them dominion over the Saxons and Britons that were then the inhabitants of the country. All descended from the Normans were freemen, not subjects by conquest. Insofar as the law applied to Normans and other subjects alike, and it became harder over time to distinguish these from one another, in practice there came to be no difference in their respective freedom or privileges.[10] But supposing – which seldom happened according to Locke – conquerors and the conquered did not become over time one people under the same laws and freedom, what then was the power of a lawful conqueror over the subdued?

Locke addressed this question in a number of steps. Any such power over the subdued was 'despotical'; the lives of defeated opponents were forfeit, but not those of their families or property. This Locke, admitted, 'at first sight will seem a strange doctrine, it being so quite contrary to the practice of the world'. Locke reasoned that it was wrong to punish children for the sins of fathers, wives for the crimes of husbands, wrong to seize their goods and property through which nature 'willith the preservation of all mankind'. A conqueror, Locke argued, was entitled to reparations, 'to the utmost farthing'. War inevitably destroyed a couple of years' worth of harvest; reparations were part of this cost but even if these amounted to the equivalent of five-years produce this was of little account set against the perpetual productive value of land. Nothing in 'a state of nature' ('as all princes and government are in reference to one another') could give the conqueror the power to dispossess to posterity of the vanquished, and turn them out of that inheritance, which ought to be in the possession of them and their descendants for generations. Such were the arguments that Molyneux drew upon in *The Case for Ireland*.

Locke's *Second Treatise* expanded on a doctrine of rule by consent that emerged during the Middle Ages to protect the rights of the privileged nobility against an absolutist conception of monarchy.[11] What Locke meant by consent was something akin to acquiescence. This connected the idea of a social contract with a Protestant emphasis on voluntarism. Both served to promote the belief that obedience to authority could only be legitimate if it was based on the voluntary submission of those subject to the exercise of authority. His moral philosophy was therefore an admixture of natural law and the positive moral law tradition that flourished after the Reformation.[12]

For Locke, as for earlier natural law philosophers like Aquinas, some understanding of God's will, His plan and the basis of a moral law antecedent to human laws could be acquired through the exercise of reason. Locke defined Natural Law as 'the decree of the divine will discernable by the light of nature' as understood by what reason tells us 'what is and is not in conformity with rational nature'. Moral law was understood to accord with human nature but not in a way that could ever discard reference to God's will. Locke at times emphasised the importance of moral positivism; in particular, the revelation of divine law contained in the Bible with its presumed emphasis upon obedience and acquiescence and upon the threat of divine sanctions.[13] Early positive law theorists such as Hobbes and Bentham emphasised coercion as the basis of moral and legal authority. For Locke however, a natural law emphasis on voluntarism won out over a fear of God's sanctions. A person did not just obey God's will because he or she is coerced. The capacity of a person to understand, through reason, his or her duties and obligations was emphasised. This translated in the secular realm into an emphasis on consent as the principle that underpins the legitimacy of civil authority. A person did not just obey a sovereign because he or she was coerced; they acquiesced or consented to such rule.

Locke's understanding of natural law emphasised the primacy of a right of self-preservation. This superseded duties to others or to a transcendent order. Within Locke's moral philosophy rights and duties coexisted but rights came first. Rights took priority over the will or authority of those with power who would deny others access to resources needed for self-preservation. Locke reasoned that the natural condition of mankind was a state of equality. As stated in the second of his *Two Treatises of Government*:

> A state also of equality, wherein all the power and jurisdiction is reciprocal, no one having more than another: there being nothing more evident, than that creatures of the same species and rank promiscuously born to all the same advantages of nature, and the use of the same facilities, should also be equal one amongst another without subordination or subjection, unless the Lord and Master of them all, should by any manifest declaration of his will set one above another.[14]

For Locke, there existed a state of moral equality, a basic notion of human worth that translated into a political theory of an equal right to freedom of the person and the right to self-government.[15] However, Locke and contemporaries like Molyneux read less into this presumption than did subsequent generations of readers committed to democratic politics. Locke's understanding of consent equated with voluntary assent or acquiescence.[16] His presumption about the primacy of a right to self-preservation and the existence, by implication, of a right to equality was tempered by an acknowledgement, rooted in moral positivism, that such rights are dependent upon the will of God. He suggested that inequality could be justified *if* it were in accordance with such will or if it emanated from the consent or the will of the people.

The case of Ireland stated

Theories of conquest and of the rights of the conquered had obvious application to Irish history. But Molyneux's interest was predominantly in the claims of Irish Protestants; in defence of these he marshalled arguments drawn from historical precedent – about the constitutional rights to property and representation of the still-Catholic pre-Reformation English Irish – alongside a case built line-by-line upon Locke's writings on conquest in *The Second Treatise*. Molyneux's prose was often convoluted by comparison to Locke's and weighed down by chains of rhetorical questions framed negatively. An exception was his conclusion where this method worked to powerful effect:

> Does it not manifestly appear by the Constitution of Ireland, that it is a compleat Kingdom within itself? Do not the Kings of England bear the Stile of Ireland amongst the rest of their Kingdoms? Is this agreeable to the Nature of a Colony? Do they use the Title of Kings of Virginia, New England, or Mary-land? Was not Ireland given by Henry the Second in a

Parliament at Oxford to his Son John, and made thereby an absolute Kingdom, separate and wholly independent on England, until they both came united again in him, after the Death of his Brother Richard without Issue? Have not Multitudes of Acts of Parliament both in England and Ireland, declared Ireland a compleat Kingdom? Is not Ireland stiled in them all, the Kingdom, or Realm of Ireland? Do these Names agree to a Colony? Have we not a Parliament, and Courts of Judicature? Do these Things agree with a Colony? This on all hands involves so many Absurdities, that I think it deserves nothing more of our Consideration.

The essence of Molyneux's precedent case for Ireland was that the settlement in the reign of Henry II that gave Ireland its parliament was a contract not a conquest. Ireland, Molyneux emphasised, was a kingdom, not a colony. His argument changed little from Locke's other than to substitute the word invader for conqueror. Suppose, Molyneux wrote, 'a just invader, one that has Right on his Side', attacks 'a Nation in an hostile Manner' and that 'those who oppose him are in the Wrong, let us then see what Power he gets, and over whom. First, 'Tis plain he gets by his Conquest no Power over those who conquered with him; they that fought on his Side, whether as private Soldiers or Commanders, cannot suffer by the Conquest, but must at least be as much Freemen, as they were before. If any lost their Freedom by the Norman Conquest, (supposing King William the First, had Right to invade England) it was only the Saxons and Britons, and not the Normans that conquered with him.' Molyneux distinguished between the rights of the conquered Irish and their conquerors, the English who settled in Ireland who had become, he argued, the vast majority of the Irish or, more accurately, those Irish who should be counted as having rights from precedent:

> Supposing Hen. II. had Right to invade this Island, and that he had been opposed therein by the Inhabitants, it was only the Ancient Race of the Irish that could suffer by this Subjugation; the English and Britains, that came over and conquered with him, retain'd all the Freedoms and Immunities of Freeborn Subjects; they nor their Descendants could not in reason lose these, for being successful and victorious; for so the State of both Conquerors and conquered shall be equally slavish.
>
> Now 'tis manifest that the great Body of the present People of Ireland, are the Proginy of the English and Britains, that from time to time have come over into this Kingdom; and there remains but a meer handful of the Ancient Irish at this Day; I may say, not one in a Thousand: So that if I, or any Body else, claim the like Freedoms with the Natural Born Subjects of England, as being descended from them, it will be impossible to prove the contrary. I conclude therefore, that a just Conqueror gets no Power, but only over those who have actually assisted in that Unjust Force that is used against him.

There were several echoes of Locke's *Second Treatise* here. Locke had argued that after the Norman Conquest both Normans and Saxons had become indistinguishable before the law and had culturally assimilated over the generations. Molyneux claimed that just one in a thousand of the Ancient Irish remained and inferred that these had either been destroyed, assimilated or were somehow excluded from the jurisdiction of natural rights. Catholics at that time constituted at least two-thirds of the Irish population. None of these were old Gaelic Irish; many were in fact old English.

Molyneux's overwhelming concern was with the parliamentary rights of the Protestant Irish, rooted by precedent in those of the pre-Reformation English Irish.[17] These, he argued, had lost no rights by Conquest. He asserted that the just conqueror has an absolute Power over the lives and liberties of the conquered, because the conquered, by putting themselves in a state of war and using unjust force, had thereby forfeited their lives: 'For quitting Reason, (which is the Rule between Man and Man) and using Force, (which is the Way of Beasts) they become liable to be destroy'd by him against whom they use Force, as any savage wild Beast that is dangerous to his Being.' But not, paraphrasing Locke, their families; nor was their property forfeit:

> The Father, by his Miscarriages and Violence, can forfeit but his own Life, he involves not his Children in his Guilt or Destruction. His Goods, which Nature (that willeth the Preservation of all Mankind as far as possible) hath made to belong to his Children to sustain them, do still continue to belong to his Children. 'Tis true indeed it usually happens that Damage attends unjust Force; and as far as the Repair of this Damage requires it, so far the rightful Conqueror may invade the Goods and Estate of the conquered; but when this Damage is made up, his Title to the Goods ceases, and the Residue belongs to the Wife and Children of the subdued.

It is less than clear from the text which fathers and which sons Molyneux had in mind in evoking Locke's argument. He had no concern for the Irish Papists who rose 'against the King and Protestants of Ireland'. After the Rebellion of 1641 several Acts of Parliament in England were made for reimbursing the costs of their defeat by disposing of their lands. What then of *their* dispossessed sons? Who amongst the Irish should pay reparations? Leave that, he proposed, to an autonomous Irish Protestant parliament.

How the Protestant Irish might dispose of Catholic property or whether or not they would dispossess Catholic sons from the sins of their fathers hardly needed explanation. In 1695, three years before *The Case for Ireland* was published, the first of the Penal Laws was enacted by the Dublin Parliament in which Molyneux sat. Another Act to Prevent the Further Growth of Popery became law in 1704. This prohibited the inheritance of land by Catholics. Sons who wished to realise their natural rights would have to convert.

Molyneux's constitutional history of Ireland made copious references to 500 years of case law in disputing the subordination of Ireland – meaning Protestant Ireland – to the English Parliament. King John had been crowned as king of Ireland some twenty-two years before accession to the Crown of England. Thereafter the Crowns of Ireland and England were united in the royal Person of King John and his successors. John's son, King Henry III, on 12 November 1216, during the first year of his reign, granted to Ireland a *Magna Charta*, 'exactly agreeable to the *Magna Carta* which he granted to *England* eight years later; only in ours we have *Civitas Dublin*, & *Avenliffe*, instead of *Civitas London*, & *Thamesis*; with other Alterations of the like kind where needful'.[18] The Great Charter of Ireland secured rights for the King's Anglo-Norman subjects in Ireland.[19]

Molyneux's aim in charting this constitutional history was to build the case for Irish parliamentary autonomy. He drew upon the Lockean principle of rule by consent as well as upon precedent. That Ireland should be bound by Acts of Parliament made in England, was against Reason and the common Rights of all Mankind:

> All Men are by Nature in a State of Equality, in respect of Jurisdiction or Dominion. This I take to be a Principle in itself so evident, that it stands in need of little Proof. It is not to be conceived, that Creatures of the same Species and Rank, promiscuously born to all the same Advantages of Nature, and the Use of the same Faculties, should be subordinate and subject one to another; these to this or that of the same Kind.

Molyneux's innovation was to extend the principle of rule by consent to nations, a term he used repeatedly in cases where Locke had referred to individual men:

> No one or more Men can by Nature challenge any Right, Liberty or Freedom, or any ease in his Property, Estate or Conscience, which all other Men have not an equally just claim to. Is England a free People? So ought France to be. Is Poland so? Turkey likewise, and all the Eastern Dominion ought to be so: And the same runs throughout the whole Race of Mankind.

He argued that the principle of consent was breached when laws made in the English Parliament were applied to Ireland. This went against the Common Laws of England that were in force in both England and Ireland. The Irish were not represented in the English Parliament but had its laws applied to them. The result was, according to Molyneux:

> we are neither personally, nor representatively present . . . Whether it be not against Equity and Reason that a Kingdom regulated within itself, and having its own Parliament, should be bound without *their Consent*, by the Parliament of another Kingdom, I leave the Reader to consider.

The constitutional problems that vexed Molyneux turned on Poynings' Law, named for the then Viceroy of Ireland, enacted by the Irish Parliament in 1495, in the tenth year of Henry VII. Poynings' Law remained in place until 1782 when Ireland achieved legislative independence. In Molyneux's summary it stated that no Act of Parliament should pass in Ireland, before it was first certified by 'the chief Governor and Privy Council here, under the broad Seal of this Kingdom, to the King and his Privy Council in England, and received their Approbation, and by them be remitted hither under the broad Seal of England, here to be passed into a Law'. In effect, Poynings' Law hamstrung the Irish Parliament. It could veto bills and rubber stamp legislation but not propose it; the Lieutenant Governor drafted such legislation for submission to the King.

In 1692 some members of the Irish House of Commons sought to increase its legislative role. On the 27th of October the Irish House resolved that it had the undoubted right to determine the ways and means of raising money and that it had the sole and undoubted right to prepare heads of bills to do so. In protest it refused to pass fourteen bills proposed in the usual way by the Lieutenant Governor during its 1662 sitting. A compromise was agreed in 1695 that gave the Irish Parliament a role in drafting bills, as distinct from the sole right its members sought.

However, Molyneux envisaged future constitutional dangers arising from Poynings' Law. As the power of Parliament in England grew and that of the King waned, Ireland's aspiration to be recognised as an autonomous kingdom under the same King was increasingly in jeopardy. Ireland's status as a Kingdom meant less and less as the constitutional authority of the King declined. The original purpose of Poynings' Law, he argued, had been to prevent anything 'passing in the Parliament of Ireland surreptitiously, to the Prejudice of the King, or the English Interest of Ireland'. But this was a needless caution, insofar as the King and Parliament of England had power at any time to revoke or annul any such proceedings. He did not object to this legislative veto per se. Several times and in a number of ways he attacked the right of the King and English Parliament to make Acts in England that bound his subjects in Ireland without their consent and emphasised the dangers of doing so:

> If the Religion, Lives, Liberties, Fortunes, and Estates of the Clergy, Nobility and Gentry of Ireland, may be disposed of, without their Privity and Consent, what Benefit have they of any Laws, Liberties, or Privileges granted unto them by the Crown of England? I am loth to give their Condition a hard Name; but I have no other Notion of Slavery, but being bound by a Law to which I do not Consent.

If Irish Protestants were, in Molyneux's rhetoric, in danger of becoming slaves what then of Catholics? Locke subscribed to natural rights but not universal rights. Natural law philosophy since Aristotle held that certain categories of persons including children, slaves and persons of diminished capacity for reason possessed lesser natural rights. In this tradition, Locke's *Second Treatise* offered some justifications for slavery.[20] As put in *The Second Treatise*:

> But there is another sort of servant which by a peculiar name we call slaves, who being captives taken in a just war are, by the right of Nature, subjected to the absolute dominion and arbitrary power of their masters. These men having, as I say, forfeited their lives and, with it, their liberties, and lost their estates, and being in the state of slavery, not capable of any property, cannot in that state be considered as any part of civil society, the chief end whereof is the preservation of property.[21]

The just war argument hardly applied to the slave trade. Locke had benefited personally as a substantial shareholder in the Royal African Company (where he had invested 600 pounds) and also invested a lesser amount in a company of Bahama Adventurers for the purchase of several slaves. Locke was well versed in the economics of slavery.[22] For all this the opening sentence of his *First Treatise* proclaimed that slavery was such a vile estate in man that it was hardly to be concieved that an Englishman should plead for it.[23] But in various writings Locke fudged distinctions between servitude, indenture and slavery to infer that the rights of the master in each case resulted from a contract between both parties and so implied that slaves had somehow consented to intergenerational bondage.[24] Lockean conceptions of rights only came to be deployed against slavery when it came to be argued that natural rights were universal rights. But in post-1691 Ireland, where Penal Laws were being enacted, the putative rights of Irish Catholics stood on no such bottom. They were, by Molyneux's inference, justifiably enslaved under the rules of conquest and were of no consequence in any deliberation about the future of Irish civil society. What Molyneux meant rhetorically by slavery was the denial of rule by consent to the Irish Protestants who comprised this civil society. Various interpreters have argued that the denunciation of slavery that opened Locke's *First Treatise* was no less a rhetorical flourish, a salvo directed against political tyranny and the absence of rule by consent.[25]

In his conclusion Molyneux argued that it would prove 'highly inconvenient for England to assume this Authority over the Kingdom of Ireland', that it was dangerous to make light of the constitutions of kingdoms; 'it is dangerous to those who do it, it is grievous to those that suffer it'. He then evoked the dangerous potential consequences of an absence of rule by consent:

> If England assumes a Jurisdiction over Ireland, whereby they think their Rights and Liberties are taken away; that their Parliaments are rendered merely nugatory, and their Lives and Fortunes depend on the Will of a Legislature, wherein they are not Parties, there may be ill Consequences

of this. Advancing the Power of the Parliament of England, by breaking the Rights of another, may in Time have ill Effects.

He argued that the rights of Parliament should be preserved sacred and inviolable, wherever they are found. Echoing Locke's defence of the Glorious Revolution in *The Second Treatise*, he argued that:

> parliamentary government, once so universal all over Europe, is now almost vanished from amongst the Nations thereof. Our King's Dominions are the only Supporters of this noble Gothick Constitution, save only what little Remains may be found thereof in Poland. We should not therefore make so light of that Sort of Legislature, and as it were abolish it in one Kingdom of the Three, wherein it appears; but rather cherish and encourage it wherever we meet it.

Molyneux, Locke and the case of Ireland restated

The specific case for Irish parliamentary autonomy advanced by Molyneux was built upon ideas that really only entered the domain of mainstream political argument several decades later. Ian McBride suggests that the rise and fall of the popularity of *The Case of Ireland* during the eighteenth century served as a barometer of eighteenth-century Irish constitutional tensions and patriotic feeling.[26] *The Case of Ireland* found an audience 'with each burst of Irish national sentiment throughout the century'; it was cited by Swift, Charles Lucas, Grattan and even Wolfe Tone.[27] An anonymous 1779 pamphlet described *The Case for Ireland* as 'the manual of Irish liberty'.[28] But rising interest in Moylneux over time and the trajectory of Protestant patriotic politics coincided with the rising influence of Locke, particularly in America. American influence upon Irish political aspirations during the 1770s and early 1780s should not be underestimated.

As a result of Molyneux's influence, Locke's *Essay on Human Understanding* became part of the curriculum at Trinity College Dublin in 1682. It would take another eighty-eight years for it to be joined by his *Two Treatises on Government*. Yet, Locke framed philosophical and theological questions that variously preoccupied Bishop Berkeley, Francis Hutcheson and Edmund Burke.[29] In 1724, in his fourth Drapier letter, Swift cited Locke and Molyneux as dangerous authors, 'who talk of Liberty as a blessing to which the whole race of Mankind hath an Original Title; wherof nothing but unlawful force can divest them'.[30]

Molyneux was an unusually early adopter and adapter of Locke's political philosophy. Only a handful of English acquaintances or correspondents are known to have mentioned *The Two Treatises* with Locke's approval during his lifetime.[31] What Locke made of Molyneux's use of his *Second Treatise* is unknown; until his death in 1704 Locke went to considerable lengths to protect his anonymity. He gained public identification as a major political authority in Ireland before he did so in England even though he was intellectually influential amongst the emerging Whigs during his own lifetime.[32] A few early engagements with *The Two Treatises* came from pamphleteers writing in response to Molyneux. The most notable was Charles Leslie's 160 page long *Considerations of importance to Ireland in a letter to a member of parliament thereupon the occasion of Mr Molyneux's later book* (1698) dedicated to 'the Modern English Nobility, Gentry, and Protestant Inhabitants of Ireland'.[33] By the mid-eighteenth century *The Two Treatises* loomed large in Whig histories of the Glorious Revolution, notably in the writings of David Hume.[34] By the end of the eighteenth century Locke emerged as the most frequently cited authority in Irish pamphlet literature generated by the debate preceding the Act of Union.[35] From the end of the eighteenth century Locke's ideas increasingly came to be viewed through the lens of Tom Paine's *The Rights of Man*, first published in 1791. He was also cited in a number of pamphlets during the 1770s. These took from Locke what Molyneux did, refutations of the notion that claims based on conquest conveyed power over the descendants.[36]

Following the original 1698 edition *The Case of Ireland* was reprinted in 1706, 1719, 1720 and 1725. After a twenty-four year gap it was again republished in 1749. A further four editions were published between 1770 and 1782. The 1770 edition added a long foreword, supposedly written by Henry Flood and praised by Benjamin Franklin as 'shrewdly written'.[37] This restated Molyneux's sense of grievance at having been driven temporarily abroad. It argued that inadequate parliamentary autonomy had rendered the interests of Ireland a pawn on the chessboard of English parliamentary politics. It distinguished the Irish, meaning the Protestant patriot Irish, from 'the wild ferocious Natives of Ireland'. Although Molyneux had not described the Catholic Irish in such terms it was true to his Lockean rationale for not considering their entitlement to rule by consent.

At a 1791 celebration of Bastille Day in Belfast, Molyneux was the sole Irishman other than Grattan to be toasted. Locke was toasted but so too was Tom Paine, who defined the principle of rule by consent in wider terms.[38] In April 1782 Grattan secured the Irish Parliament that Molyneux wished for. In May that year the London Parliament rescinded Poynings' Law and passed various other Acts that gave independence to Irish judges subject to the Irish House of Lords. In his April 1782 speech that divined the Spirit of Molyneux at work Grattan optimistically summarised the new political settlement:

> There is not a man of forty shillings freehold that is not associated in this our claim of right, and bound to die in its defence; cities, counties,

associations, Protestants and Catholics; it seems as if the people had joined in one great national sacrament; a flame has descended from heaven on the intellect of Ireland, plays round her head, and encompasses her understanding with a consecrated glory.

Catholics gained some important freedoms under the 1782 settlement. However, the Irish Parliament was still defined by the Penal Laws and the Protestant patriot mindset proposed by Molyneux at the end of the previous century. For example, Irish Catholics could not hold elected office and efforts by Catholics or on their behalf to redress such exclusions were depicted as seditions. It took eighteen years for Grattan's Parliament to fall asunder. Some of the architects of its downfall were the Protestant United Irishmen influenced by Lockean ideas of natural rights as these had come to be understood in the era of the American and French revolutions. But it was also the case that the spirit of Molyneux – his case for exclusively Protestant privilege, parliamentary autonomy and the denial of natural rights to Catholics – had failed to invoke a viable future.

CHAPTER FOUR

Edmund Burke and the case for Union

Edmund Burke was most likely born in 1730, a year after the publication of Swift's *Modest Proposal*. He died in 1797 in Bath, having lived in a milieu recognisable from Jane Austen's early nineteenth-century novels, loyal to the hierarchies she depicted and a defender of rank as her characters understood it. He came to be esteemed as a political philosopher, a great prose stylist and – always a stumbling block for his Irish reputation – as a great Englishman. The focus of this chapter is upon Burke's writings on Ireland from the 1760s until his death. Burke was a Protestant critic of what came in his lifetime to be called the Protestant Ascendancy. In a letter to his son Richard in 1794 he pondered the meaning of ascendancy. Rank had its duties; Burke understood 'ascendancy' to denote a moral rather than civil or political basis of authority. It signified influence obtained over the mind of some other person legitimised by love or reverence, by artifice even, or by seduction. Ascendancy, on any such basis, offered a legitimate basis for authority and hierarchy. On such criteria the Irish Protestant Ascendancy had earned no such legitimacy:

> It is neither more nor less than the resolution of one set of people in Ireland to consider themselves as the sole citizens in the commonwealth and to keep a dominion over the rest by reducing them to absolute slavery under a military power, to divide the public estate, which is the result of general contribution, as a military booty solely among themselves.[1]

One month before his death in 1797 Burke wrote to one Dr Laurence that the system of military government in Ireland was 'mad to the extreme, made worse in the mad hands in which it is placed'. He railed against governmental incapacity wrought by jobbery propped up and paid for by England; 'as long as they can draw on England for indefinite aids of men and sums of money' such corruption will persist.[2] Earlier, in March 1796, he complained to another correspondent that Ireland was in a truly unpleasant situation. The Irish government was ineffective, false in its maxims, totally ignorant in the art of governing. He had received letters from the fast friends of Irish Catholics – the reality being that Catholics then needed Protestants to speak on their behalf – to solicit government in England. Such petitions were rebuffed: 'neglect, contumely, and insult, were never the ways of keeping friends; and they add nothing to force against an enemy'.[3]

This enemy at the gates, Burke had made clear in his 1790 *Reflections on the Revolution in France*, was the kind of revolution that would sweep away the *ancien régime*. He usually described this threat as 'Jacobin', a word with shifting meanings in the Irish case. The Catholic and old English in Ireland who allied with James II and Louis XIV did so for a Catholic cause but revolutionary France, Burke argued, opposed all religion and all kings. In 1795 Burke wrote that his 'whole politics' turned on what would most depress the cause of Jacobinism:

> The Jacobins have resolved to destroy the whole frame and fabric of the old societies of the world, and to regenerate them after their fashion. To obtain an army for this purpose they everywhere engage the poor by holding out to them as a bribe the spoils of the rich. This I take to be a fair description of the principles and leading maxims of the enlightened of our day, who are commonly called Jacobins.[4]

In a 1796 letter Burke made what was for him an important distinction between Protestant Jacobinism – the kind that was speculative in its origins and arose 'from wantonness and fullness of bread' might possibly be kept under by firmness and prudence – and its attractions to Irish Catholics under grievous oppression. Such Jacobinism arising 'from penury and irritation, from scorned loyalty and rejected allegiance' had roots shot into the depths of hell. It constituted a radical evil born in local evil circumstances: 'All the evils of Ireland originate within itself'. The United Irishmen had in their irresponsibility (Burke used the word 'folly'), represented these evils as English in origin when 'in truth, its chief guilt is in its total neglect, its utter oblivion, its shameful indifference and its entire ignorance of Ireland, and of everything that relates to it, and not in an oppressive disposition towards that unknown region'.

The folly of Protestant United Irishmen had sprung from that of the Irish Directory, the Protestant Ascendancy 'junto' in power. The latter sustained a system that would never be abandoned as long as it brought them advantage. In 1796, in his last major letter on Ireland, Burke once again detailed the oppressions and grievances of the Catholic majority but, here as before, insisted that revolt against lawful authority, however tyrannical, was not a viable option. Their riots, disorders and rebellious disposition furnished new arguments for English support for the authority of the

Directory: 'So long, therefore, as disorders in the country become pretexts for adding to the power and emolument of a junto, means will be found to keep one part of it, or another, in a perpetual state of confusion and disorder'. This was the traditional policy of such men. They used the discontents that, under them, broke out amongst the people, to hold their situation. Specifically the Directory used religious persecution to cement their power. In doing so they fuelled the Jacobinism that Burke regarded as an even greater tyranny.[5]

Burke's concluding argument on Irish affairs was that liberty for Irishmen was more likely to be achieved under the British constitution, through closer political connections with England – exemplified by the Act of Union three years after his death – and by bringing Ireland under English constitutional norms. Let English law apply properly to Ireland with its reforms and franchises, extend the benefits of the constitution to Irish Catholics doubly oppressed by religious discrimination and woefully ineffective and malicious rule by the Irish Protestant Directory of Dublin's Parliament, and this would create a basis of freedom more meaningful and less destructive than that Irish freedom as proposed by the example of France.

The laws on popery and the malign ascendancy that sustained them

To seek to pigeonhole Burke as Protestant, Anglo-Irish or arch-conservative would be simplistic. Burke's mother Mary Nagle was Catholic. Her grandfather Garret Nagle was a Jacobite; he had fought for James II but managed to retain his property after the defeat of 1691.[6] Burke's sister, Julianna was raised as a Catholic. In 1757 he married Jane Nugent, the Catholic daughter of a Catholic doctor who became a father figure and close friend Burke, according to one biographer, lived according to his beliefs that 'man was a pre-eminently a sociable animal, best able to fulfil his nature in groups, in families, in extended kinship networks, in larger national and religious loyalties'. Elsewhere the same biographer wrote that throughout his life, Burke sought to belong and be accepted.[7] Conor Cruise O'Brien wrote that the 'clan' at whose head Burke marched was shot through with Catholicism at a time when Protestantism might be feigned but Catholicism, being socially and economically disadvantageous, must be presumed to be sincere.[8] In 1793 a contemporary, Sir George Eliot, wrote sneeringly that Burke had gathered around him at his house in England 'such a train after him as would sink anybody but himself'; this included a brother who was 'rather oppressive with animal spirits and brogue' and a companion of his wife who was 'the most perfect She Paddy ever caught'.[9] On the home front no less than in the public domain Burke never denied his Irish roots. His layered loyalties to family, Ireland, and to England fascinated his peers and ideological opponents. Let me purloin the 1797 quotation used by Luke Gibbons on the closing page of his *Edmund Burke in Ireland*.[10] Wolfe Tone describes a conversation with Tom Paine:

> I mentioned to him that I had known Burke in England, and spoke of the shattered state of his mind in consequence of the death of his only son Richard. Paine immediately said that it was the *Rights of Man* which had broke his heart, and that the death of his son gave him occasion to develop the chagrin, which had preyed upon him since the appearance of that work. I am sure the *Rights of Man* have tormented Burke exceedingly, but I have seen myself the workings of a father's grief on his spirit, and I could not be deceived. *Paine has no children.*[11]

In his *Reflections on the Revolution in France* Burke contrasted the costs of revolution ('plots, massacres and assassinations'), its drama and spectacle with 'cheap, bloodless reformation, a guiltless liberty' that must appear vapid and flat to putative revolutionaries.[12] Burke's conservative political vision emphasised, above all else, stability and security sustained by a viable social contract. As put in *Reflections in the Revolution in France*, writing in the persona of an Englishman to an imagined French audience:

> You would have had a free constitution; a potent monarchy; a disciplined army; a reformed and venerated clergy; a mitigated but spirited nobility, to lead your virtue, not to overlay it; you would have had a liberal order of commons, to emulate and to recruit that nobility; you would have had a protected, satisfied, laborious, and obedient people, taught to seek and to recognise the happiness that is to be found by virtue in all conditions; in which consists the true moral equality of mankind, and not in that monstrous fiction that inspires false ideas and vain expectations into men destined to travel in the obscure walk of laborious life, serves only to aggravate and imbitter that real inequality, which it can never remove, and which the order of civil life establishes as much for the benefit of those it must leave in a humble state, as those whom it is able to exalt to a condition more splendid, but not more happy.[13]

Burke's anti-Jacobin politics have an antecedent in Saint Augustine who wrote his *City of God* amidst the chaos of the fall of the Roman Empire. Augustine, like Burke, would pay a premium for stable government. Augustine likened states to robber bands and indeed acknowledged that many small kingdoms originated from such. Both, he argued, were held together by a social contact. Both maintained a form of order and a form of earthly justice. Kings operated much like robbers when engaged in conquest but on a larger scale. The king was distinguished from the robber by the nature of his legitimacy amongst those he ruled and by his capacity to bring order. Augustine maintained that the state and its instruments of punishment were divinely ordained institutions designed as remedies as well as punishments for the sinful condition of fallen man. God uses the evil desires of fallen man as a means for the establishment of earthly peace and for the just punishment of mankind's vices. The state, even when ruled by evil men and populated by the unredeemed, was therefore a gift from God to man. The authority of the ruler over his subjects was therefore derived from God. Life on earth was best thought of as a proving ground for the soul. The institutions of social, economic and political life, at best, might hold the dark passions of sinful men in check and thus provide a measure of peace and stability. The breakdown of social and political order through disobedience or rebellion was therefore the worst of all possible earthly evils.[14] Augustine summed up his fatalistic politics in the following terms:

> It would be better for good administrators of the commonwealth to make … provision by the free consent of the people than by extorting it from the conquered. But as to those things which truly confer dignity, namely security and good morals, I entirely fail to see what difference it makes, aside from the most empty pride of human glory, that some men should be conquerors and other conquered.[15]

Burke, no less than Augustine, feared the chaos that might erupt if established authority failed. Various writings on Burke have sought to chart the influence of terror and chaos in Ireland upon Burke's political conservatism. For example, Luke Gibbons connects the 'anxious aesthetics' of Burke's 1757 *A Philosophical Enquiry into the origin of our Ideas of the Sublime and the Beautiful* to the colonial terrors in the Ireland of Burke's time.[16] Burke defined the sublime as a feeling analogous to feelings of terror, fear and pain. Gibbons emphasises how in 1766 Fr Nicholas Sheehy, a relative of Burke through marriage, was hung, drawn and quartered for alleged involvement in a Whiteboy murder but finds other incidents before 1757 which suggest that there was nothing abstract about Burke's understanding of colonial terror.[17]

Burke had imbibed a keen sense of colonial injustice in Ireland. In July 1746, then a sixteen-year-old university student, Burke wrote to a friend that he had embarked on the study of 'the history of Ireland, our own poor country'.[18] In 1759 he fell out with David Hume following a 'violent' disagreement about Irish historiography. Hume's *History of England from the Invasion of Julius Caesar to the Revolution of 1688* mobilised claims that in 1641 barbaric Catholics had committed large-scale massacres of Protestants to justify the legitimacy of subsequent campaigns in Ireland.[19] Such massacres occurred but never, according to John Curry and Charles O'Connor, two Catholic antiquarians whose arguments against Hume Burke endorsed, in such vast numbers.[20] Burke's understanding of Irish history departed considerably from Hume's Whig history of the English

Constitution which both cherished even if, for both, the Constitution, as put back on track by the Glorious Revolution, was part of a history of progress.[21] Generations of Whig historians have depicted 1688 as a bloodless revolution whereby the transfer of sovereign power from King James II to William of Orange was peaceably approved by Parliament.[22] Such happy history, Burke was all too aware, hardly pertained to Ireland; Burke's writings on Irish affairs sought to reconcile this history of British liberty with an Irish one that included 'terrible exterminatory periods'.[23]

In his 1775 *Speech on Conciliation with America*, Burke argued that the legitimacy of English authority lay in it being the guarantor of liberty in accordance with its own constitution. 'Let the colonies always keep the idea of the civil rights associated with your government', he argued, 'and no force under heaven will be of power to tear them from their allegiance.'[24] Burke's case for concessions to American colonists drew from the same well as the case for Ireland made by Molyneux. English conquest, he declared, gave Ireland a parliament. The *Magna Carta* applied to Ireland as well as England. English colonisation, 'changed the people', 'altered the religion' but 'never touched the form or vital substance of government' or ever formally imposed taxes on Ireland for all the 'irregular things done in the confusion of mighty troubles'.[25] Burke urged England to trust, as he did, in its own Glorious Revolution in its dealings with its colonies. America, he argued to the English Parliament, was entitled to all the constitutional liberties accorded to Ireland. His 1775 speech sidestepped the constitutional status of the Catholic Irish no less than Molyneux did eighty years earlier in making his case for a Protestant Parliament.

Burke's first major writings on Ireland were his uncompleted and unpublished *Tracts on the Popery Laws*, some seventy pages composed between 1760 and 1765. These reveal an intense interest in the genesis and consequences of discrimination against Catholics in politics, education and the ownership of property. Five chapters were planned according to an outline found in Burke's papers. The first introductory chapter aimed to depict the Popery Laws as 'one leading cause of the imbecility of the country'. The second sought to clearly explain these laws. A rhetorical flourish in Chapter Two declared: 'We found the people heretics and idolaters; we have by way of improving their condition, rendered them slaves and beggars.' The third was envisaged as an account of who these were targeted ('a body which comprehends at least two-thirds of the whole nation; it amounts to 2,800,000 souls'); it would describe their damaging effects ('corrupted morals, which affect the national prosperity'). The fourth sought to explain how they served to undermine 'national security'. The fifth aimed to set out the reasons why the laws were supported by government and to make arguments against these.

Burke rehearsed at considerable length the laws that prevented Catholic ownership of property. Catholics were only permitted temporary leases, thus preventing inheritance and undermining industry:

Allow a man but a temporary possession, lay it down as a maxim that he can never have any other, and you immediately and infallibly turn him to temporary enjoyments; and these enjoyments are never the pleasures of labour and free industry ..., they are, on the contrary, those of a thoughtless, loitering and dissipated life. The people must be inevitably disposed to such pernicious habits merely from the short duration of their tenure which the law has allowed.[26]

Laws aimed at vanquishing Catholicism had instead undermined the fabric of Irish society. The Laws against Popery were 'corrupt contrivances' aimed at keeping Irish society in an unnatural state as distinct from one that could be legitimately and peacefully sustained. The problem was not simply that the Penal Laws were unjust, it was that they were unjust to a large majority of the population and, as such, undermined the perceived legitimacy of the constitution. A society could weather injustice towards some of its members and remain stable. Injustice towards a large majority of the population served to undermine social cohesion.

A law against the majority of the people is in substance a law against the people itself; its extent determines its invalidity; it even changes its character as it enlarges its operation; it is not particular injustice but general oppression, and can no longer be considered as a private hardship which might be borne, but spreads and grows up into the unfortunate importance of a national calamity.[27]

A law directed against the 'mass of the nation' was unreasonable, it lacked authority 'for in all forms of government the people is the true legislator'; the consent of the people – either actual or implied – was essential to the validity of law. Legitimacy was a necessary bedrock of any viable law or binding constitution.

This was how he saw it in the 1760s. Three decades later the Penal Laws had to some extent been relaxed but Ascendancy intransigence kept alive the damage they did. In 1792 Burke reiterated much of the analysis of *Tracts on Popery* in his 1792 pamphlet, *A Letter to Sir Hercules Langrishe*, written as an open letter to a leading member of the Ascendancy Parliament:

Their declared object was to reduce the Catholics of Ireland to a miserable populance, without property, without estimation, without education. The professed object was to deprive the few men who, in spite of those laws, might hold or retain any property amongst them, of all sort of influence or authority over the rest. They divided the nation into two distinct bodies, without common interest, sympathy or connection. One of these bodies was to possess *all* the property, *all* the education; the other was to be composed of drawers of water and cutters of turf for them. Are we to be astonished when, by the efforts of so much violence in conquest, and so much policy in regulation, continued without intermission for near a hundred years, we had reduced them to a mob; that whenever they came to act at all, many of them would act like a mob, without temper, measure or foresight?[28]

'You', he wrote to Langrishe, 'have made three mistakes'. The first was to conflate the religious question, to depict Catholics as the enemy when they might be allies against the greater Jacobin enemy to all religion. The second was to resist Catholic access to property and status:

> Next to religion, *property* is the great point of Jacobin attack ... When the Catholics desire places and seats, you tell them that this is only a pretext (though Protestants might suppose it is just *possible* for men to like good places and snug boroughs for their own merits); but that their real view is to strip Protestants of their property ... if you treat men as robbers, why robbers sooner or later, they will become.[29]

The third was to seek to punish Catholics for the ideas and seditious propositions of dissident Protestants ('I may mistake, for I have not the honour of knowing them personally, but I take Mr Butler and Mr Tandy not to be Catholics, but members of the Established Church'). It would be strange, he argued, that 'the tempter should escape all punishment, and that Catholics who, under circumstances full of seduction and full of provocation, have resisted the temptation, should incur the penalty'.[30]

The Irish constitution and its enemies

Langrishe had proposed a limited 'reform' of the Penal Laws proposing that Catholics should enjoy everything *under the state* but not be of the state. Catholics were to be treated as denizens rather than citizens. Langrishe was what legal scholars would now describe as a constitutional originalist.[31] He considered the constitution to be settled as it had been established at the 1688 Glorious Revolution; this declared the State to be Protestant; it was so provided in the Acts for settling the succession of the crown. By law the King and every other magistrate and member of the State, legislative and executive, were bound under the same obligation.

Burke disagreed. There was much ambiguity in the word *State*. Sometimes the term was used to signify the whole commonwealth, sometimes just the higher and ruling part of the commonwealth commonly called the government. Under the first meaning to assert that Catholics ought not to be the State was at best a state of civil servitude to absolute masters whereby men were subject to the State without being citizens. Under the second, the exclusion of whole classes of men from government, a lower and degraded state of citizenship was implied, 'such as existed (with more or less strictness) in countries in which a heredity nobility possess the exclusive rule'. England, Burke explained, was no longer such a country and such a system, if applied to Ireland, would neither work for Protestants nor Catholics. In countries where such *ancien régime* (Burke did not use that term here) systems persisted they did so, he argued, because the system of rule was perceived by plebeians as well as aristocrats to be a legitimate one. In such cases the separation of the estates meant that plebeians had freedoms in their domains; aristocrats got to rule, nobles had the monopolies of honour but were in turn excluded from commerce, manufacturing and the farming of land. Because plebeians had freedoms in such domains a balance of sort was struck; a kind of compensation was furnished to those who, *in a limited sense*, were excluded from the government of the State. This was not so in the Irish case where the Penal Laws had distorted the kinds of relationships between the estates that would be required to make Langrishe's scheme viable:

> The Protestants in Ireland are not *alone* sufficiently the people to form a democracy; and they are too *numerous* to answer the ends and purposes of *an aristocracy*. Admiration, that first source of obedience, can only be the claim or the imposture of the few. I hold it to be absolutely impossible for two million plebeians, composing certainly, a very clear majority of that class, to become so far in love with six or seven hundred thousand of their fellow citizens (to all outward appearance plebeians like themselves, and many of them tradesmen, servants, and otherwise inferior to some of them) as to see with satisfaction, or even with patience, an exclusive power vested in them, by which *constitutionally* they become the absolute masters, and by the *manners* derived from their circumstances, must be capable of exercising upon them, daily and hourly, an insulting and vexatious superiority. Neither are the majority of Irish indemnified (as in some aristocracies) for this state of humiliating vassalage (often inverting the nature of things and relations) by having the lower walks of industry wholly abandoned to them. They are rivalled, to say the least of the matter, in every laborious and lucrative course of life; while every franchise, every honour, every trust, every place down to the very lowest and least confidential (besides whole professions) is reserved for the master caste.[32]

Burke's response was very much that of what would now be called a judicial activist. In essence his approach to the constitution prefigured the way in which feminist, disability or gay activists have argued for deeper understandings of rights and liberties enshrined in constitutions. Burke argued that much of what occurred at the Revolution was inconsistent with its constitutional principles: 'Many things were done from the necessities of the time, well or ill understood, from passion or from vengeance.' Amongst these he highlighted the 'deprivation of some millions of people of all the rights of citizens' that these should have had from birth under the constitution.[33]

Clearly, the constitution operated differently in England and Ireland. England witnessed the struggle of the great body of the people for the establishment of their liberties against the efforts of a small faction who would have oppressed them. In Ireland the power of a smaller number was established at the expense of the civil liberties and properties of the far greater part, and at the expense of the political liberties as a whole. In Ireland the 1688 Glorious Revolution was not a revolution but a conquest: 'The Protestants who settled in Ireland considered themselves in no other light than as a sort of colonial garrison to keep the natives in subjugation.' The Penal Laws, he argued, were an 'unparalleled code of oppression' and 'manifestly the effects of national hatred and scorn towards a conquered people'.

In his 1792 letter to Langrishe Burke invoked the *Magna Carta* as the basis for constitutional reform in Ireland. Two years earlier in his *Reflections on the Revolution in France* Burke mapped a Whig constitutional history of asserting liberties from the *Magna Carta* to the 1688 Declaration of Right.[34] This inheritance, he repeated to Langrishe, provided that no man shall be deprived of his liberties and free customs other than by the judgement of his peers or the laws of the land. *Magna Carta* provided that any statutes contrary to this shall be void. The franchises instigated by *Magna Carta* were, he insisted, integral to the constitution. No subsequent 'secondary or subsidiary laws', he argued, should be taken to supersede this fundamental law be it 'the rabble of statutes' instigated by Henry VIII, Acts instigated by Elizabeth to assert the supremacy of the crown or 'things made against treason' in the time of Charles II; laws against Catholics were subsidiary to the fundamental provisions of the constitution.

'Let us take care' he entreated Langrishe, of the dangers of 'preventing better people from any rational expectations of partaking in the benefits of that constitution *as it stands*.'[35] Langrishe's proposal (in reality, Ascendancy intransigence) would cut the matter short. The maxims he would establish offered no meaningful remedy to the 'persons who seek relief' or to the 'proper or improper means by which they seek it'; 'They form a perpetual bar to all plans and to all expectations.'[36]

Burke then argued that liberty for Catholics would be better fostered by closer ties with England than by Irish liberty as understood by either Jacobites or Protestant patriots:

> Our constitution is not made for great, general, and proscriptive exclusions; sooner or later it will destroy them, or they will destroy the constitution. In our constitution there has always been a difference between *a franchise* and *an office*. Franchises were supposed to belong to the *subject*, as *a subject*, and not *as a member of the governing part of the State*. The policy of government has considered them as things very different; for whilst Parliament excluded by the Test acts (and for a while these Test Acts were not a dead letter, as now they are in England).

Protestant dissenters from all civil and military employments, they *never touched their right of voting for members of parliament or sitting in either House* – a point I state, not as approving or condemning, with regard to them, the measure of exclusion from employments, but to prove that the distinction has been admitted in legislature as, in truth, it is founded in reason.[37]

Ireland's constitutional problem was that unlimited power was placed in the hands of a privileged minority who treated the excluded people with contempt. Ireland, he argued, was badly governed because of such exclusions and governed so as to deliberately perpetuate them:

In a country of miserable police, passing from the extremes of laxity to the extremes of rigour – among a neglected, and therefore disorderly, populace – if any disturbance or sedition from any grievance, real or imaginary, happened to arise, it was presently perverted from its true nature, often criminal enough in itself to draw upon it a severe appropriate punishment; it was metamorphosed into a conspiracy against the State, and persecuted as such.

In 1792 Burke had appealed for electoral reform that would ameliorate the alienation of Catholics. He argued to Langrishe that placing Catholic voters on a similar footing to Protestant dissenters would lead change only by slow degree. The effect in favour of Catholic power would be 'would be infinitely slow. But it would be healing; it would be satisfactory and protecting. The stigma would be removed.' His second open letter to Langrishe in 1795 attacked the 'pretended fears' of Irish Protestants, that if any ground was ceded to Catholics, then the result would be a Popish system and Popish representation capable of overturning the establishment. Burke wrote of a sense of impending calamity, of sanguine hopes blasted and of terrible disappointment with the state of Irish affairs. He could 'hardly overstate the malignity of the principles of Protestant Ascendancy as they affect Ireland'.[38]

Burke's Irish future

The native Irish and Catholic English in Ireland had lost three wars during the seventeenth century. These defeats, Burke argued, were final. All that could be done was to work with the constitution of the victors, to obtain the liberties that they granted each other and to swap the destruction of colonial misrule for the benefits of the British constitution. In *Reflections on the Revolution in France* writing in the persona of an English beneficiary of this constitution, Burke argued that there was always a constitutional alternative to revolution. He had in mind a French audience but would hardly have changed his script for an Irish one. The privileges of the French constitution though discontinued were not lost from memory. ('Your constitution was suspended before it was perfected; but you had the elements of a constitution very nearly as good as could be wished.') It had 'suffered waste and dilapidation' but its foundations still existed. Using the metaphor of a ruined castle he argued that a new one could have been built on the old one's foundations.[39] But this was no longer possible after 1789. The French Revolution had set in train a political case for an Act of Union. With each passing year the dangers of Protestant intransigence fuelling Irish Jacobinism seemed to increase.

In 1794, in a letter to his son Richard, Burke argued that the Protestant Parliament needed to become a patriot parliament. It needed to somehow represent the heterogeneous population under a form of constitution 'favourable at once to authority and to freedom; such as the British constitution boasts to be, and – such as it is, to those who enjoy it'. Because it was incapable of doing so the Ascendancy Parliament had no legitimacy and no viable future:

> The result is – you cannot make the people Protestant – and they cannot shake off a Protestant government. This is what experience teaches, and what all men of sense, of all descriptions, know. Today the question is this – are we to make the best of this situation, which we cannot alter? Or ... shall it be aggravated by stripping the people ... so as to leave them naked of every sort of right, and of every name of franchise; to outlaw them and cut from the constitution, and to cut off (perhaps) three millions of plebeian subjects without reference to property, or any other qualification, from all connection with popular representation of the kingdom?[40]

In 1795, in a letter to William Smith, another member of the Irish Parliament, Burke argued that Catholics were natural allies against Jacobinism.[41] All three religions (Catholic, Church of Ireland and Presbyterian) 'all ought to be countenanced, protected and cherished; and that in Ireland particularly the Roman Catholic religion should be upheld in high respect and veneration ... and not tolerated as an inevitable evil'. The serious and earnest practice of religion, in any of its forms, constituted 'the most effectual barrier, if not the sole barrier against Jacobinism'. What Marx would later call the opium of the people was the glue that would bind the Catholic masses to constitutionalism.

> The Catholics form the great body of the lower ranks of your community, and no small part of these classes of the middling that come nearest to them. You know that the seduction of that part of mankind from the principles of religion, morality, subordination, and social order is the great object of the Jacobins. Let them grow lax, sceptical, careless and

indifferent with regard to religion, and so sure as we have an existence, it is not a zealous Anglican or Scottish Church principle, but direct Jacobinism, which will enter into that breach. Two hundred years dutifully spent in experiments to force that people to change the form of their religion have proved fruitless. You now have your choice, for full four-fifths of your people, of the Catholic religion or Jacobinism.[42]

Burke had in a sense anticipated the rise of Catholic and Christian Democrat parties hostile to socialism, the nineteenth- and twentieth-century successor to Jacobinism as he understood it. He had also contributed to its birth in Ireland. He had a long association with the Catholic Association founded by Curry and O'Connor. His son Richard became employed as its political agent. In December 1796, a few months before his death, Burke wrote to Dr Hussey, the founding President of the Catholic seminary at Maynooth, who had served as a broker between the Catholic Association and Burke. They had become regular correspondents since 1793 when Burke had become involved with the campaign to establish Maynooth.

Burke hugely admired him and sent him a memento of his dead son Richard. Hussey was born in Ireland in 1741 but educated in the Irish College in Salamanca. He became a Trappist monk and then a missionary priest in Spain. He became chaplain to the Spanish Ambassador in London, a friend of Dr Johnston and Burke whilst stationed there; he moved successfully in diplomatic circles and was employed by George III to represent British interests in Spain during the American war. He became a fellow of the Royal Society and worked on the preparation of the 1791 Catholic Relief Bill. He acted on behalf of the Irish Catholic Association to recruit Burke's son Richard as their political agent.[43] In 1795 *The Act for the Better Education of Persons Professing the Popish or Roman Catholic Religion* received Royal Assent.[44] That same year Hussey became the founding President of Maynooth College.

Burke's correspondence with Hussey concerned the provocation of Catholic soldiers in the British army; Hussey was given charge of the appointment of army chaplains and charged with addressing the grievances of Catholic soldiers at the same time Lord Fitzwilliam was appointed as Viceroy to Ireland in 1794. Fitzwilliam was soon recalled by Pitt; the policy of conciliation towards Catholics proved short-lived. Fitzwilliam overreached himself in his challenges to the Irish Parliament; Dublin Castle prevailed. Burke reiterated many points of his despairing analysis of the state of Ireland and discussed new provocations against Catholics raised by Hussey. One such issue was the whipping of a Catholic soldier in Carrick-on-Suir for attending mass. This, according to Burke, reflected 'the systematic ill-treatment of Catholics'; as the country grew more discontented 'new arguments were furnished for giving vigorous support to the authority of the Directory'. Sick and in despair, he urged Hussey to counsel Catholics to formulate achievable demands and to avoid 'those very disorders which are made pretexts for further oppression'.[45] This was Burke's last counsel to advocates of Irish liberty:

> They must . . . make themselves independent *in fact*, before they aim at a *nominal* independence. Depend upon it, that . . . joined to a different system of manners, they would grow to a degree of importance, to which, without it, no privileges could raise them, much less any intrigues or factious practices. I know well that such a discipline, among so numerous a people, is not easily introduced, but I am sure it is not impossible. If I had youth and strength, I would go myself over to Ireland to work on that plan; so certain that I am that the well-being of all descriptions in the kingdom, as well as of themselves, depends upon a reformation amongst the Catholics. The work will be new, and slow in its operation, but it is certain in its effect. There is nothing which will not yield to perseverance and method.[46]

It fell to Daniel O'Connell to work out that plan. By the time of Burke's death, all provocations notwithstanding, the Catholic hierarchy had begun to bask in the tepid affection of the authorities.[47] An *Act for the Relief of His Majesty's Popish or Roman Catholic Subjects in Ireland* was passed in 1793. The Catholic Archbishop of Dublin, Thomas Troy, stated in his 1793 pastoral letter, *On the Duties of Christian Citizens* that Catholics had a duty to obey the Crown. Not all did so in 1798. The 1793 Relief Act was constructed along the lines endorsed by Langrishe and disparaged by Burke as inadequate to secure the stability of Ireland. It removed prohibitions upon Catholic rights to own and inherit property. It also extended the right to vote to Catholics who met property ownership enfranchisement criteria. The right of Catholics to sit in Parliament and to hold various offices of the state, to be as Langrishe put it 'of the state' – Catholic emancipation as it came to be known – was not achieved until 1829.

CHAPTER FIVE

Thomas Malthus and Catholic emancipation

The Reverend Thomas Robert Malthus (1766–1834), known to friends and family as Robert or Bob, is remembered as the prophet of human overpopulation. He died a decade before the great Irish Famine, an event he did not predict. He was regarded by his critics as the giver of alibis to governments that shirked responsibility for addressing poverty and hunger and as the influential champion of punitively parsimonious poor laws. William Hazlitt wrote in 1807 that Malthus's name hung suspended over the heads of the poor like a baleful meteor and that his influence might yet prove fatal to them.[1] This notoriety stemmed from his 1798 *Essay on the Principle of Population as it Affects the Future Improvement of Society with Remarks on the Speculations of Mr Godwin, M. Condorcet and Other Writers.*[2] The long title of what became known as *The Essay on Population* warrants attention. It grew out of debates with his father, 'a gentleman of good fortune, attached to a country life, but much occupied in classical and philosophic pursuits' – he was a devoted admirer of Rousseau – who subscribed to the theories of the perfectibility of mankind advanced by William Godwin and other Enlightenment figures.[3] He instilled in his son an independence of mind that led Robert to challenge the doctrines of the New Philosophy. For Malthus, Godwin, the husband of Mary Wollstonecraft and father of Mary Shelley, exemplified the kind of speculative philosopher, 'with eyes fixed on a happier state of society, the blessings of which he paints in captivating colours', who indulged in bitter invectives against the status quo without seeming to be aware of the tremendous obstacles that opposed the progress of man towards perfection.[4] Like Edmund Burke's *Reflections on the Revolution in France*, the *Essay on the Principle of Population* rallied conservative opposition to the New Philosophy and the political ideologies of the Enlightenment.[5]

The principle of population that Malthus invoked was the potential for arithmetic increase, a doubling, every generation: 'Taking the population of the world at any number, a thousand millions, for instance, the human species would increase in the ratio of – 1, 2, 4, 8, 16, 32, 64, 128, 256, 512 etc.' The potential for crisis resulted from the inability, as he then believed to be the case, of food production to keep pace with population growth. Overpopulation, where population growth outstripped the food supply, imposed cruel correctives:

> By that law of our nature which makes food necessary to the life of man, the effects of these two unequal powers must be kept equal. This implies a strong and constantly operating check on population from the difficulty of subsistence. This difficulty must fall somewhere and must necessarily be severely felt by a large portion of mankind. Through the animal and vegetable kingdoms, nature has scattered the seeds of life abroad with the most profuse and liberal hand. She has been comparatively sparing in the room and the nourishment necessary to rear them. The germs of existence contained in this spot of earth, with ample food, and ample room to expand in, would fill millions of worlds in the course of a few thousand years. Necessity, that imperious all pervading law of nature, restrains them within the prescribed bounds. The race of plants and the race of animals shrink under this great restrictive law. And the race of man cannot, by any efforts of reason, escape from it.[6]

Much of *The Essay on Population* was a response to Godwin's utopian ideals. These included a doctrine of the progressive improvement of the human mind and of progress towards a state of society in which everything would be subject to the control of reason.[7] Malthus disparaged Godwin's vision of a future society where benevolence was the master-spring and moving principle as 'little better than a dream, a beautiful phantom of the imagination'.[8] He argued that progress towards equality as defined by Godwin would promote a catastrophic expansion of population. Improvement in conditions amongst the poor living on the cusp of hunger would encourage these to marry earlier and have more children. Under ideal conditions of 'great equality' where 'the means of subsistence were so abundant that no part of the society could have any fears about providing amply for a family, the power of population being left to exert itself unchecked, the increase of the human species would evidently be much greater than any increase that has been hitherto'.[9] Redistribution encouraged ongoing population growth without increasing the overall food supply. The more humane the treatment of the poor the greater the danger was of future catastrophe. In Hazlitt's disparaging summary, Malthus represented the improvement of society as an evil; the most extensive improvement of society would only prepare the way for the most deplorable wretchedness.[10]

In his *Enquiry Concerning Political Justice and its Influence on General Virtue* Godwin presumed that, as mankind moved towards his ideal state, mind would triumph over matter and the passion between the sexes would be dampened thus allowing for a benign check on population.[11] Malthus retorted that even the highest minded aesthetes were not exempt from sexual impulses. Even the most rational being, 'though he may determine to act contrary to it' was a compound being; 'The cravings of hunger, the love of liquor, the desire of possessing a beautiful woman, will urge men to actions the fatal consequences of which, to the general interests of society, they are perfectly well convinced, even at the very time they commit them. Ask them their opinion of the same conduct in another person, and they would immediately reprobate it. For anybody – rich aesthete or pauper – the decision of the compound being would differ from the convictions of the rational being.'[12] Malthus, then still unmarried, revelled in intellectual pleasures but confessed that when he passed an evening with a pretty woman, he truly felt alive.[13] His frankness about sexual motivation allowed opponents such as Hazlitt great scope for caricature. Malthus's whole doctrine rested on the malicious supposition that all mankind was 'like so many animals in season' (Hazlitt hoped that the reader would pardon 'the grossness of expression').[14] Malthus, Hazlitt warned, would shut up the workhouse, deny them any relief from the parish and preach lectures to them on the newly invented crime of matrimony.[15]

What Malthus had to say about the Irish case where population was rising at a rate unknown elsewhere in Europe has also been misrepresented. And no wonder! He included a trite reference to Ireland in the second 1803 edition of his *Essay*, now entitled *An Essay on the Principle of Population Or A View of Its Past And Present Effects on Human Happiness With An Inquiry into Our Prospects Respecting The Future Removal Or Mitigation Of The Evils Which It Occasions*. Attacks on Godwin were set aside for new and expanded case studies. Scotland received fourteen pages but Ireland warranted but a single paragraph. This stated that the widespread cultivation of the potato – a cheap and nourishing root that could feed a family from a small piece of ground – 'joined to the ignorance and barbarism of the people, which have promoted them to follow their inclinations with no other prospect than an immediate bare subsistence, have encouraged early marriage to such a degree, that the population is pushed much beyond the industry and resources of the country; and the consequence naturally is, that the lower classes of people are in the most depressed and miserable state'.[16] One Irish critic of the 1803 *Essay* wrote that 'it does not appear that he ever saw the country, consulted a document, or asked such a simple question about such an important part of the United Kingdom'.[17] In a later edition Malthus expunged the word 'barbarism' and changed a reference to the 'wretched and degraded state of the common people' of Ireland to their 'depressed state'.[18]

Malthus did not read up on Ireland until 1808. What he subsequently wrote differed hugely from perspectives often attributed to him in the post-Famine era when critics blamed Malthusianism for a non-interventionist mindset that justified government inaction and blaming the Irish peasantry for their own deaths. In an 1808 article, in another the following year and in his *Principles of Political Economy*, first published in 1820, he variously described the political oppression of Catholics as 'disgusting', 'evil', 'the radical cause of the present moral and political degradation of the Irish poor'. From 1808 he was adamant that Irish land and population problems were the result of a malign system of exploitation and neglect made possible by the Penal Laws.

Great hunger, little room

Near the beginning of his 1798 *Essay on the Principles of Population* Malthus acknowledged that the Europe of recent centuries had witnessed at most only a slow growth of population; 'instead of doubling their numbers every twenty-five years they require three or four hundred years, or more, for that purpose. Some, indeed, may be absolutely stationary, and others even retrograde'. The cause of such low rates of increase could hardly be traced to a decay of the passion between the sexes. That natural propensity, according to Malthus, existed still in undiminished vigour. Why then had Europe not experienced a geometric rate of population expansion?

His answer examined the social mores of his own social class. He compared the calculations these made to discipline their biological reproduction to the manner in which decisions to marry were made by the poor. Jane Austen began her 1813 novel *Pride and Prejudice* with the proposition that: 'It is a truth universally acknowledged, that a single man in possession of a good fortune, must be in want of a wife.' In 1798 Malthus had observed that a man of his own social standing who lacked sufficient fortune to support a family would ordinarily defer marriage rather than descend the rungs of the English class system:

> The preventive check appears to operate in some degree through all the ranks of society in England. There are some men, even in the highest rank, who are prevented from marrying by the idea of the expenses that they must retrench, and the fancied pleasures that they must deprive themselves of, on the supposition of having a family. These considerations are certainly trivial, but a preventive foresight of this kind has objects of much greater weight for its contemplation as we go lower. A man of liberal education, but with an income only just sufficient to enable him to associate in the rank of gentlemen, must feel absolutely certain that if he marries and has a family he shall be obliged, if he mixes at all in society, to rank himself with moderate farmers and the lower class of tradesmen. The woman that a man of education would naturally make the object of his choice would be one brought up in the same tastes and sentiments with himself and used to the familiar intercourse of a society totally different from that to which she must be reduced by marriage. Can a man

consent to place the object of his affection in a situation so discordant, probably, to her tastes and inclinations?[19]

Most men of his class would not. Others, guided either by a stronger passion, or a weaker judgement, broke through such restraints, for 'it would be hard indeed, if the gratification of so delightful a passion as virtuous love, did not, sometimes, more than counterbalance all its attendant evils'. But the general consequences of such marriages were, he believed, 'calculated to justify rather than to repress the forebodings of the prudent'.[20]

Likewise, the sons of tradesmen and farmers were exhorted not to marry until they became settled in some business or farm that enabled them to support a family. Some deferred marriage until very late in life; the scarcity of farms was a very general complaint in England. And the competition in every kind of business was so great that it was not possible that all should be successful.[21] The calculus facing the poorer classes was again similar but starker:

> The labourer who earns eighteen pence a day and lives with some degree of comfort as a single man, will hesitate a little before he divides that pittance among four or five, which seems to be but just sufficient for one. Harder fare and harder labour he would submit to for the sake of living with the woman that he loves, but he must feel conscious, if he thinks at all, that should he have a large family, and any ill luck whatever, no degree of frugality, no possible exertion of his manual strength could preserve him from the heart-rending sensation of seeing his children starve, or of forfeiting his independence, and being obliged to the parish for their support.[22]

Malthus argued that a preventive check to population operated, albeit with varied force, amongst all of England's social classes. In various ways social restraints upon marriage involved both sexes in inextricable unhappiness. Men turned to vice, often without sanction, but unmarried women were severely penalised when they broke societal rules of sexual conduct. The institution of marriage, 'or at least, of some express or implied obligation on every man to support his own children', had a functional purpose or, as Malthus put it, was a natural response of any community confronted with the relationship between unchecked sexual impulses and poverty.[23] So too was the 'superior disgrace' or stigma placed upon unmarried or deserted mothers. When a woman became connected with a man who took no responsibility to maintain her children and then deserted her, her children became either a burden on society or they would starve.[24] He argued that rules of sexual conduct and social sanctions had developed as a check on population. These sanctions were especially directed towards women because the offence was 'more obvious and conspicuous in the woman'; she was always identifiable, whereas the father of her children was not: 'Where the evidence of the offence was most complete, and the inconvenience to the society at the same time the greatest, there it was agreed that the large share of blame should fall', however harsh, cruel and unfair this might appear.[25]

He believed that education could foster such a sense of responsibility amongst the poor – in the language of the day 'improve the poor' – but believed that it would be 'a gross absurdity' to suppose that any amount of education would extinguish the passion between the sexes and immoderate indulgence in the pleasures of sensual love. Yet, he believed that the expansion of education would go some way towards encouraging people to calculate the consequences of such indulgence. He argued – describing this as 'the principal argument' of his *Essay on the Principles of Population* – that it was highly improbable that the lower classes of people in any country should ever be sufficiently free from want and labour to obtain any high degree of intellectual improvement.[26]

In *The Crisis*, an earlier unpublished essay – a prototype of *The Essay on the Principle of Population* written in 1786 – Malthus exhibited considerable sympathy with improving the conditions of the poor. Whilst their dependency upon the parish should not be made too agreeable it was the duty of society to maintain such of its members who were unable to maintain themselves and 'assistance should be given in the way that is most agreeable to the persons who are to receive it'. The industrious widow with four or five children that she had hitherto brought up decently should be kept out of the workhouse and supported to keep living in her own home. And it seemed particularly hard upon old people, who perhaps had been useful and respectable members of society in their day and 'have done the state some service' to be obliged to quit the village where they have always lived, their friends, children and grandchildren, as soon as they were unable to work and be forced to spend 'the evening of their days in noise and unquietness among strangers, and wait their last moments forlorn and separated from all that they hold dear'.[27]

By 1798 Malthus favoured the gradual abolition of the Poor Law. He attacked the Speenhamland System and then-current proposals for a weekly allowance of a shilling for each additional child for poor families with more than three children.[28] The poor, so defined, were the families of men who were fully employed but still unable to keep their children from hunger. He described the prevalence of child mortality and widespread malnourishment amongst the peasantry. Of the former 'much too great a proportion belongs to those who may be supposed unable to give their offspring proper food and attention, exposed as they are occasionally to severe distress and confined, perhaps, to unwholesome habitations and hard labour'. Large families on low incomes inevitably faced distress:

> The sons and daughters of peasants will not be found such rosy cherubs in real life as they are described to be in romances. It cannot fail to be remarked by those who live much in the country that the sons of labourers

are very apt to be stunted in their growth, and are a long while arriving at maturity. Boys that you would guess to be fourteen or fifteen are, upon inquiry, frequently found to be eighteen or nineteen. And the lads who drive plough, which must certainly be a healthy exercise, are very rarely seen with any appearance of calves to their legs: a circumstance which can only be attributed to a want either of proper or of sufficient nourishment.[29]

But artificially raising the incomes of the poorer classes would not necessarily address their poverty. Suppose instead an eighteen pence a day tax on the rich increased the rate of pay for labourers to five shillings. It might be imagined that now they could have meat every day for their dinners. But this would be a very false conclusion. Such a rise in wages would not increase the quantity of meat in the country. And if there was at present not enough for all to have a decent share nor would there be enough to go around if the poorest could afford to pay more. Under conditions of scarcity what mattered was who could pay the most and who could pay the least. Increased incomes would stimulate the production of additional food to only a limited extent. Because agricultural land was finite in supply – in 1798 Malthus believed that the limits of agricultural production had nearly been reached – any additional demand for meat could only be addressed at the expense of growing corn, which would be a very disadvantageous exchange, for it is well known that the country could not then support the same population. Whether the lowest members of society earned eighteen pence of five shillings they must at all events be reduced to live upon the hardest fare and in the smallest quantity.[30] Under most circumstances Malthus perceived redistribution from rich to poor as a zero sum game because he presumed that land and its productive capacity was finite. The only means of reducing the numbers in poverty would be to bring additional land into cultivation:

> It may at first appear strange, but I believe it is true, that I cannot by means of money raise a poor man and enable him to live much better than he did before, without proportionally depressing others in the same class. If I retrench the quantity of food consumed in my house, and give him what I have cut off, I then benefit him, without depressing any but myself and family, who, perhaps, may be well able to bear it. If I turn up a piece of uncultivated land, and give him the produce, I then benefit both him and all the members of the society, because what he before consumed is thrown into the common stock, and probably some of the new produce with it. But if I only give him money, supposing the produce of the country to remain the same, I give him a title to a larger share of that produce than formerly, which share he cannot receive without diminishing the shares of others.

Efforts to improve the conditions of the poor clearly mitigated some cases of very severe distress yet these tended to increase population without increasing the food for its support. They made it possible for a poor man to marry with little or no prospect of being able to support a family in independence.[31] The poor laws, he argued, had 'powerfully contributed to generate that carelessness and want of frugality observable among the poor, so contrary to the disposition frequently to be remarked among petty tradesmen and small farmers'. If the labouring poor could not be educated out of their improvidence they could be encouraged to feel stigma and shame:

> Hard as it may appear in individual instances, dependent poverty ought to be held disgraceful. Such a stimulus seems to be absolutely necessary to promote the happiness of the great mass of mankind, and every general attempt to weaken this stimulus, however benevolent its apparent intention, will always defeat its own purpose. If men are induced to marry from a prospect of parish provision, with little or no chance of maintaining their families in independence, they are not only unjustly tempted to bring unhappiness and dependence upon themselves and children, but they are tempted, without knowing it, to injure all in the same class with themselves. A labourer who marries without being able to support a family may in some respects be considered as an enemy to all his fellow-labourers.[32]

Malthus repeatedly emphasised the harsh, precarious and unfair conditions under which the poorest lived. The very laws necessary for a society to function – that protected the security of property and the institution of marriage – also imposed conditions of great inequality:

> Those who were born after the division of property would come into a world already possessed. If their parents, from having too large a family, could not give them sufficient for their support, what are they to do in a world where everything is appropriated? We have seen the fatal effects that would result to a society, if every man had a valid claim to an equal share of the produce of the earth. The members of a family which was grown too large for the original division of land appropriated to it could not then demand a part of the surplus produce of others, as a debt of justice. It has appeared, that from the inevitable laws of our nature some human beings must suffer from want. These are the unhappy persons who, in the great lottery of life, have drawn a blank.[33]

To prevent the recurrence of misery, was, 'alas! beyond the power of man'. All Malthus could suggest were some palliative measures. And if these appeared cruel they were ultimately less so than the irresponsible benevolence of poor laws which failed to discourage the poor from bearing children likely to die of malnourishment. More positively, he argued that any measures that would increase the available food supply should be supported. Every means should be employed to weaken and destroy all rules and institutions that caused the labours of agriculture to be worse paid than the labours of trade and manufactures.

Existing legislation, aimed at preventing newcomers settling in parishes where they might become a burden on the poor-rates, hampered labour mobility. He argued that the poor should be allowed to settle without interruption anywhere there was better prospect of employment or a higher price for labour.[34] Incentives should be given for the expansion of cultivated land and to encourage agriculture above manufacture and to tillage above grazing, so that more could be fed. Such arguments reflected his country gentleman background.[35] For all that Malthus railed against poor laws, presenting these as a trap for the poor, he nevertheless allowed that for cases of extreme distress, county workhouses with harsh regimes might be established, supported by rates upon the whole kingdom, and 'free for persons of all counties, and indeed of all nations' where also the able bodied poor 'whether native or foreigner, might do a day's work at all times and receive the market price for it'.[36]

The *Essay on the Principles of Population* set out a back and forth debate proposing the removal of the poor laws with one breath, universal access to just such a system with another. Malthus opposed any measures that fostered an increase in the population without increasing the food supply. So whilst he opposed supports and subsidies on the incomes of the poorest (these would only make food more expensive) he supported reforms and freedoms that would enable the poor to grow more food or travel to find work. Such opposition to restrictions imposed upon the eighteenth-century English peasantry were consistent with his later opposition to the Penal Laws that affected Irish Catholics.

Malthus lived half his life in the eighteenth century and half in the nineteenth. His later writings acknowledged that huge agricultural improvements had occurred in England.[37] As such, his analysis of the population question shifted considerably over time. There was, he argued in his *Political Economy* (I cite the 1836 edition) 'no state in Europe, or in the world' which could not support ten times as many inhabitants as were supported at present.[38] This expanded breeding room meant that there was more breathing room. When he came to write on Ireland, a decade after the 1798 *Essay on the Principles of Population* first appeared, his arguments were quite different than might be supposed by those who had read only the *Essay* or read about it.

The condition of Ireland

In 1808 and 1809 Malthus published essays on Ireland in *The Edinburgh Review*. The first responded mostly to an 1805 book by Thomas Newenham, *A Statistical and Historical Inquiry into the Population and Magnitude of Ireland*.[39] The second responded to a 1809 follow-up book by Newenham,

A View of the Natural, Political and Commercial Circumstances of Ireland.[40] In his 1805 book Newenham pulled together a mass of data on Ireland's economy and demography reaching back to the writings of William Petty and forward to 1837 when he projected Ireland would have a population of 8,413,224. Malthus trusted Newenham's figures. Newenham estimated that Ireland had a population of 5,400,000 in 1804, one that had quadrupled over the previous century. Malthus contrasted the 'extraordinary phenomenon' of Ireland's population growth with the slumbering or nearly stationary populations of many European countries.[41] He cited Newenham's assessment that potatoes required just one quarter of the land needed to feed a person on wheat.[42] In his later *Political Economy* he similarly wrote that without the potato Ireland's population would not have much more than doubled, instead of much more than quadrupled during the last century.[43] Simply put, the population quadrupled in a century because food production could keep pace with the rising population. But it could not do so indefinitely. As land holdings became smaller and food became relatively more expensive the size of families would become smaller as a result of later marriages. Yet, his 1808 forecast for Ireland was for a soft landing, at least by comparison with what transpired. Malthus anticipated a slow-down in the increase of population, one that lagged behind the increase in the food supply but he did not refer to the possibility of famine. He believed that food shortages would impose gradual pressures for a very long time before the growth in population would stop:

> It is difficult indeed to conceive a more tremendous shock to society, than the event of its coming at once to the limits of the means of subsistence, with all the habits of abundance and early marriages which accompany a rapid increase in population. But, happily for mankind, this never is, nor ever can be the case. The event is provided for by the concurrent interests and feelings of individuals long before it arrives; and gradual diminution in real wages of the labouring classes of society, slowly, and almost insensibly, generates the habits necessary for an order of things in which the funds for the maintenance of an order of things in which the funds for the maintenance of labour are stationary.
>
> We may be quite certain, therefore, that, without external violence, the period when the population of Ireland will become stationary is yet at a very considerable distance; that in the mean time it will continue increasing, with a movement sometimes quicker and sometimes slower, from varying circumstances, but on the whole, gradually retarded; and that the causes of its regulation will be generally felt, and generate a change of habits long before the period in question arrives.[44]

It was conceivable that Ireland's population would grow to 20 million by the end of the nineteenth century. It would be unsurprising on the basis of past astonishing increases if Ireland became the most densely populated country yet known to the world. Yet, it was more likely that this growth would somehow be checked. Malthus anticipated that rents would rise until the usual quantity of land considered necessary to support a large family could not be obtained for less than the average earnings of a year's labour. Land holdings would be subdivided and the cottier system would gradually be destroyed and replaced by one like the English farm labourer system but where potatoes remained the principal food. The price of food would continue to rise compared to the cost of labour. The size of a family that an Irish peasant could afford to feed would shrink from ten to five persons and this would check the habit of early marriages. But such measures would only slow down the rate of increase.[45]

Malthus specifically focused on how such a rapid increase could have occurred 'amongst a people groaning under a penal code of singular severity, and oppressed for three fourths of the period in a manner of history does not furnish a second example'.[46] As later summarised in his *Political Economy*:

> On the introduction of the potato into that country, the lower classes of society were in such a state of oppression and ignorance, and were so little respected by others, and consequently had so little respect for themselves, that as long as they could get food, and that of the cheapest kind, they were content to marry under the prospect of every other privation.[47]

In his articles on Ireland Malthus was particularly concerned with the political causes and implications of Irish population increases. The likely decline in Irish standards of living wrought by population increases occurred alongside economic, political and religious grievances. In this context poverty would be the final straw rather than the root cause of insurrection. Poverty without other aggravating factors did not result in insurrection. However, when 'other and removable causes of complaint' existed at the same time, it made matters ten times worse:

> The distress of the common people of Ireland will ever continue to be a weapon of mighty and increasing force in the hands of the political agitator, till it is wrested from him, or its point turned aside, by the complete abolition of all civil distinctions between the Protestant and Catholic subjects of the British empire. If to this consideration be added, that of the rapidly increasing physical force of the Irish Catholics, it seems scarcely possible to imagine a case in which the views of policy and security so imperiously dictate the same line of conduct of justice and humanity.[48]

His underlying political arithmetic, if not his conclusions, recalled that advanced by William Petty. Catholics, 'because of their great and growing numbers, could not fail to effect either a change to the current system of penal laws or a separation of the two countries'.[49] Every year the proportion of Catholics to Protestants rose, 'a circumstance to be contemplated without fear if they were once conciliated; but, till that time arrives, must be regarded with increasing apprehension'.[50] Every year 50,000 Irish youths came of military age in Ireland, adding to the disposition and the power of Ireland to resist the wrongs she suffered. Ireland's population increase would, he argued, give it a growing comparative advantage over England and unless current policy be exchanged, 'and that very shortly', for one of kindness and conciliation, England would inevitably have to rue her folly.[51]

Here, Malthus uncharacteristically emphasised the advantage numerically larger populations gave nations over their enemies, a common argument at the time of the Napoleonic wars. In 1808 England needed soldiers but, he argued, the conditions enjoyed by English agricultural workers and the wages available to artificers provided little incentive to enlist. Not so in Ireland where the size of the redundant agricultural population was rapidly increasing, where wages were below army rates and where the habitations and food of the peasantry made a British camp appear as an abode of much superior comfort, and the fare of the common soldier, a luxurious repast.[52]

Alongside Newenham's book he reviewed a pamphlet on the injustices of tithes imposed upon Catholics.[53] Every effort, he insisted, should be used to relieve Catholics of the injustice of tithes payable to the Protestant Church of Ireland. So also should the Penal Laws be revoked:

> Every principle that is known to influence human conduct, seems to assure us, that if the Irish Catholics were raised from their present political degradation, and admitted to all the rights and privileges of British subjects; if the career of honours and distinctions of every kind were fully and fairly opened to them, and they were allowed to feel the same motives of love and veneration for the Government under which they live, as their Protestant brethren, – they would soon be amongst the most loyal, willing and powerful supporters of the Crown and empire.[54]

In his second July 1809 article on Ireland he argued that the future of Ireland was daily risked by 'the inhuman cry of no popery' and 'by the bigotry and littleness' of its administration:

> It is really sickening to think that at a period when every heart and hand is wanted to rally round the last remains of liberty in Europe, a set of men should be found at the head of affairs, who are either absolutely incapable, from the narrowness of intellect, of profiting by the great lessons of experience that are daily unfolding themselves; or, whatever their opinions may be, are willing to sacrifice them and their country at the shrine of present place and emolument![55]

Newenham identified five springs of his country's misfortune: (1) The ignorance, (2) the poverty, (3) the political debasement of the inferior orders, (4) the Catholic code, and (5) the provinciality of the government. Malthus differed with him about the relative importance of each: 'We should without hesitation say, of these five causes of Irish misery, that the Catholic code, and the provinciality of government, had produced the political debasement of the inferior orders; and that this political debasement had been the chief instrument in producing the peculiar ignorance and poverty of the lower classes of the Irish.' Root causes had to be addressed first: 'To begin with ignorance and poverty, is to begin at the wrong end, and to labour in vain.'[56]

Malthus argued that the Penal Laws and what Newenham called 'the provinciality of the government' were invariably found to be 'the primary and radical causes of the mischiefs we deplore' and without the removal of the former and reform of the latter no effort to relieve the misfortunes of Ireland could succeed.[57] He argued that the causes of the degradation of the Irish were independent of soil and climate, that in Ireland the improvement of the poor could be fostered by the removal of Catholic grievances, and that this in turn would foster an improvement in the condition of the poor. It was, he argued, 'probable, that the decent pride occasioned by a superior political condition' would raise the aspirations of the lower classes in terms of diet and industry.[58] The experience of Irish Catholics under the Penal Laws, which had reduced most of the population to bare subsistence and impeded the emergence of a Catholic middle class, offered a model for future European despotism:

> Universally it will be found, that political degradation is accompanied by excessive poverty; and that the opposite state of society is the most efficient cause of the spread of comforts amongst the lower classes. We have little doubt that the political degradation of the Irish poor powerfully contributed to make them adopt potatoes as their principal food; and in the curious question, whether, at a future distant period, the greater part of the population of Europe will be supported upon potatoes? Much will depend on the character of the governments in which the present convulsions may terminate. The establishment of an universal despotism, and the exclusion of the lower and middle classes of society from all share in government, by annihilating in a great degree individual importance and dignity, would have a strong tendency to make the poor submit to the lowest and cheapest kind of sustenance; and it is quite certain that once they consent to produce an adequate supply of labour on the cheapest kind of food, they never will be able to obtain anything better.[59]

His assessment of the Irish case emphasised at least three variables that were not part of his 1798 *Essay*. Firstly, he had revised upwards his estimates about the potential future productivity of land by a factor of ten. Secondly, he argued that the potato had driven down the cost of labour in Ireland and increased the cost of land. It cost one-quarter what other foodstuffs cost and insofar as workers only received enough land to cultivate to ensure their bare subsistence, it drove up the population alongside the price of that land. Thirdly, he emphasised how the ability of the Irish to check their population had been impeded by the radical evils of the Catholic code and malign government.

In this context the future expansion of Ireland's population was likely to be checked in one of two ways. The first, a population check resulting from 'aggravated poverty *alone*', was not to be contemplated. The alternative means was 'by such an elevation in the character and condition of the lower classes of society, as will make them look forward to other comforts besides the mere support of their families on potatoes'.[60]

In his 1798 response to Godwin Malthus had been sceptical that the English poor could ever afford the education in prudential habits they would need to break the cycle of early marriages and large families. For that reason he focused on reducing their poor law supports. Ireland, in any case, did not have a poor law system or the social structure needed to maintain one. The only hope the Irish had of retarding future distress was to establish prudential habits. 'If we allow ourselves to indulge in hope of this kind', he argued, 'it is quite clear, that the first step towards its accomplishment must be the full and complete emancipation of the Catholics, as the radical cause of the present moral and political degradation of the mass of the Irish poor.'[61]

Malthus argued against government action to reduce the exorbitant rents which apparently impoverished the Irish. To do so without otherwise reforming the Penal Laws against Catholics would merely drive up the population. Civil and political freedom, would, he hoped, foster respect for the Irish and the self-respect which would lead the Irish to expect higher living standards.

He had some grounds for believing so. His April 1808 article noted that Ireland had excellent natural resources and climate. Ireland consisted of more than 19,439,960 acres. Of these 13,454,375 were considered as cultivated and fertile land, 4,800,000 acres had yet to be reclaimed. A further 1,185,585 acres consisted of lakes, rivers, towns and roads. Ireland's cultivated land was disadvantaged by 'want of capital, and want of skill'. Citing Newenham he argued that 'uncommon fertility of soil' combined with 'excessively bad management' of Irish lands where even the basics of crop rotation were neglected. Clearly there was massive scope for improvement.

He was much taken by evidence presented by Newenham about the extent of education in Ireland and of rising standards of living amongst Catholics in some areas. In his July 1809 article he noted that in the Diocese of Cloyne and Ross alone there were 316 Catholic parochial schools that were attended during the summer by 21,892 scholars, some 6,000 more than the entire roll call of Protestant pupils in Ireland. Newenham attributed the expansion of education to the care and industry of the Catholic clergy. Malthus, the Anglican clergyman, was most impressed with reports of the work of his Catholic equivalents to improve the situation of the poor:

> We should rejoice to hear, that the check to the present rapid increase of population, which must necessarily soon take place, had begun to operate from an increasing taste for comforts and conveniences, before it was forced from the absolute want of food; but we own we have not much hope of any marked and striking change of this kind, till the Protestant and Catholic are in every respect put on a level.[62]

He revisited the case of Ireland in his *Political Economy*, first published in 1820. This reiterated many of the arguments of his 1808 and 1809 articles but focused more on economic patterns of exploitation of the Irish peasantry. The cultivation of the potato meant that the Irish labourer could command the support of a larger family at subsistence level than upon the wheat of the labourer in England.[63] It was also to blame for Ireland's huge population increases. He contrasted the impact of cheap food in the Irish case with what had happened in England during the first half of the eighteenth century where the price of corn fell and the price of labour rose. A great increase of command over the necessities of life did not, in the English case, produce a proportionate increase in population. Rather it found the people of the country 'living under good government, and enjoying all the advantages of civil and political liberty in an unusual degree'. Unlike in the Irish case the lower classes of people had been in the habit of being respected, both by the laws and the higher orders of their fellow citizens, and had learned in consequence to respect themselves. The result was, he argued, that their increased corn wages, 'instead of occasioning an increase in population exclusively, were so expended as to occasion an elevation in the standard of their comforts and conveniences'.[64]

In Ireland, in the absence of such voluntary checks, population increases pushed up rents for ground fit for the growing of potatoes and increased the supply of labour. Competition for land led to high rents, competition for work led to low wages. This dilemma often resulted in the Irish cotter being unable to pay the rent he contracted for. Landlords benefited, however, from being able to charge high rents and pay low wages:

> The wheat, oats, and cattle of Ireland are sold in England, and bear English money prices, while they are cultivated and tended by labour paid at half the money price; a state of things which must greatly increase either the revenue derived from profits, or the revenue derived from rents; and practical information assures us that it is the latter which has derived the greatest benefit from it.[65]

Ireland had come to support a much greater population than it could employ, resulting in 'the very general prevalence of habits of indolence'. However, Malthus sought to vindicate the character of the Irish peasant:

> In defence, however, of the Irish peasant, it may be truly said, that in the state or society in which he has been placed, he has not had a fair trial; he has not been subjected to the ordinary stimulants which produce industrious habits. In almost every part of the island, particularly in the south and west, the population of the country districts is greater than the actual business to be done on the land can employ. If the people, therefore, were ever so industriously inclined, it was not possible for them all to get regular employment in the occupations which belong to the soil.[66]

By way of example he described how a small farm in the Kerry mountains might support perhaps a large family, amongst whom are a number of grown-up sons, but the business to be done upon the farm was a mere trifle. The greatest part of such work fell to the women. The men were underemployed, unskilled, unable in any case to access resources to improve their lands and homes and unsurprisingly demotivated:

> What remains for the men cannot occupy them for a number of hours equal to a single day in the week; and the consequence was they are generally seen loitering about, as if time was absolutely of no value to them. They might, one should suppose, with all this leisure, employ themselves in building better houses, or at least improving them, and keeping them neat and clean. But with regard to the first, some difficulties may occur in procuring materials; and with regard to the second, it appears from experience, that the object is neither not understood, or not considered as worth the trouble it would cost.
> They might also, one should suppose, grow or purchase the raw materiels of clothing, and work them up at home; and in fact this is done to a certain extent. Most of the linen and woollen they wear is prepared by themselves. But the raw materiels, when not home grown, cannot be purchased without great difficulty, on account of the low money prices of labour; and in preparing them for wear, the temptations to indolence will generally be too powerful for human weakness, when the question is merely about a work which may be deferred or neglected, with no other effect than that of being obliged to wear old clothes a little longer, when it can be done without any violation of the customs of the country.[67]

Malthus doubted whether most people living under such circumstances in any country might ever acquire industrious habits. However, to break out of such circumstances, 'to keep themselves constantly and beneficially employed, it was necessary to exercise a great degree of providence, energy and self-command'. In his 1808 and 1809 articles he emphasised that the removal of the Penal Laws was a necessary first step in the improvement of the Irish but his account of the condition of the Irish in his *Political Economy* focused mostly on barriers resulting from the structure of the Irish economy.

The status quo that impoverished most of the population secured incomes for landowners through high rents, low wages and exports to England. It was also characterised by scant investment in and improvements of Irish lands. Malthus considered that additional investment of capital in Ireland would not ensure the employment of the Irish people even though there was a great want of capital. One difficulty was the absence of a domestic market for manufactured goods. The potato had resulted in low wages, with little left over for the purchase of goods, a want of demand. The tastes and habits of such a large body of people would be slow to change. The domestic market aside, 'unjust and impolitic restrictions by England' prevented or circumscribed the demand for Irish manufacture abroad.[68]

Malthus was adamant that Ireland could produce enough food to feed its entire population with a relatively small amount of the available labour. Ireland, he argued, had great natural resources. If its agriculture could become more efficient then even more could potentially be released to work in manufacture. If the productive potential of Ireland's land and labour could be harnessed, if the people 'instead of loitering on the land were engaged in manufactures and commerce carried out in great and flourishing towns, Ireland would be beyond comparison richer than England'.[69]

As things stood demand was blocked by the poverty of peasants and barriers to exports. Immense capital was needed but it could only be effectively introduced gradually. Of even greater importance was 'a change in the tastes and habits of the lower classes of people'. In effect he meant a change in the overall class structure. In a footnote Malthus stated that, 'there is nothing so favourable to effectual demand as a large proportion of the middle classes of society'.[70]

Palliatives

Malthus wrote his two essays on Ireland some years after the Act of Union that ended Ireland's Ascendancy parliament. In 1808 and 1809 Malthus argued for repeal of the Penal Laws and the extension of full rights to Irish Catholics in accordance with the spirit of the Union, 'or what ought to have been its spirit'.[71] The case he made for Catholic emancipation was of the kind Burke argued would never be heard in Ireland under Ascendancy rule. Support for Catholic emancipation was not unusual in the Whig intellectual circles in which he moved although Malthus only became exercised by injustices towards Irish Catholics when he began to research his 1808 article for *The Edinburgh Review*. However, the rationale he offered for Catholic emancipation, as being crucial to the avoidance of a population crisis in Ireland, was distinctive.

He did not predict the great calamity that killed one million of the eight million on the island by 1841 and precipitated the century-long decline of Ireland's post-Famine population. Instead he envisaged a process whereby population would begin to slow down its rate of expansion in belated response to the rising costs and relative shortfall of food and increased hardships. There was scope, he believed, to improve the Irish even though he had argued against Godwin in 1798 that there was little possibility for the English poor to be raised through education. Believing this at the time he focused on the removal of the poor laws as a means of discouraging large families amongst the improvident. In the Irish case, where there were no poor laws to begin with, he focused upon political obstacles to their improvement.

Nobody could accuse Malthus of rigid consistency. In 1798 he had influentially insisted that poor laws encouraged early marriage and larger families amongst the poorest classes. In 1807 he admitted that in England, there was 'decisive evidence that the poor laws do not encourage early marriages *so much* as might naturally be expected'.[72] He acknowledged that some of his arguments applied better to agricultural societies than to emerging industrial ones capable of manipulating nature and mankind to an extent not previously understood.[73] The potential for arithmetic expansion was the fixed element of his principle of population. Various iterations of his theory emphasised different factors in different times and places that might modify the rate of increase of population. This depended upon specific social, economic, and as he emphasised in the Irish case, political contexts.

The habits of subsistence, as these varied over time and from place to place, depended not just on 'material the physical causes of climate and soil but still more perhaps on moral causes, the formation and action of which are owing to a variety of circumstances'. In essence, he argued that the same economic stimuli – he gave the example of high wages – might induce different responses under different circumstances. These might result in either (a) a rapid increase of population, with spending chiefly spent on maintaining large families, or (b) an improved standard of living without a proportionate increase in the growth of the population.[74]

The first outcome (a) was produced by circumstances which rendered the lower class of people unable or unwilling to reason from the past to the future, and ready to acquiesce, for the sake of present gratification, in a very low standard of comfort and respectability. The second outcome (b) came about under circumstances which tended to elevate the character of the lower classes of society, which makes them act as beings who 'look before and after', and 'who consequently cannot acquiesce patiently in the thought of depriving themselves and their children of the means of being respectable, virtuous and happy'.[75] Education, he argued, played a crucial role in the development of 'preventative foresight' and more generally fostered human capabilities (not a term he used but one used now by developmental economists influenced by Malthus and Adam Smith) to improve their circumstances. But such calculations were also influenced by perceptions of the nature and extent of freedom and opportunity. As put in his *Political Economy*:

> Of all the causes which tend to generate prudential habits among the lower classes of society, the most essential is unquestionably civil liberty. No people can be much accustomed to form plans for the future, who do not feel assured that their industrious exertions, while fair and honourable, will be allowed to have free scope; and that the property which they either possess, or may acquire, will be secured to them by a known code of just laws impartially administered. But it has been found by experience that civil liberty cannot be permanently secured without political liberty. Consequently, political liberty becomes almost equally essential; and in addition to its being necessary in this point of view, its obvious tendency to teach the lower classes of society to respect themselves by obliging the higher classes to respect them, must contribute greatly to aid all the good efforts of civil liberty.[76]

Catholic emancipation was achieved almost two decades before the Great Famine. But the intervening period did not witness the dividend from prudential habits inspired by liberty he hoped for. He did not predict a potato famine but did anticipate an ongoing deterioration of the lives of those who sought to subsist on what he once called the 'never failing bellyful'. In 1808 Malthus had accepted Newenham's prediction that Ireland's population would exceed 8 million by 1837 and did not disparage his forecast that this could grow to 20 million by the end of the nineteenth century. Yet, he anticipated that one way or another the rate of increase would be checked during the nineteenth century. Something would have to give.

CHAPTER SIX

Richard Whately and the end of ascendancy

Richard Whately (1787–1863) was parachuted into Irish political and ecclesiastical life as Church of Ireland Archbishop of Dublin in 1831, skipping the rank of bishop, having been the second ever Professor of Political Economy at Oxford. The university, a nineteenth-century biographer wrote, was thrown on its beam-ends by the shock.[1] It seems obligatory that all writings about him, from early biographies to more recent scholarly analyses, include some sketch of the idiosyncrasies that together with his intellectual positions set him apart from his peers. 'It was the fate of Dr. Whately', his daughter Jane wrote in her two volume biography (giving many examples), 'to have portions of his character and opinions much misunderstood'. He could 'never refrain from bringing forth his entire opinion on any topic'.[2] He reportedly trained his dogs to climb trees and jump down on undergraduates out walking with girls. 'In common rooms and at college dinners', Whately's presence 'was enough to discomfort the polite, anger the complacent and embarrass the bashful'.[3] For all that many of his fellow academics found him abrasive and iconoclastic he was in his element at Oxford. Why he accepted the Dublin position that he described as the 'call to the helm of a crazy ship' remains something of a mystery.[4]

His lack of experience as a bishop made him an unexpected candidate. That said, at Oxford he had been president of St Alban's Hall, an office that had once been filled by a former Archbishop of Dublin, Dr Narcissus Marsh. The Established Church was very much in his blood. His father was the Reverend Joseph Whately who was in turn descended from 'a puritan divine of some eminence'.[5] At St Alban's Whately's deputy and protégée was John Henry Newman, who had yet to convert to Catholicism. Both had been close friends but Newman broke with his mentor over Whately's campaign on behalf of Robert Peel. Catholic emancipation had become a heated issue in the university with most of the faculty being vehemently opposed. Peel, who had conceded reform of the Penal Laws, 'fell into great odium with his learned constituents at Oxford' with Whately standing beside him 'almost alone'.[6] Newman took umbrage at what he saw as an attempt by Whately to bully the university. The break came when Whately, having seated Newman amidst some of the least intellectual men in Oxford at a university dinner, asked him if he was proud of his friends.[7]

Whately's stand against Oxford's Tory majority commended him to Charles Grey, the Whig Prime Minister, as a possible head of the Established Church in Ireland. Grey's own great achievement in the making, the 1832 Reform Act, had been blocked by the bishops in the House of Lords. Whately had advocated an agenda of Church Reform. His 1826 pamphlet, *Letters on the Church, by an Episcopalian*, advocated the separation of Church and State.[8] In 1832 he wrote to Grey that, in blocking the Reform Bill *en bloc* against popular opinion and the government, the bishops had 'rendered themselves excessively obnoxious', had threatened a constitutional crisis and had undermined the Established Church in the House of Lords.[9] This was in essence the analysis of many Whigs, including Grey, at the time.[10] Whately's view that bishops should not be in the House of Lords, his opposition to slavery and the Penal Laws, his advocacy of penal reform, of the betterment of the poor through education, of laissez-faire economics and his endorsement of a restrictive poor law, all were compatible with the reforming liberal spirit of the time.

He was part of an Oxford circle, led by his mentor Edward Copleston, that advocated the robust intellectual education of clergymen in order to best defend the Church of England. In 1829 he became Oxford's second ever Professor of Political Economy, a subject he defined as inquiry into the nature, production and distribution of wealth, not its connection with virtue and happiness.[11] Before long, he believed, political economists of some sort or other would come to run the world alongside professionals in other fields like physicians and lawyers. Nobody without some kind of professional expertise would be taken seriously.[12]

For all his reputation as an arch-liberal he was also in many respects a conservative. In his private journal he sketched the character of Lord Melbourne, another Whig Prime Minister 'to whom any change was a great evil'. Melbourne had 'what most conservatives have not, shrewdness enough to perceive when it was unavoidable, and then he always welcomed it with so much gladness that many people were alarmed with a dread of his going too far'. In appreciating such qualities in Melbourne, Whately highlighted virtues that he himself aspired to for all his reputation for abruptness. Thinking of Melbourne, using an analogy he was fond of, he mused that a man is not a traitor for surrendering a town to the enemy when untenable, instead of waiting to have it stormed and sacked, 'though in doing so he is acting with those who wish the enemy to have possession of it, while his feelings are with those who are holding out and dying in the breach'.[13]

Whately felt similarly misunderstood. The Established Church in Ireland was such a town.

Whately was appointed to Dublin by a Whig government needing to address the consequences of Catholic emancipation. He succeeded Archbishop Magee, an arch-practitioner of the old Ascendancy politics that had long blocked reform. His instincts were to protect his Church through conciliation with Catholics where possible. In his responses to Catholic emancipation, as in his advocacy for penal reform and the abolition of slavery, he emphasised the need to address knock-on consequences. What to do with a prisoner who could no longer be executed? How was a society that set free its slaves or emancipated its Catholics to function? Such were the predicaments he addressed in various writings before and during his first years in Ireland.

He advised the Howard Society for Removing the Penalty of Death that capital punishment could not be feasibly done away with unless the issue of secondary punishments to fit formerly capital crimes had been thought through.[14] In an 1832 pamphlet on such punishments he described the transportation of criminals to Australia as a failed experiment.[15] Punishments needed to be judged on their ability to prevent crime. They needed to inflict as little useless suffering as possible. They should lead to as little moral debasement as possible and, unlike transportation, needed to be cost effective.

An 1833 letter to the Anti-Slavery Society argued that most of those who swelled the cry for immediate emancipation were ignorant of the chief evil of slavery – its making and keeping the slave unfit for freedom. It was unhappily the case that slave owners were the best placed to equip slaves for freedom. The repeal of slavery was not just a matter of freeing slaves but ensuring that they lived viable lives and that their owners not be ruined. Whately recommended that slavery be abolished gradually by means of schemes that would make it in the economic interest of owners to prepare slaves for freedom and part-replace taxes on colonial produce with equivalent taxes to be levied upon slave owners.[16]

He opposed slavery but endorsed the coercion of the poor if this would foster their improvement. Whately supported the replacement in England of the Elizabethan poor laws with a penitentiary workhouse system aimed at removing what liberals of his era understood as incentives to indolence amongst the able-bodied poor. Such 'penitentiaries for vagrants' were worthwhile only if they could achieve some clear goal.[17] In an 1832 letter to Nassau Senior, his predecessor as Professor of Political Economy in Oxford, he proposed that any female receiving relief should have her hair cut off. Firstly, a good head of hair would fetch enough to pay for about a fortnight's maintenance. Secondly, it would be a powerful disincentive against dependency on the parish. One of his maids, he explained, became ill and though her life was in danger she refused to part with her hair and would have cheerfully worked and fared hard for any length of time to save it.[18]

Whately had given little though to Irish affairs before being posted to Dublin. Writing to Nassau Senior in August 1831 he described the Irish migrants he had seen in Oxford: 'a continual ebb-tide of returning Irish, some labourers, and some beggars, but mostly *both* by turns, who seldom go home empty handed. At the mendacity office in Oxford, where a great majority of the applicants were Irish, they were sometimes, on being searched, found to have one, two, or three sovereigns in their rags. They held onto their money and, if possible, begged their way home. By such remittances capital flowed from England to Ireland. In the absence of poor laws in Ireland many presented themselves in England as persons of distress and could not be told, as might be said to Englishmen, "Go to your Parish".' Or else they outbid Englishmen for work: 'May it not also be said that the Irish labourers, whose standard of decencies is so low, tend to bring down the English to the same level? If I am an English labourer, and am outbid by an Irishman, who lies on straw and lives on potatoes, I must accept the same wages (unless I go to the Parish), and live the same piggish kind of life.'[19]

Giving to beggars, he repeatedly argued, 'was, in fact paying a number of wretched beings to live in idleness and filth, and to neglect and ill-treat the miserable children whose sufferings formed part of their stock in trade'.[20] He agreed with the essence of Malthus's case against Poor Law relief in England, having read the first (1798) edition of the *Essay on the Principle of Population*. He praised Malthus to Senior in an 1835 letter, at the height of his involvement in the *Commission for Inquiry into the Conditions of the Poorer classes in Ireland*, known as the Whately Commission ('I wish justice be done to him – 1st, against his enemies; 2nd, much more against his professed friends, who have made him a tool for their noxious purposes'). Malthus, he thought, would have saved himself much grief if he had been more careful in his use of language, if instead of arguing that war and pestilence were necessary to keep the population within the bounds of subsistence, to use the word unavoidable. This was hardly a deep reading of Malthus's *Essay*.[21] Senior, more so than Malthus, had 'Malthusian concerns' about Irish overpopulation but both believed that a poor law along English lines could only worsen the condition of the Irish poor.[22]

Whately's opposition to the introduction of poor relief in Ireland was hardly original. In 1804, 1819, 1823 and 1825 select committees on the state of Ireland dominated by political economy orthodoxies – expressed by experts like Senior and influenced by Malthus – had on all occasions recommended against any extension of English poor laws to Ireland.[23] Nor were they challenged by Daniel O'Connell who made some vague statements in support of an Irish poor law in 1824 and 1828 yet remained decidedly ambivalent towards the introduction of one. In 1830 he professed to be 'particularly sensitive to the argument that poor laws modeled on that of England tended to promote immorality, most especially in the form of sexual laxity'.[24] By 1831 his position towards the introduction of an Irish poor law was fundamentally antagonistic.[25] Whately considered that comprehensive poor law entitlements were an evil in the English case that, realistically, could be diminished but not eradicated. In the Irish case, the introduction of a poor law would be 'a gratuitous mischief'.[26] In Ireland there was no rationale for a punitive system like that introduced by the 1835 Poor Law: 'The difficulty in Ireland is not to make the able-bodied look for employment, but to find it profitably for the many who seek it ... we see that they are therefore, and not from any fault of their own, in permanent want'.[27] In a letter to Senior in late 1837 he remarked that the feeling of the English towards Ireland on the passing of the Outdoor Relief Bill was a mixture of revenge, compassion and self-love. They pitied the suffering poor of Ireland; they had a fierce resentment against Irish landlords, whom they hastily judged to be the sole authors of these sufferings; and they dreaded calls on their own purse.

He likened the imposition of the English system upon Ireland to the maid in an anecdote by Swift. She was sent to open a drawer but was unable to find the right key. She forced the lock and broke the key because her mistress would think her a fool if she had done nothing. 'And such a mistress did the Commissioners find the British Public.' But what many in England really sought were:

> measures that might prevent the periodical immigration of Irish labourers to England for the harvest-work, 'to take the bread out of the mouths of the English labourers,' and 'to carry away with them English money into Ireland' – as if it were not plain that if the work they did were not worth more than that money, it would not be worth any one's while to employ them.[28]

After a few years in Ireland he became irked by the preconceptions of visitors to the country – travellers like Gustave de Beaumont and English liberal reformers who came to see things with their own eyes – the 'distress and dirt, and drunkenness' – and then declare the opinions they had formed 'of Ireland, its evils, and their remedies'. They brought with them, Whately declared, their ready-made theories and plans then declared that everything they had heard or seen had confirmed their convictions.[29]

Catholic emancipation, no less than the repeal of slavery or ending the death penalty, had knock-on consequences. These included the burning issues that he faced on arrival, Catholic grievances about having to pay tithes to the Established Church and reform of the government-funded sectarian education system run by the Kildare Place Society. His approach was to address the consequences of Catholic emancipation both in terms of relations with Catholics – avoid antagonisms, break the cycles of past conflict and enmity – and in preparing Irish Protestants intellectually and spiritually for a future where there was no moral or practical case for a Protestant Established Church.

In pursuing this goal the main battleground was education. Whately's proudest achievement was his stewardship for over two decades of the National School system introduced by the Whigs in 1832. His 1850 book, *The Past and Future of Ireland as indicated by its Educational System*, described how a blatantly sectarian government-funded system of often appalling schools run by the Kildare Place Society had come to be reformed. His vision of a secular education system was not to be. By 1853, after two decades in charge of the Education Board, he was swept aside as a condition for the cooperation of the new Catholic Archbishop of Dublin, Paul Cullen. Whately had presided over a huge expansion in the numbers of children educated, from 107,042 pupils in 789 state-funded schools in 1833 to 432,884 pupils in 3,246 schools by 1845.[30] For all the shenanigans of defensive Protestants and of increasingly forceful Catholics he oversaw something of a golden age of cooperation between both. If the ideal of a secular school system fell short of reality it had served, alongside other accommodations promoted by Whately, to cushion the peaceful decline of Protestant Ascendancy. Although he died more than half a century before Irish independence and some years before the final disestablishment of the Anglican Church he was a kind of post-colonial figure, a prototype of those charged with winding down the British Empire more than a century later.

The consequences of Catholic emancipation

Catholic emancipation in March 1829 signaled the end of Protestant Ascendancy even though it was accompanied by measures aimed at checking Catholic power. A bill suppressing the Catholic Association was introduced a month before. Another abolished the right of forty shilling freeholders to vote thereby reducing the Irish electorate from 230,000 to just 14,000 who qualified as having freeholds worth £10 or more. A third bill introduced a new oath of allegiance making it possible for practicing Catholics to be members of parliament and hold all offices except those of regent, chancellor and lord lieutenant. The oath obliged Catholics to 'adjure any intention to subvert' the Established Church 'or weaken the Protestant religion or Protestant Government'.[31] Whately arrived in Ireland in October 1831 to head up an institution whose status he viewed as indefensible for all that he was cast in the role of its leading defender. As put in his personal journal:

> The establishment of a Protestant Church in Ireland, which by many thoughtless Liberals and designing demagogues is spoken of as a burden to the Irish nation, and which the ultra-Protestants speak of as nothing to be complained of by the mass of people, should be viewed, though no burden, yet as a grievance, as being an insult.[32]

His appointment was part of a package of measures aimed at addressing the government of post-Emancipation Ireland, most notably the secular National School system inaugurated just a week later.[33] His arrival in Ireland was represented as 'a heavy blow to the cause of Protestant liberty'.[34] The contrast he made with his Irish Ascendancy predecessor Dr Magee was striking. Magee had been hostile to Catholic emancipation and had actively campaigned against it.[35] In an 1822 sermon Magee had proclaimed a 'Second Reformation' on the anniversary of the Gunpowder Plot in strident terms not witnessed in Ireland since the beginning of the nineteenth century. His stance was widely interpreted as a spiritual war on Catholics and Presbyterians.[36] A nineteenth-century biographer of Whately wrote that: 'So completely inoculated were the Protestant clergy of Dublin with the virus of Dr. Magee's retrogressive view, that the liberal principles of Dr. Whately startled them every day more unpleasantly.'[37] Magee had also viewed tithes as 'an inalienable right' and urged his congregation to resist to their 'last breath' any attempt at reform.[38] Whately, for his part, supported changing the laws that obliged Catholics to pay tithes to the Established Church. Ireland, he emphasised, was the only country in Europe where the Established Church was the religion of a 'small and inconsiderable minority'.[39]

Catholic agitation against tithes payable to the Established Church had spread across the country following a confrontation in Graiguenamanagh in County Killkenny in 1830, although resentments had been building for some years. A bad harvest, falling agricultural prices and local friction with the Reverend Luke McDonnell, an unpopular curate 'exceptionally lacking in judgement and tact', had precipitated demands for a reduction in tithes. These were refused by a number of parsons – the legal formula for setting amounts allowed rates to be set for several years without review – so the farmers refused to pay at all. That McDonnell was prominent in Magee's New Reformation also emerged as a bone of contention in evidence given to the Select Committee of the House of Commons on Tithes which met in 1831 and 1832.[40]

A number of proselytising Protestant Societies had been formed to convert the Catholic peasantry during the 1820s – 'to persuade people of the errors of their ways and the deceit of the priests'. Their mobilisation coincided with that of Catholic priests in support of Daniel O'Connell's campaign against the Penal Laws. The tithe strike that spread across the country vented Catholic resentments and was to a considerable extent a manifestation of wider sectarian conflicts as well as a further expression of the political mobilisation that had pushed for Catholic emancipation. One submission to the select committee described how over the previous few years a body of men comprised principally of clergy of the Established Church, with some laymen, had gone through Ireland with the avowed purpose of correcting the errors, as they termed them, of the Catholic Church ('They assailed invariably the religion of the Roman Catholics, heaping upon it every opprobrium and abuse it was possible to convey').

Doing so stirred up much resentment amongst Catholics. Catholic emancipation 'had been delayed, till it was perilous to delay it longer'.[41] When Whately landed in Dublin turbulence and vitriol were at levels that surpassed, on one account, 'even the height of '98'.[42] There was considerable anger amongst Irish Protestants about the appointment of 'a Whig and an Englishman who supported Sir Robert Peel in his apostasy', who was, his Protestant Ascendancy critics complained, 'an alien by blood and birth'.[43]

His immediate problem was the danger of escalating violence resulting from the tithe strike. A letter of 14 January 1832 to the Lord Lieutenant excoriated a proposal to appoint an agent from Scotland to collect arrears from Catholics, to be jointly funded by the government and the Established Church. In default of payment the agent's employees were to seize cattle for sale in Scotland or elsewhere in Ireland. Allowing such contractors to do the work of government, he argued, was likely to kindle a civil war.[44] A letter to Copleston a few days later reiterated the same argument. The government should act decisively lest its authority be usurped. If there was to be a showdown better that this be between the government and subjects than between parties of subjects. It would the sooner and more effectually be put down, and would have less disastrous results. But the crucial need was to lance the boil of sectarian conflict:

> I think it not unlikely that the Orange party-spirit, if called into action in the manner you speak of, may crush the opposite party for a time but the permanent pacification of Ireland, through the Orange party, can only take place by the total extermination of the Roman Catholic population. This is not so generally *acknowledged* here as is *readily known*: and in England it is not understood. There are many instances on record of a conquering and a conquered nation or faction quietly amalgamating together; but then, that is by the exercise of some degree of moderation, firmness and prudence on the part of the victors. Now, in all three of these requisites we are remarkably deficient. The English apply all they hear about the Irish national character to the Roman Catholics, and imagine that Protestants – men of their own church – are much such men as themselves; whereas a Roman Catholic and an Orangeman (with, of course, individual exceptions) are much more like each other than either of them to an Englishman: the chief difference, in respect of the present point, is implacability.[45]

Within months of arriving in Ireland he took to explaining to English correspondents how much Ireland was misunderstood in England and how different Irish Protestants were from English ones. Irish Protestants never wearied of tyrannising over the conquered and of rubbing salt into the wounds of the Catholics their ancestors had defeated. Generation after generation they trampled on, insulted and tormented the fallen foe rather than letting the conflicts of previous generations be forgotten.

The very name of Orangemen is a sign. It is chosen *on purpose* to keep up the memory of a civil war, which every friend of humanity would wish to bury in oblivion. It is doing what amongst the heathen was reckoned an accursed deed, keeping a trophy *in repair*. The English would have too much, if not Christian feeling, at least of good taste, to assemble in Paris to celebrate the Battle of Waterloo. Here we parade Orange flags and decorate King William's statue, and play the tunes of insulting songs under the noses of the vanquished, till they are goaded to madness; and it is curious that they are more studious to provoke than to disable their enemies; they are like sportsmen who preserve foxes on purpose to hunt them.[46]

In another letter to Copleston in 1832 he emphasised that Ireland was fundamentally misunderstood in England:

I do not know what to think of the state of this country. Besides other difficulties, the English, who are in fact its legislators, do not understand the peculiarities of the people; they are surrounded by those who wish to mislead them; and when they meet with one who tells them the truth, they will not believe him. In particular, they will cling to the belief that Protestant *ascendancy*, or the ascendancy of any one party would pacify the country, which, as I have lately explained to you, could only be through the complete extermination of its opponents. As long as *any* of the adverse sect remained, the victors would never cease insulting and goading them, till they bought on a fresh rebellion; and so there would be, as for the last six hundred years, a perpetual sucession of battle, murder, and sudden death. But this is never adequately understood by the English nation, who are perhaps haughty and selfish governors of the vanquished, but not restless and wanton tormentors.[47]

A conquered enemy of the English, he continued, was an ox yoked to the plough to drudge; of the Protestant Irish, a bull to be tied to the stake to be bated. In the shadow of such habitual provocation Catholic emancipation would not, he believed, resolve Ireland's political problems:

You may remember I was a true prophet respecting the Catholic relief Bill, in saying that it would not satisfy the people of Ireland; I always felt sure it could not, under any circumstances, unless accompanied by other measures. And it was granted so late, so ungraciously, and so avowedly from intimidation, that whatever good it might have done was more than prevented.[48]

Unlike his predecessor, Whately cultivated cordial relations with his Catholic opposite number, Archbishop Daniel Murray, and with Catholic clergy more generally.[49] Both Murray and Whately endeavoured to rein in the sectarianism of their own bishops and clergy. Whately was regarded as a dangerous interloper by many of his own clergy. He had little time for the more evangelical members of his flock who engaged in proselytising and blaming Catholics for the evils of the world in the same breath. In an 1832 letter he wryly observed the tendency of some of these to attribute a cholera epidemic and other natural disasters as divine retribution for the transgressions of their enemies: 'one man, in a sermon which friends of mine heard, attributed the wet harvest to the passing of the Roman Catholic Relief Bill; some, in this country, attribute the cholera to the superstitions of the Church of Rome'.[50] In 1836 he sought to block efforts by Evangelical Protestants to invite the Reverend L. J. Nolan, a former Maynooth seminarian who had converted to Protestantism, to preach in his diocese. But the correspondence on the issue, much of it with Archdeacon Magee, son of Whately's predecessor, illustrates how little direct control he had over his clergy.[51] His authority depended to no limited extent on the perceived legitimacy of his position on a given issue.

Whately's initial preferred solution to the tithes crisis was that incomes should be provided to Catholic priests as well as to Protestant clerics 'not, as some puzzle-headed bigots are accustomed to say, by a Protestant government, but out of the revenues of a nation, partly Protestant, partly Romish, revenues to which both contribute and in which both have a right to an equitable share'. Tithes payable to the Established Church should be reformed into a tax payable to the state that would fund a National School system as well as provide incomes for clerics of all denominations. This would be in keeping with what was now the law of the land, the right of parents to educate their children in their own faith.[52]

Irish Protestants, Whately reported to Lord Melbourne in May 1835, were very worried that reform of tithes would create incentives for future violence against their clergy. From debates in the House of Commons it was believed that the revenues of the Established Church would be transferred over time to the Education Board; as incumbent clergy 'became deceased' their livings would revert. 'What alarms us', he wrote, were the incentives such a system of the apportioning of the revenues of the Church and the Education Board to the varying proportions of the Roman Catholic population to the Protestant – 'the principle of making the funds for national education contingent upon the death of incumbents' – might create for agrarian violence and murder. It would 'place the clergy so circumstanced in a most invidious and, in this country, a most dangerous situation. No one who knows anything would like to reside here surrounded by his heirs, on whom his income was to devolve at his death'.[53] 'Better, far better', he argued in the context of all too real fears of agrarian violence, 'would it be to confiscate at once and for ever all the endowments held by the clergy, and leave them to be supported by voluntary contribution, or by manual labour. However impoverished, they and their congregations would at least have security for their lives.'[54]

What he sought was a scheme that would allocate a proportion of the revenues collected in lieu of tithes to the Church as a government grant and that the rest should be immediately dispersed by the government in grants towards primary education. Let grants be made at once to the Education Board instead of letting the Irish nation understand that a great national advantage must be postponed in great measure till the deaths of certain Protestant clergymen. These should become life-pensioners of the government in exchange for giving up the basis of their livings. That would, he mused, still leave various issues to be resolved in the future, namely how to adjust the funds given by the government to the Established Church as the number of Protestants in congregations rose or fell. He envisaged parishes where there might be just fifty or so Protestants. These would be unable to support their own ministers. A system might be put in place to build houses for such ministers and to augment their wretchedly poor livings.

He counseled expediency, to prevent this issue being used to keep Ireland in a state of perpetual turmoil. Anything that allowed Catholics to believe that they still funded the Established Church would perpetuate a sense of grievance.[55] The formula approved by Westminster in 1838 was along lines supported by Whately since 1833. Tithes were to be converted into a 'charge' payable by landlords, who would then pass the cost onto their tenants as part of their rent. Arrears in tithes were annulled.[56]

Whately was primarily preoccupied with salving the wounds of sectarian conflict. But his office and the income that came with it allowed him to promote other interests; he endowed a Chair in Political Economy at Trinity College and subsequently founded the Dublin Statistical Society. His status along with his expertise in political economy led to his appointment to the Commission on Poor Law. For all that the Whately Commission produced more than 5,000 pages of evidence on the lives of the Irish poor and on the economic needs of the country it is easy to conclude from his correspondence that he was more exercised by the needs of impoverished clergy – often privately giving large sums from £50 to £1,000 to deserving cases – than with the condition of the Catholic Irish poor.[57] Not for the first or last time in Irish history did a political focus on sectarian problems drive out consideration of social and economic ones. The Whately Commission's finely detailed accounts of the lives of the Irish poor and destitute seem to have had little impact on Whately's approach to Irish affairs. He had made his mind up before coming to Ireland about what to do about their kind. This boiled down to promoting their betterment though education and removing incentives to idleness.

Education against sectarianism

Catholic emancipation created an impetus to educational reform. The primary education system set up by the Kildare Place Society in 1811 had, within a decade of its foundation, become bogged down in denominational acrimony. Catholics had been represented on its Board but were a small minority. From 1820 the Society gave funding to schools that had avowedly proselytising aims and the Society encountered rising opposition from the Catholic Church. In 1820 Daniel O'Connell, then a member of the Kildare Place Society, criticized the spirit of proselytism he believed was at work in its schools.[58] Thirty years later, in *The Past and Future of Ireland as Indicated by its Educational History*, Whately explained how the charter schools run by the Society came to be avoided by Catholics for other good reasons. Not only were these run on sectarian principles but the quality of education was very poor and the treatment of pupils was brutal. Inspections of such schools in 1824 on behalf of a Royal Commission on Education revealed these as akin to Dotheboys Hall in Charles Dickens' 1838 novel *Nicholas Nickleby*. Amongst the abuses cited by Whately was the habitual practice of the master at Sligo of seizing 'the children by the throat, press them almost to suffocation and stricke them with a whip or his fist, on the head or face, while his passion lasted'. 'In Stradbally, one little boy was flogged with a leather strap, nine times in one day, suffering 100 lashes for a sum of long division'; 'In the same boarding school, eight boys had been flogged till their backs were frightfully lacerated, because two of them had been looking at the policemen playing ball in an alley near the school. The master had three farms and left the school to a brute of an usher, who thus conducted himself.' In the same school seventeen out of a class of twenty thirteen-year-old boys had never heard of St Paul. This, he thundered, was the system defended by those who opposed the new one on religious grounds.[59]

The old system had been unsound and corrupt; officials were bribed by the masters of schools: 'Hence all communications inculpating the latter were cushioned, or sent to the accused; in which case the boy who had complained was publicly flogged as a warning to others and became forever after a special victim, the scapegoat of the school.' The commissioners warned that 'no offence which a charter-school child can commit seems to be less pardonable than daring to utter a complaint'. For all the difficulty of punishing delinquent masters, which was never done without legal proof, so enormous were the abuses of the system that between 1800 and 1825, no less than thirty-two masters were dismissed for misconduct and seventeen more resigned to avoid the same fate. No wonder that some Protestants and most Catholics preferred to send their children to *pay* schools in cabins and stables rather than to the Kildare Place Society, where they would be taught for free.[60]

Whately was particularly concerned about the inability of such schools to foster religiosity. The Bible was taught as a 'dry verbal task for the memory' that frequently created an aversion to that sacred book not easily removed. He cited evidence to the 1824 commission that even the more advanced boys did not have a tolerable understanding of the New Testament. Although the Kildare Place schools were open to charges of proselytism Whately thought that most of these were hardly capable of managing this.[61]

The replacement National School system had come about largely due to Catholic activism and support. In January 1826 the Irish Catholic bishops drew up resolutions, backed by the Catholic Association, supporting a 'Mixed Education' school system. Their proposals endorsed the admission of Protestants and Catholics into the same schools 'provided sufficient care be taken to protect the religion of the Roman Catholic children and furnish them with adequate means of religious instruction'. The 1824 Royal Commission on Education documented the kinds of materials used by Catholic schools: mostly Catechisms, prayer books, works of religious instruction, church histories and devotional works such as *The Imitation of Christ* by Thomas a Kempis along with a small number of Douay Bibles.[62] The 1826 proposals required that the master of each school in which the majority of pupils profess the Roman Catholic faith, be a Roman Catholic and that, in schools in which the Roman Catholic children form only a minority, a permanent Roman Catholic assistant be employed. The other main safeguard related to curriculum materials.[63] These proposals were worked into a bill by Thomas Wyse, a Catholic Association MP, and this bill was subsequently reworked by E. G. Stanley, the chief Secretary for Ireland and Lord Grey's Whig government.[64] A petition on educational reform from the Irish Catholic Hierarchy on educational reform was presented to both Houses of Parliament in 1830. The influential Bishop of Kildare and Leighlin, Dr John Doyle (J. K. L.), stated in 1830 to the Parlimentary Committee on the State of Ireland that he did not believe that peace would ever be established in Ireland if children were religiously segregated:

> I do not know any measure which would prepare for a better feeling in Ireland than uniting children at an early age, and bringing them up in the same school, leading them to commune with one another, and to form those little intimacies and friendships which often subsist through life. Children thus united know and love each other, as children brought up together always will; and to separate them is, I think, to destroy some of the finest feelings in the hearts of men.[65]

The reformed system was described to Parliament as 'a denominational system with a conscience clause'.[66] For a number of years it was trenchantly opposed by the great bulk of the Protestant clergy 'as a scheme for subverting the Protestant Establishment of Ireland'. In March 1837 Whately was petitioned by 3,000 lay members of his own flock. The petition complained of 'certain novelties of discipline, recently promulgated'.[67] The teaching of religion, or matters that touched on religious doctrines, proved contentious for Protestant and Catholic interest groups alike. Whately considered that many such complaints from Protestants – who demanded that the full text of the Bible be placed on the curriculum – were humbug, given the poor quality of religious education under the old Kildare Place system. Catholics objected to the reading of scripture in the classroom without doctrinally sound commentaries. In 1837 following much negotiation between Whately and Murray the Board adopted a primer of readings from the New Testament, *Easy Lessons on Christian Evidences*.[68] Whately was very involved in designing elements of the curriculum and became the focus of criticism from both sides.

He saw his role over these two decades as circumventing sectarian demands that would foster respective Catholic and Protestant 'hotbeds of bigotry and religious animosity'. The Catholic Church initially supported the system but became increasingly ambivalent towards it over time. Initially, 'Presbyterians and the Orangemen clamoured for a return of the old system'. In 1832 the Synod of Ulster raised the cry of 'the bible unabridged and unmutilated' and held back from the Board's schools. The appearance of neutrality was crucial in managing the politics of demands for control by both sides. By 1840 enough of the demands of Presbyterians had been acceded to for these to become staunch supporters of the Board. Whilst Murray supported the National School system other Catholic bishops, notably Archbishop McHale of Tuam, campaigned for a system of Catholic denominational schools and stepped up their demands over time.[69] In 1839, to counter such demands, Murray requested that a legate be sent from Rome to evaluate the system. This was conducted the following year by the future Catholic Archbishop of Dublin Paul Cullen who concluded at the time that the schools 'could not have been more Catholic than they are'.[70]

The system worked very differently in practice than as represented by the Education Board. One incident described in William Fitzpatrick's 1864 biography of Whately, in the key of a short story by Sommerville and Ross, illustrated the underlying fudge that governed the workings of the Education Board. The inspector of schools in the overwhelmingly Catholic County Clare was a Protestant. He was treated with considerable hospitality by the Catholic priests of the county; they used to drive him from district to district in their gigs; he liked them and the priests got fond of him. The inspector was disciplined by a new zealous superior, a Catholic committed to the anti-sectarian principles of the Education Board: 'He had visited the schools, and saw a sight which well-nigh made the hair stand on his head. At one of the doors a holy-water pot, filled to repletion was placed! Another building, used as a school, had been the Roman Catholic chapel of the parish until the erection of a new church supplanted its purpose. A number of Catholic emblems, however, had never been removed, including several crosses and a picture of the blessed Virgin Mary.' The hapless county inspector was summonsed to Dublin; 'Thither he repaired, and casting one longing, lingering look behind at visions of old port, roast turkeys, and poteen punch, of which he had a painful presentiment were never again to be realized.'[71]

Whately chaired the hearing and asked the man to answer to the charges against him. The inspector produced a petition signed by all the parish priests in Clare and by Dr Kennedy, the Roman Catholic Bishop of Killaloe, an influential Whig. 'Now', asked Whately, what should one think 'of the rats signing round-robins testifying to the efficiency of the cat?' The irregularity was strongly condemned but the inspector was treated leniently. The control Whately could exercise over the system was limited. But it prevented the diffusion of an amount of 'superstition' (here he was thinking of Catholics), 'bigotry, intolerance' (here Protestants) and 'religious animosity' (and here both).

Once Cullen succeeded Murray in 1852 he sought to lever confrontation. He made the removal from the curriculum of a religious primer compiled by Whately in 1837, *Easy Lessons on Christian Evidences*, a price for his membership of the Board of National Schools. By proscribing Whately's primer – banning its use by all Catholic teachers and children – Cullen, in effect, levered his resignation.[72] In a flurry of correspondence with the Lord Lieutenant in July 1853 Whately railed ineffectually against the shifting ground beneath his feet; he protested that *Easy Lessons* had been sanctioned by the Education Board and approved by Murray. He defended his track record against efforts by Protestants to subvert the National Education system but nowhere did he acknowledge Cullen's power play.[73] In correspondence with a Vatican cardinal in August 1853 Cullen exulted that: 'The downfall of the Archbishop is very favourable to us because in the first place he was a very subtle and crafty enemy and second because it has shown to the other commissioners that they cannot injure our religion with impunity.'[74]

Education and the new ascendancy

Murray died in 1852 at the age of eighty-four having been Archbishop of Dublin for forty-two years. He had seen out the Penal Laws and had achieved parity with the Established Church in the administration of the National School system. His achievements came to be denigrated in the new era of assertive Catholicism. Although he had cooperated with Dublin Castle he had overseen the building of more than ninety churches and had supported the establishment of the Christian Brothers, the Sisters of Mercy and the Jesuits in Dublin. Where Murray sought parity his successor in Dublin, Archbishop Cullen, sought ascendancy. Cullen had been ordained in Rome and from 1833 became the agent of Irish bishops in the Vatican where he also 'guided and defended' Daniel O'Connell. After O'Connell's death he became the de facto leader of Catholic Ireland.[75] He founded a new Catholic University of Ireland together with John Henry Newman. Newman had been Whately's protégé in Oxford but Cullen became his mentor in Rome following Newman's conversion to Catholicism.

Cullen kept sniping at Whately long after he ousted him from the Education Board, complaining in 1860 that Catholic children were using textbooks 'replete in anti-Catholic spirit, compiled from Protestant sources, under the direction of a rationalistic dignitary of the Protestant Establishment'.[76] In an 1863 letter Whatley was described as opportunistically spreading 'unscriptural darkness by publishing scripture lessons'.[77] In a pastoral of 21 January 1867, he depicted Whately as the arch-proselytiser: 'You will recall that Dr Whately always professed great liberality and was extolled by his party as a model of just dealing, impartiality and integrity, in whom Catholics might put implicit confidence in everything connected with that most important of all matters, the education of their children. Yet, this straightforward, liberal, high-minded man was supporting national education with the view of undermining our religion, of supplanting what he calls *vast fabric of the Irish Roman Catholic Church, and of weaning*, as he says, *The Irish from the abuses of popery*; and he was doing all this covertly and insidiously, professing at the same time, to be anxious to give fair play to Catholics.' 'Should we not look with great suspicion and with even fear', Cullen continued, 'on the mixed system declared by Dr Whately, one of the most acute reasoners of our times, to be the fittest engine for supplanting the true faith and undermining the true church? And should we not insist on having Catholic schools, Catholic colleges and a Catholic university?'[78] Whately was dead four years by then and had been displaced fourteen years earlier.[79]

The future, referred to in his 1850 book *The Past and Future of Ireland*, was exemplified by the new undenominational Queen's Colleges established by Peel in 1845 in Cork, Galway and Belfast. Like the National School system set up in 1831 these were supported by Archbishop Murray but opposed by some of the other Catholic bishops. Cullen led a long campaign against the 'godless colleges' although he remained behind the scenes, having mobilised the Archbishop of Cashel, Michael Slattery, and the Archbishop of Tuam, John McHale, as the public face of opposition.[80] Correspondence between Catholic bishops from 1845 to 1850 reveals conflicts behind the scenes.[81] Curran secured a papal condemnation of the Queen's Colleges in October in 1847. Murray continued to support the Queen's Colleges and made a counter-petition to Rome in January 1848, stating in effect that the Pope had been inadequately briefed on Irish affairs by his opponents. The Pope, Cullen complained in June 1848, was 'so anxious to please the English that he will not again condemn the godless colleges'.[82]

The Past and Future of Ireland was dedicated to Peel, 'the patron of Ireland and Liberal Education, the friend of Ireland and the founder of the Queen's Colleges which auger for that country a future of peace, content, prosperity and true glory'. Its final chapter described the courses offered by the new institutions and set out profiles of their presidents. Queen's College in Belfast was headed by the Reverend Dr P. Henry, a member of the Synod of Ulster who had supported the national schools 'on the principle of united unsectarian education'. The President of the new Cork University was Robert Kane, an eminent chemist, a Catholic who had been educated at

Trinity College Dublin. That of Galway was the Reverend Joseph Kirwin, 'one of the most eminent Roman Catholic divines in Ireland', a former parish priest in County Galway who, according to Whately, had been frequently threatened with excommunication for his association with the Queen's Colleges. Galway fell under the jurisdiction of McHale, the Archbishop of Tuam. McHale worked with Cullen to undermine Murray's advocacy of the new colleges but in turn encountered dissent in his own patch.

Whately, for his part, hoped that the lecture-halls of the new institutions would be crowded with young Catholic men 'thirsting for knowledge, exulting in freedom, and resolved on surpassing the glory of the Celtic name in the brightest era of its history ere the gloom, barbarism and tyranny of the feudal ages had infused the spirit of *serfdom* into the souls of the Irish people'. Dare, he exhorted, to be Burkes, Goldsmiths, Sheridans, O'Connells or Kanes: 'The young Catholics of Munster and Connaught have before them in their own church the example of a Kane: let them trod boldly in his footsteps, and they too will have the reward of a life of usefulness and happiness, and it may be, in productions of genius which posterity will not let die.'[83]

Whately argued that academic education for the middle classes – comprehensive, liberal, practical, suited to the times, the kind not supplied by Trinity College – had long been badly needed in Ireland. Irish students needed access to fellowships, scholarships and bursaries on the same basis and for the same reasons that enriched the universities. He also advocated the reform of Trinity which was still endowed as a divinity school. The time for it to be restricted to clergy and gentry of the Established Church had passed.

Cullen had lost the battle but went on to have huge influence in the shaping of post-1850s Ireland. After Murray's death, Whately lost his remaining influence over education. In the last decade of his life the once-boisterous archbishop suffered poor health. He became somewhat bitter in his last years. His personal notebooks suggest that he found much about Ireland perplexing and infuriating. As an often-unpopular man, one certainly who lacked the common touch, Whately could not understand the admiration the Irish heaped upon an unnamed fellow countryman – it could only have been O'Connell – for possessing a 'fluent bluster and fine-sounding superficial declamation' when so many of them anyway – perhaps three out of four – had this talent themselves.

I suppose there *is* some much greater difference than I perceive; and that their appearing to me so nearly on a par with each other is just like the mistake of those who are being unused to negroes fancy they are all alike ... But some kind of talent there must be always in everyone who accomplishes an object which many others *would* accomplish if they could but *cannot*.[84]

Such asides taken together with his powerful arguments against colonial racism in *The Past and Future of Ireland*, point to one of Whately's great strengths: a self-awareness that mobilised the character flaws and eccentricities observed by others to break with convention. He endeavoured to challenge his own prejudices and those of others towards Ireland and the Irish. He championed liberal education as an antidote to religious ascendancy in Ireland, the old Protestant variant and the rising Catholic one exemplified by Cullen. In *The Past and Future of Ireland* he also made a case for the new cultural nationalism as an antidote to colonial hubris:

> That the imagination of a people so long afflicted as the Irish should dwell much in the past, and clothe their ancient state in too bright a glory, is but natural. It is an extreme to which they would be driven by the systemic efforts made, in past times to vilify and degrade their forefathers, to destroy their ancient monuments, to proscribe their primitive and noble language, and to abolish their national institutions, laws, and customs.[85]

The proper study of Irish history, he argued, offered the intellectual tools to contest colonial prejudices. When the claims that the beleaguered Irish made about their past were examined in a critical light 'enough of authentic history' would remain 'to testify that for many ages after the fall of the Roman empire, Ireland stood at the head of the nations of Europe, as the dispenser of learning and civilisation'. The Irish nation possessed a 'genuine history several centuries more ancient than any other European nation possesses, in its present spoken language'.

Whately used his account of this history in *The Past and Future of Ireland* to disparage claims about Irish inferiority: 'A great deal of unsound philosophy has been written and spoken of late on the subject of *races,* and of the virtue of Saxon blood' but 'The boast of superior blood is one of the silliest forms of prejudice'. There was something in the notion of differences in cultural temperament, for example between Celts and Saxons, but history showed how little of this affected national character compared to other causes: 'What race is there that has not, in its turn, been elevated by Christianity, and degraded by religious despotism and social oppression?'[86]

He insisted that character and temperament were crucially affected by education and social conditions; even amongst the 'so-called inferior peoples' a sound education and free institutions would in the course of a few generations obliterate every trace of their aboriginal inferiority. A proper regimen and exercise, combined with a right moral education, tended to enlarge the volume of the brain, to give power to the intellectual faculties, health and purity to the moral feelings, and so to develop a noble character whilst 'semi-starvation, ignorance and slavery, will have an effect quite opposite'. He argued that 'the ancient Egyptians, from whom Europe learned the rudiments of her civilisation, were undoubtedly men of colour' and commented that 'the once noble Greeks were the modern Irish of Rome in the days of Juvenal'. At a time when the Irish were spreading learning across Europe the very Saxons from which the now powerful and apparently superior English were descended from had been degraded: 'The slave of yesterday becomes the lord today'.[87]

He emphasised the value of preserving, studying and translating Gaelic manuscripts and 'the stupidity of despising the Irish language'.[88] At the same time he was adamant that the Irish would not find their future in their past:

> Now instead of proscribing the native tongue, professors are endowed to inculcate it. Let us rejoice in this as one of the many signs that we have entered on a new era. But as to the Irish language, toleration and patronage have come too late. It cannot be saved alive by any human power. It is at present confined to about one-third of the peasantry, and these are the most ignorant and uncivilised. As a spoken language, it can hardly survive the present generation. The fathers and mothers will retain it till their death, but by the children it will be neglected and forgotten. The time for educating them in their native language has gone by forever. It is not the language of business, of modern civilisation, and will not enable a man to get on in the world. However we may regret that any language, especially one so primitive, so expressive, so powerful as the Gaelic, should cease to live, its doom is inevitable. Had it been the vehicle of education and of modern literature, its fate would have been different. Had Protestants taken it up a century ago in a kindly and national spirit, it would have greatly aided their religion; but to take it up now, when its owners have laid it aside as a cast-off instrument, is preposterous. In the rudest districts, reading in English can be just as well taught as reading in Irish; while, in the former case, you open the mind to all the treasures of knowledge, and all the mighty resources of civilisation; and in the latter, only shadowy reminescences of a by-gone state of existence, and of an imperfect civilisation, which has perished, and will never know a resurrection.[89]

He 'hoped to convince those who have influence over the destinies of the United Kingdom that there was no inherent deficiency in the Celtic mind', that it is not incapable of the highest attainments in literature and science, or of steady progress in the peaceful and prosperous arts of Christian civilisation. If Ireland was to break with the tragedies of its past, it could only do so by means of an education system designed and implemented so as to subordinate the sectarian prejudices that had held it back. Doing so, he argued in the *The Past and Future of Ireland*, meant acknowledging just how destructive the systems of government and education put in place since the Reformation had proved. England's Glorious Revolution had imposed an oppressive penal code that had 'scarce a parallel in European history' and that had 'poisoned the vital springs of society'. In this context, the education system that he had been given responsibility for was inherently compromised.[90]

CHAPTER SEVEN

Friedrich Engels and the crisis of Irish character

Irish immigrants loom large in Friedrich Engels' *The Condition of the Working Class in England*, written in 1844 when he was just twenty-four.[1] Engels first wrote about the Irish the previous year for a German newspaper edited by Karl Marx whom he had yet to meet. To write his book on the poor of England he strip-mined the books and pamphlets of others, particularly *Chartism* by Thomas Carlyle.[2] The People's Charter of 1838 had called for the universal franchise and parliamentary reform and, like the campaign for Catholic emancipation in Ireland a decade earlier, resulted in mass political agitation. Engels appropriated Carlyle's accounts of the Irish emigrant poor and the dilemmas Carlyle believed these posed for English society. Neither had been to Ireland prior to the publication of their respective polemics. But both could observe at first hand the hundreds of thousands of Irish emigrants pouring into English cities. The 1841 census identified some 415,000 in England and Scotland, a figure that did not include seasonal migrants and the children of earlier migrants.[3] Carlyle viewed Irish immigrants as a trial deservedly visited on England for the injustices it had perpetrated upon Ireland, but one to be lamented nevertheless. Engels took much of the content and tone of his account of the dissolute Irish in English cities from Carlyle and saw in them the capacity to drag down the conditions of and corrupt the character of the English proletariat.

Engels in his public and private lives embodied, in the words of one biographer, 'contradictions of Hegelian proportions'.[4] He was a fox-hunting bon viveur who gained access to both of the two nations described in Benjamin Disraeli's 1845 novel *Sybil*. Until he was able to retire in 1869 at the age of forty-nine and live off the profits from his capital, Engels worked for his father's company. Running Ermen and Engels, manufacturers of cotton twist, gave him an insight into the owners and controllers of the means of production which was denied to many socialists. The class from which he emerged were stolid burghers, devoted to religion, business and civic duty, demanding of yet concerned about the skilled artisans their families employed for generations and leery of many of the changes associated with the industrial revolution.[5] According to another biographer industrial England perturbed him with its brutal dissolution of mankind into monads or atoms. In the turmoil of its streets there was 'something repulsive, something against which human nature rebels'.[6]

Young Friedrich rebelled against a safe but stifling home. The terms of his Bremen business apprenticeship, which included a stock of beer in the office and a hammock for after-lunch naps, gave him ample time to cut a dash about town and immerse himself in the radical ideas that were convulsing Germany: cultural nationalism and other expressions of Romanticism, the radicalism of the Young Germany movement and, in particular, the writings of Goethe and Hegel. At the age of nineteen he wrote some articles (under the pseudonym Friedrich Oswald so as to not distress his family) about how international competition and new industrial techniques had undermined work conditions in the Rhenish textile industry.[7] These vivid 'Letters from Wuppertal' provided a template for *The Condition of the Working Class* five years later. A year of undemanding military service in Berlin enabled him to mix in socialist circles and imbibe Hegel on religion (God as the invention of man), history (the unfolding of the idea of freedom in human affairs) and progress (the product of reason and rationality as evidenced in language, culture and the spirit of the people).[8] His early writings as Oswald exulted in the idea of Germany's life-blood 'throbbing in the veins of world history'.[9] In January 1841 he declared his support for a German manifest destiny by conquest if necessary:

> For I am of the opinion, perhaps in contrast to many whose standpoint I share in other respects, that the reconquest of the German-speaking left bank of the Rhine is a matter of national honour, and that the Germanisation of a disloyal Holland and of Belgium is a political necessity for us. Shall we let the German nationality be completely suppressed in these countries, while the Slavs are rising ever more powerfully in the east?
>
> ... We want to chase all these crazy foreign habits and fashions, all the superfluous foreign words back whence they came; we want to cease to be the dupes of foreigners and want to stand together as a single, indivisible, strong, and with God's will free German nation.[10]

The very first line of *The Communist Manifesto* declared that all history was the history of class struggles. But such struggles intertwined with those of nations and on this, Engels argued elsewhere, history played favourites. In 1849 he described the Slavs as non-historic peoples destined for and deserving of extermination. He professed little sympathy for 'those numerous small relics of peoples which, after having figured for a longer or shorter period on the stage of history, were finally absorbed into one or the other powerful nations'. Slav leaders, he wrote, talked 'drivel about the equality of nations'. They rose up in 1848 to achieve their national independence but in doing so suppressed the socialist German-Magyar revolution. As such they were counter-revolutionary. They were on the wrong side of history as this was understood by Hegelians in two ways: against German nationalism and against socialism. The coming times, he wrote with relish, would 'wipe out all these petty hidebound nations, down to their very names'. The next world war would 'result in the disappearance from the face of the earth not only of reactionary classes and dynasties, but also of entire reactionary peoples. And that, too, is a step forward'.[11]

Engels' 1849 list of non-historic peoples included the Scottish Gaels, the Bretons and the Basques. There was, he explained, no country in Europe which did not have in some corner or other one or several ruined fragments of peoples, the remnant of a former population that was suppressed and held in bondage by the nation which later became the main vehicle of historical development. Citing Hegel he argued that these relics of nations were mercilessly trampled underfoot in the course of history – these *residual fragments of peoples* – 'always become fanatical standard-bearers of counter-revolution and remain so until their complete extirpation or loss of their national character, just as their whole existence in general is itself a protest against a great historical revolution'.[12]

In *The Condition of the Working Class*, the question of whether the Irish were on the right or wrong side of history simmered in the background. For all his professed sympathy for Ireland's plight and the condition of the Irish in England, Engels remained at best ambivalent. He considered Daniel O'Connell to be profoundly reactionary. He portrayed the Irish in Britain as a corrupting influence on the proletariat, for all that their disrupting presence might hasten the crisis of capitalism. But history and serendipity weighed in their favour. What Hegel in an 1831 essay called the cankers of Ireland – the legacies of centuries of exploitation – could not but influence the future of world-historic England.[13] Ireland came to exert a sentimental influence on Engels through his conjugal relationships with Mary Burns and her sister Lizzie. The Burns family, to use Burke's term, became his own little platoon. Home for Engels was not his official Manchester residence but a succession of smaller houses in which he installed the Burns sisters, ate his Irish stew (supposedly his favourite meal) and discussed the twists and turns of Irish politics. Mary became his 'underworld Persephone' to the factories and slums of Manchester.[14]

Within the pages of *The Condition of the Working Class* Carlyle's analysis of England's social crisis, the German romantic nationalist ideals of Engels' intellectual formation and a preoccupation with the Irish poor jostled with a socialist critique of liberal political economy. In his seminal essay *Outlines of a Critique of Political Economy*, written in late 1843, Engels attacked the premises of what he called 'this sham philanthropy produced by Malthusian population theory', the modern slavery of the factory system and the licence granted by the principle of private property to exploit those who sold their labour. Malthus's error was to confuse the means of subsistence with means of employment. The incomes of the labouring poor, Malthus argued, were driven to subsistence levels because the available land for rent was finite. Malthus, he argued, 'failed to see that surplus population or labour power was invariably tied up with surplus wealth, surplus capital and surplus landed property'. Population questions, Engels argued, could not be considered in isolation from other factors. Nations had been known to starve in the midst of plenty. Malthus and other laissez-faire liberals had found no fault in the principle of private property. But private property, the economist's 'most beloved daughter whom he ceaselessly caresses' was a Medusa.[15]

The condition of England

Carlyle's works, Engels argued in an 1844 review of his *Past and Present*, were the only ones worth reading amongst 'all the fat books and thin pamphlets that had appeared in England for the edification of educated society, the multivolume novels and bible commentaries that were the staples of English literature and the dry works of history and science which one studies, but does not read'. He described to his German audience an England where everything was 'as fixed and formalised as in China'. For all the impressive bustle of the Houses of Parliament, the English free press and tumultuous popular meetings all questions had just two answers, a Whig answer and a Tory answer. The Whigs had vested interests in industry and legislated to protect and expand it. The Tories, whose dominance of English society had been broken by industry and whose principles had been shaken by it, hated it and saw it at best as a necessary evil. Some 'philanthropic Tories' had taken the part of factory workers against the manufacturers. Carlyle, Engels explained, was originally such a Tory: 'A Whig would never been able to write a book that was half so humane as *Past and Present*.'[16]

In James Anthony Froude's summary, in his *Life of Carlyle*, the 1832 Reform Bill was to have mended matters, but the poor were no happier. The power of the state had been shifted from the aristocracy to the mill owners and merchants. The Liberal theory, as formulated by its political economists, was that laissez-faire would bring about the best of all possible worlds.[17] In Carlyle's vivid narratives of the devastation wrought by liberal political economy, Engels identified an ally. But the solution proposed by his enemy's enemy – a return to virtue and spiritual renewal – held little appeal for Engels. The piety of the Middle Ages, Carlyle argued, had been abandoned and nothing had taken its place but a Godless utilitarianism: 'God's Laws are become a Greatest Happiness Principle', Man had lost his soul and vainly sought 'antiseptic salt in killing Kings, in Reform Bills, in French Revolutions, in Manchester Insurrections'.[18] Engels was taken with Carlyle's faculty for coining vivid Germanic compound terms like 'MammonGospel' for laissez-faire ('the shabbiest Gospel ever preached on Earth'), the aforementioned 'workhouse Bastilles' and 'sanspotatoes' – a play on *sanscullottes* – for the Irish poor who were flocking to industrial England. Engels cited some of Carlyle's vitriolic accounts of industrial injustice – the shirtless workers who toiled in mills making millions of shirts, 'the working millions at liberty to die by want of food' – and the stupidity that accompanied such injustice. He quoted an account from *Past and Present* of a poor Irish widow who with her children had been refused help from the charitable establishments of Edinburgh. She sank down in typhus fever; died and infected her lane so that seventeen other persons died in consequence. Would it not have been *economy*, protested a doctor that Carlyle had cited, to help the widow? She was treated as if she had no place in the wider community. Yet by fatally infecting seventeen others she had proved that social bonds were all too real.

The Condition of the Working Class cited the same Dr Alison, and several Irish physicians that Alison had cited, to demonstrate how privation resulting from commercial crises or bad harvests had fuelled typhus epidemics in Ireland as in Scotland, and how the fury of the plague fell almost exclusively on the working class.[19]

Engels took analysis as well as tone and evidence from Carlyle. His review of *Past and Present* quoted the following summary of the condition of England in 1843:

An idle landowning aristocracy which 'have not learned even to sit still and do no mischief'. A working aristocracy submerged in Mammonism, who, when they ought to be collectively the leaders of labour, 'captains of industry', are just a gang of industrial buccaneers and pirates. A Parliament elected by bribery, a philosophy of simply looking on, of doing nothing, of *laissez-faire*, a wornout crumbling religion, a total disappearance of all general human interests, a universal despair of truth and humanity, and in consequence a universal isolation of men in their own 'brute individuality', a chaotic, savage confusion of all aspects of life, a war of all against all, a general death of the spirit, a dearth of 'soul', that is of truly human consciousness, a disproportionately strong working class, in intolerable oppression and wretchedness, in furious discontent and rebellion against the old social order, and hence a threatening, irresistibility advancing democracy – everywhere chaos, disorder, anarchy, dissolution of the old ties of society, everywhere intellectual insipidity, frivolity and debility – That is the condition of England.

Engels agreed with most of this. *The Communist Manifesto* declared that the new economic order had: 'pitilessly torn asunder the motley feudal ties that bound man to his "natural superiors", and has left remaining no other nexus between man and man than naked self-interest, than callous "cash payment". It has drowned the most heavenly ecstasies of religious fervour, of chivalrous enthusiasm, of philistine sentimentalism, in the icy water of egotistical calculation. It substituted naked, shameless, direct, brutal exploitation in place of numberless indefeasible chartered freedoms'.[20]

Carlyle admitted that he had no panacea for curing the ills of society but believed that these would persist unless, somehow, mankind could recover its soul. But such spiritual recovery was unlikely. What he called atheism, was not so much disbelief in a personal God but disbelief in the inner essence, the infinity of the universe, disbelief in reason and despair of the intellect. Many of Carlyle's reference points here were those of Engel's own recent intellectual formation, in particular Hegel's bible of universal history and Goethe's cult of the perennial nobility and even sacredness to be found in work. The potential of work to offer what Carlyle called a 'lifepurpose' – his examples came from the monasteries of the Middle Ages – stood in contrast with lives of despair in factories and the wider spiritual deadness of the age.

For all that Engels disputed Carlyle's bucolic account of the 'godly' Middle Ages in *Past and Present* as skipping over the miseries of serfdom. And while Carlyle depicted the nineteenth century as Godless, Engels complained that it was saturated with religion. God, Engels insisted, was a human invention – 'a more or less indistinct and distorted image of man himself' – that had outlived its purpose. Man had only to understand himself and to organise the world in a truly human manner according to the demands of his nature. Had Carlyle not 'divided mankind into two lots, sheep and goats, rulers and the ruled, aristocrats and rabble, lords and dolts, he would have seen the proper social function of talent is not in ruling by force but in acting as a stimulant and taking the lead'. But both men were elitists. Engels was captivated by great men like Napoleon and Cromwell he thought had shaped history. Carlyle advanced a 'great man' theory of history but despaired about the growing political significance of the suffering masses. Engels believed these could be influenced by a revolutionary elite to play their part in advancing human history.

The Irish against the proletariat

Irish peasants had fled rural poverty for lives of urban poverty and exploitation. Engels considered that those who travelled to English cities and those who had moved to Dublin had essentially similar experiences. Dublin, he wrote, was a city of great attractions, with its beautiful bay compared by the Irish to the bay of Naples, with better and more tastefully laid out aristocratic districts than any other British city. It also had poorer districts amongst the most hideous and repulsive to be seen in the world.

'True', he wrote, 'the Irish character, which, under some circumstances, is comfortable in the dirt, has some share in this; but as we find thousands of Irish in every great city in England and Scotland, and as every poor population must gradually sink into the same uncleanness, the wretchedness of Dublin is nothing specific, nothing peculiar to Dublin, but something common to all great towns'.[21]

In Manchester a hollow surrounded by factories known as 'little Ireland' was home to some 4,000 human beings, most of them Irish. Engels gave a partially first-hand account of its decrepit cottages, an atmosphere poisoned by the effluvia of refuse, offal and sickening filth and by the smoke from a dozen factory chimneys.[22] A horde of ragged women and children swarmed about, 'as filthy as the swine that thrive amongst the garbage heaps and the puddles'. Drawing on public heath reports he described conditions of chronic overcrowding ('pens containing at most two rooms, a garret and perhaps a cellar prone to flooding where, on average twenty people lived', '120 persons having to share a single privy') where often whole Irish families crowded into one bed, 'often a heap of filthy straw or quilts of old sacking cover all in an indiscriminate heap'. 'Often the inspectors found, in a single house, two families in two rooms. All slept in one, and used the other as a kitchen and a dining room in common.' Many families who had but one room to themselves received lodgers and boarders: 'such lodgers of both sexes by no means rarely sleep in the same bed with the married couple'; Engels referred to six documented cases cited in Manchester public health report where a man, his wife and his sister-in-law shared the one bed.[23] Again from such reports Engels described common-lodging houses – some 267 in Manchester – each with about thirty guests, where five to seven beds in each room lie on the floor: 'What physical and moral atmosphere reigns in these holes I need not state. Each of these houses is a focus of crime, the scene of deeds against which human nature revolts, which would perhaps never be executed but for this forced centralisation of vice.'[24]

The Condition of the Working Class drew heavily on analysis of the consequences of Irish immigration set out in Carlyle's *Chartism*. As put by Carlyle:

That the condition of the lower multitude of English labourers approximates more and more to that of the Irish competing with them in all markets; that whatsoever labour, to which mere strength with little skill will suffice, is to be done, will be done not at the English price; at a price superior as yet to the Irish, that is superior to scarcity of third-rate potatoes for thirty weeks yearly; superior yet hourly, with the arrival of every new steamboat, sinking near to an equality with that. . . . the giant Steamengine in a giant English Nation will here create violent demand for labour, and will there annihilate demand. But alas, the great portion of labour is not skilled: millions are and must be skill-less, where strength alone is wanted; ploughers, delvers, borers; hewers of wood and drawers of water; menials of the Steamengine, only the *chief* menials and immediate *body*-servants of which require skill. English commerce stretches its fibres over the whole earth; sensitive literally, nay quivering in convulsion, to the farthest influences of the earth. The huge daemon of Mechanism smokes and thunders, panting at his great task, in all sections of English land; changing his *shape* like a very Proteus; and infallibly at every change of shape, *oversetting* whole multitudes of workmen, and as if with the waving of his shadow from afar, hurling them asunder, this way and that, in their crowded march and course of work or traffic; so that the wisest no longer knows his whereabouts. With an Ireland pouring daily in on us, in these circumstances; deluging us down to its own waste confusion, outward and inward, it seems a cruel mockery to tell poor drudges that *their* condition is improving.[25]

The Irish in Ireland had become degraded by economic exploitation and made miserable by injustice but it was possible, Carlyle insisted, for them to recover their character though strength of will and spirit. England was guilty of tyrannising over Ireland and now with the onset of large-scale immigration 'reaps at last, in full measure, the fruit of fifteen generations of wrong-doing'. But Carlyle also saw the arrival of the Irish and simultaneous emigration of Englishmen to America of symptoms of the English decline in a soulless, utilitarian, industrial, laissez-faire age. His imagined America, for he had never been there, was that of his friend Emerson where resolute English yeomen who had quit industrial England in disgust and now cleared untilled forests rather than sink, like the Irish, from decent manhood to squalid apehood. But the poor Irish could not stay at home and starve. It was just and natural that they came hither as a curse on England. The result was a sad circuitous revenge of their sore wrongs.

In June 1843 Engels penned his first article about Ireland for a German newspaper. That he had never been there did not prevent him from writing a vivid 'eye witness' account of Daniel O'Connell's monster meetings and torch-lit rallies. He wrote disparagingly about O'Connell but in rapt wonder at his army of supporters ('And what a multitude of people are at his disposal! The day before yesterday in Cork – 150,000 men, yesterday in Nenagh – 200,000, today in Kilkenny – 400,000, and so it goes on. A triumphal procession lasting a fortnight, a triumphal procession such as no Roman emperor ever had'). Halfway through, his article switched from images of torch-lit parades that he could have only heard about second-hand to his impressions of the actual Irish he had seen in Manchester:

> Two hundred thousand men – and what men! People who have nothing to lose, two-thirds of whom are clothed in rags, genuine proletarians and *sansculottes* and, moreover, Irishmen, wild, headstrong, fanatical Gaels. One who has never seen Irishmen cannot know them. Give me two hundred thousand Irishmen and I will overthrow the entire British

monarchy. The Irishman is a carefree, cheerful, potato-eating child of nature. From his native heath, where he grew up, under a broken-down roof, on weak tea and meagre food, he is suddenly thrown into our civilisation. Hunger drives him to England. In the mechanical, egoistic, ice-cold hurly-burly of the English factory towns, his passions are aroused. What does this raw young fellow – whose youth was spent playing on moors and begging at the roadside – know of thrift? He squanders what he earns, then he starves until the next pay-day or until he again finds work. He is accustomed to going hungry. Then he goes back, seeks out the members of his family on the road where they had scattered in order to beg, from time to time assembling again around the teapot, which the mother carries with her.[26]

In the Ireland of Engels' imagination the grievances of five hundred years of oppression were so keenly felt by the Irish peasantry that 'their eyes burned with a perpetual thirst for revenge'. Add to this the violent national hatred of the Gaels against the Saxons, the orthodox Catholic fanaticism fostered by the clergy against Protestant-Episcopal arrogance – in such a context O'Connell could have achieved anything he wanted! In a number of articles Engels and Marx argued that O'Connell was a false leader, not serious about the welfare of the Irish people, not concerned with abolishing poverty, not even sincerely concerned with 'wretched Repeal'. Such was O'Connell's power, such were the crowds at his disposal, Engels argued, that the British authorities could not but capitulate to any demands he might choose to make:

> If O'Connell were really the man of the people, if he had sufficient courage *and were not himself afraid of the people*, i.e., if he were not a double-faced Whig, but an upright, consistent democrat, then the last English soldier would have left Ireland long since, there would no longer be any idle Protestant priest in purely Catholic districts, or any Old-Norman baron in his castle. But there is the rub. If the people were to be set free even for a moment, then Daniel O'Connell and his moneyed aristocrats would soon be just as much left high and dry as he wants to leave the Tories high and dry. That is the reason for Daniel's close association with the Catholic clergy, that is why he warns his Irishmen against dangerous socialism, that is why he rejects the support offered by the Chartists, although for appearances sake he now and again talks about democracy – just as Louis Philippe in his day talked about Republican institutions – and that is why he will never succeed in achieving anything but the political education of the Irish people, which in the long run is to no one more dangerous than to himself.[27]

In the same 1843 article he described 'half-savage' Irish proletarians locked in contradiction with themselves in the civilised environment they now found themselves. The raw fellows who knew nothing of thrift and who squandered with they earned were presumably the same as those who marched on their thousands under torchlight in Ireland, 'attended public meetings and worker associations, knew what Repeal was and what Sir Robert Peel stood for'.[28] However, the Irish as he described them in *The Condition of the Working Class* hardly seemed capable of such activism. Their characters and circumstances were depicted as so debased that these threatened to drag down the English proletarians:

> For work which requires long training or regular pertinacious application, the dissolute, unsteady drunken Irishman is on too low a place. To become a mechanic, a mill-hand, he would have to adopt the English civilisation, the English customs, become, in the main, an Englishman. But for all simple, less exact work, wherever it is a question of more strength than skill, the Irishman is as good as the Englishman ... And even if the Irish, who have forced their way into other occupations, should become more civilised, enough of the old habits would cling to them to have a strong degrading influence on their English companions in toil, especially in view of the general effect of being surrounded by the Irish. For when, in almost every great city, a fifth or a quarter of the workers are Irish, or children of Irish parents, who have grown up amongst Irish filth, no one can wonder if the life, habits, intelligence, moral status – in short the whole character of the working-class assimilates a great part of the Irish characteristics.[29]

Like Carlyle, Engels asserted that competition from Irish immigrants had 'degraded the English workers, removed them from civilisation, and aggravated the hardship of their lot'. Unlike Carlyle he welcomed the social crisis fuelled by their presence. By driving down wages they had deepened the chasm between the workers and the bourgeoisie and hastened the approaching crisis.[30] The 'still-somewhat civilised' Englishman was being dragged down by economic competition with 'the Irishman who goes in rags, eats potatoes and sleeps in a pig-sty'.[31] Irish immigrants, already debased by poverty, had grown up almost without civilisation. They were accustomed from youth to every sort of privation. They had brought all their brutal habits with them into a class of the English population which itself had little inducement to cultivate education and morality.[32] As put by Carlyle in one of many quotes cited by Engels:

> The uncivilised Irishman, not by his strength, but by the opposite to strength, drives the Saxon native out, takes possession of his room. There he abides, in his squalor and unreason, in his falsity and drunken violence, as the ready-made nucleus of degradation and disorder. Whoever struggles, swimming with difficulty, may now find an example how the human being can exist, not swimming but sunk.[33]

Carlyle's descriptions of the Irish were, Engels maintained, true except for his 'exaggerated defamation of the Irish character'. Engels nevertheless rode on the coat-tails of Carlyle's hyperbole and offered no caveats to the following assertions in *The Condition of the Working Class*:

> Filth and drunkenness too, they have bought with them. The lack of cleanliness, which is not so injurious in the country, where the population is scattered, and which is the Irishman's second nature, becomes terrifying and gravely dangerous through its concentration here in the great cities.[34]
>
> And since the poor devil must have one enjoyment, and society has shut him out of all others, he betakes himself to the drinking of spirits. Drink is the only thing which makes the Irishman's life worth having, drink and his cheery care-free temprement; so he revels in drink to the point of the most bestial drunkenness. The southern facile character of the Irishman, his crudity, which places him but little above the savage, his contempt for all humane enjoyments, in which his very crudeness makes him incapable of sharing, his filth, his poverty, all favour drunkenness.[35]

What else, Engels asked, should the poor devil do? How could society blame him when it placed him in a position in which he almost of necessity becomes a drunkard; when it leaves him to himself, to his savagery? For all that he borrowed from Carlyle Engels purported not to endorse Carlyle's most *outré* disparagements of Irish character but his prognosis was in effect the same: 'Such a people circulates not order but disorder, through every vein of it; – and the cure, if it is a cure, must begin at the heart; not in his condition only but in himself must the patient be all changed. Poor Ireland!'[36]

Carlyle concluded that the time had come 'when the Irish population must either be improved a little, or else exterminated'. They could not survive in the midst of civilisation 'in a state of perennial ultra-savage famine'.[37] They were out of step with a modern world that Carlyle despised. Their only hope was assimilation into Englishness but this too was under threat. Carlyle romanticised the English as ingenious, methodical, rational, truthful and capable Saxons. With this 'strong silent people' the Irish had now found a common cause. In the same breath he argued that the wretched English poor and wretched Irish poor were now in the same boat. The Irish population, he continued, 'must get itself redressed and saved, for the sake of the English if for nothing else'. All of this minus the romanticism of English character found its way into *The Condition of the Working Class*. The Irish were clearly in need of some kind of uplift but Engels did not see scope for this under the conditions of industrial capitalism.

With Marx in *The German Ideology* (1845) he coined the term *Lumpenproletariat* to denote the rabble or raggedy proletarians unlikely to achieve class consciousness and who would therefore impede revolutionary struggle. Marx in *The Eighteenth Brumaire of Louis Bonaparte* (1852) defined the *Lumpenproletariat* as 'the refuse of all classes,' lost to socially useful production, that included swindlers, confidence tricksters, brothel-keepers, rag and bone merchants, organ-grinders, beggars, and other flotsam of society. The Irish as depicted in *The Condition of the Working Class* posed a danger to the proletariat and an impediment to socialism. If all history was the history of class struggles then the peasant Irish in the English cities and the lumpen-peasants that had followed O'Connell back in Ireland were a people on the wrong side of history.

The future of Irish character

Engels travelled to Ireland for the first time in 1856 in the company of Mary Burns. His itinerary took him from Dublin to Galway to Limerick and Killarney, then back to Dublin. In an account of his visit in a letter to Marx he wrote that he never imagined that famine could be so tangibly real:

> Throughout the west, but particularly the Galway region, the countryside is strewn with these derelict farmhouses, most of which have only been abandoned since 1846. . . . Whole villages are deserted; in between the splendid parks of the smaller landlords, virtually the only people still living there, lawyers mostly. Famine, emigration and clearances between them have brought this about. The fields are empty even of cattle; the countryside is a complete wilderness unwanted by anybody. In County Clare, south of Galway, things improve a bit, for there's some cattle at least and, towards Limerick, the hills are excellently cultivated, mostly by Scottish farmers, the ruins have been cleared away, and the country has a domesticated air. In the south-west, numerous mountains and bogs but also marvellously luxuriant woodland; further on, fine pastures again, especially in Tipperary and, approaching Dublin, increasing signs that the land is occupied by big farmers.

The Irish countryside, he explained to Marx, was covered in ruined buildings of one kind or another. These bore witness to the destruction of several hundred years of English wars of conquest that had utterly ruined the country. For all their fanatical nationalism, the Irish no longer felt at home in their own country. Emigration would continue 'until the predominantly, indeed almost exclusively, Celtic nature of the population has gone to pot'. How often had the Irish set out to achieve something and each time been crushed, politically and industrially! In this artificial manner, through systematic oppression, they had come to be a completely wretched nation and now, as everyone knew, they have the job of providing England, America and Australia with whores, day labourers, pickpockets, swindlers, beggars and other wretches.[38]

From his first 1843 article on O'Connell he followed the twists and turns of Irish politics for more than forty years. Although he saw scant signs of revolutionary potential amongst the Irish peasantry he saw the Irish question as crucial to the future of socialism in England. From his writings on the 1848 Magyar revolt onward Engels never supported revolution for its own sake. He believed that repeal of the Act of Union would galvanise progressive socialist politics and opposed Irish acts of insurrection that worked to undermine parliamentary progress toward such ends. For example, in November 1867 he wrote to Marx that 'the vile deeds of the English must not allow us to forget most of the Fenian leaders were jackassess and some of them were exploiters'. The context was the execution of three of their followers, William Allen, Michael Larkin and Michael O'Brien, the 'Manchester Martyrs', who had killed a policeman whilst attempting to rescue some compatriots. Their deaths had a galvanised effect upon Irish nationalism. Even Catholic priests, Engels informed Marx, had condemned the executions from their pulpits. Black for mourning and green for Ireland, he wrote, were the prevailing colours in the house he shared with the Burns.[39]

His home life being as it was, Engels became steeped in Irish affairs. He made various efforts to explain Irish affairs to his socialist friends. In 1870 he compiled preparatory material for a history of Ireland, a project that was never completed. The outline was structured into several periods, the penultimate of these entitled the period of the small peasants (1801–46) and the final (1846–70) was labelled the period of extermination.[40] The material he had compiled suggest some shift away from stereotypes expressed in *The Condition of the Working Class*. If the Irish, after all, had a part to play in the march of history it was because they kept up their revolutionary struggles against the English. By contrast the Scottish Celts since 1745 had been destroyed as a separate people. Somehow the same Irish 'race' who fetched up as a deracinated *Lumpenproletariat* in English cities could also manifest an indomitable national character. To explain 'the enormous resilience of the Irish race' Engels invoked one of the great Irish historical clichés:

> After the most savage suppression, after every attempt to exterminate them, the Irish, following a short respite, stood stronger than ever before: it seemed they drew their main strength from the very foreign garrison forced on them in order to oppress them. Within two generations, often within one, the foreigners became more Irish than the Irish, *Hiberniores ipsis Hibernicis*. The more the Irish accepted the English language and forgot their own, the more Irish they became.[41]

He had never included the Irish in his list of non-historical peoples. Yet, his 1840s account of displaced Irish peasants in English cites cast these as a *Lumpenproletariat* standing in the way of history. His 1856 letter to Marx foretold the destruction of an Irish national character. Deracinated Irish were fated to become the whores and vagrants of the British Empire as they had become the detritus of English cities a decade earlier. But the successes of Irish cultural and political nationalism in the post-1850s period challenged his earlier conclusions about the likely 'extermination' of a distinctive Irish nation. Nor could his thinking on Irish affairs be understood in isolation from that of Marx. In 1870 Marx wrote (in a letter to Sigfrid Meyer on 9 April 1870) that after studying the Irish question for many years he now concluded that the decisive blow against the English ruling classes 'cannot be delivered in England but only in Ireland'.

Both argued that Ireland was the bulwark of the English landed aristocracy. It derived from Ireland much of its material wealth and its greatest moral strength. Domination over Ireland was the cardinal means by which the English aristocracy maintained their domination in England itself. Their downfall in Ireland, where the destruction of the aristocracy would be so much easier, would bring about their downfall in England. And this would provide the preliminary condition for the proletarian revolution in England. Hence the importance of the Irish land question and the parliamentary Irish nationalist movements that pursued it.

Writing in 1870 Marx portrayed the impact of Irish emigration to England in much the same terms as Engels did twenty-five years earlier. The English bourgeoisie continued to have a vested interest in competition between English workers and the Irish who had been displaced from the land: 'Ireland constantly sends her own surplus to the English labour market, and thus forces down wages and lowers the material and moral position of the English working class'. As a result the working class in England was divided 'into two hostile camps'. The response of the English working class to the Irish was 'the same as of the "poor whites" to the Negroes in the former slave states of the U.S.A.'. The Irishman paid him back in kind: 'He sees in the English worker both the accomplice and the stupid tool of the English rulers in Ireland.' This antagonism was 'artificially kept alive and intensified by the press, the pulpit, the comic papers, in short, by all the means at the disposal of the ruling classes'. Something crucial had shifted in the quarter century since *The Condition of the Working Class*. The Irish in England were now to be regarded as proletarians.

How this had come to pass was touched upon in a letter from Engels to Marx's daughter Jenny written in February 1881. Those who managed to stay in Ireland found access to levels of education denied to those who migrated to the English cities and to the English urban proletariat more generally. Referring to a 1812 report that there were 4,600 hedge schools in Ireland he argued that: 'The Irish, neglected by the English government, had taken the education of their children into their own hands'; 'At the time when English fathers and mothers insisted on their right to send their children to the factory to earn money instead of to the school to learn, at that time in Ireland the peasants vied with each other in forming schools of their own.'[42]

An 1882 letter to Karl Kautsky reappraised the role of nationalism in aiding and hindering the revolutions of 1848. He argued that one of the real tasks of the revolution of 1848 was 'the restoration of the oppressed and disunited nationalities of Central Europe in so far as they were at all viable, and, in particular, ripe for independence'. It was 'historically impossible for a great people' to seriously address their internal circumstances 'so long as national independence is lacking'. Engels had come to believe that international socialism was possible only within independent nations. He argued that two nations in particular – Ireland and Poland – 'were not only entitled but duty-bound to be national before they are international'. Deprive the Poles of the prospect of restoring Poland and then their interest in the European revolution would be at an end. At the same time it was the destiny of non-viable European nations to be forcibly incorporated into others. In the same letter to Kautsky he wrote:

> Now you may perhaps ask me whether I have no feeling of sympathy for the small Slav peoples and fragments thereof which have been split apart by those three wedges – the Germans, the Magyar and the Turkish – driven into the Slav domain? To tell the truth, damned little.[43]

What then of Ireland? In an 1882 letter to Eduard Bernstein he traced a history of Irish agrarian violence – by the Ribbonmen, the Whiteboys and Captain Moonlight – back to the seventeenth-century Tories, as he explained the dispossessed Catholic 'brigands' of the seventeenth century were known. The names had changed but not the essence of resistance even if new tactics such as boycotting were used against hated landlords and their agents. The period after the Act of Union saw the emergence of 'the liberal-national opposition of the urban-bourgeoisie', who as in other agrarian European countries found their leaders in the lawyers but who needed the political support of the farmers. Engels sketched a brief history of the politics of the Irish land question from O'Connell to Parnell, seeing the Land League as more revolutionary in its aims than its predecessor movements, its aim being the elimination of landlords. The political climate was such that frightened landlords were clamouring 'the speediest possible redemption of farmland in order to save what can be saved while Gladstone, for his part is declaring a greater measure of self-government for Ireland to be altogether admissible'.[44]

Alongside these tendencies he now savoured the possibility of a Fenian military victory. There were hundreds of thousands of Irish solidiers who fought in the American civil war 'with the ulterior motives of building up an army for the liberation of Ireland'. American political parties were 'coquetting with the Irish vote, making many promises to support Irish independence but abiding by none. Why would they when America benefited so much from Irish emigrants. But in twenty years' time America would be the most populous, wealthy and powerful country in the world, and *might* take a different view of military support for Irish independence. And should the danger of a war with America arise, England would give the Irish anything they asked, 'with both hands'.

In the meantime, the only recourse remaining to the Irish was 'the constitutional method of gradual conquest', whereby one position is taken after another; and here the lurking threat of armed Fenian conspiracy was politically useful. Yet, in 1882 he opposed actual manifestations of physical force Fenianism just as he had done in 1867. He lamented the assassination of two Dublin Castle officials, the chief secretary Lord Frederick Cavendish and his undersecretary T. H. Burke, by the Invincibles, a Fenian splinter group. Engels viewed the Phoenix Park murders as counterproductive. All these managed to do was to frustrate a compromise between the Land League and Gladstone that represented, he believed, the best option for Ireland. In an 1888 interview conducted in New York he was asked what he thought were the future chances of socialism in Ireland. He replied:

> A purely socialist movement cannot be expected in Ireland for a considerable time. People there want first of all to become peasants owning a plot of land, and after they have achieved that mortgages will appear on the scene and they will be ruined once more. But this should not prevent us from seeking to help them to get rid of their Landlords, that is, to pass from semi-feudal conditions to capitalist conditions.[45]

The Condition of the Working Class was first published in English in 1887 in New York. A second English language edition was published in London in 1892. The condition of England, he admitted, had changed greatly since the 1840s, a period he now described as a juvenile period of capitalist exploitation. England's world market for its manufactured goods was unparalleled. Manufacturing industry had become apparently moralised. Industry and employment became regulated, working conditions had improved and trades unions were accepted. Some kinds of exploitation had abated in England, even if these were now to be found in other parts of the world, where primitive industrial conditions resembled those in England four decades earlier. Certain kinds of petty thefts upon the working people were no longer deemed to pay. Repeated visitations of cholera, typhus, smallpox, and other epidemics had shown the British bourgeois the urgent necessity of sanitation in his towns and cities, if only to save themselves and their families. As a result, the most crying abuses described in *The Condition of the Working Class* had either disappeared or had been made less conspicuous. Some of the worst slums described, such as Little Ireland, had disappeared even if new slums had emerged elsewhere. Only the pigs and the heaps of refuse were no longer tolerated. The bourgeoisie had made further progress in the art of hiding the distress of the poor. But some parts of the working class were clearly better off.

The Condition of the Working Class presented the Irish as the debased people of the abyss, to use a term coined by late-Victorian social explorers a generation later. The inference of Engels' 1892 foreword was that these had become assimilated into the English working class. When writing *The Condition of the Working Class* Engels was drawn to lurid accounts of the Irish poor. Nuance was the first casualty in his war against English capitalism. Historians now consider that the experiences of the Irish in urban England were more varied than Engels insisted, especially in Manchester from where so much of the stereotype was drawn.[46] Clearly Mary Burns, his guide to the raggedy Irish, was no lumpenproletarian. The Irish in Manchester and in other cities came to be mobilised against their urban squalor by the Catholic Church more so than by socialism. The Irish in Ireland became mobilised by an increasingly Catholic nationalism in support of land reform. Irish living standards rose hugely in the half century after the Famine notwithstanding folk memories of the period.[47] The Famine killed more than a million people and exacerbated an already heavy flow of emigration. Its cruel lesson in political economy altered marriage and inheritance patterns amongst the shrinking remainder. Ireland's population shrunk from an estimated 8,175,124 in 1841 to an all-island one of 4,704,750 by 1891. Its economy remained mostly agricultural but there was a massive shift from labour-intensive tillage to pasture. The most vulnerable were displaced from the countryside but the incomes and education levels of those who hung on were raised. It is striking that none of his occasional writings on the Irish from the 1850s onwards invoked the stereotypes that dominated *The Condition of the Working Class*. Irish national character had been improved even if the Irish, preoccupied with land ownership, were hardly model proletarians. Those swept away by hunger and poverty were lost from Irish history and to the onward march of world history as understood by Engels.

CHAPTER EIGHT

John Mitchel and the last conquest of Ireland

John Mitchel (1815–75) came to be credited by Patrick Pearse as one of the apostles of a new testament of Irish nationalism, the prophet of old being Daniel O'Connell. Mitchel's writings from 1845 to 1847 in the Young Ireland periodical *The Nation* and his *Jail Journal* heavily influenced later generations of nationalists. The *Jail Journal* documented the decline of O'Connell's Repeal Association, the rise of Young Ireland, the failed 1848 Rising, Mitchel's transportation to Tasmania for sedition, his dramatic escape and his arrival in New York in November 1853 determined to oppose the influence of what he called 'the British system' in America. By this he meant the liberal politics and political economy that he blamed for the Famine in Ireland. In *The Last Conquest of Ireland (Perhaps)* Ireland's most illiberal and bloody-minded nineteenth-century Northern Protestant nationalist – the point being he was one of a kind – made the case for a reactionary patriotism that found common cause with slaver-owners in the American South.[1] His dream of Tara was the antebellum Tara of Margaret Mitchell's *Gone With the Wind* as much as it was the wasted opportunity, as he saw it, of O'Connell's 1843 monster meeting on the actual hill of Tara. 'We, for our part wish', he wrote in 1854, 'we had a good plantation well-stocked with healthy negroes, in Alabama'.[2]

Mitchel despised Abolitionism and other expressions of liberal philanthropy, seeing these as part of the same system that he blamed for the Famine. In this he was heavily influenced by the writings of Thomas Carlyle. *The Last Conquest of Ireland* drew upon agrarian reactionary ideas in Carlyle's work that Engels rejected in *The Condition of the Working Class*. Engels, like Mitchel, saw Carlyle as his enemy's enemy, the real enemy being liberal political economy. While Engels rejected the reactionary conservative alternatives to nineteenth-century capitalism Carlyle proposed in *Past and Present* Mitchel took these more seriously that Carlyle ever did. While

Mitchel hated the English system he also despised those Irish who prostrated themselves before it, the great 'Pacificator' being O'Connell. The last conquest of Ireland had been furthered by an insidious system of ideas that had become so pervasive that rebellion required great hatred of all those, including Irish nationalists, who were complicit in their dominance.

Mitchel, the son of a Unitarian minister and descendant of Planter stock, grew up in Newry in County Down and went to Trinity College Dublin in 1830 at the age of fifteen. His father hoped that he would take Holy orders. Instead he apprenticed to a solicitor in Banbridge. His work in the courts brought him to Dublin where in 1841 he met Thomas Davis and other founders of the Young Ireland movement. Davis and Charles Gavan Duffy founded *The Nation* in October 1842. In *The Nation* Davis championed a new cultural nation-building project which was in step with the *Zeitgeist* of European romantic nationalisms and which rejected the utilitarian liberalism of O'Connell. The 'weapons' of nationalism he advocated were cultural ones:

> *National* books, and lectures and music – *national* painting and busts and costume – *national* songs, and tracts, and maps – *historical* plays for the stage – *historical* novels for the closet – *historical* ballads for the drawing room – we want all these, and many other things illustrating the *history*, the resources and the genius of our country, and honouring her illustrious children, living and dead. These are the seeds of permanent nationality and we must sow them deeply in the People's hearts.[3]

In 1844 Mitchel was commissioned to write one such national book, a biography of Hugh O'Neill for *The Nation*'s Library of Ireland series. When Davis died in 1845 Mitchel moved to Dublin to work for *The Nation* full-time. Where Davis penned rousing ballads like *A Nation Once Again*, Mitchel wrote rousing revolutionary polemics at odds with O'Connell's 'moral force' politics even though *The Nation* was technically an organ of the Repeal Association. A 25 October 1845 article, 'The People's Food', threatened the landlords of Ireland that if they tried to collect rents from hungry tenants they could expect the 'blood and terror' of more extensive agrarian outrage than had ever been previously witnessed. Irish landlordism, he promised, had reached its latter days, and would shortly be in its grave.[4] The same issue of *The Nation* carried a record of a Repeal Association meeting at its Conciliation Hall headquarters that ran for several pages. This included dozens of letters and reports from around the country – all reverently addressed to 'the Liberator' – that were read into the records. Each issue sold more than 10,000 copies but, as distributed by the Repeal Association, reached an audience estimated at a quarter of a million people.[5]

Inevitably there was conflict between O'Connell's insistence on peaceful protest and Mitchel's fiery rhetoric. On 22 November 1845, in an article entitled 'Threats of Coercion', Mitchel quoted Robert Peel from the *Morning*

Herald as saying that one of the advantages of the new Irish railway system was that it would soon put every part of Ireland within six hours of the garrisons in Dublin. In an attack on repressive government responses to O'Connell's monster meetings – coercive proclamations from Dublin Castle and war steamers in Irish harbours – he proposed that instructions for blowing up the railways be promulgated throughout the country. Just as the Dutch once broke the banks of their dams to prevent their country from being overrun by French armies, 'and in one day those fertile plains, with all their waving corn, were a portion of the stormy German Ocean', so too Ireland's railways were better destroyed than allowed to become a means of transport for invading armies. Mitchel proposed that every railway within five miles of Dublin could easily be destroyed. Tracks could be lifted and tunnels filled. Railway cuttings, he advised, made good sites from which to ambush troop trains. He invited his readers to imagine an ambush of rocks and trees ready to roll down on a train carrying a regiment of infantry, its engine panting nearer and nearer to its destruction.[6]

For all such rhetoric Mitchel's primary rebellion was one against O'Connell and the ideas he stood for. His anti-colonial literary project necessitated the annihilation of O'Connell's reputation as Ireland's Liberator and the demolition of his political legacy. *The Last Conquest of Ireland (Perhaps)* opened with the fall from grace of O'Connell and the rise of Young Ireland. In 1843 O'Connell was at the height of his popularity and power: 'The people believed he could do anything; and he almost believed it himself.' The year 1843 was to be the 'Repeal year'. O'Connell held a series of vast open-air meetings at which the peasantry were accompanied by their priests. The meetings were peaceful and orderly and good humoured: 'Father Matthew's temperance reformation had lately been working its wonders; and all the people were sober and quiet.' Repeal Wardens everywhere organised an 'O'Connell Police', and any person of the immense multitude who was even noisy was instantly and quietly removed. O'Connell sought to achieve Repeal, Mitchel quoted him: 'by legal peaceable and constitutional means alone', 'by the electricity of public opinion', without 'the expense of a single drop of human blood'.[7]

O'Connell the Agitator had whipped his multitudes to the brink. Then his 'moral force' reined them in. His power, Mitchel explained, lay in his perfect knowledge of the people he addressed, their ways of life, wants and aspirations and 'the passions of the mighty multitudes rose and swayed and sunk again beneath his hand, as tides beneath the moon',[8] Mitchel cited a report of a meeting in Connaught where O'Connell declared that, he often heard the poor woman say, when about to be turned out of the cabin, that it was there she lighted the first fire in her own house, – it was there her children were born and brought up about her, – there her husband reposed after the hard toil of the day, – there were all her affections, centred, because they called to her mind all the pleasing reminiscences of early life; but her tears were disregarded, her feelings scoffed at; and the tyrant mandate was heard to issue – 'Pull down the house!' So when O' Connell exclaimed: 'Did you ever hear of the tithes?' he knew what long and bitter memories of blood and horror the question would call up. 'Did you ever hear of the tithes?' O'Connell called out again, 'They call them Rent-Charges now; do you like them any better since they have been newly christened?' And when curses of his audience had subsided, he shouted:

> Well; repeal the Union, and you get rid of that curse: no widow woman's stack-yard will ever more be plundered by the police and red-coats, to pay a clergyman whom she never saw, and whose ministration she would not attend. Repeal the Union, and every man will pay the pastor of his choice. I don't want Protestants to pay our Catholic clergy; – why should we be compelled to pay theirs?

Language, Mitchel added, which generally seemed to his audience perfectly fair.[9] They followed him for years with 'patient zeal, self-denial, and disciplined enthusiasm'. The 'great Liberator' told them that 'no political amelioration was worth one drop of human blood'. They did not believe this, Mitchel insisted. All O'Connell had to do was give the word that at Tara and at Mullaghmast in 1843 hundreds of thousands of fiery eyed supporters seemed to crave. And when he walked in triumph out of his prison in September 1844, 'at one word from his mouth they would have marched upon Dublin from all the five ends of Ireland, and made short work with police and military barracks'.[10] By contrast one sympathetic biographer quoted an unnamed comrade of Mitchel's from 1848: 'He either did not know or could not sufficiently bear in mind what the mass of men are, and was subject to a perpetually recurrent surprise at finding they were not of his temper.'[11] In Mitchel's new testament of nationalist history all blame lay with O'Connell:

> If it be asked whether I now believe, looking calmly back over the gulf of many years, that O'Connell's voice could indeed have made a revolution in Ireland, I answer, beyond all doubt, Yes. One word of his mouth, and there would not, in a month have been one English epaulette in the island. He had that power.[12]

But instead he sought to dissolve the proscribed Repeal Association, in order to shut out its more radical members. He occupied his weekly speeches with collateral issues like the Colleges Bill – matters that would have been of importance in any self-governing nation, but mattered little in the circumstances – or 'he poured forth his fiery floods of eloquence in denunciation, not of the British Government, but of American Slavery, with which he had nothing on earth to do'.[13] As the Famine took its toll O'Connell made 'helpless' speeches but in his very last letter to the Repeal Association he regretted (the inference being he knew he was wrong) that more had not been done to save a sinking nation before hundreds of thousands had died: 'How different would be the scene be if we had our own Parliament to take care of our own people, of our own resources'.[14] In Mitchel's damning judgement:

> He had used all his art and eloquence to emasculate a bold and chivalrous nation: and the very gratitude, love, and admiration which his early services had won, enabled him so to pervert the ideas of right and wrong in Ireland, that they believed him when he told them that Constitutional 'Agitation' was Moral Force – that bloodshed was immoral – that – to set at naught and defy the London 'laws' was a crime – that, to cheer and parade, and pay Repeal subscriptions, is to do one's duty – and that a people patient and quiet under wrong and insult is a virtuous and noble people, and the finest peasantry in the universe. He had helped the disarming policy of the English by his continual denunciations of arms, and had thereby degraded the manhood of his nation to such a point that to rouse them to resistance in their own cause was impossible . . . . To him and to his teaching, then, without scruple, I ascribe our utter failure to make, I do not say a revolution, but so much as an insurrection, two years after, when all the nations were in revolt, from Sicily to Prussia, and when a successful uprising in Ireland would have certainly destroyed the British Empire, and every monarchy in Europe along with it. O'Connell was, therefore, next to the British Government, the worst enemy that Ireland ever had – or rather the most fatal friend.[15]

In February 1848, coinciding with the revolution in France, Mitchel founded his own paper, *United Irishman*, and declared himself a republican. The stated aim of *United Irishman* was to overthrow British rule. Issue after issue during the four months it ran spewed forth belligerent propaganda aimed at provoking a response from the government.[16] It got Mitchel arrested under the freshly minted Treason-Felony Act. By June 1848 sentence had been passed and he was dispatched 'in chains' to Barbados, a celebrated 'martyr', a second Robert Emmet, who lived to tell the tale in his *Jail Journal*. In 1853 he escaped to America from Tasmania (to where he was rerouted from Barbados). The original edition of *Jail Journal* ended in despair about the apparent failures of Young Ireland nationalism:

> The very nation that I knew in Ireland is broken and destroyed; and the place that knew it shall know it no more. To America has fled the half-starved remnant of it; and the phrase that I have heard of late, 'a new Ireland in America', conveys no meaning to my mind. Ireland without the Irish – The Irish out of Ireland – neither of these can be our country.[17]

America then became the battleground where Ireland's future might be determined. The aim of *The Citizen*, where the *Jail Journal* was first serialised, was 'to lay before our Irish-Americans, from week to week the true nature of British policy in Europe, in America, and in Ireland, and to refute and expose the treacherous representations of all these things which were constantly put forward by the English Press, and too often adopted upon trust by that of the United States'. The editors of *The Citizen*, he wrote at the end of the *Jail Journal*, refused to believe that, prostrate and broken as the Irish nation was now, the cause of Irish independence was utterly lost. They also refused to admit 'that any improvement in the material condition of those Irishmen who have survived the miseries of the last seven years (if any improvements there be) satisfies the honour, or fulfils the destiny, of an ancient and noble nation'.[18] Having first declared war on O'Connell, then on the British Empire in 1848, he now declared war on the nineteenth century itself, on all its ideas of social and economic progress, on British claims that Ireland was 'improving and contented' now that it had come through the Famine. In this conflict his great ally, his enemy's enemy, would be Thomas Carlyle.

Against progress, anti-slavery, racism and colonialism

Mitchel's literary heroes were Charles Dickens and Thomas Carlyle. He shared with Dickens a predilection for first serialising his books in periodicals he edited. The *Jail Journal* which recounted his Young Ireland experiences, his arrest, trial and transportation, his escape from Van Diemen's Land and arrival in New York was first serialised in *The Citizen*. Each chapter of *The Last Conquest of Ireland (Perhaps)* ended in a kind of cliffhanger; all had been initially published in *The Southern Citizen*, a short-lived pro-slavery paper that he founded in 1857.[19] From the outset his writings had been modelled on those of Carlyle. The first draft of Mitchel's *Life of Aodh (Hugh) O'Neill* had been, in the view of Duffy and Davis, too much in thrall to his style. But the very project of presenting O'Neill as a great Irish hero was no less influenced by Carlyle's great man theory of history.[20] An April 1849 entry in Mitchel's *Jail Journal*, written aboard the *Neptune*, a prison ship then anchored off Barbados, declared that Carlyle was 'the only man in these latter days who produces what can properly be termed books'.[21]

A deputation of admiring Young Irelanders had visited Carlyle in April 1845. His early writings, influenced by German romanticism, had struck a chord.[22] They were drawn by his calls for 'Justice for Ireland' in *Chartism* but challenged its pejorative depictions of Irish character. Carlyle admired the 'young heroic hearts of Ireland' but not their political goals.[23] Duffy considered that Carlyle had little or no concrete knowledge of Irish affairs and embarked on a project to correct that. Carlyle received an invitation to Dublin which he accepted and a subscription to *The Nation*. He read the paper diligently. He commented on its contents in many letters to Duffy. He consulted Duffy on the text of the second edition of his *Life of Cromwell*. Duffy gave him advice on Irish geography and place names that he accepted and gave him a nationalist perspective on Irish history that he rejected outright.[24] 'I do not admit the Irish to be a nation. Really and truly that is the fact,' he wrote to Duffy. 'I cannot find that the Irish were in 1641, are now, or until they conquer all the English, ever again can be a "nation" – any more than the Scotch Highlands can, than the parish of Kensington can.' So much then for Davis's proclamation-in-song: 'A Nation Once Again'.

Carlyle influenced Duffy in one direction, Mitchel in another. In Young Ireland Carlyle identified the future leaders of Ireland, and advised them to step into positions of responsibility within the Union. He professed to love Mitchel but 'read with pain his wild articles', expected that he would hang but declared to Mitchel that 'they would not be able to hang the immortal part of him'.[25] Mitchel's extremism irritated him very much.[26] He saw the more moderate Duffy as a protégé. But when both were imprisoned for sedition in 1848 Carlyle lobbied Lord Clarendon, the viceroy of Ireland, on behalf of Mitchel as well as Duffy.

Duffy was released and restarted *The Nation*. A manifesto he published in 1849, 'Wanted a Few Workmen', drew ecstatic praise from Carlyle. True service to Ireland, Duffy argued, now involved active involvement in the day to day government of the country. Ireland needed efficient ministers and administrators not rhetoricians. There was no country in Europe where there was so little practical genius, practical skill, or fruitful practical knowledge as in Ireland. O'Connell had moulded Ireland's public men into 'ruthless speechifiers' well able to fire the Irish imagination but incapable of seizing the reins of day to day government. True proof of Irish greatness was to be found amongst the emigrants in Australia and America who were clearing forests and building cities. Ireland needed workmen of this calibre at home.[27] Duffy was elected to the House of Commons in 1852 but resigned in 1856. He then emigrated to Australia. He was elected as Premier of Victoria in 1871 and knighted in 1873.

Carlyle responded to Duffy's manifesto with 'Trees of Liberty' which was published under a pseudonym in *The Nation*. Many Irishmen, he began, talk of dying for Ireland but before doing so, he exhorted, think about in 'how many quiet strenuous ways you might beneficially live for it'. Each and every one, through theirs, might plant their own tree of industry. Each such tree would be, of a surety, *his* tree of liberty.[28] In the shadow of such rhetoric Carlyle argued Ireland had been failed by its landlords, aristocrats and political leaders. In the face of such malign stewardship the best available future was one despised by Mitchel: to 'render Ireland habitable for capitalists, if not for heroes; to invite capital, and industrial governors and guidance (from Lancashire, from Scotland, from the moon, and from the Ring of Saturn), what other salvation can one see for Ireland?'

Mitchel shared with Carlyle a contempt for Whig optimism in social, economic and moral progress and a tendency to idealise agrarian societies.[29] Both supported slavery. Carlyle's *Occasional Discourse on the Nigger Question* (1849) attacked 'the unhappy wedlock of liberal philanthropy and the dismal science' (his coinage) of political economy and the hypocrisy of Abolitionism when half of England's workers were near starvation. Carlyle declared that his own servants would be better off if they were permanently bound to him and to who he was bound.[30] Mitchel's efforts to attack Abolitionism in *The Nation* were blocked by Duffy.

The Nigger Question was Carlyle's response to the emancipation of slaves in the West Indies which he declared had been turned into a 'Black Ireland'. As put in the section that coined the term 'dismal science':

> Our own white or sallow Ireland, sluttishly starving from age to age on act-of-parliament 'freedom,' was hitherto the flower of mismanagement among the nations: but what will this be to a Negro Ireland, with pumpkins themselves fallen scarce like potatoes! Imagination cannot fathom such an object; the belly of Chaos never held the like.[31]

The Negroes would be better off as secure chattel than left to the tender mercies of liberal political economy and reliant on their own inferior capabilities. They had only to observe the 'free' evicted Irish citizens dying in ditches. Such were the spurious benefits of freedom under laissez-faire conditions. Carlyle's 1843 book *Past and Present* argued that European peasants fared better under the stable hierarchies of feudalism than their descendants were doing under industrial capitalism. Both yearned for stable societies that would act as bulwarks against what Mitchel called the British Model. He viewed the British Empire as a vehicle for the doctrine of political economy.[32] Like Carlyle he blamed Irish hunger on the implementation of laissez-faire. Both believed that economic and political freedom were of themselves meaningless. But while Carlyle offered no panacea except to yearn for a return to virtue – calling for more responsible elites and invoking a pre-industrial social ideal – Mitchel actively sided with actual enemies of nineteenth-century economic and social modernisation. In effect he rejected the nineteenth century.[33]

A December 1853 entry in Mitchel's *Jail Journal* surveyed the New York press. He considered the *Tribune* to be an 'admirably written newspaper', but 'very abhorrent for its philanthropy, human progress, and other balderdash'.[34] Even before arriving in America he had been drawn to the cause of the southern secessionists. They, he believed, best exemplified an equivalent opposition in America to the British ideas that had dominated Ireland with O'Connell's blessing. The American South appeared to have rejected the false promises of progress. Slavery had to be defended because Abolitionism was the ideological jewel of the system of ideas he argued had devastated Ireland and killed or exiled millions of its people. But even in the antebellum South Mitchel was a voice in the wilderness. In the *Jail Journal* he described giving an address to a graduation ceremony at a university in Virginia on 24 June 1854 on 'Progress in the Nineteenth Century'. The drift of it was to show that there was no such thing, that for all the trappings of progress – gas, steam, the printing press and telegraphs – men were no wiser, happier, or better than they were thirty centuries ago. His audience, Mitchel, recorded, were courteous but did not share his conclusions.[35] Mitchel never did anything by halves. In September 1854, in *The Citizen*, he argued that the slave trade with Africa should be reopened; the 'ignorant and brutal negroes' would enjoy 'comparative happiness and dignity' as plantation hands.[36] In 1857, at a meeting of the Southern Commercial Convention in Knoxville, he championed, with the support of local 'men of substance', plans for doing so.[37]

At the same time he was trenchantly critical of Carlyle's disparagement of the Celtic Irish during and after the Famine. Carlyle had described Ireland as a starved rat that had crossed the path of an elephant ('what is the elephant to do? – squelch it, by heaven! squelch it!). From this time, Mitchel argued, commenced that most virulent vilification of the Celtic Irish, in all the journals, books, and periodicals of the 'sister island'. English writers busied themselves with the differences of 'race' between Celt and Saxon, differences which proved to their own satisfaction that the former were born to be ruled by the latter. These were then faithfully reproduced ('like all other British cant') in America, where it gave venom to Know-Nothing agitation.[38] The 'Know Nothings' were nativist groups hostile to the immigrant Irish in New York. In effect, Mitchel argued that anti-Irish racism (beliefs that the Celtic Irish were an inferior race) was proactively mobilised to justify the colonisation of Ireland and to undermine sympathy for the 'starved-out Celts'. The 'bitterness and spite exhibited against the Irish Celt in all British literature, especially since 1848' had a clear motive. The British literary classes were:

> . . . painfully aware that myriads upon myriads of the exterminated Irish, having found refuge here in America, have filled this continent with cursing and bitterness against the English name; and a strong political necessity is upon them to make Americans hate us, and, if possible, despise us, as heartily as they do themselves. As for us, expatriated and exterminated Irish, we have every day occasion to feel that our enemy pursues us into all lands with unrelenting vengeance; and though we take the wings of the morning, we can never escape it – never until Ireland shall become, as Scotland is, a contented province of the British Empire, thoroughly subdued, civilized, emasculated, and 'ameliorated' to the very heart's core.[39]

Ironically then, for all his advocacy of slavery in America, Mitchel was the architect of an anti-racist critique of colonialism. If Carlyle was a reactionary imperialist Mitchel was a reactionary anti-imperialist. Slavery was justifiable in America because it was integral to a social order that stood in opposition to liberal political economy that Mitchel saw as the true engine of nineteenth-century colonialism. But denigration of the Irish race fuelled this engine.

For all that Mitchel attacked Carlyle's portrayals of the Irish he could not have but agreed with his idol's depictions of 'sallow Ireland, sluttishly starving from age to age on act-of-parliament "freedom"'. Much of his rage against Famine, one of his biographers suggests, stemmed from a sense of shame that the Irish peasantry had accepted their fate with passivity.[40] O'Connell had also described the Irish peasantry as supine. Writing to a friend in 1839 a few years before the Repeal campaign:

> I will never get half credit enough for carrying Emancipation, because posterity never can believe the species of *animals* with which I had to carry on my warfare with the common enemy. It is crawling slaves like them that prevent our being a nation.[41]

Mitchel blamed O'Connell for encouraging their shameful placidity. He attacked the British literary classes for denigrating them. In death and in exile they became sanctified within his 'new testament' history of Irish Nationalism as a people who would have eventually risen ('because O'Connell was not immortal') had the Famine not killed so many. He argued that their very existence had threatened the 'integrity of the Empire'. But after the Famine it would never again be menaced by half-million Tara meetings: 'Those ordered masses of the "Irish Enemy," with their growing enthusiasm, their rising spirit, and their yet more dangerous discipline, were to be thinned, to be cleared off.'[42] Mitchel portrayed the events that killed them as a war against Ireland worse than any seven or thirty year European war: 'No sack of cities ever approached in horror and desolation the slaughters done in Ireland by mere official red tape and stationery, and the principles of political economy.'[43]

The last conquest

In *The Last Conquest of Ireland (Perhaps)* Mitchel distinguished between the means of oppression by which Ireland was policed – an 'iron grip' that could nevertheless be shaken off – and new insidious means of colonisation in which O'Connell and the Catholic elite were implicated. The opening of *The Last Conquest* itemised at length such means of oppression: an army of thirty or forty thousand, an armed police cantoned in small barracks around the country, a corps of detectives to spy on the people, a system of workhouses built like fortresses, each with a gang of well-paid officers, all humble servants of the government and a system of National Education under the management of a board of Commissions appointed by the government, under the Protestant archbishop, Dr Whately. All this, he argued, could have been cast aside with just one word from O'Connell.[44] But what he referred to as the last conquest had been brought about by the intellectual and material dominance of liberal political economy that he sometimes referred to as the English system. Its consequences included land clearances, famine-related death and emigration.

In explaining this Mitchel firstly argued that Catholic emancipation was anything but. The post-1829 settlement ushered in a new phase of conquest that bound better-off Catholics to the British Empire and led directly to the clearance of many poorer ones from the land. In effect it drove a wedge between the interests of such peasants and the wealthier and educated Catholics who benefited from access to the professions, politics and official posts. Catholic emancipation, he insisted, was a measure for the consolidation of the British Empire.

The Roman Catholic Relief Act (1829) admitted Catholics to parliament and the professions but the deal struck disenfranchised the forty-shilling freeholders who had been the mainstay of the movement for Catholic emancipation. Before 1829 landlords needed the political support of their tenants. The 'low franchise' had induced them for the sake of securing political power, to subdivide farms and create voters: 'After this franchise was abolished there was no longer any political use for the people; and it happened about the same time that new theories of farming became fashionable. There was to be more grazing, more green cropping; there were to be larger farms; and more labour was to be done by horses and by steam.' But consolidation of many small farms could not be effected without clearing off the 'surplus population'. And then, as there would be fewer mouths to be fed, so there would be more produce for export to England. Catholic emancipation, Mitchel argued, had triggered a large-scale and ongoing land clearance that economically benefited England:

> Reflect one moment on the established idea of there being a 'surplus population' in Ireland; – an idea and phrase which were at that time unquestioned and axiomatic in political circles; while, at the same time, there were four millions of improvable waste-lands; and Ireland was still, this very year, exporting food enough to feed eight millions of people in England. Ireland, perhaps, was the only country in the world which had both surplus produce for export and surplus population for export; – too much food for her people, and too many people for her food.[45]

Secondly, Mitchel depicted the Irish Poor Law as a deliberate instrument of dispossession and land clearance. No farmer could apply for outdoor relief until he had first given up all his land to the landlord except for one quarter of an acre. Farms were thereafter daily given up without the formality of a notice to quit or a Court summons. Mitchel argued that the way in which schemes of public works were introduced and withdrawn displaced many thousands from the land: 'On the 6th of March 1847, there were 730,000 heads of families on the public works but provision had been made to dismiss these in batches. So on the 10th of April, the number was reduced to 500,723 and thereafter rapidly declined. Many of these had nothing to fall back upon but outdoor relief but were ineligible if they held onto their tenancies.'[46] The Poor Laws 'were a failure for their professed purpose – that of relieving the famine; but were a complete success for their real purpose, that of uprooting the people from the land, and casting them forth to perish'.[47]

He described the programme of public works as chaotically mismanaged. 'Confused and wasteful attempts at relief' were organised by 'bewildered barony sessions striving to understand the voluminous directions, schedules, and specifications that determined how they might use their own money to relieve the poor at their own doors', hampered by 'insolent commissioners and inspectors, and clerks snubbing them at every turn, and ordering them to study the documents', where efforts to expend some of the rates at least on useful works – reclaiming land, or the like – were always met with flat refusal and a lecture on 'political economy'. For 'political economy', it seemed, declared that the works must be strictly useless until many good roads became impassable on account of pits and trenches, with plenty of jobbing and speculation all this while; and the labourers, having the example of a great public fraud before their eyes, themselves defrauding their fraudulent employers, 'quitting agricultural pursuits and crowding to the public works, where they pretended to be cutting down hills and filling up hollows, and with tongue in cheek received half wages for doing nothing. So the labour was wasted; the labourers were demoralised, and the next year's famine was ensured'.[48]

Thirdly, he argued that the potato blight, and consequent famine, placed in the hands of the British Government an engine of state by which they were eventually enabled to clear off two and a half millions of 'surplus population'.[49] Mitchel repeatedly blamed the Famine on British political economy, policy and misrule:

> Further, I have called it an artificial famine: that is to say, it was a famine which desolated a rich and fertile island, that produced every year abundance and superabundance to sustain all its people and many more. The English, indeed, call that famine a 'dispensation of Providence'; and ascribe it entirely to the blight of the potatoes. But potatoes failed in like manner all over Europe; yet there was no famine save in Ireland. The British account of the matter, then, is first, a fraud – second, a blasphemy. The Almighty, indeed, sent the potato blight, but the English created the famine.[50]

He cited a report that recorded decreases during 1847 in the numbers of farms. That year, 24,147 small farms vanished. There was also a reduction of 4,274 farms between fifteen and thirty acres. In all seventy thousand occupiers, with their families, numbering about three hundred thousand, were rooted out of the land. However, by the end of 1847 the number of farms larger than thirty acres had risen by 3,670.

That year in Connaught, where the clearances were most severe, 9,703 farms between one and five acres out of a total of 35,634 and 12,891 of the 76,707 farms between five to fifteen acres were cleared; 2,121 of the 12,891 farms between fifteen and thirty acres also vanished in 1847. In all 26,499 tenants and their families were removed in Connaught in a single year. Such reports, Mitchel emphasised, took no account of famine-related deaths of the landless peasants who were most severely affected. Many landlords gained possession without so much as an ejectment, because the tenants died of hunger.

But many resident landlords, Mitchel acknowledged, devoted themselves to the task of keeping their poor people alive. Many remitted their rents and ladies kept their servants busy and their kitchens smoking with continual preparation of food for the poor. Local committees purchased all the corn in the government depots (at market price, however), and distributed it free of charge. Clergymen, both Protestant and Catholic, 'generally did their duty'. Many a poor rector and his curate shared their crust with their suffering neighbours and priests, after going round all day administering Extreme Unction to whole villages at once, all dying of mere starvation, often themselves went supperless to bed.[51] Many landlords, encumbered by debt and the pressure of the poor-rates, 'generally had no more control over the bailiffs, sheriffs, and police, who plundered and chased away the people, than one of the pillars of their own grand entrance gates'. [52]

The fault, Mitchel insisted, was England's. Even in 1847 when the Famine was at its most severe the Whig Government, 'bound by political economy, absolutely refused to interfere with market prices'. Merchants and speculators were never so busy on both sides of the Channel. Fleets of ships sailed with every tide, carrying Irish cattle and corn to England. He argued that much of the grain brought into Ireland had been previously exported *from* Ireland, and came back – laden with merchants' profits and double freights and insurance – to the helpless people who had sowed and reaped it: 'This is what commerce and free trade did for Ireland in those days.'[53]

Again and again Mitchel pounded home the argument that the mismanagement of Famine relief suited government policy ('the calculations of political circles') of clearing Irish lands. Charitable people in England and in America, 'indignant at the thought of a nation perishing of political economy', did contribute generously, believing that every pound they subscribed would purchase twenty shillings worth of bread:

> In vain! 'Government' and political economy got hold of the contributions (of prayers and blessings neither Government nor political economy takes any account), and disposed of them in such fashion as to prevent

their deranging the calculations of political circles. For example: the vast supplies of food purchased by the 'British Relief Association,' with the money of charitable Christians in England, were everywhere locked up in Government stores. Government, it seems, contrived to influence or control the managers of that fund; and thus, there were thousands of tons of food rotting within the stores of Haulbowline, at Cork Harbour; and tens of thousands rotting without. For the market must be followed, not led (to the prejudice of our Liverpool merchants)! – private speculation must not be disappointed, nor the calculations of political circles falsified![54]

Drawing on an 1847 report of the then-Chancellor of the Exchequer Sir Charles Wood, Mitchel argued that England had feasted while Ireland starved. Wood had reported 'with great satisfaction' that the English people and working classes were 'steadily growing more comfortable, nay, more luxurious in their style of living'. Their consumption of goods such as coffee, tea, butter, beer, bread, beef, bacon and currants had hugely increased during Ireland's famine years. Currants, Wood explained, had become one of the necessaries of life to an English labourer, who must have his pudding on Sunday. Wood's statement came at the end of a long speech on measures to address famine in Ireland.[55] Mitchel made much of the contrast between English living conditions and those in which many Irish died:

> One would not grudge the English labourer his dinner and his tea; and I refer to his excellent table only to remember during the same three years, exactly as fast as the English people and working classes advanced to luxury, the Irish people and working classes sank to starvation: and further, that the Irish people were still sowing and reaping what they of the sister island so contentedly devoured to the value of at least £17,000,000 sterling.[56]

But when Carlyle visited Dublin in 1846 he commented on the excellent table at Mitchel's house on Upper Leeson Street, a recently built 'four-storied brick set over a good basement'.[57] During the Famine the Young Irelanders and their ladies attended banquets of the elite 82 Club – named in honour of the Irish Protestant Volunteers of 1782 – in the Rotunda. The women took refreshments under crystal chandeliers as their menfolk filed in wearing uniforms designed by Thomas Davis. Mitchel's cost twelve guineas. It consisted of a dark green suit lined with white satin. Crowds of Dublin's poor came to catch sight of their favourites and catch thrown coins.[58]

Just as Catholic emancipation produced its winners (the Catholic middle class) and losers (Catholic peasants) so later did the Famine and the land clearances it precipitated. An Encumbered Estates Act was introduced in 1849 to speed up the sale of indebted estates. The aim, Mitchel argued was to facilitate a 'New Plantation' of Ireland. The English Press anticipated 'a peaceable transfer of Irish land to English and Scotch capitalists'. However the great bulk of purchasers were mainly Catholic Irishmen. He quoted 1851 figures of total sales of more than £3.5 million. But less than 10 per cent (£319,486) were to English and Scottish purchasers. The 1857 figures he cited revealed a similar pattern. Of a total of 7,216 purchasers, 6,902 were Irish.[59] A new elite could be seen to have emerged along the lines advocated by Carlyle and Duffy. There was much liberality towards Catholics of the educated classes. Mitchel listed a Mr Wyse who became ambassador to Greece and a Mr More O'Ferrall who became Governor of Malta. Many Catholic barristers, 'once loud in their patriotic devotion at Conciliation Hall' received government appointments. He could have added Duffy, who became Premier of Victoria, to this list.

By these various means, Mitchel concluded in his last chapter, the last conquest of Ireland had been consummated: 'England prosperous, potent, and at peace with all the earth' had 'succeeded (to her immortal honour and glory) in anticipating and crushing out of sight the last agonies of resistance in a small, poor, and divided island, which she had herself made poor and divided.'[60] Ireland was now depicted as 'improving' and 'prosperous'. It could not be denied that the survivors had begun to live better. With three million people dead or driven off there was a smaller supply of labour. Wages were higher. There was more cattle and grain for export to England, because there were fewer mouths to feed. The middle classes, he concluded, had been extensively corrupted 'and neither stipendiary officials nor able-bodied paupers ever make revolutions'.[61] With this Mitchel drew his 'very dismal and humiliating narrative' near to its close. But the final paragraph of *The Last Conquest of Ireland (Perhaps)* introduced a note of defiance:

> The subjection of Ireland is now probably assured until some external shock shall break up that monstrous commercial firm, the British Empire; which, indeed, is a bankrupt firm, and trading on false credit, and embezzling the goods of others, or robbing on the highway, from Pole to Pole, but its doors are not yet shut; its cup of abomination is not yet running over. If any American has read this narrative, however, he will never wonder hereafter when he hears an Irishman in America fervently curse the British Empire. So long as this hatred and horror shall last – so long as our island refuses to become, like Scotland, a contented province of her enemy, Ireland is not finally subdued. The passionate aspiration for Irish nationhood will out-live the British Empire.[62]

In 1874, the year before his death, Mitchel returned to Ireland where he stood as a candidate in a Tipperary by-election. He professed himself as 'savage' against the idea of Home Rule as he had been 'vicious' against Repeal. He won the election by a huge margin (receiving 3,114 votes out of a total of 3,860 votes cast) but did not take up his seat. No man in Tipperary or Ireland, he declared, really supposed that he was going to creep up to the bar of the English House of Commons and crave permission to take oaths in order to do so.[63]

Mitchel had little political influence in his day. He was unwilling to lead those like the Fenians who wished to follow him (he abhorred secret societies) and was not cut out to be a politician. But he exercised considerable intellectual influence over late nineteenth-century cultural nationalists such as Douglas Hyde and within the Sinn Fein movement that emerged a decade before the 1916 Rising. In 1892 Hyde delivered a seminal address, 'The Necessity for De-Anglicising Ireland,' that led to the formation of the Gaelic League.[64] A year earlier he praised *The Last Conquest of Ireland (Perhaps)* declaring that Mitchel would have made a rebel out him if he was not one already.[65] 'Most of us', Hyde wrote to a friend in 1910, 'want to produce a race of spirited nationalists who would go as far as Michel or Wolfe Tone if the opportunity offered'.[66]

In his preface to the 1913 edition of *Jail Journal* Arthur Griffith, the founding President of Sinn Fein, described Mitchel as having introduced 'an element of reality unto the Irish politics of his time'; 'the Ireland he preached to shrank from the preacher' preferring 'to die of hunger on its hearthstone – but in Peace'. 'In a land so lost to reason, the voice of sanity was deemed mad.' Griffith described him as a 'sane Nietzsche'.[67] Mitchel might well have cheered Nietzsche's denunciation of the 'pig philosophy' of liberal utilitarianism. He advocated a kind of bloody-minded equivalent to Nietzsche's 'will to power' over and a fierce intolerance of oppressive ideas and systems. Nietzsche had advocated the destruction of inner slave mentalities and the need to obliterate ways of thinking that would encourage such enslavement.[68] Mitchel depicted the conquest of Ireland as the consequence of mental as much as physical domination.

Ireland, Griffith proclaimed on the first page of his preface, 'failed Mitchel because it had failed in manhood'.[69] In 1915 Pearse wrote that 'Mitchel's *Jail Journal* was the last gospel of the New Testament of Irish Nationality, as Wolfe Tone's Autobiography is the first'. [70] Pearse had previously referred to the *Jail Journal* in such terms in November 1914 at the Thomas Davis Centenary meeting of the Trinity College Gaelic Society. He did so in reply to William Butler Yeats who condemned Mitchel for preaching hate of England rather than love of Ireland.[71] But Yeats was as much steeped in Mitchel as Pearse was. In 'Under Ben Bulben', a poem meant as his own epitaph and elegy in his final collection of poetry, Yeats recalled the power and influence of Mitchel's spirit as a call to violence:

You that Mitchel's prayer have heard,
'Send war in our time, O Lord!'
Know that when all words are said
And a man is fighting mad,
Something drops from eyes long blind,
He completes his partial mind,

For an instant stands at ease,
Laughs loud, his heart at peace.
Even the wisest man grows tense
With some sort of violence.
Before he can accomplish fate,
Know his work or choose his mate.[72]

Early twentieth-century Sinn Fein took his excoriations of O'Connell, his rejection of nineteenth-century liberalism, his account of the Famine and his understanding of colonialism as articles of faith. Post-independence Ireland was shaped by his case for intellectual isolationism as well as by that made by cultural nationalists. Each reinforced one another. The new Irish state seemed to define itself in terms of the agrarian anti-modern ideal that Mitchel adapted from Carlyle. This found elegiac expression on St Patrick's Day 1943 when Éamon deValera gave a radio address on his ideal of Ireland. Incorrectly remembered for an imaginary reference to comely maidens dancing at the crossroads, deValera's dream was of an agrarian society 'bright with cosy homesteads, whose fields and villages would be joyous with the sounds of industry,' a vision he described as in keeping with that of Young Ireland and the Gaelic League. But by then the clearances and rural depopulation described by Mitchel had been ongoing for a century and nationalist struggles against what Mitchel called the last conquest of Ireland had definitely run out of steam. Subsequent Irish governments explicitly championed ideas of progress that Mitchel would have despised.

CHAPTER NINE

James Connolly and Catholic nationalism

James Connolly (1868–1916) was born in Edinburgh to Irish parents. He enlisted in the British Army at the age of fourteen and was stationed in Ireland for nearly seven years. On his return to Scotland he became a labourer in Edinburgh, a trade unionist and student of Marxism. He was sent to Ireland in 1896 by Kier Hardie to set up a Dublin branch of a British Socialist Party.[1] But within a month of arriving he founded the Irish Socialist Republican Party (ISRP) and in 1898 founded its newspaper the *Worker's Republic*. In his 1897 pamphlet *Erin's Hope: The End and the Means* he argued that socialism in Ireland could not be realised without national independence although the interests of workers were identical all over the world. Each country, he argued, needed to work out its own salvation 'on the lines most congenial to its own people'.[2] Initial efforts to get the ISRP recognised at the Second International Socialist Congress were rejected – the view being that Ireland was part of Britain – but in 1900, when each 'nation' was given two votes, Connolly managed to win separate recognition for the ISRP from the English delegation.[3]

Following his resignation from the ISRP in 1903 (and unable to provide for his family) he moved to New York. He remained in the United States until 1910, working as an 'agitator' (his own description of his occupation) for the Socialist Labour Party of America and the International Workers of the World (IWF). Whilst in America he still wrote extensively about Ireland and in 1907 he founded an Irish Socialist Federation.[4] A section of his 1909 pamphlet *Socialism Made Easy* was directed at Irish Americans. *Labour Nationality and Religion* (1910) addressed where socialism stood in relation to Catholic social thought. He also founded *The Harp*, a periodical aimed, as its name suggested, at influencing Irish-American and Irish opinion. He was unhappy in America, partly because of political and ideological infighting and partly because of the dire poverty his family often experienced.

In 1910 he returned to Dublin and worked as an organiser of the Irish Transport and General Workers' Union (ITGWU). He co-founded the Irish Labour Party in 1912 and the Irish Citizen's Army in 1913 with James Larkin. He founded the *Irish Worker* and when it was suppressed in December 1914 for opposing Britain's involvement in the Great War he revived the *Worker's Republic*, the title he had founded in 1898.

His books included *Labour in Irish History* (1910) and *The Re-Conquest of Ireland* (1915). The former sought to emphasise the potential common purpose between nationalism and socialism. The latter declared that the goal of the Labour Movement was a re-conquest that would take possession of the entire country: 'all its power of wealth-production and natural resources and organising these on a cooperative basis for the good of all'. By 'conquest' Connolly meant the dominance of a capitalist conception of law from the seventeenth century.[5] Modern Irish history, he argued in *Labour and Irish History*, began with the Cromwellian settlement of 1654. The final conquest of Ireland was exemplified by the rise to fortune of William Petty, ancestor of the 'noble Landsdowne family', his acquisition of vast swathes of Kerry land with an annual rent of £18,000, and the corresponding dispossession and transplantation of many original inhabitants from that region.[6] The result of this conquest had been social and political slavery, 'mastery of the lives and liberties of the people of Ireland by forces outside of and unresponsive to the people of Ireland'.

His analyses of patriotic political revolutions from the 1640s emphasised how little these had to do with the conditions of ordinary Irish people. Victory for the Gaelic and Jacobite aristocrats who were defeated respectively by Oliver Cromwell and William of Orange would only have substituted one set of masters for another. The Ascendancy parliament advocated by William Molyneux and realised by Henry Grattan was concerned only with the interests of the property-owning classes. He was no less critical of Daniel O'Connell's Repeal Movement and of most of Young Ireland. Connolly's fusion of socialism and Irish nationalism built on John Mitchel's critique of nineteenth-century liberalism, though hardly upon the paternalist agrarianism Mitchell advocated. He argued that previous movements for Irish 'freedom' failed because these ignored the interests of Ireland's most oppressed people. So too, he insisted, would any future patriot revolution that did not contest class exploitation in Irish society. As he put in *Socialism Made Easy*:

> Let us free Ireland, says the patriot who won't touch Socialism.
> Let us all join together and cr-r-rush the br-r-rutal Saxon. Let us all join together, says he, all classes and creeds.
> And, says the town worker, after we have crushed the Saxon and freed Ireland, what will we do?
> Oh, then you can go back to your slums, same as before.
> Whoop it up for liberty!

And, says the agricultural workers, after we have freed Ireland, what then?

Oh, then you can go scraping around for the landlord's rent or the money-lenders' interest same as before.

Whoop it up for liberty!

After Ireland is free, says the patriot who won't touch Socialism, we will protect all classes, and if you won't pay your rent you will be evicted same as now. But the evicting party, under command of the sheriff, will wear green uniforms and the Harp without the Crown, and the warrant turning you out on the roadside will be stamped with the arms of the Irish Republic.

Now, isn't that worth fighting for?[7]

Yet the 1916 Rising for which Connolly was executed had little to do with socialism and Connolly knew that this would be the case. There was no reference at all to socialism in his play *Under Which Flag?*, which was premiered just a month before the Rising by the ITGWU-sponsored Irish Workers' Dramatic Company in Liberty Hall. The play was set in rural Ireland during the Fenian Rebellion of 1867. The closing lines of the play, spoken as the Green Flag with the golden harp was raised on stage, were; 'Under this flag only will I serve. Under this flag, if need be, will I die.'[8] But, the flag of the Citizen Army had been the Plough and the Stars which Sean O'Casey, a founder member of the Citizen Army, took as the title of his 1924 classic play. By the time Connolly replaced Larkin as its leader in late 1914 he had, according to O'Casey, 'stepped from the narrow byways of Irish Socialism on to the broad and crowded highway of Irish Nationalism'. O'Casey also wrote of Connolly that the 'high creed of Irish nationalism became his daily rosary, whilst the higher creed of international humanity that had so long bubbled from his eloquent lips was silent forever, and Irish Labour lost a leader'.[9]

Connolly's most influential intellectual achievement was not as he hoped, to inject socialism into the mainstream of Irish nationalism, but an account of Irish history that classified constitutional nationalism as false patriotism that helped keep alive a dissident Republicanism that perceived the Free State created by the winning side of the civil war as a betrayal of the Irish people. Connolly's posthumous influence cannot be understood without consideration of the stronger influence of Patrick Pearse upon Irish Republicanism. Both contributed to what Pearse called the new testament of Irish Nationalism, a canon that included Wolfe Tone, Robert Emmet and John Mitchel.

Various writings about Connolly by socialists have emphasised a declaration he made in 1908 that he was not a practicing Catholic, yet Catholicism formed a third corner of the triangle of his loyalties alongside socialism and nationalism.[10] In America he opposed anti-Catholicism amongst socialists, writing in the same 1908 letter that he respected the good Catholic more than the average freethinker. He took care that his responses to clergy who criticised socialism would not label him as anti-Catholic. In April 1890 he wrote a 'scolding letter' to his future wife Lily Reynolds, a Protestant, insisting that in accordance with what his Church required, she agree never to interfere with his observance of his religion and that any children born of their union be baptised into the Catholic Church.[11] On the eve of his execution he asked her to promise him that she would receive instruction in the Catholic faith and, if she could do so, be received into the Catholic Church. Lily did so and subsequently became active in social work with Frank Duff, founder of the Legion of Mary.[12] In *The Harp* he argued that it was capitalism rather than socialism which was hostile to religion.[13] However, the Irish Church remained trenchantly opposed to what he meant by socialism. Catholic social thought developed explicitly to address the threat of Marxism, one that was mostly imaginary in the Irish case. Connolly's Socialist Republicanism proposed solidarity between Ireland's Catholic and Protestant working classes but in the wake of Unionist militancy against Home Rule, it became for all intents and purposes an instrument of Catholic nationalism. And in a sense Socialism died for Ireland alongside Connolly, Pearse and the other Catholic nationalist signatories of the 1916 Proclamation.

History for the Irish working classes

In *Labour in Irish History* Connolly sought to demonstrate how little past generations of Irish patriots and the historians who praised them cared for the sufferings of the ordinary people. He sought to remedy 'the deliberate neglect' of social issues and economic questions by such historians. He positioned himself as the heir of both John Mitchel and William Thompson, an Irish socialist thinker who he intellectually located between Robert Owen and Karl Marx, whose writings on surplus value Thompson had influenced to a considerable extent. In his efforts to fuse Irish nationalism and socialism Connolly sought Irish precedents for socialist ideas. He wrote for an Irish audience versed in Mitchel's critique of colonialism and engaged in a project of cultural decolonisation exemplified by Douglas Hyde's 1892 manifesto *The Necessity of De-Anglicising Ireland* and D. P. Moran's *The Philosophy of Irish-Ireland* (1905).[14] As put in the foreword of *Labour in Irish History*:

> If we would understand the national literature of a people, we must study their social and political status, keeping in mind the fact that their writers were a product thereof, and that the children of their brains were conceived and brought forth in certain historical conditions. Ireland, at the same time as she lost her ancient social system, also lost her language as the vehicle of thought of those who acted as her leaders. As a result of this twofold loss, the nation suffered socially, nationally and intellectually from a prolonged

arrested development. During the closing years of the seventeenth century, all the eighteenth, and the greater part of the nineteenth, the Irish people were the lowest helots in Europe, socially and politically. The Irish peasant, reduced from the position of a free clansman owning his tribeland and controlling its administration in common with his fellows, was a mere tenant-at-will subject to eviction, dishonour and outrage at the hands of an irresponsible private proprietor. Politically he was non-existent, legally he held no rights, intellectually he sank under the weight of his social abasement, and surrendered to the downward drag of his poverty.[15]

Connolly's inference that pre-seventeenth-century Ireland was a socialistic Eden pressed the same buttons as did the champions of the Gaelic Revival. His materialist interpretation of Irish history hardly endorsed the essentialist claims of many Gaelic revivalists about the distinctive cultural and national character of the Irish people, but in seeking to woo Irish nationalists he often played along with such assertions. In his 1897 pamphlet *Erin's Hope* he addressed the difficulties of making such an account of pre-seventeenth-century Irish society fit with the Marxist scientific interpretation of history. This emphasised progression from chattel slavery to feudalism to wage-slavery as preparation for the highly ordered society of the future.[16] From such a perspective Connolly acknowledged that the Irish system of clan ownership constituted a state of retarded economic development that would have hindered such progress. Left alone it would have given way to a private ownership system of capitalist-landlordism in any case. But 'coming as it did in obedience to the pressure of armed force from without, instead of by the operation of economic forces within', the change had been 'bitterly and justly resented by the vast mass of the Irish people', many of whom still mixed with their dreams of liberty futile longings for a return to the ancient system of land tenure.

Various strands of nationalism sought pre-seventeenth-century inspiration. Undoing the Reformation appealed to Catholics. Cultural nationalists emphasised the linguistic restoration of Gaelic. Connolly's own valorisation of pre-seventeenth century Irish society was a Trojan horse aimed at inserting radical socialist ideas into a wider nationalist politics that was often conservative and often cared little more about social and economic injustice than did past generations of Irish patriots.[17] What mattered was that Irish nationalists came to understand this history as one of capitalist colonisation and that they realised that the only viable Gaelic restoration, or re-conquest of Ireland as he termed it, was a socialist revolution that gave real freedom to the ordinary people who had suffered social and economic oppression since the time of Cromwell.

Connolly depicted the Jacobites – supporters of King James – as little better than traitors for their action in seducing the Irish people into a war on behalf of a foreign tyrant. These Catholic gentlemen and nobles had no greater entitlements to Irish lands than the Cromwellian or Williamite adventurers who usurped them. The lands they held were tribe lands which in former times allegedly belonged to the Irish people. Successive waves of Irish patriotism, from the settler nobility in the time of Henry II, to the Ascendancy descendants of seventeenth-century planters and adventurers represented the interests of Irish landowning classes:

> At once they became patriots, anxious that Ireland – which, in their phraseology, meant the ruling class in Ireland – should be free from the control of the Parliament of England. Their pamphlets, speeches, and all public pronouncements were devoted to telling the world how much nicer, equitable, and altogether more delectable it would be for the Irish people to be robbed in the interests of a native-born aristocracy than to witness the painful spectacle of that aristocracy being compelled to divide the plunder with its English rival. Perhaps Swift, Molyneux, or Lucas did not confess even to themselves that such was the basis of their political creed.
>
> The human race has at all times shown a proneness to gloss over its basest actions with a multitude of specious pretences, and to cover even its iniquities with the glamour of a false sentimentality. But we are not dealing with appearances but realities, and, in justice to ourselves, we must expose the flimsy sophistry which strives to impart to a sordid, self-seeking struggle the appearance of a patriotic movement.

He described such Protestant patriotism as 'flimsy sophistry' that masked the 'sordid self-seeking' of its exponents. In the same vein Connolly argued that many of the better-off beneficiaries of Catholic emancipation were also less than credible patriots. These sought constitutional reform 'whilst leaving untouched the basis of national and economic subjugation.' He argued that Daniel O'Connell had sided with the Irish capitalist and professional classes and worked to quash efforts by Chartists to establish an Irish trade union movement. Echoing Mitchel, Connolly insisted that 'all except a few men had elevated landlord property and capitalist political economy to a fetish to be worshipped, and upon the altar of that fetish Ireland perished'. During the Famine, free trade filled the stores of speculating capitalists with corn but left those who have sown and reaped it without a meal. Free trade 'unpeopled villages and peopled poorhouses'; it 'consolidated farms and glutted the graveyards with famished corpses'.

The 'crowning absurdity' of 1848 had been the leadership of William Smith O'Brien. A splenetic passage of *Labour in Irish History* described how Smith O'Brien wandered through the country telling the starving peasantry to get ready, but refused to allow them to feed themselves at the expense of the landlords who had so long plundered, starved and evicted them: 'at Mullinahone he refused to allow his followers to fell trees to build a barricade across the road until they had asked permission of the landlords who owned the trees; when the people of Killenaule had a body of dragoons entrapped between two barricades he released the dragoons from their dangerous situation upon their leader assuring him that he had no warrant for his (Smith O'Brien's) arrest; in another place he surprised a party of soldiers in the Town Hall with their arms taken apart for cleaning purposes, and instead of confiscating the arms, he told the soldiers that their arms were as safe as they would be in Dublin Castle'. Such a recital, in the midst of a Famine that killed a million, read 'like a page of comic opera'. Smith O'Brien had been 'vehemently solicitous for the rights of his class, and allowing his solicitude for those rights to stand between the millions of the Irish race and their hopes of life and freedom'.

Two chapters in *Labour in Irish History* celebrated nineteenth-century efforts to promote socialist ideas in Ireland. One described the ideas and social experiments of William Thompson, 'a forerunner of Marx', 'a Socialist who did not hesitate to direct attention to the political and social subjection of labour as the worst evil of society; nor to depict, with a merciless fidelity to truth, the disastrous consequences to political freedom of the presence in society of a wealthy class'. Thompson's analyses of labour, capital and surplus value anticipated conclusions drawn by Karl Marx. As put by Thompson in an 1824 work cited by Connolly:

> As long as the accumulated capital of society remains in one set of hands, and the productive power of creating wealth remains in another, the accumulated capital will, while the nature of man continues as at present, be made use of to counter-act the natural laws of distribution, and to deprive the producers of the use of what their labour has produced . . . As long as a class of mere capitalists exists, society must remain in a diseased state. Whatever plunder is saved from the hand of political power will be levied in another way, under the name of profit, by capitalists who, while capitalists, must be always law-makers.[18]

Thompson had brushed aside the economic fiction maintained by the orthodox economists and declared that profit was due to the subjection of labour and the resultant appropriation, by the capitalists and landlords, of the fruits of the labour of others. In an 1827 pamphlet *Labour Rewarded, the Claims of Labour and Capital Conciliated; or, How to Secure to Labour the Whole Product of its Exertions* he declared that for about twelve years he had been 'living on what is called rent, the produce of the labour of others'.[19] His 1825 pamphlet, *Appeal of one-half of the Human Race – Women – against the Pretensions of the other half – Men – to retain them in Political and thence in Civil and Domestic Slavery* had demanded the extension of voting rights to all the adult population. In 1830 he published his *Practical Directions for the Speedy and Economical Establishment of Communities on the Principles of Mutual Co-opertion*.[20] When he died in 1833 he left the bulk of his fortune to endow the first co-operative community to be established in Ireland. His relations successfully contested the will on the ground that 'immoral objects were included in its benefit'.

Such a community had in fact been established in County Clare. Robert Owen visited Dublin in 1832 and held a number of meetings to explain the principles of socialism. His audiences were mainly composed of the well-to-do. At the time, 'socialism was the fad of the rich instead of the faith of the poor'. The meetings led to the establishment of a short-lived Hibernian Philanthropic Society to promote Owen's co-operative ideas. Owen himself subscribing £1,000 and further donations were raised from other sources. One member, Arthur Vandeleur, went on to establish a socialist colony on his estate at Ralahine, County Clare. The Rules of Association of the Ralahine Agricultural and Manufacturing Co-operative Association provided that no member be expected to perform any service or work disagreeable to their feelings but that all should assist in agricultural operations, particularly in harvest, that all the youth, male or female, should learn a useful trade, that the expenses of the children's food, clothing, washing, lodging and education be paid out of the common funds of the society until the age of seventeen when they became eligible to become members.

For a time the Ralahine Association looked like it was going to be a success. It introduced the first reaping machine to be used in Ireland. It had been envisaged that the co-operative would eventually purchase the land it leased. But Vandeleur had gambling debts and problems and fled in disgrace. The ensuing bankruptcy proceedings broke up the Association and treated its members as common labourers. The failure of Ralahine and the frustration of Thompson's bequest to found a similar co-operative were, Connolly emphasised, due to laws of property. If Ralahine had been owned by the people who worked its land it would surely have been viable.

In *Labour in Irish History* Connolly sought to emphasise a history of rebellion from below where 'the peasant, labourer, or artisan, banded himself with his fellows to strike back at their oppressors in defence of their right to live in the land of their fathers'. Their enemies included the Irish 'respectable' classes, led by Daniel O'Connell, who under 'the deadly embrace of capitalist English conventionalism' deplored such actions. He described how in County Clare, whilst the Ralahine experiment was underway, lodges of the secret Ribbon Society 'made midnight raids for arms upon the houses of the gentry, assembled at night in large bodies and ploughed up the grass lands, making them useless for grazing purposes, filled up ditches, terrorised graziers into surrendering their ranches, wounded and killed those who had entered the service of graziers or obnoxious landlords, assassinated agents, and sometimes, in sheer despair, opposed their unarmed bodies to the arms of the military'. Such conflicts highlighted the crucial underlying issues that had shaped Irish politics for centuries:

> As we have again and again pointed out, the Irish question is a social question, the whole age-long fight of the Irish people against their oppressors resolves itself, in the last analysis into a fight for the mastery of the means of life, the sources of production, in Ireland. Who would

own and control the land? The people or the invaders; and if the invaders, which set of them – the most recent swarm of land-thieves, or the sons of the thieves of a former generation? These were the bottom questions of Irish politics, and all other questions were valued or deprecated in the proportion to which they contributed to serve the interests of some of the factions who had already taken their stand in this fight around property interests. Without this key to the meaning of events, this clue to unravel the actions of 'great men', Irish history is but a welter of unrelated facts, a hopeless chaos of sporadic outbreaks, treacheries, intrigues, massacres, murders, and purposeless warfare.

In his fight for the soul of Irish nationalism Connolly sought to undermine the then-standard narrative of Irish history that made heroes and patriots out of seventeenth- and eighteenth-century aristocrats and more recent middle-class nationalists who had kept the ordinary people in a state of abasement and sycophancy. *Labour in Irish History* emphasised an alternative nationalist pantheon that included Wolfe Tone, Robert Emmet and John Mitchel. Tone's contribution was an anti-sectarian United Irishmen ideal. Emmet, Connolly explained, believed the 'national will' was superior to property rights, and could abolish them at will. Mitchel had preached a 'holy hatred' of the capitalist system that sustained the British Empire. Connolly distinguished between the false patriotism of elites and constitutional nationalists who were complicit in the exploitation of the poorer classes and the 'real nationalists of Ireland, the Separatists', who had 'always been men of broad human sympathies and intense democracy' who kept faith with the revolutionary spirit of their times whether this was the French Revolution, the spirit of 1848 or that now expressed through socialism.

Socialism and nationalism

Much of the analysis and argument in *Labour and Irish History* dated from the immediate period after he returned to Ireland as a union organiser in 1897. An editorial by Connolly described *The Worker's Republic* as 'primarily a missionary organ' aimed at presenting to the working class an 'understanding of the scientific principles of socialism'.[21] But from the outset Connolly declared himself an Irish patriot. 'I rather like that intense desire to conserve the honour or freedom of a particular country', he wrote in a 1900 article where he also professed himself a believer in the brotherhood of all men in the international solidarity of labour.[22] Through the ISRP he produced a series of five pamphlets to mark the centenary of the 1798 Uprising. These reprinted *United Irishmen* writings from that time including an attack on Grattan's Parliament extracted from Tone's *An Argument on behalf of the Catholics of Ireland* (1791). An August 1898 editorial in *The Worker's Republic,* headlined 'The Men We Honour', declared that

Tone had refused to 'prostitute his genius in the cause of compromise and time-serving'. For this he had been crucified in life and idolised in death by Irishmen who, had he been still alive, would have repudiated him as a dangerous malcontent.[23] Tone, Connolly argued, grasped that British dominion in Ireland could only be dislodged by a radical revolution in step with the ideals of the French Revolution of his day.

In an 1897 article entitled 'Socialism and Nationalism' he argued that a successful national movement could not be built on 'a morbid idealising of the past; it needed a political and economic creed capable of addressing the problems of the present and the wants of the future'. As a socialist he was prepared to do all that one man could to achieve for his motherland her rightful heritage – independence; but would decline if asked 'to abate one jot or title of the claims of social justice, in order to conciliate the privileged classes.[24] Other 1897 articles like 'Patriotism and Labour' and the 1897 pamphlet that bought these materials together, *Erin's Hope* all made the case for a Socialist Republic.[25] To nationalists he argued that a revolution that merely hoisted the Green Flag over Dublin Castle would win no real independence for Ireland because it would not benefit ordinary Irish people. To socialists he argued that national independence was an indispensable prerequisite to the emancipation of the working classes. The Irish people, he argued in an 1899 article entitled 'Physical Force in Irish Politics', at various times had glided from constitutionalism into insurrectionism, 'meeting in each the same failure and the same disaster'. Every revolutionary effort in Ireland, he argued, had drawn the bulk of its supporters from the disappointed followers of some defeated constitutional movement without any substantial rethinking of political goals. A willingness to use physical force on its own did not make for an advanced nationalism. That was determined by the ends sought rather than means employed. Connolly's concern was that the many of those who might fight for Irish freedom were in fact reactionary nationalists.[26]

Connolly's departure to America in 1903 was tinged with bitterness. Many men, he wrote, had been driven out of Ireland by the British Government or by landlords, he was the first driven forth by socialists.[27] The ISRP had never been more than 'a few kindred souls' whose subscriptions Connolly depended upon to feed his family and keep *The Worker's Republic* going.[28] In 1903 Connolly fell out with other members over the use of the party's precarious funds. He complained to a Scottish comrade about their lack of initiative and their resentment of him and asserted his determination that this would make no difference to him:

> I know that if any comrade acts with any degree of initiative and originality he will be accused of bossing, and of running the party for his own benefit just as I was, or of striving to advertise himself just as you were, but we do not expect to have a party of angels or of brotherly love, and the man who knows he is serving the cause to the best of his ability can treat such

littleness with contempt. In everything somebody must move first, or take the lead, and in the Socialist movement the man who moves first earns the hatred of the capitalist, and the spite of the 'comrades.' Such is life.[29]

Two years later in America, recalling events in 1903, he wrote that he regarded Ireland, or at least the socialist part of Ireland ('which is all I care for') as having thrown him out and he did not 'wish to return like a dog to his vomit'. [30] But Connolly escaped from the frying pan into the fire. He still experienced periods of intense economic hardship. He soon found himself in conflict with Daniel De Leon, leader of the Socialist Labour Party of America. De Leon had intellectually influenced Connolly who was taken by his syndicalist principle of organising socialist activism through 'One Big Union'. But in practice both got on with one another badly. Personality conflicts aside, Connolly viewed De Leon's methodology for achieving socialism as very inflexible and dogmatic. De Leon attacked Connolly for not holding 'orthodox' socialist positions (as De Leon defined these) on Catholicism and marriage. Connolly for his part had become 'wearied until death listening to Socialist speeches and reading Socialist literature about materialism and philosophy, ethics, sex, embryology, monogamy, physiology' and not hearing enough from his American comrades about the daily struggles of the workers and how they might be organised.[31] He became embittered by his experiences with American socialism. He had come to regard his emigration to America as the great mistake of his life and he declared that he had 'never ceased to regret it'.[32]

In 1907 he established an Irish Socialist Federation and edited its periodical *The Harp*. Within three years he had published *Socialism Made Easy* (published with shamrocks and the Irish harp on its cover), *Socialism, Nationalism and Religion* and *Labour in Irish History*. At the time (April 1909) he was in such economic dire straits, having lost his job, that he was 'frightened' that his family would starve in New York. He put in train a plan to print *The Harp* in Dublin, have it circulated by post to America, and manage it by correspondence from America at his own expense. In response to scepticism from Irish acquaintances about the viability of the project he vented in a letter to an Irish socialist friend, William O'Brien, 'I am old enough to know what I am doing, and my days for guileless trust in the comradeship of Socialists is long over'.[33] Six issues of *The Harp* were published in Dublin from January 1910. Connolly returned to Ireland with no firm offer of employment in July 1910. He gave a series of lectures and received some financial support for Jim Larkin's ITGWU and moved his family to Belfast. A poster for his 1910 lectures under the banner Cumannacht Na hEireann (Socialist Party of Ireland) declared in Irish and in English the party's goal of creating an organised Commonwealth of Ireland in which the land, railways, and all other instruments of production, distribution and exchange would be owned by the whole people and included the following quote from Connolly:

Ireland as distinct from her people is nothing to me; and the man who is bubbling over with love and enthusiasm for 'Ireland', and can yet pass unmoved though our streets and witness all the wrong and suffering, the shame and the degradation wrought upon the people of Ireland – aye wrought by Irishmen upon Irish men and women, without burning to end it, is, in my opinion, a fraud and a liar in his heart, no matter how he loves that combination of classical elements he is pleased to call 'Ireland.'[34]

Connolly returned to Ireland still enamoured by De Leon's syndicalist ideal of the One Big Union. For the next few years he was heavily involved in promoting trade unionism in Belfast and elsewhere in Ireland. He also became involved in reviving the Socialist Party of Ireland (SPI), a successor to the ISRP that had been limping along with a small squabbling membership. Under Connolly's leadership the SPI published a new manifesto in September 1910 with the stated aim of 'organising itself politically and industrially with the end of gaining control and mastery of the entire resources of the country' but (unlike the doctrinaire De Leonites he became disillusioned with in America) leaving itself free to adapt its methods to suit the circumstances it encountered.[35] As in America, many of the frictions he experienced had to do with personality rather than ideology. He found himself in conflict with Larkin and portrayed him in correspondence as an unbearable bully over money matters within the ITGWU and as consumed with jealousy and hatred of anyone – meaning Connolly – who would not cringe before him.[36]

In his writings he repeatedly emphasised the need for solidarity between Protestant and Catholic members of the working class. In a 1913 article he noted that according to all socialist theories North-East Ulster, the most developed industrially, ought to be where class politics had become most pronounced.[37] In practice such working class solidarity proved impossible to realise when 'the mental atmosphere of the early seventeenth century' was being heavily promoted by the Orange Order. In 1915 in a chapter of *The Re-Conquest of Ireland* on conditions in Belfast he described how poverty and dire working conditions affected the health and safely of male and female workers and their children. Due to poor housing conditions consumption was rife and many lost life or limb in industrial accidents:

It has been computed that some seventeen lives were lost on the *Titanic* before she left the Lagan; a list of the maimed and hurt and of those suffering from minor injuries, as a result of the accidents at any one of those big ships would read like a roster of the wounded after a battle upon the Indian frontier. The public reads and passes on, but fails to comprehend the totality of suffering involved. But it all means lives ruined, fair prospects blighted, homes devastated, crippled wrecks of manhood upon the streets, or widows and orphans to eat the bread of poverty and pauperism.

However, solidarity with the Northern Protestant working class proved difficult in practice. In 1913 he argued that socialism could not be built by temporising in front of a dying cause such as that of the Orange ascendency and declared to the Orange workers of Belfast that 'we', meaning Irish socialism, 'stand for the right of the people of Ireland to rule as well as to own Ireland, and cannot conceive of a separation of the two ideas, and to all and sundry we announce that as Socialists we are Home Rulers, but on the day the Home Rule Government goes into power, the Socialist movement in Ireland will go into opposition'.[38] In effect, Connolly was asking the Protestant working class to support Irish Republicanism. He stood as an independent candidate in the January 1913 Belfast Municipal Elections in the Dock Ward where many Belfast members of the ITGWU lived and where the majority of the population were Protestant. His supporters were overwhelmingly Catholic and the Catholic *Irish News* endorsed him. Unsurprisingly his Orange opponent won with 1,523 votes to 905; the ratio of votes resembled that of the Protestant to Catholic ratio of population in the ward.[39] Socialism also split along sectarian lines. Belfast Independent Labour Party members remained part of the British socialist movement and became Unionists.

Industrial agitation in Dublin came to a head in 1913. During what came to be known as the Dublin Lockout 24,000 trade union members were suspended by a federation of some 400 Dublin employers led by William Martin Murphy, the city's leading business magnate and publisher of *The Irish Independent*.[40] The Lockout occurred when a strike spread from the tram company to other Dublin businesses owned by Murphy. The strikers in Dublin received considerable financial support from the British Trade Unions Congress but not enough to alleviate widespread hunger and hardship during the winter of 1913. Nor did the British trade unions declare the general sympathetic strike that Connolly had anticipated. The strikes in Dublin failed to achieve any concession from Dublin employers and left the ITGWU demoralised and indebted. The following year Larkin left for America and Connolly became the leader of a trade union movement incapable of further mass industrial action.

In the aftermath of the Lockout the Irish Citizen Army, a small militia established to protect strikers modelled on the Ulster Volunteers, became Connolly's primary focus. Its manifesto (drafted by the future playwright Sean O'Casey) declared that it stood for 'the absolute unity of Irish nationhood' and that membership was open to 'all who accepted the principle of equal rights and opportunities for the Irish people'.[41] His campaigns for socialism coalesced into one against Britain in the Great War between the most socialist nations on the Earth. Connolly repeatedly attacked Britain's involvement in the Great War in *The Irish Worker*. A fanciful (given the bruising experiences of the 1913 Dublin Lockout) August 1914 article contemplated a general strike and 'even armed battling in the streets' to prevent the export of Irish agricultural produce to England, this being 'the immediately feasible policy of the working-class democracy'. Such a revolution 'might yet set the torch to a European conflagration that will not burn out until the last throne and the last capitalist bond and debenture will be shrivelled on the funeral pyre of the last war lord'.[42]

But in late 1914 he came to believe that the Great War had undermined all hopes for socialist internationalisation and any possibility of general strikes. He wrote eloquently on how socialists in the armies on both sides now had to kill each other. He opposed Home Rule support for Britain in the war. He argued that Germany had never harmed Ireland whilst England had.[43] He also made an anti-conscription case for rebellion in Ireland. No rebellion, he argued, could conceivably lead to such slaughter of Irish manhood as would result from John Redmond's call to Home Rulers to enlist in the British Army.[44]

Meanwhile Connolly was drawn increasingly into revolutionary nationalist circles. Two companies of the Citizen Army had attended a Wolfe Tone commemoration in Dublin alongside the Irish Volunteers in June 1914. Both organisations provided guards of honour at the funerals of those killed by British soldiers on Bachelors Walk following the landing of arms for the Irish Volunteers by the Asgard in July 1914. Along with Pearse and several other signatories of the 1916 Declaration Connolly founded the Irish Neutrality League in September 1914, a front for subsequent revolutionary mobilisation.[45] Together with these he was one of the committee that organised the funeral of the Irish Republican Brotherhood leader O'Donovan Rossa on 1 August 1915. Pearse's oration dedicated the Irish Volunteers to the realisation of Irish freedom as understood by Tone and Mitchel. In an accompanying pamphlet Connolly declared that the Irish Citizen Army pledged its members to fight for a Republican Freedom for Ireland.[46] Sean O'Casey, in *The History of the Irish Citizen Army: 1913–1916*, argued that under Connolly's leadership the Citizen's Army became subsumed into the Irish Volunteers, an organisation he saw as dominated by enemies of socialism rather than elected representatives of the working class.

In 1915 Connolly wrote a series of articles aimed at instructing these putative rebels on insurrection and warfare. His choices were past conflicts that seemed to offer useful military instructions for the Irish revolution he anticipated. These included lessons on urban street fighting from the 1905 Moscow and 1848 Paris insurrections and the defence of the Alamo in 1836 against an overwhelming force of 10,000 Mexican troops. Connolly argued that the Alamo 'was one of those defeats which are often more valuable to a cause than many loudly trumpeted victories'.[47]

Three months before the 1916 Rising in *The Worker's Republic* Connolly recalled the socialist programme he had pursued since 1896 – to organise Irish labour and make it revolutionary, to gather into Irish hands in Irish trade unions the control of all the forces of production and distribution in Ireland – that had been set back by the Great War.[48] But the Republic, for Connolly, now came first. In January 1916 Connolly spent three days in intense secret discussion with other leaders of the Easter Rising (after which he wrote 'What is Our Programme'. When asked where he had been by Countess Markievicz, he cryptically replied, 'I have been in Hell, but I have conquered my enemies.' Various interpretations of what he meant by this are cited by Donal Nevin in his monumental biography of Connolly.[49] As put by a historian of the Irish trade union movement, C. Desmond Greaves:

> He had suffered successive blows. The European proletariat had not risen. Ireland [in 1913] had refused to act as a trigger ... When the military committee [of the IRB] had approached him, his own plans were in ruins. The workers were simply not ready for a rising that would put an end to throne, debentures and warlords.[50]

And as put in Desmond Ryan's account of the Rising:

> He was in a mood of bitter disillusion because the Socialist and Labour movement in which he had given so many years of work and propaganda had collapsed in face of the war, because his union, the Irish Transport and General Workers Union, was also bankrupt in members and funds after the Dublin struggle of 1913, because the attitude of British Labour and Irish nationalism alike had angered him during the very bitter and stubborn lockout.[51]

The operative word here is 'propaganda'; Connolly could write again and again that the Irish workers demand this or understand that but it was mostly just Connolly who demanded this and thought so. He could write, as he did in *The Re-Conquest of Ireland*, that the Gaelic Leaguer 'realises that capitalism did more in one century to destroy the tongue of the Gael than the sword of the Saxon did in six'. But all this meant was that the Gaelic Leaguer *should* realise capitalism was the enemy. By the time he returned from America in 1910 the trade union movement was ripe for expansion but it proved incapable of taking on Irish capitalism. Most of its members were staunch Catholics. Connolly had opposed the Home Rule movement because it sought independence without social or economic reform. He opposed the militant Unionist opponents of Home Rule because they would impose a sectarian divide in Irish politics that would undermine the future of the Socialist Republic he believed in. His socialism was in strong theoretical solidarity with Protestant workers. In practice, it developed a sectarian solidarity with the Catholic majority that he argued were the true Irish working class. And then, too few of this Catholic working class expressed an interest in socialism.

The age of labour solidarity he proclaimed had failed to come to pass in Ireland. Connolly seems to have been grieving the death of any real chance for a Socialist Republic. Having gone through some of the various stages of grief – denial, anger and despair – he came to accept a nationalist revolution that paid bare lip service to the values and beliefs for which he had fought for decades, a revolution exemplifying the basic fault he attributed to previous failed Irish revolutions; it had little to do with emancipating the ordinary people of Ireland from the exploitation they experienced at the hands of the owners of Irish property.

In February 1916 he wrote that a destiny not of our fashioning has chosen this generation as the one called upon for the supreme act of self-sacrifice – 'to die if need be that our race might live in freedom.'[52] In March he wrote of the awe-inspiring but glorious thought that those martyrs whom Ireland gave to the cause of freedom were weighing and judging the actions of those who invoked their memories in 1916.[53] On Easter Monday 1916 Connolly led 200 members of the Citizen Army into a week of fighting. Although Pearse was nominally in charge Connolly made most of the decisions about deployments and gave most of the orders. Towards the end a wounded Connolly was evacuated to a 'cottage' near the corner of Moore Street and Henry Street which was occupied by Thomas McKane, his wife and their ten children. A bullet fired into the lock of the front door by a volunteer killed sixteen-year-old Bridget McKane and seriously wounded Thomas. Connolly, when he was brought in, asked Mrs McKane to make him a cup of tea, and told her she was a brave woman. Connolly died bravely himself when executed on 12 May.

The triumph of Catholic nationalism

Connolly had settled for a revolution without any clear socialist programme. In 1909 he wrote that socialists had no sympathy with Sinn Fein's economic policies of self-reliance because these did not address the redistribution of wealth amongst the Irish people and followed capitalist ideas of progress.[54] The gulf between nationalist economic policy as mooted by Arthur Griffith and the socialist ideal mooted by Connolly was one between economic isolationism and anti-capitalism, between tariff barriers to protect Irish businesses and the redistribution of property amongst Irish people.

But, in a 1913 article that criticised the treatment of the Dublin poor during the Lockout, Pearse concluded that there was 'something to be said for the hungry man's hazy idea that there is something wrong somewhere'. He declared that a free Ireland would drain the bogs, harness the rivers, plant the wastes and would nationalise the railways and waterways.[55] Yet Pearse hardly advocated socialism as this was understood by Connolly; a free Ireland, he added, would also improve commerce. Both were the main authors of the 1916 Proclamation of the Irish Republic. This declared the right of the people of Ireland to the ownership of Ireland, a resolve to pursue the happiness and prosperity of the whole nation and, famously, to cherish all children of the nation equally. In his March 1916 pamphlet *The Sovereign*

People Pearse referred to Tone's appeal to 'that numerous and respectable class', the 'men of no property', and stated that a nation may determine as many modern nations had that all its railways and waterways were the public property of the nation to be administered for the general benefit. A nation, he continued, may go further and determine that all sources of wealth whatsoever were the property of the nation, the operative word being 'may' rather than 'should'.[56]

Peter Berresford-Ellis in *A History of the Irish Working Class* – a 1972 book faithful to Connolly's interpretation of the pre-1910 past that applied his critique of the failures of constitutional patriotism to post-independent Ireland – argues that 'the political gulf between Pearse and Connolly was extremely narrow when they signed the 1916 Proclamation'.[57] Such a claim exemplified the intellectual fudge between two quite different positions that has played out in the post-independence Irish Republican Army and Republican Socialist movements over several decades. The 1916 Proclamation contained phrases that could be read as endorsements of socialism. So also did the Democratic Programme adopted by the Dáil in 1919. This reiterated the words of the 1916 Proclamation and in the language of Pearse declared that the nation's sovereignty extended to 'all its material possessions, the nation's soil and all its resources, all the wealth and wealth-producing processes within the nation; and with him, we reaffirm that all rights in private property must be subordinate to the public right and welfare'. The authors of this document were Seán T. Ó Ceallaigh, Ceann Comhairle (Speaker) of the first Dáil and future President, Thomas Johnson, secretary of the Labour Party and Connolly's old comrade and confidant William O'Brien.[58]

Here was a serious attempt to inject some socialist vision into the constitution of the putative Republic. But it could only be done by invoking Pearse. And the problem with using Pearse as a proxy for socialism was that he was not a socialist. Richard English draws a helpful distinction between the communalist ideals of Pearse, as expressed in *The Sovereign People,* and Connolly's socialist ideals.[59] The former sought to promote harmony between the social classes whilst the latter advocated redistribution to the working class. The influence of the former could for example be seen in the IRA's 1934 *Constitution and governmental programme for the Republic of Ireland.* This reiterated claims contained in the 1916 Proclamation and the 1919 Programme that the nation's soil and rivers, lakes and waterways, were the property of the people. The 1934 IRA programme favoured the co-operative organisation of agriculture and generally a strong role for the state, but it also would permit private enterprise, encourage home ownership and promised that farmers would not be compelled to collectivise their land. Within the IRA at the time socialists like Peadar O'Donnell were in the minority.

The problem for Republican socialists remained the same as encountered by Connolly in all his dealings with nationalists. Connolly declared common cause between socialism and progressive nationalism. Socialist ideals could be read into the record book of Irish nationalism at various stages but if most nationalists had scant socialist leanings it hardly mattered in practice. However, the invocation of such ideals from the margins of Irish nationalism served to legitimise an ongoing struggle against new generations of false and corrupt patriots. Just as Connolly distinguished the false patriotism of Jacobite landowners, the Protestant Ascendancy Parliament, Daniel O'Connell's constitutional Repeal Movement and the constitutional Home Rule movement from the true patriotism of Wolfe Tone, the United Irishmen, Captain Moonlight, John Mitchel, the Fenians and, of course, the rebels of 1916, so it now became possible for Republicans from the civil war onwards to invoke Connolly's socialist standard for true patriotism against the constitution of the Irish Free State.

Socialism was also smothered by Catholicism. In January 1916 in *The Worker's Republic* Connolly made much of a 'splendid speech' by the Capuchin priest Father Laurence in Dublin to an audience of Catholic working men and women. Connolly professed himself to be unable to identify any fundamental differences between Laurence's views and those of Irish socialists. In describing these similarities Connolly's phrasing echoed the language of Catholic natural law: 'We accept the family as the true type of human society. We say that as in the family the resources of the entire household are at the service of each, as in the family the strong does not prey upon the weak.' Laurence's willingness to engage with the concerns of the people, Connolly argued, as a sign that the Church recognised that if it did not move with them, the people would move without the Church, as had happened in France.[60]

Similarly, in *The Re-Conquest of Ireland* he claimed common cause with the co-operative movement being promoted by George Russell (AE), the Jesuit Thomas Finlay and Sir Horace Plunkett, which he described as in keeping with the Utopian experiment of Ralahine and the operation of Catholic monasteries. He noted that over 100,000 Irish farmers were now organised in co-operative societies. There existed co-operative creameries, co-operative marketing, co-operative banks and projects for co-operative fishing. Their members, he claimed, shared the ideal of a Co-operative Commonwealth with the militant workers of the world. He argued that 'the earnest teacher of Christian morality sees that in the co-operative commonwealth alone will true morality be possible'.

But Catholic social thought as exemplified by the 1891 Encyclical *Rerum Novarum* was explicitly designed to undermine the appeal of socialism to the industrial working classes. A 1919 article 'Socialism and Catholic Teaching' by Finlay maintained that the programme that the Irish Republican Socialist Party was one that Leo XIII had explicitly condemned. At the same time he stated that the nationalisation of railways or coal mines or state ownership of some land by the Congested Districts Boards was not necessarily contrary to Catholic doctrine.[61] The first major analysis of

Connolly's writings by another Jesuit, Lambert McKenna, *The Social Teachings of James Connolly* (1921), maintained that some of these were in accordance with Catholic social thought.[62] Yet, in another article the same year McKenna called the inner cadre of the Communist Party 'Mullahs who lead the Faithful of this new Islamism.'[63] Just as Connolly claimed Catholic interest in social justice for socialism so McKenna maintained that Connolly was hardly a historical materialist in the full sense of believing that religion was merely the expression of material conditions. In other words, he was not a true Marxist. Here the distinction between communalism and socialism again played out. Catholic support for the former developed after independence into advocacy of corporatist vocationalism; what this meant is explained in Chapter 11. Its aim was to promote solidarity between social classes. The Church proactively sought to counter the appeal of socialism. Catholic social thought came to dominate the teaching of social sciences in Irish universities for decades after independence. It also dominated industrial relations, beginning with schemes to educate Catholic trade unionists that explicitly copied those of the British trade union movement, whilst keeping socialism at bay.[64]

CHAPTER TEN

Hanna Sheehy Skeffington versus the Free State

The place of women in various aspirations for future Unionist, Home Rule or independent Irelands became politicised during the first and second decades of the twentieth century. Campaigns for suffrage for Irishwomen were by no means intellectually rooted in Ireland. However, these found distinctive expression in the heady, febrile, politically militant decade before Irish independence. The first Irish suffrage groups had been founded in the 1870s; one in Belfast by Isabella Tod, a staunch Unionist, the second in Dublin by Anna Haslam, a Quaker. The subaltern position of women was exemplified by thinner trails of pamphlets and books through which their understandings of the predicaments facing Irish society were documented. It was hard for women to become public intellectuals where they were debarred from or stifled within the public sphere. For this reason feminist historical scholarship is often preoccupied with recovering marginalised voices. But Hanna Sheehy Skeffington (1877–1946) was born into a well-documented milieu of writers and politicians. Her own life coincided with crucial events in modern Irish history. Sheehy Skeffington's writings and activism exemplified – but did not solely personify – a running battle between prominent women activists and the mainstream politics of Home Rule and of the Free State.

She was the eldest daughter of Irish Party nationalist MP, David Sheehy, who had been a Fenian in his youth and was jailed on six occasions during the Land War. Later as member of the Irish political establishment he was implacably opposed to her campaigns for female suffrage. She was a founding member of the Irish Women's Franchise League (IWFL) in 1908 and a sometime-editor of its periodical. *The Irish Citizen* had been founded in 1912 when the IWFL adopted the militant tactics of English suffragists. Whilst Sheehy Skeffington was on hunger strike in Mountjoy Prison in June 1912 her father was one of thirty-eight Irish Parliamentary Party MPs who backed a new law that allowed such protesters to be force fed. She was hugely influenced by her uncle, Father Eugene Sheehy, a leading member of the Land League and a senior member of the Irish Republican Brotherhood. One of her earliest memories (at the age of four) was visiting 'the rebel priest' in Kilmainham prison.[1] In 1912 he visited her in Mountjoy jail. Imprisonment and hunger strikes became recurring motifs of her political activism. At the beginning of the Rising she delivered supplies to rebel combatants. Father Eugene volunteered as a Chaplain. Her husband Frank Sheehy Skeffington, a pacifist described by Sean O'Casey as the Irish Gandhi, was arrested during the Rising after attempting to prevent looting. He was murdered by a British officer who was subsequently court-martialled and judged insane.

From October 1916 she embarked on an almost two-year-long American tour speaking about 250 times to the text of her pamphlet *British militarism as I have known it* (1917). This described her husband's murder and the response to the British government in order to make the case for Irish independence. Before the death of her husband she had been scathing about the tendency of Irish political parties to betray the interests of Irish women and insisted that rights for women would not be delivered if deferred in order to secure Home Rule. It was the duty of suffragists, she wrote after the outbreak of war in 1914, to refuse to set aside their goals for patriotic 'war work' as many English suffragists did. But after the 1916 Rising Sheehy Skeffington did likewise believing that an independent Irish Republic would honour the commitments to equal citizenship for women set out in the 1916 Proclamation.

She was arrested in June 1918 on her return from America and imprisoned alongside Constance Markievicz who had been a combatant in the Rising. Fellow prisoners included Kathleen Clarke, the widow of Tom Clarke – one of the leaders – and Maud Gonne McBride, whose husband Major John McBride was also executed. Hanna went on hunger strike and was quickly released by a British government mindful of her international profile. She was elected as a Sinn Fein councillor in the 1920 local elections, a limited female franchise having been introduced by the Westminster Parliament in 1918. She vehemently opposed the Treaty that established the Free State. During the civil war she was sent by Eamon de Valera on a second speaking tour of the United States to campaign against Partition. In September 1923 she was dispatched by de Valera to the League of Nations where she called on member countries to reject Free State membership. The response of the Free State to its female enemies was at once deeply misogynist but also a bitter fruit of the civil war.

In 1926, along with Markievicz, Clarke and Margaret Pearse, the mother of Patrick Pearse, she became a member of the founding executive of de Valera's Fianna Fáil party. She resigned from the party soon after when Fianna Fáil determined to participate in the Dáil and, in effect, accept the Free State status quo. After 1926 she aligned herself with radical Republicans including Peadar O'Donnell. She became an assistant editor of *An Phoblacht*. She was imprisoned in 1933 for a month in Northern Ireland for giving a public speech on behalf of Republican prisoners. She trenchantly opposed the 1937 Constitution introduced by de Valera. She stood unsuccessfully in the 1943 general election and received only a minute percentage of the female vote.

However, according to the historian Diarmaid Ferriter, she dazzled the later generations of Irish feminists who wrote about her.[2] One of her three female biographers, Margaret Ward, describes her as the most significant of all Irish feminists who fought for women's rights to equality before, during and after the war of independence.[3] But she fostered schisms within Irish feminism that excluded Unionist women and non-militants. She pursued her activism 'with an unremitting defiance that several times captured world headlines'.[4] A photograph of her in *The San Francisco Chronicle* in 1938 carried the caption 'Mrs Hanna Sheehy Skeffington excels at being a rebel'. The accompanying article described her as a woman who could make 'strong men and their governments shudder'. It also described her as willing to talk about Clark Gable as well as about Irish freedom.[5]

Home rule for women

In 1866 a petition seeking female suffrage was presented to the House of Commons by John Stuart Mill. It included the signatures of twenty-five Irish women including Anna Haslam who went on to found the first suffrage society in Dublin in 1876. In 1870 the first women suffrage bill passed its second reading in the House of Commons but was blocked by the Liberal Government. In 1875 another such bill was defeated by only a narrow majority.[6] Most of the initial forty-three members of the Dublin Women's Suffrage Association were Quakers like Haslam. By 1911 membership of what became, after a few name changes, the Irish Women's Suffrage and Local Government Association (IWSLGA) peaked at 647.[7]

The first actual suffrage society in Ireland was founded in 1871 by Isabella Tod in Belfast. Tod initially campaigned to promote the secondary and university education of women.[8] In 1867 she presented a paper titled *Advanced education for girls of the upper and middle classes*.[9] In 1874 she published another pamphlet, *On the Education of Girls of the Middle Class*.[10] She played a leading part in the climate of reform that enabled some well-to-do women of Hanna's generation to attend university. With Anna Haslam she campaigned for the repeal of the Contagious Disease Acts of 1864, 1866 and 1869 which permitted the compulsory inspection of prostitutes for venereal disease. The Acts applied solely to women, leaving the soldiers these were designed to protect unhindered. A successful campaign of opposition was motivated by unease about civil liberties, anger about double standards and concern that the Acts licensed vice. In 1871 Tod founded the Northern Ireland Society for Women's Suffrage. Her greatest success was winning a fourteen-year campaign that extended the municipal franchise to some women in Belfast under an 1887 Act concerned with drainage plans for the city.[11] She was founding member of the Belfast Women's Temperance Association. In 1886 Tod organised a protest against the first Home Rule Bill and founded a Liberal Women's Unionist Association. She argued that Ulster should become a separate jurisdiction with some freedom from the Home Rule Parliament that seemed a real possibility before the fall of Charles Stewart Parnell.[12]

Parnell's sister Anna, founder of the Ladies Irish Land League, would have been a more obvious role model for Sheehy Skeffington given her family political history. The Land League was founded in 1881 when Parnell and other male leaders of the Land League were imprisoned. It briefly took over much of the day to day running of the organisation.[13] Within a year some 400 short-lived branches had been set up around Ireland. Michael Davitt, who supported its formation, wrote that 'the idea was laughed at by all' and vehemently opposed by Charles Stewart Parnell and John Dillon as a 'dangerous experiment'.[14] Anna Parnell in her posthumously-published *The Tale of a Great Sham* described a climate of hostility towards the Ladies Land League by Land League men that 'increased instead of diminishing over time'.[15]

Hanna and her sisters grew up in a socially ambitious family around leading members of the Catholic intelligentsia. She was part of the small elite of Irish women who benefited from expanded Catholic access to university education in the wake of the Royal University of Ireland Act of 1878. During the last quarter of the nineteenth century educational opportunities for middle-class women had improved considerably. She was an excellent student with a particular aptitude for languages. She received her BA degree from the Royal University of Ireland in 1899. During her student years she travelled several times to Germany and France. In 1902 she attained a first class honours MA.[16] James Joyce as a youth was a regular visitor to Sunday evening soirées at the Sheehy home, a four-storey house just off Mountjoy Square. Other socially respectable well-to-do Catholic nationalists lived nearby. Various Sheehys found their way into *Ulysses* and *Stephen Hero*. Joyce got a rave review in *The Freeman's Journal* for his performance as Geoffrey Fortescue, 'An Adventurer' in a 1901 performance of a one-act 'comedy' written by Margaret and Hanna Sheehy. In *Cupid's Confidante* Eva, a young woman in possession of a fortune, must choose between two suitors that, she worries, only care for her riches and her rank. Dick, whom she chooses in the end, vows to go to Africa to make his fortune in order to be worthy of her. She begs him to wait until she is able to go with him. The daughters of the Home Rule elite were also daughters of an Empire.[17] Mary Sheehy married Tom Kettle, the great hope of the Irish Party. Kettle was killed whilst serving on the Western Front a few weeks after the Easter Rising. Katherine Sheehy married Francis Cruise O'Brien.

Francis 'Frank' Skeffington, the second cleverest man at University College Dublin, as Joyce put it, produced a pamphlet with him in 1901 consisting of two articles that had been rejected by a University College Dublin magazine.[18] Joyce's 'The Day of the Rabblement' condemned the parochialism of Irish theatre. Skeffington's 'A Forgotten Aspect of the University Question' argued that female students should have equal status to men. Skeffington resigned in 1904 as Registrar of University College Dublin because it refused to admit female students on the same terms as men. Joyce called him the 'hairy Jaysus'. Frank had embraced vegetarianism, pacifism and feminism and grew a beard. When Frank took his wife's surname he invoked the ire of his own father for appearing as a Sheehy (and not as a Skeffington) in Thom's Directory, which listed significant landowners, civil servants, churchmen, military officers and other establishment people in Ireland.[19]

Frank wrote a florid novel, *In Dark and Evil Days*, which eulogised the 1798 Rebellion in Wexford. It was serialised anonymously and not published under his own name until 1936.[20] A less pacifist and feminist novel would be hard to imagine for all that Hanna's foreword listed his credentials on both scores. But it went to show how even pacifists and feminists were steeped in the pugnacious nationalist culture of their time. Esmond, the hero of *In Dark and Evil Days*, wants nothing to with the United Irishmen although his fiancée Dora urges him to join the rebellion. He is provoked into joining the rebels by the murder of his parents by British soldiers. He kills Dora, as he had promised to do, so as to prevent her being raped – a fate worse than death! He swears vengeance and slays many English soldiers including, in a swordfight, Colonel Kingsborough who was responsible for the murder of his family. The scenario resembles somewhat that of Mel Gibson's film *The Patriot* (2000). A man who wants peace joins his neighbours in rebellion when provoked beyond endurance into an orgy of justifiable violence. After achieving his vengeance Esmond resolves to martyr himself for Ireland. He urges his brother-in-law to raise up a race of Irish Americans to hate the Saxon, to revere Ireland as their wronged mother and to live to avenge these wrongs. John Mitchel would surely have approved. Esmond dies heroically alongside his servant Dan whose final mawkish words are: 'Sure it's grand to be dyin' for the sake of the oul' sod!'[21]

Sheehy Skeffington had, by her own account, given female suffrage little or no thought before becoming a university student and meeting her future husband. In her *Reminiscences of an Irish Suffragette* she described joining Anna Haslam's IWSLGA after being introduced to John Stuart Mill's *Subjection of Women* by Frank.[22] She came to prominence in 1908 as co-founder and leader of the IWFL. Irish suffragists were predominantly middle class or upper middle class and 'solidarity with their working class sisters was never a reality'.[23] In December 1913 *The Irish Citizen* carried an advertisement for an annual suffrage conference at the Rotunda Concert Rooms in Dublin. Admission was two shillings and sixpence with tickets for a debate with anti-suffragettes costing an additional one or two shillings. An

Ibsen play put on as a conference entertainment cost two shillings and sixpence. Suffragists were urged to do all their shopping for presents at the conference Christmas fair – fancy articles, books, turkeys and suffragist toys.[24] Excluding any Christmas shopping this came to about a week's wages for some women in Dublin. *The Irish Citizen* published articles that stated that some women were earning as little as four shillings a week, though a forewoman might get ten shillings a week and a typist twelve shillings and sixpence.[25] The first issue of *The Irish Citizen* published a suffragist's catechism which accepted that votes for women should be restricted along class lines on the same principle applied to men:

> What do suffragists want?
> Votes for women.
> What does that mean?
> That women should be allowed to vote at the elections of members of Parliament, just the same as the men are.
> Does that mean you want every woman to have a vote?
> No
> Why not?
> Because every man has not got a vote. Men have to qualify for the vote in certain ways – they have to be owners or occupiers of certain property, or lodgers in rooms of a certain value. What we ask is that women who qualify in the same way should have the same right to vote as the men who qualify.[26]

On such criteria members of the IWFL would be entitled to vote but not their servants. As things stood Irishwomen were entitled to vote subject to property qualifications in local elections under the Local Government (Ireland) Act 1898. In the 1909 election thirty-one women were elected as councillors. Further rights to vote in local elections followed in 1911.

Breaking glass

The Irish Parliamentary Party (IPP) saw the suffrage question as a threat to Home Rule which depended on its alliance with the Liberal Party. The Liberal Prime Minister Herbert Asquith had threatened to resign if women became enfranchised. Fearing that if Asquith's government fell Home Rule would also, supporters of the suffragists in the IPP such as Hanna's brother-in-law Tom Kettle toed the party line. But many senior IPP figures opposed suffrage on principle. Sheehy Skeffington in her *Reminiscences* recalled John Dillon stating that women's suffrage would be the ruin of Western civilisation ('It will destroy the home, challenge the headship of man, laid down by God. It may come in your time – I hope not in mine!').[27] Not one IPP member of Parliament supported the 1912 suffrage bill, not even those who were on the cross party committee that drafted it. As she put it some years later:

> Here were good Irish rebels, many of them broken in to national revolt, with all the slogans of Irish revolution and its arsenal of weapons – Boycott, Plan of Campaign, Land for the People, and so on, the creators of obstruction in Parliament – yet at the whisper of Votes for Women many changed to extreme Tories or time-servers who urged us women to wait till freedom for men was won.[28]

Suffragists were to split on the Home Rule question. In an account of a mass meeting between various factions on 1 June 1912 in *The Irish Citizen* Hanna tried to paper over the cracks:

> Some weeks ago – when, in fact, we first learned that we were excluded from the Home Rule Bill – the Irish Women's Franchise League conceived the thought of rallying all Irish suffragists under a common standard to voice our common demand. Suffrage societies and other women's organisations throughout the length and breadth of Ireland instantly responded. Constitutional joined militant – for the day at least; Unionist was allied to Nationalist, Party claims (so dear to our loyal women) were for once subordinated to sex principle.[29]

The meeting passed a resolution calling on the Government to amend the Home Rule Bill to include a woman's right to vote. Copies were circulated to all the Irish MPs to no avail. The IPP voted as a man to exclude the Votes for Women clause. The IWFL turned to militant protest. On 13 June 1912 eight women were arrested for breaking the windows of various public buildings including the Custom House, the GPO and, in Hanna's case, Dublin Castle for which she was sentenced to three months' imprisonment.[30] *The Irish Citizen* published a cartoon of a suffragist exuberantly breaking a window with a hammer (the punch line – 'Nothing for their Panes').[31] Between 1912 and the beginning of the Great War in August 1914 thirty-three convictions were secured in Ireland against suffragists, mostly involving damage to government property.[32] As recollected by Hanna:

> Educated, articulate rowdyism (as they would call it) from the comfortable classes, from respectability dressed women, stupefied them . . . Militancy, required a willingness to damage government property, to go to jail, and, more usually, to meet hecklers on their own ground and to be capable of facing down 'bombardments of rotten eggs, over-ripe tomatoes, bags of flour, stinking chemicals' with good humour.[33]

'Suffs', she recalled with more than a little nostalgia, 'were good sports'.[34] A 1913 *Irish Citizen* article by Hanna described a suffragist tour of Longford,

Leitrim and Roscommon, places where 'no suffrage speaker had ever penetrated'. In Longford the Bishop used his influence to prevent the hiring of a hall. It did not help that the local newspaper was owned by an MP, 'a pronounced anti' who had been heckled a few weeks beforehand. But for all that the Longford meeting was pronounced a success ('a crowded hall, an enthusiastic meeting. Many converts who had come to jeer remained to join'). In Carrick an attempt to hold a meeting outdoors was interrupted by a 'howling, raging mob, led by a drunken virago'. The Canon had denounced them at first Mass on the previous Sunday. In Boyle the local paper printed an advertisement that falsely declared that the meeting was cancelled. Shopkeepers were bullied to withdraw posters from their windows. The meeting was interrupted by some boys who scattered red pepper and broke yards of glass. Afterwards rival factions used the occasion for a fight, during which they rolled in the mud on the main street. Five police baton charges took place. One of the combatants declared the next day: 'Shure, we hadn't such a grand time since the Parnell split.'[35]

In print Sheehy Skeffington exulted in such rowdyism. A 1912 article 'penned on the eve of prison' in *The Irish Review*, argued that stone and the shillelagh had an honoured place in the armoury of Irish argument. Women gathered aprons and stockings full of shards, glass and flints to hurl at the Williamites during the siege of Limerick and Tipperary. Stone-throwers were proverbial in Land League times. 'No doubt', she added in an anti-Unionist aside, 'the followers of Sir Edward Carson, when preparing the last ditch, will not neglect to stock this homely ammunition'. 'We women of a younger generation', she declared, 'are somewhat in a hurry for reform, why, if it falls asleep at its post, we shall wake it with a stick'.[36]

When Asquith visited Dublin in July 1912 he encountered a number of suffragist demonstrations. A party of women with a megaphone and votes for women placards went out in a boat to meet the ship he arrived on. Frank disguised himself as a clergyman in order to get into the Theatre Royal where Asquith was due to share a platform with John Redmond. When he heckled the Prime Minister demanding votes for women he was ejected. Three English members of the Women's Social and Political Union (WSPU) had followed Asquith to Dublin. One of them threw a hatchet into the Prime Minister's carriage ('it was blunt and meant symbolically', according to Hanna in her *Reminiscences*. 'It skimmed between Asquith and Redmond and grazed the latter's ear'). The Englishwomen also tried to burn down the Theatre Royal the day before the event by setting fire to some curtains. They also planted some kind of bomb which went off in the theatre a few minutes later. When arrested they were found to have explosives in their lodgings.[37]

Not only did the militancy of the IWFL pale in comparison to that of their English sisters, so too was their treatment by the authorities milder. Mary Leigh and Gladys Evans, the women who attacked Asquith were sentenced to five years' hard labour. They went on hunger strike. In solidarity Hanna and other IWFL women in Mountjoy also went on hunger strike.

The authorities were loath to force feed the Irishwomen and treated them with kid gloves.[38] Only when they were released were the Englishwomen subjected to force feeding. Privately, Hanna had disapproved of the WSPU attacks on Asquith. She 'deplored the fact that they had not left the heckling to the Irishwomen'.[39] Connections with the WSPU and the influence of English militants were used as sticks to beat the IWFL with by its Home Ruler opponents. The IWFL was accused of promoting alien ideas. *The Irish Citizen* retorted that the IWFL represented the true Land League and Fenian spirit that the IPP had abandoned.

Women at war with women

Suffragists in the pages of *The Irish Citizen* variously expounded liberal theories of equality, socialism and presumptions that women were morally superior to men. Some wanted a fundamentally different type of social system where the 'womanly virtues' of peace, love and cooperation would replace war, hate and competition.[40] Some were nationalists, others internationalists and many others were Unionists. In 1909 a branch of the Conservative and Unionist Suffrage Association was founded in Belfast – subsequently renamed as The Irish Women's Suffrage Society. By 1913 fifteen suffrage groups from around the country had affiliated to the non-militant Irish Women's Suffrage Federation including several from the North: Belfast, Armagh, Portrush, Derry, Bushmills, Lisburn and Warrenpoint.[41] In Ulster in 1912 some 218,806 men signed the Ulster Covenant against Home Rule. At the instigation of the Ulster Women's Unionist Council 228,991 women signed a similarly worded declaration.[42] In September 1913 the leadership of the Unionist Party let it be known that women would be given the franchise under their plans for a provisional government in Ulster. This vague pledge was hardly a concession to suffragists but rather an acknowledgement of the importance of women within Unionism.[43]

Nationalism also competed successfully with feminism for women's political loyalties. Cumann na mBan (the women's club or party) was founded in April 1914. It 'pledged to work for the establishment of an Irish Republic'. Some members were suffragists but many like Markievicz and Gonne McBride were not.[44] The outbreak of the First World War further undermined suffragism in Ireland and Britain. Suffragists, Hanna argued, had a duty to preach peace, sanity and votes for women, to direct their guns against the war-mongering government rather than the Germans.[45] An editorial by Frank in *The Irish Citizen* blamed 'the anti-feminist canker' in the heart of modern civilisation for the war. Those who, yesterday, were horror stricken at the destruction of a stained glass window were contemplating 'without protest and in some cases with joy' the inevitable loss of millions of human lives.[46]

However, the WSPU became 'violently patriotic' and agreed to suspend its suffragist activism for the duration of the war.[47] The Irish Women's

Suffrage Federation also decided to suspend active suffrage propaganda once war was declared, a policy that drove some members to resign, most notably Mary MacSwiney who argued in *The Irish Citizen* that most in the league were 'Brits first, suffragists second and Irishwomen perhaps a bad third'.[48] The IWSLGA got involved in fundraising on behalf of Belgian refugees and in charitable work aimed at relieving distress caused by the war. In an acerbic article 'The Duty of Suffragists' Sheehy Skeffington urged women to resist the advice of newspapers to knit soft woollen comforters for departing soldiers or to patch up the shattered victims of machine guns and torpedoes. Taking up war work, she argued, could only lead to the kind of betrayal that occurred at the hands of the Home Rule movement in 1912. But women, she insisted, had also betrayed themselves:

> At every crisis suffragists must be alive to insidious dangers that threaten to swamp the cause. War is the favourite method employed by governments hard pressed at home and eager to shelve their responsibilities. The rock of party politics on which so many suffragists in the past suffered shipwreck they now, thanks chiefly to the militants, have learned to avoid. We smile now when we are told to put the needs of the party first, not to embarrass the Government or Home Rule of the Union by pressing our claims . . . We know by bitter experience that the women who heed these cries are traitors to their cause, and that it is their supineness which is largely responsible for our voteless condition.[49]

Prior to the 1916 Rising Sheehy Skeffington opposed violence as a means to political ends. She hardly viewed breaking the windows of government buildings in such terms. However, following the murder of her husband she identified intensely with the executed leaders of the Easter Rising, particularly with James Connolly who had been a supporter of the IWFL. Her eulogy to them in the September 1916 edition of *The Irish Citizen* declared that the Irish Volunteers and Citizen Army were Suffragists almost to a man and that women prominent in the movement were all convinced and practical exponents of the doctrine of equality of the sexes.[50] Her 1917 pamphlet *British Militarism as I have known it* described how on the first day of the Rising Frank had tried to help the wounded and to organise a civic police to protect the city from looting. He was arrested on the second evening and used as a hostage by Captain Bowen-Colthurst on a patrol through Rathmines, where he witnessed Bowen-Colthurst shooting an unarmed youth. The following morning Bowen-Colhurst murdered Frank at Portobello Barracks along with two Unionist journalists who had been arrested during the patrol. When the incident was reported to Dublin Castle an order was given to bury the bodies without an autopsy or giving any information to relatives. Bowen-Colhurst was not reprimanded but was allowed to conduct a raid on the Sheehy Skeffington house which was ransacked whilst Hanna was at home with her son. The facts came to light when a British officer, Sir Francis Vane, 'horrified at the indifference of Dublin Castle' to the murders committed by Bowen-Colhurst, went to London to report these directly to the War Office. Following a meeting with Lord Kitchener Bowen-Colhurst's arrest was ordered. Vane was subsequently dismissed from his post and Bowen-Colhurst was court-martialled and found to be insane. Her pamphlet depicted the killings as part of 'an organised pogram' involving the deaths of more than fifty unarmed prisoners and civilians by soldiers during Easter Week. By contrast she described all military actions by the rebels as justified:

I knew the Irish Republican leaders, and am proud to call Connolly, Pearse, MacDonagh, Plunket, O'Rahilly and others friends – proud to have known them and had their friendship. They fought a clean fight against terrible odds – and terrible was the price they had to pay. They were filled with high idealism. They had banks, factories, the General Post Office, the Four Courts, their enemies' strongholds, for days in their keeping, yet bankers, merchants and others testified as to the scrupulous way in which their stock was guarded. A poet A. E. said,

'Your dream, not mine,
And yet the thought, for this you fell,
Turns all life's water into wine.'

Their proclamation gave equal citizenship to women, beating all records, except that of the Russian Revolutionists, and their revolution came later.[51]

Their dream became hers. Her emotional identification with the executed leaders of the Rising was intense. She depicted her pacifist husband as a martyr to the Irish Republic they proclaimed. This Republic had promised to fully include women as citizens. In a 1922 article in *The Irish World* she recalled the Rising as 'something glorious'. She evoked the Tricolour as a symbol that portrayed Connolly, Pearse and her husband as dying in the same breath for the same cause. With Connolly's death 'labour was shot down because it dared to be discontented with bad housing and miserable wages'. Pearse the idealist surrendered to superior forces to save his countrymen and was shot down because he 'dared to dream greater dreams than were allowed to small nationalities'. Frank was shot down by a lunatic 'because he got in the way of militarism'. Together their deaths stood for 'Labour, Idealism and Pacifism.'[52] In a 1928 article (one of many) that eulogised Constance Markievicz as Ireland's Joan of Arc she proclaimed that 'our best die on the scaffold, in exile, in prison cell, in action on the battlefield, in dreary hospital ward, of broken hearts'.[53]

The Irish Citizen folded in 1920, having gone from a weekly, to a monthly and finally to a quarterly publication. Writing in the February 1920 edition, Hanna described its decline as a symptom of the waning of the women's movement. She identified two reasons. The Representation of the People Act 1918 gave the right to vote in parliamentary elections to women of thirty years of age and over, who were householders, the wives of householders, were possessed of a five-pound qualification or were graduates. The result was that middle-class women, if not most Irishwomen, had the franchise. Secondly, and crucially in her case, 'the national struggle had come to overshadow all else'.[54]

Enemy of the Free State

Free State leaders proved more hostile to the demands of women activists than the Home Rulers had been a decade earlier. Sheehy Skeffington and other Republican women picked the losing side in a bitter civil war and suffered politically for this. P. S. O'Hegarty's pro-Free State polemic *The Victory of Sinn Fein* (1924) described them as 'unlovely, destructive-minded, arid begetters of violence, both physical violence and mental violence', a conclusion according to O'Hegarty, 'that was shared by Cosgrave's entire cabinet'.[55] All six female members of the Dail voted against the Treaty including Mary MacSwiney, whose brother Terence had died on hunger strike during the war of independence, Margaret Pearse, Kathleen Clarke and Constance Markievicz. In a chapter entitled 'The Furies', O'Hegarty wrote that in the worst phases of the war: 'Dublin was full of hysterical women, living on excitement, enjoying themselves in the thought of ambushes and *stunts*.'[56] Elsewhere in the book he described the women of Sinn Fein as implacable and irrational upholders of death and destruction:

> To them the Truce was nothing but a trick played upon the British, and to them peace was a loveless thing, and no life so good as the life of war. They became practically unsexed, their mother's milk blackened to make gunpowder, their minds working on nothing save hate and blood.[57]

Anti-Treaty activism by women – in this Hanna was a prominent propagandist – engendered a palpable misogyny amongst Free State leaders. Kevin O'Higgins' eulogy at Michael Collins' funeral in August 1922 berated 'the fanatics and doctrinaires and pseudo-intellectuals (a list for him that included her) who knew they were menacing the life of the nation by setting it an impossible task'.[58] Before, during and after the civil war Hanna wrote vitriolic anti-Free State columns for *The Irish World*. The claims she made as to where women stood mirrored those of O'Hegarty:

> There are families in Ireland in which wives, daughters and sisters are in one camp (Republican) and their men-folk in the other (Free State). This difference of opinion along sex lines is significant. As Michael Davitt said

of the women in the land war of the 80's: 'Women are more uncompromising than men.'[59]

In March 1922 Arthur Griffith rebuffed a delegation of women including Hanna that had sought to extend the franchise to women under thirty years, claiming that their real purpose was 'queer the pitch of the Treaty'.[60] Women, if they could vote would, she hoped, bring down the Free State. She told her Irish-American readers that the women deputies who voted in the Dail against the Treaty 'were typical of Irish womanhood generally' but in effect she argued that the only women whose views mattered were Republican women ('I exclude, of course, loyalist women and others who are not Sinn Feiners. Almost all the women I know in the movement are against the Treaty'). Their organisation Cumann na mBan, she informed her readers, had rejected it by more than seven to one.[61]

Article after article throughout 1922 poured vitriol on what she called the 'Freak State' (Northern Ireland was 'Carsonia').[62] One in April described the Free State as holding Ireland for its imperial masters.[63] In May she inferred that a civil war was justified against the so-called Free State that had subverted the Republic.[64] A June article declared that there could be no truce that accepted the Free State, no election either. Seats in the Dail, she wrote, 'are nothing to us . . . The Republic is everything. A nation's (like an individual's) honour is above even a nation's life'. Irrespective of any election outcome, she declared the Treaty could not be accepted by true Republicans.[65] An August 1922 article 'Ireland's Military Dictatorship' declared that the Irish Republic was 'in the grip of a double tyranny, the tyranny of Irishmen reinforcing the foreign invader'.[66] In another August 1922 article she declared that an indefinite guerrilla war against the Free State was justified.[67] A notebook found in her papers from this period contained an unpublished alphabet where 'A' was 'for the Army who never asked for pay./Fighting for Ireland's cause: Up the I.R.A!' and 'F' was for the 'so-called Free state that England gladly gave/That grants to Irish freemen the status of a slave.'[68]

Various 1922 articles in *The Irish World* directed jibes at Unionist women and a whiff of anti-Semitism against the enemies of the Republic. An April article claimed that the Free State had given a contract for army uniforms to Jewish firms using a turn of phrase ('and those are being made by sweated labour') employed in a 1904 Dublin Trades' Union campaign against Jewish tailors in Dublin.[69] A May article disparaged thrifty Unionist or Free State housewives ('for now the terms are sadly synonymous') who engaged in panic buying of groceries around the anniversary of the 1916 Rising, out of fear of some commemorative outbreak of violence.[70] The tone of this propaganda aimed at Americans was very different from that of her earlier writings in *The Irish Citizen* and for Irish audiences more generally.

Pre-independence legislation in 1919 had extended the duty of serving on juries to women as well as men. This was undermined by a 1924 Act that permitted women to exempt themselves from jury duty. Another bill introduced by Minister of Justice Kevin O'Higgins in 1927 sought to remove the right of women to serve on juries. The main rationale put forward was an administrative one – the chance to avoid the expense of maintaining a register of women willing to serve and of providing separate accommodation for women jurors. O'Higgins claimed that most women were unwilling – noting that fewer than forty had served as jurors in 1925 – but the 1924 Act was most likely an explanation for this low number. He also argued that women should be spared from extremely unpleasant cases 'of indecent assault, of rape, and occasionally, of sodomy', matters that 'one would not like to discuss with feminine members of one's own family'.[71] However, these were the very cases *The Irish Citizen* had repeatedly argued that would receive more balanced consideration if women were included on juries. O'Higgins's argument was, according to one contemporary (male) critic, 'sentimentality that did duty to the Victorian age' and was designed to mask a dislike of activist women.[72]

Many articles in *The Irish Citizen* emphasised that the representation of women on juries, in the legal profession and in the judiciary was necessary to ensure the fair treatment of women. A recurring theme concerned how the courts did not take seriously cases of child abuse and wife beating because no women participated in the deliberation of these.[73] A July 1914 article – part of a campaign to monitor court cases involving sexual offences against young girls – emphasised the need to hear the woman's point of view in the courts where judges saw 'the natural and irresistible impulses animating the man' as mitigating circumstances in their rulings.[74] A 1915 article by the same author argued for women jurors, lawyers and judges ('A man who beats his wife, or outrages a child, answers to men alone for his crimes.')[75] A June 1915 article reported on a 'seduction case' where the victim, a shop girl, died in childbirth, having concealed her pregnancy. The article emphasised a lack of empathy by the male court and expressed the hope that in brighter days to come, there might be women jurors, women counsel and women judges too.[76] O'Higgins argued to the deputation that included Sheehy Skeffington that women in certain cases would be loath to convict.[77] However, a recurring argument in *The Irish Citizen* was that sentences for offences against women and children were too lenient. This was illustrated in the May 1919 issue of *The Irish Citizen*:

> Recently in the Dublin Courts the foreman of a jury declared that the list of criminal offences was very light, there being only one 'light' offence on the calendar, 'that of indecent assault upon a child.' Unfortunately this mentality is by no means uncommon both in juries and on the bench. We believe that men as a rule are disposed to be over lenient to such offences, which to women are far more revolting than attacks upon property. It is but another instance of the need for women lawyers, women jurors, women on the bench.[78]

A September 1919 article, 'Wife-Beating', identified a marked tendency by magistrates to let the aggressor off with a light fine or a very short prison sentence; the reason usually given was that the wife and family could not live without his earnings. It made the case for fit punishment in such cases – 'a long term of hard labour' – with, if necessary, the maintenance of the family from public funds.[79] Such arguments were dismissed by O'Higgins as a 'minority demand' from 'self-appointed spokeswomen'.[80] Whatever social and political capital they had derived from their family origins, social class and years of prominent activism quickly evaporated in the post-civil war Free State.

No country for old women

Under de Valera overt misogyny was succeeded by a heavy blanket of paternalism. Hanna was under no allusions about his conservatism even when she became a founding member of Fianna Fáil. In an article about the 1937 Constitution she described his 'mawkish distrust of women'. He was the only commander during the 1916 Rising, she added, who refused the help of women, whereas James Connolly and his Citizen Army would have welcomed women as soldiers had they been so minded. No woman appeared to have been consulted on the wording of the constitution.[81] By contrast, de Valera consulted the Jesuits at length on its wording.[82] Writing in a style often used by Connolly, when attributing to the working class demands he wished they would make, Sheehy Skeffington declared that de Valera was 'up against the entire body of organised women' and that never before had women been so organised as now when they were faced with Fascist proposals endangering their livelihood, cutting away their rights as human beings. Women, she hoped, would set up their own political party.[83] But there was no evidence that the small groups of educated organised women alongside which she campaigned, most notably the Woman Graduates' Association, could claim the backing of a significant proportion of Irish women.

In 1932 a ban on the employment of married women in the civil service was introduced and this was extended to one against the employment of married women as primary school teachers in 1934, an area where they had traditionally worked. The Conditions of Employment Act (1936) introduced by Minister for Industry and Commerce Sean Lemass – the portfolio first held by Constance Markievicz – gave the state various powers to limit the numbers of women employed in any branch of industry in order to protect male employment. At a protest meeting against the bill Hanna described Lemass's actions as those of a fascist dictator.

The marriage ban applied mainly to women's white collar work, affecting educated women of Hanna's social class – she had worked throughout her life as a teacher – to a far greater extent than industrial or service occupations where women were mostly employed. The powers to prevent women working in industry were never used. Just under half of the unmarried women in the Free State engaged in paid employment in 1926 (48.6 per cent) and just over half in 1936 (53.3 per cent) but the percentage of married women engaged in paid employment remained the same at just a little over one in twenty (5.6 per cent) in 1926 and 1936. However, 59 per cent of additional jobs created in manufacturing industries between 1926 and 1936 (virtually all created in that ten-year period) went to women. The overall percentage of women in manufacturing rose during that period from 26.6 per cent to 31.3 per cent.[84] Partly because it affected relatively few women the marriage ban did not prompt widespread political opposition from Irishwomen. Restrictions on married women were lifted in many countries during the 1950s when these began to experience labour shortages. However, in Ireland these persisted until the 1970s with the exception of primary teachers where the marriage bar was lifted in 1957. Discrimination in employment on the basis of gender became illegal in Ireland in 1973.

In April 1932 the newly elected de Valera delivered the eulogy at Margaret Pearse's funeral that praised her modesty and her motherly sacrifice in giving her sons for Ireland. It was what he wished for all Irish mothers: to produce good nationalist sons whilst staying out of the public arena themselves, unless exceptional circumstances required them to fulfil the work of their menfolk.[85] In a 1927 article Sheehy Skeffington wrote that the women favoured by the party machines tended to be the sisters, wives, widows or mothers of politicians, and were chosen no doubt on what men consider a 'safe' principle, because men are still afraid of 'the independent woman, who may turn out to be a feminist rather than a party henchwoman'.[86] Margaret Pearse, it could well be argued, was elected to the Dail as a proxy for her dead son. Other revolutionary women including Kathleen Clarke and Maud Gonne MacBride also owed their political status to their widow's weeds and so too, to a considerable extent, did Sheehy Skeffington. But none of this was to deny – as de Valera was intent on doing – the contribution women had made to the 1916 Rising and the war of independence. In 1932 she recalled de Valera's attempt five years earlier to depict Constance Markievicz in a similar feminine light. But Markievicz had been a combatant in 1916, a lieutenant in Connolly's Citizen's Army who held out fighting until after the surrender at the GPO. In recalling this Hanna contrasted Connolly and de Valera:

> To one, woman was an equal, a comrade; to the other, a sheltered being, withdrawn to the domestic hearth, shrinking from public life. Each viewpoint has its exponents, but none will deny the self-evident fact that Constance Markievicz, Ireland's Joan of Arc, belongs in the former category.[87]

In 1919 Markievicz became the first female MP elected in the British Isles. She was the first woman to become a cabinet minister, serving as Minister for Labour from April 1919 to January 1922. It was not until 1979 that another woman, Máire Geoghegan-Quinn, was appointed as an Irish government minister.

Sheehy Skeffington was one of four women affiliated to the WSPU who stood as independent candidates in the 1943 general election. Their platform included 'Equal pay for Equal Work', 'Equal Opportunities for women' and the removal of the marriage bar. In her account of the election in *The Bell* she described how she had built her campaign on James Connolly's imagined Republic ('which included feminism'). Her election manifesto declared that 'under the 1916 Proclamation Irish women were given equal citizenship, equal rights and equal opportunities, and subsequent constitutions have filched these, or smothered them in mere "empty formulae" '. It also emphasised her die-hard Republicanism:

> Nationally I stand for the complete independence of Ireland and for the abolition of partition which has dismembered our country. My attitude towards Ireland's right to unfettered nationhood is unchanged and unchangeable.[88]

She stood in the South Dublin constituency that she had represented twice as a Sinn Fein councillor.[89] She received just 917 first preferences in a seven-seat constituency that had 42,000 women on the electoral register; 16,000 first preferences went to Sean Lemass, enough to carry three other Fianna Fáil candidates with him. Three women were re-elected to the Dail in 1943. All three were the widows of former TDs. Irish women, she concluded, were not yet sufficiently educated politically to vote for women. For this she blamed the political parties that disregarded them except as mere voting conveniences. Certain blame also attached to the women themselves, especially those smug ones who declared that they had no interest in politics. She envisaged a long slow process of gradual penetration of party politics by women and of educating public opinion and ended her last significant publication by describing the 1943 campaign as a seed buried beneath the snow, submerged but still living, ready to germinate.

CHAPTER ELEVEN

Jeremiah Newman and Catholic decline

Jeremiah Newman (1926–95) had a keen sense of the impending decline of Irish Catholicism and waged a defensive intellectual war against this for more than four decades. As a university professor and president he exerted perhaps more influence than his more famous namesake John Henry Newman ever did. The *Dictionary of Irish Biography* recalls him as a superb university administrator who oversaw the transition of Maynooth from a seminary into a university with science and arts faculties. As Bishop of Limerick (from 1974) 'he was the most outspoken, controversial, conservative member of the hierarchy', a pro-nuclear Cold War warrior and strong supporter of the United States against Bishop Éamon Casey's call on the Irish government to break off diplomatic relations with the US over its policy in Central America. The entry also described him as a connoisseur of good food and wine before noting that illnesses had incapacitated him in his final years.[1] It seems that Newman's lifelong intellectual battles against secularism at some stage became joined by one against alcoholism. Various Irish media articles reported that he travelled in July 1994 to the United States for treatment. At his requiem mass Cardinal Cathal Daly described Newman as having been in some ways a troubled man:

> For a person of outstanding intellectual ability, he seemed to have a strange sense of inadequacy. This may have bought him his share of suffering, although I believe on the whole he was a happy man. . . . And for one who was so loveable, he seemed to have difficulties in believing that others respected and admired him. This may have engendered a certain sense of insecurity, although unjustified in the light of his many great qualities and achievements.[2]

In a 1974 interview in the *Limerick Leader* he described himself as 'a little bit of a loner, always studying and writing books'. His body of work includes more than twenty written across four decades. In 1985, when Catholic bishops were no longer automatically treated with reverence, a *Magill* magazine profile called him the 'Mullah of Limerick' (a nickname first pinned on him by Conor Cruise O'Brien), perceived in liberal Dublin circles to be on the right of Genghis Khan.[3] His obituary in the *Irish Times* described him as a firm believer in the right of the Catholic Church to intervene to influence civil laws governing both public and private morality and characterised him as a person who did not relate easily to people: 'Some felt he made himself more isolated in his bishop's palace than was necessary, believing that he had to perform the role of the aloof traditionalist bishop who must take the controversial stands he did in defence of the church because no one else would.' But he was described as 'surprisingly open to new ideas'; he could quote 'Germaine Greer as well as any feminist'.[4] His juxtaposition of hard-line conservativism with intellectual curiosity along with his prodigious output as a theologian, political philosopher and sociologist made Newman a distinctive protagonist in the battle to save Catholic Ireland. Most of his books addressed the consequences of modernisation, be it the social changes that were affecting Irish Catholicism or the secular ideas that challenged it throughout the modern world.

Jeremiah Newman was born and grew up in County Limerick, the only child of a village shopkeeper. The decline of Limerick villages and rural society later came to be the focus of his best-known sociological research. During the late 1940s he studied for the priesthood in Maynooth and was ordained there in 1950. A little over a year later, at the age of twenty-five, he was awarded a doctorate in Philosophy from the Catholic University of Louvain. He then spent a year reading sociology at Oxford whilst living in the Catholic Workers College, a well-trodden route for clerics handpicked by their superiors to hold professorships in Irish universities. He seems to have thoroughly enjoyed himself in Oxford. Free from exams he dabbled in 'social stuff': economics, sociology, anthropology and political philosophy; he already had his doctorate and recalled being 'full of himself', a champion 'like Cassius Clay'. He joined the Oxford branches of the Labour, Liberal and Conservative parties, became a member of the rationalist association and the 'very left wing' Peace Association which held meetings with the Communist Club. He also attended meetings of the Psychic Society. Newman – classically schooled in Plato, Aristotle, Saint Augustine, Aquinas, Descartes, Locke, Berkeley, Hume, Kant and Hegel – attended lectures by A. J. Ayer and Gilbert Ryle on the logical positivism that intellectually dominated Oxford.[5]

On his return from Oxford he applied unsuccessfully for the vacant Chair in Philosophy and Ethics at Maynooth and instead got a temporary job filling in for Cathal Daly, the future archbishop, teaching philosophy at Queens University Belfast. In October 1953 he was appointed Professor of Sociology at Maynooth. He became Vice-President of the university in 1967 and President a year later. Prior to 1968 the only lay students allowed into

Maynooth were those taking a teacher training course; under Newman's leadership the university opened its doors to the wider population. It was, he recalled in a 1974 interview, undergoing a crisis of declining vocations for the priesthood.[6] Tony Fahey, a former student who went on to become Professor of Social Policy at University College Dublin (UCD), recalls Newman's response to rumours that a ghost haunted a room at Maynooth where two seminarians had committed suicide. He declared that he would welcome any evidence of the supernatural.[7]

Tom Garvin, who went on to become Professor of Politics at UCD, recalls receiving a zero per cent mark for a Catholic Anthropology exam set and marked by Newman at the Institute of Public Administration in 1964. Newman in his lectures had sought to demonstrate the empirical validity of natural law understandings of social order. An example of this, addressed by Garvin in his exam script, was the near universality of monogamy in human societies. Newman had sought to demonstrate the empirical validity of the natural law through the relative rarity of polygamy and polyandry. Garvin offered an economic determinist explanation that caused Newman to fail him and to investigate (the exam scripts were anonymous) the name of the student whose soul was in mortal danger. Garvin posited that access to multiple partners by men might be a function of their wealth and that polyandry might be an outcome of poverty, occurring where diet was so poor that many women did not ovulate. On appeal an external examiner gave Garvin an honours grade.[8]

Newman for his part set out an analysis of the prevalence of monogamy, polygamy and polyandry in his 1971 book *Conscience Versus Law* which argued for the rehabilitation of natural law philosophy. He explained that Catholic moralists since Aquinas did not evaluate the purpose of human sexual intercourse from any actual study of human beings; they deduced moral teaching from general principles. There now existed greater knowledge about human sexuality and there was a need to consider changing material conditions such as the availability of contraception and concerns about overpopulation. Although relativity in morality could not be countenanced, what was moral – he gave the example of polygamy which under certain economic and social circumstances might be moral – depended to some extent on extrinsic circumstances.[9]

In Catholic Ireland, where until 1970 or so clerics dominated the teaching of the social sciences, Thomism, in essence the thought of Aristotle as interpreted by Aquinas, was taught as sociology and anthropology. Papal encyclicals such as *Rerum Novarum* (1891) and *Quadragesimo Anno* (1931) articulated natural law doctrine on the family and sexuality, the role of the state and the relationship between church and state. *Christus Rex*, the Irish journal of sociology edited by Newman, did not publish articles that did not conform to such Catholic doctrine. This included on much of the canon of secular Western sociology. From the 1970s it became no longer feasible to hope, as Newman did, for a recovery of natural law.

Newman was fascinated by social change, be it in rural Ireland, as expressed by beatniks and hippies, or the protest politics as manifested in university campuses after 1968. In a 1968 book *Race, Migration and Immigration* he examined theories of race, racial prejudice and discrimination in Britain and in the United States, racial segregation in the United States and the emergence of apartheid in South Africa and the 'White Australia' policy. Most of the chapters offered sociological or policy analysis aimed at understanding racism in order to oppose it. The conclusion addressed ethical issues from a Catholic perspective. Newman was unambiguously opposed to apartheid, racist immigration policies and restrictions on immigration that curbed family reunification.[10]

An unguarded 1985 interview with Olivia O'Leary for *Magill* did much to cement his reputation as the bête noire of Irish liberals. He provided many quotes for the prosecution. Ireland should not become 'a pale image of morally spineless Britain' though he admired Margaret Thatcher. Legislation to permit contraception was 'too high a price to pay' for accommodation with Protestants in the North. The Mullah nickname came about after he had tried, at the opening of an oratory in a Limerick shopping centre, to explain how religion should be integrated with life. It 'had to be admitted with shame' that the Muslim world was way ahead in upholding religious values in law, politics and economics. Of course he was not, he explained in the 1985 interview, in favour of public flogging or amputating hands, but Muslims had integrated religion better into their lives than had Irish Catholics.[11]

Newman's body of work included three major books on political philosophy, *Studies in Political Morality* (1962), *Conscience Versus Law* (1971) and *The Postmodern Church* (1990) where he developed and most comprehensively articulated his arguments against secular modernity. It included a number of books aimed at the general Irish public and international Catholic audiences. He also authored a number of polemics that addressed political issues of the time such as *Puppets of Utopia: Can Irish democracy be taken for granted?*[12]

He remained a stern critic of Catholic thinkers who promoted intellectual compromise of doctrinal reform to meet the exigencies of the present. But he sought intellectual allies amongst secular critics of Enlightenment positivism and Western modernity. He pressed French postmodern and poststructuralist theory – the ideas of Lacan, Foucault and Baudrillard – into the service of a new anti-modernism. If the Church could not make its peace with secular modernity it could gain something from theories that challenged Enlightenment conceptions of knowledge and truth. But such intellectual straws in the wind did nothing to save Catholic Ireland from secularism. His empirical research as a sociologist had charted social changes in rural Limerick and Maynooth that were clearly undermining Catholicism. For four decades he fought an intellectual rearguard action against this decline. More than any other Catholic conservative writer he studied the ideas to which he was opposed and tried to understand – as a sociologist and a political philosopher – what the Catholic Ireland he wished save was up against. But however much he understood and discussed the pressures for change that faced the Church in Ireland he implacably held the line against what he saw as faddish compromises by Catholic thinkers and some clerics and disobedience by the laity.

In defence of public morality

In January 1955, in a book review in *Christus Rex* Newman argued that there was an inherent tension between the principle of democracy and obedience to Catholicism.[13] He rejected the notion of the sovereignty of the people and argued against legal positivism which defined law solely in terms of man-made rules and earthly authority. He opposed separation between Church and State and argued that ideally the one true Church should be officially established by the State. But because the trend of history had been against this position, it was advisable that the Church pragmatically accept whatever constitutional status quo it was faced with without surrendering the ideal of an established Church. Catholic statesmen should act in accordance with what Aquinas called regnative prudence, 'a comparison between the evil consequences that stem from toleration and from those which the community of states will be preserved through the acceptance of the formula of toleration'.

Newman's 1962 book *Studies in Political Morality* attempted to systemise arguments he would go on to reiterate in a number of subsequent volumes. Long chapters leadenly teased out distinctions within and between the writings of relevant Catholic thinkers in a series of exhaustive and exhausting literature reviews.[14] In each case Newman sought to establish the ideal Catholic position and then typically distinguished between this and how the Church might best respond under different actual circumstances, the first typically being within a state where Catholics were in the majority and the second being where Catholics were in the minority.

Studies in Political Morality responded to Paul Blanshard, author of *American Freedom and Catholic Power* (1949) and *The Irish and Catholic Power* (1953) who argued that Catholic doctrine was incompatible with liberal democracy. So effective, Newman argued, was such anti-Catholic propaganda that Senator John Kennedy gave assurances that in the event of his becoming President of the United States there was no question that he would, as a Catholic, undermine the system of separation between Church and State.[15] In Newman's summary *American Freedom and Catholic Power* depicted Catholic theory on Church–State relations as intolerant and it castigated Catholic positions on the censorship of books, education and medical ethics as authoritarian.[16] Blanshard did not deny 'the *fact* that American Catholics are loyal to American democracy'. Rather he argued that 'given suitable circumstances, the *logical* position for the Church to adopt is one that is incompatible with American democracy'. This was precisely Newman's point in *Studies in Political Morality*.

The gist of Blanshard's argument was that whilst political democracy in Ireland was genuine an unofficial Church–State alliance permitted ecclesiastical dictatorship and political democracy to live side by side without any sense of incongruity. The Catholic Church in Ireland, Blanshard argued, had 'a program for the control of great areas of modern life which belong to democracy', in education, freedom of thought, law and medicine.[17] The Catholic ideal, Newman replied, was indeed for an established Church. It should never surrender this ideal in theoretical discussions on Church–State relations and in political theory more generally it should never surrender the primacy of theology to political theory. He faulted progressive American theologians for having done this. The demands of the Church of Christ on the State, he argued, were fundamentally doctrinal; they stemmed from the uncompromising source of theological truth.[18] The focus had to be on the political implications of theological truth rather than the other way around:

> Special recognition of the church may be necessary to secure these interests to the full in a state in which the vast majority is Catholic. It is not a question of seeking what *can* be secured from the State but what *ought* to be granted if the people's spiritual interests are to be adequately looked after in so far as their government is competent to do so. On the side of the state this, in turn, re-echoes its duty of doing whatsoever is necessary in pursuit of the political common good. It is simply erroneous to suggest that the limitation of the State to catering to the exigencies of public order means that it cannot grant special recognition to the Church.[19]

In the Irish case, where the Church enjoyed a special position closer to the ideal than in many other polities, other issues came to the fore. There had, Newman insisted, to be limits to religious tolerance. The rulers in a State comprised almost entirely of Catholics had a duty to influence legislation of the State in accordance with Catholic teaching. This included a duty to defend the religious patrimony of the people against every assault that sought to deprive them of their faith.

In 1971, in a chapter of *Conscience Versus Law* titled 'The Separation of Legality and Morality', Newman described how early positive law theorists such as Thomas Hobbes emphasised coercion as the basis of moral and legal authority. Here and in a number of other books Newman challenged the ideal of Hobbes' *Leviathan* and its presumption that the state was the final authority over the law. Newman's rogues galley included Hobbes, Jean Jacques Rousseau and Sir Francis Bacon whose justifications to King James I for the plantation of Ulster exemplified the malign use of positive law in its crudest 'might is right' form.

A chapter on the ethics of conquest addressed colonialism and the Irish case of the post-1608 plantation of Ulster. There was he argued no questioning of the moral as well as legal title to their possessions of the present-day descendants of the settlers. The passing of three centuries involved so many changes that a reversion to former ownership was unthinkable, even where the families of the earlier disposed owners could be identified. He cited and discussed a pamphlet by Sir Francis Bacon, *Considerations touching the Plantation of Ireland*, presented to James I in 1606. Bacon justified the plantation of Ireland as a means of securing the external peace for England, of civilising a 'people of barbarous manners', of ensuring England's internal peace by settling surplus population there and of securing great profit for the Crown. Bacon justified the removal and transplantation of some of the natives to ensure the civility of Irish plantations.

Newman characterised Bacon's arguments as similar to those later enumerated by the Natural Rights school of international law (meaning John Locke) but also akin to the politics of expediency professed by Niccolo Machiavelli. The legal philosophers of Bacon's England had turned expediency into international law that justified arbitrary rule in Ireland, a doctrine of might is right that preceded but anticipated the era of 'unblinking' legal positivism that followed the publication of Hobbes' *Leviathan*, 'the most thoroughgoing statement of State absolutism to come out of England'. The difference between Bacon and Hobbes on Ireland was one between duplicity – Bacon wrapped his designs in 'honour, policy, safety and utility' – and honesty. In *Conscience Versus Law* Newman highlighted Bacon's identification of justice with expediency defined in terms of the primacy of interests of the Crown.[20] He also emphasised how John Locke drew upon natural law. Locke like Aquinas stressed the capacity of a person to understand, through reason, their duties and obligations. But when God was taken out of the equation by Locke's successors – most notably by Tom Paine – this translated into an emphasis on popular consent as the principle that underpinned the legitimacy of civil authority:

> Conceived along these lines there was little alternative but that natural law should become a system of inflexible rationalisations concerning the rights and duties of man. As it was, due possibly to the influence of Protestant individualism, the catalogue came to be presented mainly as one of natural rights and the natural law, understood as a vindication of the rights of the individual. It is at this time we begin to hear so much about 'The Rights of Man' and that the French and American Revolutions produced their Declarations of Rights. In short natural law theory had become a theory of rights instead of what it used to be a theory of law.[21]

Positive law jurisprudence limited discussion of the law to a system of man-made rules. Natural rights as understood by Locke's successors depended upon what Rousseau termed a social contract and this, Newman declared, amounted to the claim that whatever was done by those in whom sovereignty of the people was invested could do no wrong. The 'General Will' of the community expressed in positive law became the only consideration of morality:

> In the political sphere once all formal connection between legality and morality had been broken, the rights of the individual were no longer guaranteed as they had been in the past by natural law and could in theory be sacrificed to the demands of the common good as dictated by the autonomous conscience of the community. An arbitrariness had entered the field of legality that could all too easily terminate in erecting the State into an absolute.[22]

Even democratic states, Newman argued, could not ensure moral government. In arguing this he gave the example of the difficulties in prosecuting Nazis for war crimes during the Nuremberg trials. Positive law did not easily allow for the prosecution of individuals who could claim they had not broken the law of the Third Reich. Instead they were prosecuted for crimes against humanity. In Newman's interpretation, the Nuremberg tribunal in effect turned to natural law in order to escape the unacceptable consequences of legal positivism.

Social change and Catholic decline

By the time *Conscience Versus Law* was published the kind of Catholic domination Newman advocated as the political ideal was clearly no longer possible in Ireland. During the 1960s Newman found his own opportunity to defend public morality as editor of *Christus Rex*, the Irish journal of sociology. In a 1959 book review in *Christus Rex* Newman observed that students of what was 'commonly called "Sociology"' in Ireland – that is, as taught by him – would be very confused by how the subject was defined in other countries.[23] In a 1961 review he complained that the author had restricted her definition of sociology to factual examination of the ethics of individual groups and as such excluded the Catholic 'Social Ethics' principles from sociology per se.[24] This approach, Newman noted, had been cultivated for a number of years by Catholic sociologists, particularly in America, in an effort to have their work accepted by secular sociologists. Newman argued that Catholic sociology should unblushingly stand by the truths about human nature represented by the Christian tradition and to seek to integrate these with factual knowledge of all kinds in an effort to solve social problems. *Christus Rex* functioned somewhat like Albania under Hoxha whilst life around it changed.[25] Newman as editor was patently unwilling to open the Pandora's box of secular social theory but by the 1960s a flood of international popular sociology had become available to Irish readers.[26]

In his own sociological research Newman was preoccupied with social changes that were likely to undermine Catholicism. His main sociological analyses were of rural Limerick where he grew up and Maynooth where he took holy orders and was later in charge of the spiritual formation of others. 1961 saw the publication of a study he led on the causes and motives of migration from some County Limerick parishes.[27] Newman argued that the findings provided 'a sober counterbalance to those critics who would have us believe that lack of adequate marriage opportunity is a primary cause of rural depopulation'. In the parishes surveyed, only 25 out of the 117 persons who had migrated between 1951 and 1956 had married by 1959. The fact that so few married after migration was taken to undermine the hypothesis that obstacles to marriage were compelling reasons for migration.[28] He argued that in the face of ongoing rural decline the only way to conserve the rural population was, 'paradoxical though it may seem', to develop a number of towns in each county with adequate social and cultural facilities. Newman formulated an index of social provision for towns and villages in County Limerick. This quantified the availability of public utilities, different kinds of commercial activities (the presence of various kinds of shops, banks, etc.), public transport, 'places of assembly' (social facilities such as Churches, libraries, public houses, cinemas) and social organisations. In short Newman's proposal was to concentrate on building up a number of sustainable communities in the county.

In a 1967 article 'Vocations in Ireland' he undertook a comparative analysis of declining vocations in various European countries. At Maynooth ordinations had peaked in 1941 at eighty-six. Irish ordinations overall had peaked in 1961 (447) and were now falling away. There were 412 in 1965. Further declines, Newman demonstrated, would follow.[29] He posited a number of causal factors. These included increased affluence and urbanisation (mirroring the conditions of other societies that experienced vocational decline), changes in the structure of the education system (resulting in the decline of influence of priests upon young people), developments in lay spirituality that encouraged marriage and the challenge of materialism to the attractions of religious life. The following year saw a similar assessment of falling female vocations.

Although Newman opened up Maynooth to lay students he was characteristically conservative on the role of the laity within the Church. In 1966, in *The Christian Layman*, one of a series of commentaries on the Second Vatican Council, he stated that the layman 'does not need the command or even the permission of his bishop before he can legitimately engage in apostolic activity. And yet, when this has been said, it must be added that his aspostalate stems from the sacramental life of which the hierarchy is guardian and that it must always remain auxiliary to that of the hierarchy.'[30] The laity, in the post-Vatican II Church, 'should be prompt to welcome in a spirit of Christ-like obedience whatever decisions their pastors may make'.[31]

In 1970 in an article that surveyed for an Irish audience the secular canon of sociology that Newman worked to keep at bay, Newman accepted that clerical control was no longer feasible.[32] He stepped down as an editor. The journal changed its name to *Social Studies* and no longer carried the imprimatur that declared that its contents were free from doctrinal and moral error. The article explicitly referenced a torrent of previously unmentioned theorists ranging from the Marxist Frankfurt School (he cited Herbert Marcuse's *One Dimensional Man*), Ferdinand Toeinnes, John Kenneth Galbraith, Desmond Morris (*The Naked Ape*), Thorsten Veblen (*Theory of the Leisure Class*), Lloyd White (*The Living City*), Marshall McLuhan (*The Medium and the Message*) to Richard Hoggart (*The Uses of Literacy*). He expanded on some of its themes in *Conscience Versus Law* the following year. Since the 1950s 'beatniks', 'hippies' and other manifestations of youth culture come to personify the revolt against contemporary society. In their extremism they were 'anti-everything – against the government, the police, the employers, university administration and the Church. Graffiti all over Paris after *les jours de mai 1968* summed it all up in the phrase *Ni Dieu ni maitre*.' They were estranged from the structures that sought to mould them to what they saw as the slavish lives of their fathers. Youth popular culture – songs by the Beatles such as 'She's Leaving Home', books like Jack Kerouac's *On the Road* – and promoted rural communes exemplified efforts to escape from the dominant material society.[33] Newman took seriously at the time the critique of Western society implied by such escapism:

> Without doubt many hippies overdo it and become the victims of dirt and drug addiction, to say nothing of idleness and promiscuity. In truth they would be saints if they did not, for man is a social animal and to drop out of society, from whatever reason, supposes either superhuman courage or despair. And many of these people do despair – of society as they know it and of its reform. For these it is all to easy to turn to drugs, as men did earlier to drink when it was cheaper than drugs. Free love, needless to say, costs nothing. As for cleanliness, it can easily become a fetish, *a va sons dire* of a chrome plated society. In this one respect perhaps, beyond all the others, the early Christian hermits are likely to have been least different from the hippies.[34]

Conscience Versus Law set out a sociological analysis of the crises facing the Church and society. This began by explaining the distinction made by Toennies between 'community' (*Gemeinschaft*) and 'society' (*Gesellschaft*) as organising principles of society. On one hand, there existed communities that were 'personal rather than interpersonal in character, unorganised without being disorganised ... in short an association of free men'. On the other societies inevitably contained some institutional aspect 'as organised and legalised by authority which if overdone can cause it to be strait-jacketed and totalitarian'. The challenge was to achieve a balance. The

Christian life was best incubated in the kind of community that he had grown up in:

> The unfortunate thing is that, as institutions, they involve relationships between individuals rather than between persons. They are created, rather than living, personal bonds. And because of this, urban-industrial society may be said to subsist primarily on impersonal structure. To a considerable degree it lacks – or rather tends to lack – *gemeinschaft*, the community life of the family and the locality, of the village, the smaller town, the owner-occupied shop, the rural church.[35]

Urban life and the impersonal social structures of modernity made community intangible and made faith difficult. With the decline of Irish *Gemeinschaft*, Newman went on to argue, a legally enforced public morality offered the only potential bulwark against the acceleration of secularisation. In a series of subsequent books he would urge the Irish State to do its duty to Ireland's Catholic majority by enforcing Catholic public morality. When it began to waver on doing so, when it was clear that Church authority was no longer what it once was, Newman's last intellectual stand would be a neo-conservative and somewhat libertarian one, implacably opposed to coercive state power.

Live free and die hard

Newman entered the 1970s keenly aware that Catholic goals in Ireland could no longer be pursued through censorship or by episcopal insistence of the primacy of Church authority in Church–State relations. The loss of Catholic intellectual monopoly in Irish sociology, the decline of vocations and the urbanisation of society meant that the threats of modernity to Irish Catholicism were no longer external. There would soon be, he anticipated, pressure for legislation to permit divorce. In *Conscience Versus Law* Newman depicted this pressure as a 'minority right' issue. The Church did not approve of divorce and in a predominantly Catholic society the state had a duty to protect the majority from legislation it would be damaged by:

> What I am getting at is the need for a patterned sociological framework which will give support to the religious and moral beliefs of the average man and thus help him live his life in accordance with them. What he needs, if you will, is a prop to his weakness, but then this is the purpose of all society in all its domains. Political society or the State is no exception. Its legal system represents a fabric of social values that are intended to sustain the individual through social living. This is the function of a constitutional provision which prohibits divorce in a society composed predominantly of people who believe it wrong to practice it.[36]

This argument had first been outlined in a 1969 issue of *Christus Rex* on the threat of divorce. Prohibition of divorce in Ireland was part of the framework provided by the Irish State that supported the conformism of the average man.[37] He argued that the emphasis of Vatican II on participation of the laity in the Church and other reforms would not ensure future high levels of religious observance in the way that had been made possible by laws underpinned by Catholic moral teaching. So defending the constitutional status quo was a priority. Social change, he believed, was inevitable. But the pace of change was fast enough without forcing it by changes to the constitution which would, he believed, further undermine Catholicism in Ireland. As he put in 1969 in *Christus Rex*:

> That diehard traditionalism is bad for society, and that there is need for a liberal stimulus to counter it, is a sound general political principle. But it should be related to society as found in the concrete. Thus the contribution of the liberal stimulus is unquestionably valuable in the context of a backward looking, quite closed, conservative society. At the other extreme, in that of a wholly liberal permissive society, there is need rather for the fostering of a sound conservativism. Today in our mixed – partly conservative and party liberal Irish society, it seems to me that one should be unusually careful about introducing a liberal stimulus in the direction of secularisation. Where has this led Britain even in our own time – from a proud empire to a giggling society?[38]

This in essence would be his mantra henceforth. For all that he acknowledged the need to understand social change he also insisted on the need to resist it, to oppose Catholic reformers who would buckle before it, to set aside concerns about the rights of non-Catholics. Newman believed that the pressure for divorce legislation and for secularisation went hand in hand. In the Irish case, Catholic politicians who advocated legislation on divorce tended to do so on grounds of promoting religious pluralism.[39] But they needed to understand that in countenancing divorce they were also endorsing the secularisation of Irish society by undermining public morality.

He drew parallels with the United Kingdom by citing the Wolfenden Report (1957) that recommended decriminalising homosexual practices between consenting adults in private (though without referring to what it was about). According to Wolfenden the function of the criminal law was to preserve public order and decency, including to provide sufficient safeguard against the corruption of those who are specifically vulnerable because they are young, or weak in body and mind.[40] In Britain the decriminalisation of homosexuality in Britain was followed by the near simultaneous revival of the penal offence of conspiring to corrupt public morals in 1961.

In a series of lectures that year, published as *Law, Liberty and Morality*, H. L. A. Hart (whose work Newman read and cited) contrasted the British change in law on homosexuality with the American tendency to retain no longer enforced legislation on the books. He noted that there seemed to be no sexual practice except 'normal' relations between husband and wife and solitary acts of masturbation that was not legally forbidden in some part of America. Fornication had not been a criminal offence in England since Cromwell's time yet it continued to be punishable in some American states even if much of the relevant legislation was dead letter law.[41] But in 1961 the courts resuscitated a long dormant eighteenth-century penal offence of 'conspiracy to corrupt public morals' following the prosecution of the publisher of a magazine that advertised the services of prostitutes. According to Hart, the ruling on the case by the House of Lords had fashioned a very formidable weapon for punishing immorality out of what had been an 'exceedingly vague and indeed obscure idea of corrupting public morals'.[42] The argument about the relationship between morality and the law endorsed by the courts reflected, according to Hart, the principle it was permissible for any society to take the necessary steps to preserve its own existence as an organised society.[43]

Newman in the Irish case did not approve of the decriminalisation of homosexuality for the same reason he opposed divorce – because doing so would erode the support of the law for Catholic social values – but his passing reference to Wolfenden suggests that he endorsed the revival of offences against public morality. As put in the preface of his 1977 book *The State of Ireland*:

> there are certain positions which, irrespective of whether the majority of people – in the Republic or a United Ireland – agree on them not, are right and should be upheld in the interests of a way of life (call it public morality if you like) which is crucial to the wellbeing of the people in Ireland.[44]

The State of Ireland argued against legislation in favour of contraception, divorce and abortion. Irish politicians who expressed support for the reform in the first two cases usually declared they would not necessarily approve of either for themselves. Whether they did or not they shielded themselves with the case for minority rights. Newman argued that in doing so they were undermining public morality understood in terms of the Catholic values of the majority. He argued that the law was a crucial bulwark against its erosion. The human being was very much shaped by environmental circumstances. These included social and cultural as well as economic and geographical factors. Environmental factors could either help or hinder the individual in living out his moral persuasions:

> Men are not pure spirits. They need help and encouragement to remain faithful to themselves even in the following of their self-confessed ideals of conduct. For government to think otherwise would be to be tragically blinkered and indeed to fail in one of its important duties.

It is precisely for this reason that the law must recognise the place of public morality, through the maintenance of a secular institutional context which responds to the needs of citizens. It was this realisation which was behind the criminal law of England so long prohibiting such matters as divorce, abortion, contraception and homosexuality.[45]

In Ireland, he implied, censorship had helped until recently to keep these debates at bay. Now public morality in Ireland was threatened by public debate on such topics. He categorically opposed change to the law in such areas for two reasons. Firstly, because ordinary people, the people he met in the course of his pastoral duties, did not want it: 'On the contrary they need what help a supportive framework of law can give them to enable them to live up to their Christian persuasions.' Secondly, Newman believed that even if the majority tended towards accepting such measures the government had a duty to conserve public morality to the best of its ability.[46]

The Republic of Ireland's Catholic moral monopoly had emerged out of the Catholic movements of the nineteenth century. Cardinal Cullen, architect of the mid-nineteenth-century devotional revolution, and other Church leaders had built up Catholic institutions but the Church had become passive in the post-independence era. The Church now faced a struggle for survival in Ireland. The rise of the influence of the Church in Ireland after Catholic emancipation had been the result of huge effort. Catholics had to stand up and be counted in order to build up the Church. The post-independence generations took this status for granted.

The State of Ireland was to a considerable extent a response to Garret FitzGerald's Towards a New Ireland (1972) which had discussed and disagreed with what Newman had to say in Studies in Political Morality.[47] FitzGerald cited the willingness of Cardinal Conway the Catholic Primate of Ireland 'to accept and even to welcome' the proposed deletion from Article 44 of the Constitution of the reference to the 'special position' of the Catholic Church as proof that there was no insurmountable obstacle to the modification of attitude by the Catholic hierarchy to accommodate Protestant sensitivities.[48] He argued that changes to the law on contraception would be approved in the Republic if these were presented as part of a package designed to create a favourable climate for reunification. Newman's opposition to such minority rights was indefatigable.

In 1983, with FitzGerald now Taoiseach, Newman published a collection of essays, Ireland Must Choose, which took its title from the Pope's sermon in Limerick on 1 October 1979. Newman argued that the relationship between Church and State had shifted from what this had been in de Valera's time – warm official relations where the State accorded a very special position to the Church because the majority of people were Catholic – to correct but informal and wary relations where both Church and State endeavoured to keep their independence but cooperated in so far as possible for the public good.[49]

The Church, Newman insisted, was not opposed to all change. There would be no objection to legislation for divorce as a lesser evil in the context of a federal solution to the Northern Conflict. But Catholics must always set their faces squarely against acceptance of the desirability of divorce, the free availability of contraceptives and the whittling away of denominational education in any way that would injure religion.[50] He repeated the mantra that in a country where Catholics were in the majority they had every democratic right to expect that in conflicts as to where rights lay, the Catholic view should prevail.

In 1987, Newman published a collection of polemic essays against the secular state and statism in general. The first essay in *Puppets of Utopia: Can Irish democracy be taken for granted?* was on George Orwell. This picked at Orwell's claim that *1984* was anti-totalitarian but not anti-socialist. The style was that of an *Encounter* or *Spectator* piece. His target was less socialism than modern states in general. Newman warned against the dangers to human freedom posed by statistical reformers whose data and tables took the place of morality and who would run mankind as a machine was run.[51] Other chapters cited other early- to mid-twentieth-century critics of socialism and totalitarianism. The material on Ireland focused on the post-1947 period when the Department of Health was established and the 'Mother and Child Scheme' which proposed state-funded health that was trenchantly opposed by the Church became politicised. Newman's revisionist argument was that Church objections to State interference in the health of the family opposed an insidious form of state coercion that had found new manifestations in hysteria about AIDS.

Whereas once he argued for a state role in defending public morality against the hidden persuaders of consumerism he now vehemently opposed state coercion as seen in proposals for a smoking ban in public places and controls over the promotion and advertising of such products as tobacco, alcohol or unsuitable food.[52] Now that there was no longer a special relationship between Church and State and that public morality was likely to be informed by secular norms Newman mounted libertarian arguments against state scrutiny and controls. Now that it had arrived with a vengeance he needed some new intellectual tools. Just as he had sought to harness the spirit of youth rebellion to his critique of secular anomie after 1968 Newman now reached for new secular allies. For example, *Puppets of Utopia* declared how in 'a remarkable series of works the French writer Michel Foucault has ably shown how medicine – particularly psychiatry – has been used over the centuries as an instrument of social control'.[53]

The Postmodern Church, published in 1990 when Newman was sixty-four years old, addressed the arguments of various philosophers who argued that the Enlightenment had failed. Modernity (here he quoted Jurgen Habermas) was a project conceived by the Enlightenment to develop objective science, universal morality and law independent of theological influences. But (quoting Theodor Adorno and Max Horkheimer) the

Enlightenment embodied a ruthlessness to dominate nature in a way that ultimately dominated human beings. It promised 'paradise on earth, by ensuring freedom of thought and the supremacy of the individual in every domain'. And now the postmodernists had pronounced it dead.[54] In essence, Newman here refined his earlier arguments about the alienating effects of secular modernity.

The best analysis of postmodernism, Newman argued, was that of Jean Baudrillard whose early work was a searing attack on the neo-capitalism and neo-modernism that had begun to overcome French life – 'the supermarkets, technocracy, mass media and the like'. Baudrillard's later work depicted, Newman explained, how the commodification of life emphasised needs that were largely artificial and had fostered lifestyle conformity, and that capitalism and Marxism, the left and the right, had come to mirror one another as expressions of modernity.[55] Newman saw postmodernism as undermining the claims made by secular modernity about rationality, truth and progress and as therefore not opposed to religious critiques of such claims:

> To the extent that Postmodernism rejects modernism and its positivist orientation, it ties up with the culture of previous eras in which science means a knowledge that was not confined to an empirical and quantifiable domain but was God-orientated and to a greater extent occupied with sacred mysteries. Even the technology of the past was largely a sacral technology, craft tools generally being of symbolic significance and artistic and architectural creations (e.g. the medieval cathedrals, pre-Reformation art, Hindu statues and Shinto temples) directly related to religious ends. The postmodern revolt against the secular technology of modernism means that it does not recognise efficiency as God.[56]

Eclecticism could be helpful and was necessary to understand the world but the Church could not be doctrinally eclectic in how it faced the postmodern world. Newman was, as before, critical of Catholic thinkers, mesmerised by the 'perestroika' of Vatican II, who bent too quickly to accommodate the intellectual and political fashions of the moment, sowing confusion in the ranks of those who listened to them with no benefit to the Church.[57]

Catholic decline and neo-conservativism

By the end of Newman's life the Catholic Church had lost what Tom Inglis called its moral monopoly over Irish life.[58] Whilst the Irish continued to strongly oppose abortion, homosexuality was decriminalised in the year of Newman's death. Contraception and divorce became legalised. Newman's thesis had been that this lax public morality would further erode Catholicism. But long before such constitutional changes came to pass Newman had been fighting rearguard actions against inevitable social change. His *Irish Times* obituary carried the headline 'Man Who Kept Fighting the Battles of Long Ago'.[59] To his opponents, the obituary continued, his was an outdated version of Catholicism, redolent of pre-second Vatican II triumphalism when 'error had no rights'. An unnamed Maynooth contemporary was quoted as saying that 'he is fighting the battles of long ago when everyone else has gone for their supper'. His obituary described him as an out of touch reactionary:

> In personal terms, too, the new bishop appeared ill-suited to his difficult new pastoral role. Here was a man who had been closeted in elite academic institutions for 30 years emerging into an Irish church trying painfully to cope with the challenges of a liberalising, secularising society, and to implement the reforms demanded by Vatican II in the face of those challenges.
>
> Dr Newman's way of coping was to state, restate and passionately and articulately defend the old fundamental truths as he saw them. His pronouncements on public affairs sounded more dogmatic and authoritarian than those of his older and more senior colleagues in the Hierarchy, and there were indications from time to time that this caused some unease.

The Church, Newman once put it, must hold onto its ideal 'whilst leaning attentively over mankind, listening to the pulse of humanity'.[60] Listen and ignore his critics might have retorted! He may have mined books on feminism for proof of the crisis of secular rationality but Newman's 1994 Lenten message warned against the dangers feminism posed to the family:

> We have seen introduced an extremist movement for women's liberation that can also injure the family. I do not refer to a balanced and welcome promotion of women's equality but the promotion of an exaggerated view of the self-sufficiency of wives which, although generally unnoticed, can tempt husbands to adopt a similar message.[61]

The year before, he noted the worrying growth of unhealthy criticism by too many Catholics of their Church.[62] Newman died not long before it became riven with scandals of clerical child abuse. Evidence now available indicates that the Catholic hierarchy in Ireland had knowledge of sexual abuse by clergy from the 1960s onwards.[63] Donal Murray, Newman's successor as Bishop of Limerick, was forced to resign in 2009 in the wake of findings of the mishandling of reports of sexual abuse that occurred in 1980 and 1981 whilst Newman was in post. Clerical sexual abuse in Ireland was denied and covered up in various ways by the Catholic hierarchy and bought to book by the secular public morality that superseded the Catholic one defended by

Newman. But the sociological purpose of that Catholic public morality, Newman emphasised again and again, was to protect the practice of Catholic faith – a means to the end of defending the Church rather than an end in itself.

Newman was both one of the last of an old breed and one of the first of a new one. His responses to modernity were also those of Pope John Paul II and his successor Benedict XVI, formerly Joseph Ratzinger, both of whom have sought to retreat from the apparent liberalism of Vatican II. None embraced it in the first place. In the Irish case Newman consciously took on the role of defending the faith from his fellow Irish Catholics who became increasingly 'a la carte' and disenchanted with the authoritarianism of the institutional Church. The writings cited here in which he did so are barely remembered and had little or no influence, but are of historical importance in understanding what was at stake from the perspective of a clerical culture that had dominated Irish society over a crucial century of modernisation.

For all that, Newman's intellectual project was a cogent one. For instance, it resonates with twenty-first-century neo-conservative politics in the United States where the Catholic Church now seeks to push public morality politics for reasons it once was in a position to do so in the Irish case. The political playbook of the Catholic Church in twenty-first-century Ireland resembles the one Newman described as fitting countries where Catholics were in a minority. In such cases, he insisted, they should hold on to the ideal of a Catholic public morality whilst pragmatically accepting the status quo and playing a long game.

CHAPTER TWELVE

The lonely passion of Conor Cruise O'Brien

Donal Conor David Dermot Donat Francis Cruise O'Brien (1917–2008) has been called with much justification the pre-eminent Irish intellectual of his generation and the most pugnacious one since George Bernard Shaw.[1] The press release that announced his appointment as Editor-in-Chief of *The Observer* in 1978 described him as 'the nearest thing to a modern George Orwell'.[2] A 2007 *Sunday Independent* profile to mark his ninetieth birthday counted six careers, 'any one of which would have occupied a lesser man'.[3] In his 1957 book *Parnell and His Party* he stated the assumption that a man's political outlook was conditioned much more by his general position in society, his 'caste', profession or employment than by the state of his purse at any given moment.[4] This certainly held in his case. He was born into one branch of Ireland's cultural and political elite and married into another. A visiting French writer recounted a conversation in the late 1960s between Sean MacEntee, veteran of the 1916 Rising and long-serving Fianna Fáil government minister, and his son-in-law O'Brien. O'Brien provoked MacEntee with a sweeping statement: '1916 was a mistake'. MacEntee responded that maybe it was, but he was glad to have been a part of it. To this MacEntee's daughter Maureen added: 'Conor, your grandfather was a member of the Irish Parliamentary Party. You were part of the elite. My father was the son of a publican. He would never have become a minister without 1916. We would not have a fine house. His children would never have been to the best schools.' 'Exactly', O'Brien replied, 'your people pushed my people aside'.[5]

But O'Brien had hardly been pushed aside. He had received an elite education (unusually for a Catholic) at an upper middle-class Church of Ireland school and at Trinity College.[6] A career in the higher civil service followed. Within a few years of his complaint to MacEntee he too would become a government minister. He took many of his intellectual preoccupations from the social milieu into which he was born. His grandfather David Sheehy, a nationalist member of parliament, was one of the 'people' who turned against Charles Stuart Parnell, the subject of O'Brien's doctorate and of his second book *Parnell and His Party* (1957). Sheehy's wife, O'Brien's grandmother, was immortalised in James Joyce's *Ulysses* as a minor character who was asked how her sons at the Jesuit-run Belvedere College were faring.[7] A Catholic priest uncle, Father Eugene Sheehy, played a prominent role in the Land War and was a childhood influence on Eamon de Valera. O'Brien came to believe that this Sheehy connection influenced de Valera's personal authorisation in 1944 of his appointment to the Department of External Affairs. Another Father Sheehy, a distant kinsman of Edmund Burke who was hung, drawn and quartered in 1766 for sedition, was claimed by O'Brien as an 'ancestor' in various works.[8]

It is almost impossible to underestimate how seriously O'Brien took nationalism. In the introduction to *States of Ireland* he argued that most history was *'tribal* history: written that is to say in terms generated by, and acceptable to a given tribe or nation'.[9] Much of his writing on Irish history and cultural politics focused on the household gods who were his real or proxy ancestors. Edmund Burke, W. B. Yeats and Maud Gonne were conscripted into O'Brien's little platoon along with various illustrious members of the Sheehy family. In O'Brien's oeuvre cultural politics and family history were intertwined. Various ancestral voices were palatable presences within his analyses of Irish nationalism. His writings on current affairs and politics drew heavily on autobiography. These recounted his experiences as a civil servant propagandist in charge of promoting the cause of a united Ireland, a diplomat representing the non-aligned diplomatic integrity of a newly-minted Republic of Ireland at the United Nations, a UN representative in post-colonial Congo, a university vice-chancellor in Ghana trying to protect academic freedoms against an increasingly despotic ruler, a government minister who used censorship against the IRA and its supporters, the editor of an English newspaper who objected to articles about Northern Ireland that he deemed too sympathetic to nationalists and the controversies he became embroiled in as an ever more combative globe-trotting public intellectual.

A 1945 essay about *Horizon*, the English intellectual periodical edited by Cyril Connolly, detailed O'Brien's own intellectual horizons at the time. Articles he considered as 'high spots' included George Orwell's 'literary slumming expeditions in *Boys Weeklies*', and the philosopher A. J. Ayer's 'difficult but rewarding exegesis of the work of Jean-Paul Sartre'.[10] He drew some unfavourable comparisons between the cosmopolitan *Horizon* and *The Bell*'s 'caution, its realism, its profound but ambivalent nationalism, its seizures of stodginess and its bad paper'. Sean O'Faolain's proclaimed mission as editor was to truthfully depict ordinary life in Ireland.[11] O'Faolain's 1933 novel was called *A Nest of Simple Folk*. O'Brien neither sprang from nor was he at all interested in simple folk. His was a nest of well-connected political families.[12] O'Brien noted that many *Horizon* writers, from the evidence of their profiles in *Who's Who*, had been educated at Eton and/or Oxford. They were from the 'Brahmin class'. O'Brien was cut from equivalent stuff.

His third book, *To Katanga and Back: A UN Case Study* (1962) addressed how he came to order UN troops, including an Irish contingent, into battle (something no Irish Taoiseach or equivalent had had to do since the civil war) to prevent the partition of the Republic of the Congo.[13] His reputation as a critic of colonialism in Africa and of the Vietnam War gave the impression he was far further to the left than he actually was. His six months in the Congo left him with 'a feeling of how thin the earth's crust and a feeling of what anarchy is like'.[14] His most enduring intellectual 'mentor' thereafter proved to be Edmund Burke. There were of course other intellectual influences. The case has been made that Albert Camus was the most important one of all.[15] By 1980 the well-received *Camus* (1970) had gone into its tenth print run.[16] But with O'Brien there is always a need to distinguish between emotional influences and intellectual sources. Camus was amongst the latter. Burke was both.

O'Brien was by no means the first to make the arguments for which he became demonised. He was, rather, a fairly late nationalist adopter of the case against a united Ireland. A review of Donald Akenson's biography of O'Brien pithily referred to the Cruiser's 'road to right thinking' on Northern Ireland as leading to Damascus.[17] O'Brien fell off his high horse several times on this journey. He had a predilection for taking positions that seemed to isolate him from the mainstream consensus of Irish politics. He set himself against what he saw as a potentially apocalyptic consensus between Northern Catholics, the Southern Republic and the Catholic Irish in America about what they thought would solve the Northern crisis. From a valid Unionist perspective, he came to insist, there could be no compromise, or as they put it, no surrender. His last significant effort to drive this point home to his own Irish Catholic 'tribe' was to become a member in 1996 of the United Kingdom Unionist Party (UKUP).

In O'Brien's analysis the siege mentality of Northern Unionists was a sincere and realistic response to their situation. He drew parallels between his own response to the IRA campaign in Northern Ireland and that of Burke to the French Revolution, seeing both as part of a larger eternal conflict between dangerous idealisms and pragmatically conservative realism.[18] Burke had to break with his political tribe, Whigs like Richard Brinsley Sheridan and Charles James Fox, who saw the French Revolution as one against despotism and as a democratic sequel to England's 1688 Glorious Revolution. Burke was committed to the general principles of the Glorious Revolution, which had bought great benefits to Britain. He sought, as the architect of the Catholic Relief Act of 1778, to extend these to Ireland, the problem being that the same Glorious Revolution had also introduced the Penal Laws against Catholics. In Ireland as in France he decried revolution. Burke's response to the French Revolution appeared to his fellow Whigs as extremely alarmist. Fox in 1791 described the French Constitution as the 'most stupendous and glorious edifice to liberty' that had ever been erected in any place or country. Within a few years, O'Brien argued, Burke was vindicated by the ensuing Regicide, the Terror and the rise of military despotism in the figure of Napoleon Bonaparte.[19]

O'Brien described this as insight bordering on prophecy. O'Brien endeavoured to become in his writings on Catholic nationalism that most unwelcome of persons – a prophet in his own land. Many of his insights were vindicated though not, happily, the conflagration he repeatedly predicted in his last years as the Northern Ireland Peace Process took hold. He never believed in that process. The passion of Conor Cruise O'Brien took the form of symbolic apostasy from his own tribe, of rubbing the noses of Southern and Northern Catholics in the ordure of unpalatable truths.

Faith, fatherland and patriot games

O'Brien's first book *Maria Cross* (1952) was a collection of essays about one Irish and seven European Catholic novelists. He had been educated in Protestant schools in accordance with the wishes of his dead father, an agnostic, who did not want his son to receive a Catholic education. He lacked experience of and had little interest in the kind of communal Irish Catholic identity depicted by writers such as Frank O'Connor or Patrick Kavanagh. His focus in *Maria Cross* was on European, and mostly French, intellectual Catholicism. Many of the essays piled on half-digested references to Catholic thinkers. A Jesuit, Father George Tyrell was mentioned as *not* having influenced Francois Mauriac. Mauriac, O'Brien blithely pronounced, 'was not going to hell for Fr. Tyrell'. O'Brien explained nothing about Tyrell except to imply that he was a kind of theological bogeyman.[20] Mauriac, the reader was told, was not theologian enough to be either an apostate or a heretic. The inference was that O'Brien was sufficiently one to pass such a judgement but all evidence was to the contrary.

Yet when it came to the only Irish writer included, he did know what he was talking about. The chapter titled 'The Parnellism of Seán O'Faoláin' seemed to belong to a different book. It foregrounded nationalist as distinct from religious sensibilities, ancestor worship rather than religious worship. It addressed a historical consciousness that permeated O'Brien's whole existence as distinct from a European Catholic intellectual sensibility that he had tried on as an ill-fitting suit of clothes:

There is for all of us a twilit zone of time, stretching back for a generation or two before we were born, which never quite belongs to the rest of history. Our elders have talked their memories into our memories until we come to possess some sense of a continuity exceeding or traversing our own individual being. The degree in which we possess that sense of continuity and the form it takes – national, religious, racial, or social – depends on our own imagination and on the personality, opinions and talkativeness of our elder relatives. Children of small and vocal communities are likely to possess it to a higher degree and, if they are imaginative, have the power of incorporating into their own lives a significant span of time before their individual births.[21]

This quote encapsulated the essential understanding of nationalism that he worked with for half a century. It explained something about O'Brien's subsequent tendency to write history in the first person, with his own familial folklore and autobiography as starting places.

O'Brien published *Maria Cross* under the name Donat O'Donnell, as he did most of his writings from 1942 when he entered the civil service until 1962 when he resigned from the Department of External Affairs. Many of his early essays and reviews were published in *The Bell* which was edited by O'Faoláin. His literary career developed in parallel with his professional and public life. His career took off in 1948 when the Interparty Government succeeded sixteen years of Fianna Fáil rule under Eamon de Valera. On leaving government de Valera went on an international tour to promote the cause of a united Ireland. This bounced the Interparty Government led by Fine Gael, into a new campaign to end partition. In 1948 the leaders of all the political parties, known as the Mansion House Committee, approved a fund-raising campaign that raised £46,000 in a church gate collection. The Minister of External Affairs O'Brien worked for was Sean MacBride, son of Maud Gonne, leader of Clann na Poblachta and former IRA Chief of Staff.

In his own *Memoir* he described anti-partition propaganda as 'the hottest political property in town'. O'Brien's work for MacBride was the making of his civil service career.[22] As put by Donald Akenson about this work, 'its seductiveness for an ambitious young man was great. And – this was crucial – Conor believed in it'.[23] In his *Memoir* O'Brien described himself as having been initially 'a willing participant' but a reluctant propagandist by 1950, ('weary of all this stuff, and beginning to feel more than a little sick about my own position with regard to it') when MacBride invited him to become managing director of the Irish News Agency.[24] This was supposed to be an international news service that promoted the Irish government viewpoint around the world. Its purpose was to 'brandish the sore thumb' of partition in the international media. MacBride in his memoir wrote that O'Brien was 'one of the intelligent people in the department', a good pen but not to be trusted. He depicted O'Brien as an unfaithful civil servant, an office-politics plotter and prone to putting his own unwelcome views forward.[25]

Reluctantly or not O'Brien played a large role in orchestrating anti-partition propaganda. The Mansion House Committee published pamphlets like *Ireland's Right to Unity* under the imprint of the All Party Anti-Partition Conference. In Great Britain 340,000 copies were distributed, 160,000 in the Republic. In 1953 O'Brien travelled to Northern Ireland to oversee the distribution of another 50,000 to Unionist families. He pitched in his own ideas for further propaganda efforts. One was a proposal to print 50,000 postcards with anti-partition slogans for sale in Ireland and America, with the profits to be invested to fund other anti-partition initiatives.[26] His efforts to end partition went beyond the call of official duty. As Donat O'Donnell he published an article entitled 'L'Unité de L'Irlande et les Irlandais d'Amérique' in the *Revue Général Belge* in July 1950.[27]

O'Brien went on some clandestine missions to the North as part of his External Affairs anti-partition brief. Their purpose included intelligence-gathering exercises, managing visits by foreign journalists and dignitaries on fact-finding missions and building up contacts with nationalist groups. He referred to the 'indoctrination' of a visiting English Jesuit in one 1954 official report. The work involved showing visitors examples of anti-Catholic discrimination and gerrymandering in order to advance the case for ending partition. Until 1956 he articulated official Irish government policy in favour of a united Ireland without giving any hint that he disagreed with this.[28]

Outside of office hours he undertook doctoral research which he completed in 1954. This led to his second well-received book, *Parnell and His Party* published in 1957. A 1945 article in *The Bell* outlined a version of the thesis for which he would be awarded his doctorate nine years later. This article, 'Parnell's Monument', took issue with the lavish application of *Fuhrerprinzip*, or great man theories of history, in Irish scholarship and folk memory alike. All the historical achievements of his day were 'cheerfully attributed to his sole personality'.[29] O'Brien excoriated the existing body of historical writing about Parnell as 'dominated by what is properly an idea for a ballad, or a Goebbels'. It left the average educated Irishman with a confused idea of what Parnell did and could have done.[30] O'Brien, after all, knew something about propaganda. Donald Akenson has argued his experience as a propagandist influenced the way he approached his doctoral research:

> Conor's work as a professional propagandist was not entirely divorced from his practice as an Irish historian. As we have seen, the conclusion that Conor presented in his work on Parnell in the mid-1950s was that he had declared in *The Bell* in 1945, long before he had done any research. This is exactly how the writing of propaganda works: the conclusions come first and the facts follow. Conor got away with this in his Parnell study because of his intuitive perception – that the mechanics of Parnell's party had been obscured by the melodrama engendered by Parnell's personality – was borne out by the facts (and this has been thoroughly confirmed by later scholars). Still, starting with one's conclusion is very risky.

And in his historical work in the mid–1950s, Conor was not yet able to deal as dispassionately with the Ulster Question as he believed he did.

This is hardly surprising, considering he was being paid at his day job to harry Northern Ireland out of existence. As a historian in the 1950s, he underestimated as a historical phenomenon the intransigence of Ulster's opposition to all forms of home rule. He believed that if Gladstone and Parnell had held strongly together, they could have forced home rule down the throats of the northern Protestants.[31]

Parnell and His Party contained just a passing couple of references to the perspectives of Ulster Protestants. The inference was that their consent was of little or no account in the politics of Home Rule. Parnell, according to O'Brien, 'acted as if he believed that the status of Ireland could be decided by negotiation between the representatives of Irish and English majorities. This belief may, in the circumstances of the 1880s, have been right'.[32] Later in the book he qualified this inference but still claimed that 'Home Rule' for a united Ireland might have been possible.[33]

O'Brien took at face value Parnell's claim that the Home Rule bill he got Gladstone to support would settle Ireland's national question. He inferred that English opinion mattered but not the views of Northern Protestants. Lord Randolph Churchill had 'played the Orange card' in an attempt to secure a 'no' verdict from the *English* people.[34] The implicit presumption here was the same as the anti-partition propaganda O'Brien was responsible for in his day job.

The 1964 reprint of *Parnell and His Party* included a preface that addressed four factual and interpretive errors in the first edition. None of these suggested any rethink of his inference that Parnell's plan for Home Rule could have worked without the consent of Ulster Protestants. However, in a belated 1981 retraction, 'Parnell and His Party Reconsidered', O'Brien wrote that he no longer believed this and that he himself had been more in the Parnellite tradition than he had realised when writing the book. He had underestimated the depth and intransigence of Ulster Protestants to incorporation in a Home Rule state. O'Brien no longer believed that even Gladstone and Parnell together could have bought about a united Home Rule Ireland, that even if the fall of Parnell had not occurred he would have had to accept some measure of partition for Home Rule to come to pass.[35]

When he wrote *Parnell and His Party* one part of him might have questioned the anti-partition propaganda he was complicit in producing but another part remained indifferent to the perspectives of Northern Protestants. Yet, in 1957 he also published an article that focused explicitly on the views of Northern Protestants on a united Ireland.

The rocky road to Damascus

'A Sample of Loyalties' (1957) appeared in the Jesuit journal *Studies* alongside a remarkable essay by Donal Barrington which set out an analysis of the Northern Ireland question that O'Brien would come to adopt.[36] Partition, Barrington argued, was not forced on Ireland by Britain but necessitated by the conflicting demands of the two parties of Irishmen. It was Ireland's crime against itself rather than England's crime against Ireland.[37] Barrington was fiercely critical of the inability of Irish politicians and diplomats to foster what de Valera once called a unity of wills in support of a United Ireland. Rather than endeavour to 'convert' Unionists to a belief in a United Ireland, Eamon de Valera, John A. Costello and particularly Sean MacBride had tried to lever international opinion in favour of Southern claims. This, Barrington implied, restated the old demand that the British should impose Irish unity. The scale of Southern misunderstanding of the North was huge. Southern efforts (the 'ill-fated Mansion House Committee') sought to fund the campaigns of anti-partition candidates. This met with a backlash in the 1949 general election. It gave the Unionist Party its biggest victory to-date and 'wiped out' the Northern Ireland Labour Party. For the first time the latter then came out against partition.[38] Barrington blamed the 'armed raids' of 1956 on the ill-considered propaganda efforts of de Valera and Costello:

> When the attempt failed, as it was bound to fail, some of our young men took the matter into their own hands. Anyone who thought at all about the history of Ireland could have expected no other result ... This propaganda has always employed emotionally charged phrases such as 'occupied Ireland', and 'the British army of occupation' with a view to isolating Britain as the party solely responsible for creating and maintaining Partition.[39]

Barrington argued that propaganda that the North was 'unfree or enslaved' did little to address the real discrimination and system of 'apartheid' experienced by Catholics in the North. He detailed the workings of gerrymandering which effectively disenfranchised Catholics in some areas, discrimination in the allocation of council houses and discrimination in appointments in the public service. Unionists had largely themselves to blame for 'the revolutionary situation' that was to be found within the Six Counties. However, Barrington insisted, this was not the whole story. Unionist bigotry had also been stoked by the Southern coercive approach to unification. So long as such threats persisted reactionary Orangemen would continue to control Unionist policy and 'ordinary Protestants' would tolerate discrimination against Catholics in ways that would be impossible were such fears absent. The constant threat from the South had kept alive sectarian bitterness in the North, had prevented the emergence there of a Liberal or Labour party and had defeated the ambitions of liberals within Unionism. Barrington argued that the Republic should formally guarantee the territorial integrity of Northern Ireland in return for effective guarantees, including electoral reform, to protect Northern nationalists against the discrimination they now experienced. Southern political leaders should discourage specifically Catholic organisations from mobilising in Northern politics and instead foster cross-border cooperation in areas such as economic policy, university education and sport. They should, Barrington argued, seek to pursue an agreement that benefited Catholics in the North and reassured the Protestant Unionist majority:

> As pointed out above, nothing is to be gained by pursuing the liberation of the Nationalist areas of the Six Counties as a separate aim of Southern policy, but if we are formally to guarantee the territorial integrity of Northern Ireland we will want in return effective guarantees to protect the Northern Nationalists against the kind of discrimination they have been suffering from hitherto . . .
>
> In return Dáil Éireann would solemnly renounce any intention of using coercion against the Northern Protestants and would guarantee the territorial integrity of Northern Ireland in much the same way as the British Parliament guaranteed it in the Ireland Act, that is to say, that the South would recognise that Northern Ireland would never enter a United Ireland without the prior consent of the Parliament of Northern Ireland. The South would also recognise the Government of Northern Ireland as an Irish Government entitled to respect not only from the people of the Six Counties but from all Irishmen.
>
> Such an agreement would be the foundation on which the new policy designed to create a unity of wills would rest. But it would merely be a beginning. It would also be necessary to call off the propaganda campaign which we have been carrying on against the Northern Government throughout the world, and it would also be wise to dissolve the anti-Partition Association, which, for all its good intentions, has done a great deal of harm.[40]

Compared to Barrington's essay O'Brien's companion piece in the same issue of *Studies* was narrow in scope and tentative in its conclusions. 'A Sample of Loyalties' analysed 'the ideas and feelings contained in a batch of essays written towards the end of 1953 by a class of 26 boys, aged 13 to 14 years attending a large Protestant secondary school in the Six Counties'. The set topic of the essay was 'Ireland'.[41] The value of the exercise for O'Brien was 'an unguarded candour and clarity' unlikely to be forthcoming from 'older or more intellectual members of that community'.[42] Twenty of the essays expressed various degrees of positive feeling towards Ireland as homeland. Many were attached to some sense of Irishness. As put by one boy who professed to like the poetry of Yeats: 'I am sort of a way attracted to its music its famousness and its green fields. We should be proud of it.' Another wrote: 'Ireland is a good country in spite of their overcrowded towns and their slums and the Roman Catholic inhabitants'.[43] Nine of the twenty-six boys stated a preference for unification. Just one of the boys came out unequivocally against it. Only four went into any specifics about what they meant by reunification. One concluded it would be good if Northern Ireland and 'Eire' were brought together under the Queen's rule. The second maintained that reunification should be under the British flag. The third suggested that Ireland should be a separate nation with a king. For the fourth, it required forgetting the seventeenth century.[44] These responses were far removed from nationalist understandings of what was meant by the unification of Ireland.

What ended O'Brien's role in anti-partition propaganda was a transfer that year to the Irish embassy in Paris. This posting was followed by a successful one to the United Nations in New York. In 1961 he was appointed as UN Representative to the Democratic Republic of the Congo. On his return he published his third book *To Katanga and Back* (1962) and resigned from the Department of External Affairs. Three years as a university vice-chancellor in Ghana was followed by three years teaching in New York. Much of his writing during this period did not concern Ireland.

Conor Cruise O'Brien, as distinct from Donat O'Donnell, properly entered Irish intellectual politics with 'The Embers of Easter', a 1966 essay on the legacies of the 1916 Rising which was first published in *The Irish Times*. 'As Pearse read the noble words of the Proclamation of the Republic to those few rows of listless Dublin faces, he must have been aware', O'Brien argued, 'of the gap between the Ireland of his ideals and the Ireland of any plausible reality'.[45] Fifty years on Dublin was the capital of a sovereign state. Soldiers in green were doing honour to his memory. Pearse and James Connolly would have been pleased, he felt, that the Dubliners of 1966 were healthier, better fed, better dressed and better housed. Neither, he thought, might be surprised that the north-east of Ireland was still part of the United Kingdom but would have been pained at the ease with which partition had come to be accepted by the southern state. O'Brien then recalled ('the present writer blushes to recall') the failed anti-partition campaign that he was part of, its roots in an Irish nationalist tradition that fought a civil war because partition was inconceivable but also inevitable:

> My generation grew into the chilling knowledge that we had failed, that our history had turned into rubbish, our past to 'trouble of fools'. With this feeling it is not surprising that the constant public praise for the ideals of Pearse and Connolly should have produced in us bafflement rather than enthusiasm. We were bred to be patriotic, only to find there was nothing to be patriotic about; we were republicans of a republic that wasn't there.

Pearse's vision was of an Ireland, 'not merely free but Gaelic as well'. By those criteria it was 75 per cent free and 0.6 per cent Gaelic in 1966. Yet, desperate games of 'let's pretend' persisted with recurring claims that Ireland was Gaelic because Gaelic was the official language, that Ireland was free because the Constitution declared that the national territory consisted of the whole island and a constitution framed in Catholic language purported to bind the Protestant majority in Northern Ireland who were not consulted about the matter at all.

Household gods and ancestral voices

During the 1940s and 1950s O'Brien had been mostly a private rather than public intellectual, a commentator rather than the pugnacious protagonist he became after he returned from the Congo and resigned from the diplomatic corps. Never again would he be accused of being a diplomat. *To Kantaga and Back* brought a degree of international renown and established the first-person voice that was never far below the surface of all his subsequent writings. It formed part of a sequence of writings exposing the cynicism of international diplomacy including a play about the Congolese crisis *Murderous Angels* (1969).[46] During the 1960s he also expounded, through a series of essays and a collection of lectures given in 1969 published a few years later as *The Suspecting Glance* (1972), the political philosophy that anchored most of his subsequent work. In *The Suspecting Glance* he described how the courses he gave as Albert Schweitzer Professor at New York University attracted a high proportion of left-wing student activists because of his well-documented opposition to the Vietnam War, his reputation as a critic of American imperialism and America's manipulation of the United Nations and his role in exposing in 1966 how the CIA had covertly funded the intellectual periodical *Encounter*.

But he considered these students to be naïve in their understandings of the consequences of the anti-authoritarianism they professed. They talked cheerfully of revolution without any sense of what one might mean in terms of human suffering, without any sense of the human cost of previous revolutions. His students disconcerted him. He saw it as his job to disconcert them. Instead of teaching them about the kind of writers who vindicated their belief that great writing should always in some way validate the revolutionary process he 'went on endlessly' about Edmund Burke, a thinker they would never have spontaneously been drawn to. In a 1966 University of Chicago lecture entitled 'Burke, Marx and History' he argued that *Reflections on the Revolution in France* foreshadowed criticisms of regimes that had resulted from Marxist revolutions.[47] In 1968 Penguin published an edition of Burke's *Reflections* edited by and including a 67-page essay on Burke by O'Brien.

In *The Suspecting Glance* O'Brien likened Burke in 1790 to a successful Negro in an American city, with roots in the black ghetto which he seldom visits but knows much about, who is accepted with reservations by the white ruling class and believes that the free enterprise system, for all its faults, is the only one that can secure people like him a place in the world. He learns that a revolution is being planned. People, including white people, are distributing literature urging the blacks to follow the example of Cuban and Chinese revolutionaries. He knows the power and ruthlessness of white society and in one sense is part of it. He knows that any black rising will be horribly crushed. He tries to combat revolutionary influences in the ghetto whilst at the same time he tries to persuade white society of the urgent need for reform, by arousing fear of the revolution he believes will happen unless reforms are realised. Reform moves ahead but then bogs down. The revolutionaries grow in influence but they are infiltrated by the authorities. His hatred for the revolutionaries becomes obsessive. He comes to hate their frivolity and the irresponsibility of those who do not know what they are doing and the callousness of those who do. He fears that revolution will threaten both parts of his life – the black world and the white – and his efforts to span both. He feels a growing pressure on the concealed crack in his own life.

This, O'Brien explained, was what life was like for Burke. For 'black' read Catholic. For 'ghetto' read Ireland. In the eighteenth century, O'Brien continued, Penal Laws made distinctions between Catholic and Protestant quite as fundamental as that between Afrikaner and Bantu under South Africa's apartheid regime. The Ireland of Burke's day was a Protestant-supremacy state in the same way that South Africa was a white-supremacy state.[48] Burke was against revolution and his writings fanned the flames of reaction in England and encouraged what he knew would be a long war with France. Such was his influence that some of his most remarkable prophesies were partly self-fulfilling. He foretold in 1790 that the Revolution, then in its liberal phase, would turn into a military despotism. It did, but only after Britain and its allies waged a war against France that was strongly urged by Burke.[49] In 1972 O'Brien's identification was Burke that was still evolving and still critical:

> Burke, having been right by force of tentativeness and exploration of circumstances, was carried, by the hubris of the successful prophet into the follies of his new crusade against the 'armed doctrine' – and carried also, in our time, into the dreary glory of being enshrined in an American pantheon of cold war ideology.[50]

O'Brien saw Burke's unremitting work for the emancipation of Irish Catholics as an expression of kinship and family affection rather than as an expression of liberalism and tolerance. He considered his own feeling for Burke to be affected by a similar tribal or national affinity.[51] The Burke he would emulate in his own interventions in Irish affairs was not so much the Burke who empathised with Catholics, the tribe from which his little platoon sprang, but the Burke at war with the revolution in France whom O'Brien described as hating the irresponsible revolutionaries and callous warmongers of his own tribe. *The Suspecting Glance* was published in the same year as

States of Ireland, O'Brien's influential reflections on the attempted IRA revolution in Northern Ireland.

His best-known essay on Yeats, the 53-page long 'Passion and Cunning' (1965), documented the poet's attraction to fascism including his time as a cheerleader for the Blueshirts in Ireland. Yeats, O'Brien argued, supported them when he thought they might win and sneered at them when they proved a flop.[52] O'Brien subsequently maintained that 'Passion and Cunning' had come to define the debate about Yeats's politics.[53] In effect, O'Brien claimed Yeats as his first major scalp in his own rise to fame as an international public intellectual. But in 1941, in *The Bell*, Frank O'Connor had already made many of the arguments upon which O'Brien built his 1965 case for the prosecution. O'Connor's 'The Old Age of a Poet', which O'Brien cited, described Yeats as a passionate nationalist, a rabid Tory, a member of the Church of Ireland who had much of the Catholic in him, a hater of reason, popular education and mechanical logic, a fascist and an authoritarian who saw in the world crises of the 1930s an opportunity to destroy the 'damned liberalism' he hated.[54] O'Brien depicted Yeats 'as near as being a Fascist as the conditions of his own country permitted' and a self-declared propagandist all his life.[55] A year after the publication of 'Passion and Cunning', a number of 1916–66 commemoration articles by other Irish intellectuals similarly focused on Yeats's poetic exhortation of blood-sacrifice.

O'Brien repeated this analysis in *The Suspecting Glance* but added a new emphasis on what he believed was the influence of Nietzsche on Yeats's elitist abhorrence of the common people of Ireland. In *The Suspecting Glance* O'Brien's ire was directed at the armchair academic cardigan-wearing champions of the 'gentle Nietzsche' who had gone to great pains to insulate him from the culture in which he was such a potent force.[56] Here, O'Brien was reacting to the popularity of Nietzsche on American campuses. Nietzsche was another dangerous mind blithely cited by the would-be revolutionary children of the 1960s social revolution. Yeats, O'Brien maintained, had times been a gentle Nietzschean and at times a fierce one. He championed in his later poetry, 'not just vague aristocracy of the spirit, but an actual social class, eugenically superior to others, and qualified to produce governments as well as works of art'.[57]

By the end of the 1960s O'Brien had acquired and articulated a political philosophy within which the political was deeply personal. His arguments about culture, nationalism, religion and identity politics would take their examples from his ancestral voices. He made an intellectual bunker from such personalised tradition, and from its specific examples he reasoned towards general defences of the traditions of others. O'Brien's lifelong preoccupation with Yeats owed something to childhood visits to the home of Maud Gonne, who had acted in Yeats's 1902 play *Cathleen Ni Houlihan* to iconic effect. O'Brien obsessed again and again about Yeats, Maud Gonne and the play in various articles and books between 'Passion and Cunning' in

1965 and his 1998 *Memoir*. For example, an account of Maud Gonne in *Ancestral Voices: Religion and Nationalism in Ireland* (1994) described how, for O'Brien, she literally personified Cathleen Ni Houlihan in how she performed the role of widow of a 1916 martyr. He described how the play electrified Dublin audiences with its summons to fight and die for Ireland and how it then entered the Irish nationalist bloodstream. Yeats had turned to Nietzsche, O'Brien argued, in the immediate aftermath of *Cathleen Ni Houlihan*'s success when its star and his muse Maud Gonne's married Major John MacBride. Under Nietzsche's influence the Yeats who declared the glory of dying for Ireland now professed fascistic elitism as a bromide against democratic vulgarity.[58]

'Passion and Cunning' had opened with a recollection of where he was when Yeats died (on 29 January 1939). He was lunching with his mother's sister Hanna Sheehy Skeffington, the widow of Frank Skeffington, a pacifist and socialist who was murdered on the orders of a British officer during the Easter 1916 Rising. The next sentence described Madame MacBride as one of his aunt's closest political friends and the rest of the opening paragraph painted a vivid portrait of her.[59] In many subsequent books and articles he restated his supposedly unique qualifications to write about this scene. Like a tomcat spraying its territory he would pepper most of his subsequent writings on Irish nationalism with quotes from Yeats's poetry or retellings of his familial connections to Maud Gonne, repeatedly reminding the reader of his place in their firmament.

In a 1989 article for the London *Times* he recalled a 1971 Dáil speech he made citing Yeats soon after the commencement of the IRA's 'offensive' in Northern Ireland, and shortly after the Arms Trial in which Charles Haughey had been acquitted of importing arms illegally into Northern Ireland (O'Brien repeatedly referring to Haughey's acquittal, never believing it was justified for a moment). He remembered quoting a few lines from Yeats's poem 'Easter, 1916'. Haughey, who was in the chamber called out loudly, 'Complete the quotation'. Doing so, O'Brien recalled, would have meant quoting lines that could be read in the spirit of *Cathleen Ni Houlihan*, lines that had entered the bloodstream of Irish republicanism, most especially the line, 'A terrible beauty is born.'[60]

States of fear

In early 1969 O'Brien resigned his chair at New York University and returned to Ireland to run as a Labour Candidate in the general election. The poll in the multi-seat Dublin constituency in which he came second was topped by Haughey, who O'Brien explained was the then Minister of Justice who had been acquitted of running guns into Ireland. When asked to write a book about Northern Ireland he found that he could not write about it in isolation from the South. Unstated was how most books about Ireland, including his own on Parnell had been written without dealing with the North.

States of Ireland described the state of Protestant–Catholic relations – the social electricity present in the air of Belfast and Derry even in times of peace – giving the example of how a person might not talk freely in a taxi or feel safe depending on the religion of the driver. In troubled times he might not take a taxi at all, unless he knew that the driver was from the same religion. A Catholic passenger would tense up if the driver took an unexpected turn onto a Protestant street and vice versa: 'And in no circumstances would either of them in the presence of the other allude to this situation, or on any subject bordering on politics or religion.'[61]

He argued that such tensions had been ignored in the interpretations of the crisis presented by left-wing and mostly Catholic activists. Their common feature was an effort to trace the evils of Northern Ireland, and the Republic, to British imperialism, understood as a still-active force, intensely concerned with keeping its grip on Ireland. Whether they were right or wrong (O'Brien thought they were wrong) such efforts to promote anti-sectarian politics in the North were in danger of further deepening the sectarian divide:

> These people are not merely non-sectarian, but sincerely and militantly *anti*-sectarian, in their conscious outlook. Their intention has been to raise the level of consciousness of the masses, in terms of class interest, up out of the sectarian bog. The effect of their efforts, gestures and language, however, have been to raise the level of *sectarian* consciousness. They have encouraged the Catholics, and helped them to win important and long-overdue reforms. They have frightened and angered Protestants, and if their efforts could be continued on the same lines, and with the same kind of success, they would bring the people of the province, and the island, not into class-revolution but sectarian civil war. And in fact, even at present, language and gestures which are subjectively revolutionary, but have appeal only within one sectarian community are objectively language and gestures of sectarian civil war.[62]

Sectarian consciousness needed to be taken seriously. The disabilities of Catholics in Northern Ireland were real, but not overwhelmingly oppressive. He did not consider that their removal was worth riots, explosions, pogroms and murder. Violence had exploded just as civil rights were in reach (he described this as frozen violence released by a thaw). Catholic civil rights marchers had perceived their actions as non-sectarian acts. Not so their assailants who saw themselves as besieged.[63] O'Brien's approach was to unmask the sectarianism of Catholic anti-colonialism, to attack the 'thumping lie' put out by left-wing civil rights campaigners that religious difference did not matter and to take seriously the siege mentality of Northern Protestants. In his *Concise History of Ireland* (yet another 1972 book) he described the leading members of the civil rights movement as a generation that had benefited from a non-discriminatory British welfare state, particularly in terms of access to education.[64]

The account of Irish history set out in *States of Ireland* emphasised how Northern Ireland Protestants considered themselves under siege. The failed 1798 revolution destroyed not only the viability of the United Irishmen's ideal but re-established amongst Protestants the old siege mentality of the seventeenth century. Orangeism replaced Ulster radicalism and subsequent nationalist movements were predominantly Catholic. A few Protestant intellectuals, notably Thomas Davis and John Mitchel, continued in the 1798 tradition and their writings did much to foster nationalism amongst Catholics, but these had little appeal to Ulster Protestants. The attempted rising in 1848, in the wake of the Famine, failed miserably. Ulster Protestants seemed now to have little to fear. Catholic Ireland seemed a hopeless, ruinous failure more to be pitied – or despised – than feared. Protestant Ulster, for its part, shared Britain's great industrial success.

From an Ulster Protestant point of view, the siege was renewed by Catholic-Irish Americans, the Fenians and Irish Catholic support for Land League and Home Rule politics in Ireland. As put by O'Brien in an analysis that departed from his earlier writings on Parnell:

> For Protestant Ulster, the eighteen-eighties constituted the renewal of the siege, in a more dangerous form than at any time since the seventeenth century. Under pressure of the Land League, using the weapon of the boycott, the landlord power – which was also the Protestant ascendancy – was decisively weakened throughout the Catholic-majority area. In terms of the siege, the outposts of Protestant Ulster were driven in. And out of the most effective mass movement in the history of Catholic Ireland, the representation of that Ireland in parliament had emerged for the first time as an effective organised force. Its leader was a Protestant, but in the eyes of Ulster Protestants – and most other Protestants at that time – he was the leader of the Catholics. And now this leader, Parnell, had bought about what seemed to Ulster Protestants an unthinkable event; the conversion of a Prime Minister of England to the idea of self-government for Ireland: self-government after Catholic emancipation and universal suffrage: implying domination of Protestants by Catholics.[65]

In 1886, in response to this renewed perception of siege, the Orange Order became the mass movement it has remained since. In *States of Ireland* O'Brien drew comparisons between this siege mentality and that of the Afrikaners who had come to preside over an apartheid state. Subsequently he wrote a book called *The Siege* (1986) about Israel and wrote articles about the dilemmas facing the apartheid regime in South Africa.[66] Ironically, he noted in *States of Ireland* that Catholic 'physical force' nationalism had been inspired by the Boer War. The Afrikaners were perceived as a small nation justly struggling to be free of the British Empire. Maud Gonne's husband Major John MacBride had fought with the Boers against the British. The notion that a better parallel might have been with the black population did not occur to most Catholic nationalists, and certainly not to Arthur Griffith who was a white-supremacist in the John Mitchel tradition.[67]

By the time of the Boer War Protestant Ulster was one of the most jingoist parts of the Empire and deeply hostile to the dourly determined Protestant Boers. Ironically then the support of Catholic nationalists for the Boers aggravated the sense of siege amongst Northern Protestants. Only later did Unionists begin to openly sympathise with whites in South Africa and Rhodesia. When O'Brien subsequently wrote about South Africa and Israel he had very much in mind parallels with the predicaments of Ulster Protestants. With respect to the former in 1986 he described the Orange/Afrikaner comparison as a fertile one, 'provided it is not being used just for the stigmatisation, or demonisation, of one community or both'.[68]

An appendix to States of Ireland set out a statement by O'Brien delivered in a public debate on 23 October 1971 with Tomás MacGiolla, President of Sinn Fein in Dublin. O'Brien acerbically pointed out that Cathal Goulding, Chief of Staff of the Official IRA, was the real leader of Sinn Fein. The party was controlled by a military elite who believed that political legitimacy sprang from the generations of dead who died for Ireland rather than springing from living voters. Unpretentious they might be in dress and manners, but the IRA elite were a military elite or aristocracy who deigned to decide who lived or died and for whom the will of the ordinary people expressed through the democratic process did not count:

> The people in Sinn Fein's vocabulary becomes a term of art, a tricky term carrying any specific meaning which it suits Sinn Fein to ascribe to it from time to time, but carrying always the general tones of a mystic and irrational concept; an imprescriptible and inalienable quality, inherent in Irish nationhood, of which the guardians, guarantors and executants are the I.R.A., whether the actual living Irish people, in any given generation, like it or not.
>
> We on the other hand, are for the little people. We reject Sinn Fein's mystical concept of the people. . . . We reject it on behalf of the living people whom we represent. . . . We reject it on behalf of the socialist tradition, concerned with living realities, and recognising always that mystical politics, the language of sacred soil and the cult of the dead, are part of the apparatus of the enemy.[69]

O'Brien argued that Sinn Fein's trajectory was towards fascism: 'the natural destination of an anti-democratic, militarist, authoritarian, ultra-nationalist movement, whose ultimate appeal is a mystique inaccessible to reason'.[70] He argued that Haughey and the other Fianna Fáil ministers who were sacked for alleged gun-running exemplified a potentially fascist right-wing Catholic nationalism:

There will be people who were attracted to you by the fascination of the gun and the bomb and the power these represent. There are also wealthy men, and ambitious politicians, who are interested in the potential of such gunmen. Alliance between that kind of wealth, that kind of politics, and that kind of gunman is not only possible: It already exists.

This alliance may not succeed. But if any kind of politics based on the use of private armies *does* succeed, that is the kind of politics it will be; not the socialism of Mr MacGiolla but the Right-wing nationalism of a Blaney, or a Haughey, or a Boland. If it triumphs here – as it might if things get bad enough in the North – then our State will be like the Greece of the Colonels. What else can be expected if we allow private armies to destroy a working democracy?[71]

His modest proposal was 'for a politics of the living, the struggle for better conditions in the here and now, without brilliant short-cuts, without blood, without the heady wine of the Apocalypse: a politics in which both reason and compassion will be vital components'.[72] At each twist and turn of the Northern crisis O'Brien would continue to warn of apocalypse.

He infuriated nationalist intellectuals, most spectacularly in the pages of *The Crane Bag*, an intellectual journal founded in 1977 whose programme owed much to his 1965 essay 'Passion and Cunning'. By then O'Brien was an establishment figure. He had been in the Cabinet since 1973 and as Minister of Posts and Telegraphs introduced a media ban in 1976 on the IRA and Sinn Fein. The main contributors to *The Crane Bag* were Catholic post-colonial literary critics and Catholic philosophers. O'Brien became their bête noire. The intellectual battle lines for him were as they were in New York in the late 1960s when he doused student revolutionary idealism with a dose of Edmund Burke. *The Crane Bag* envisaged a nuanced and discursive engagement with all shades of nationalist opinion. Instead of such talking cures Dr O'Brien prescribed his own patent shock therapy. An article by Mark Patrick Hederman tried to make sense of O'Brien from a nationalist perspective. This depicted him as a man of many parts; Cabinet Minister, influential intellectual but yet isolated from the collective Irish 'us' that *The Crane Bag* sought to identify with. *The Crane Bag* had published various articles on Yeats's advocacy of nationalist blood-sacrifice and on the Christ-like Pearse who had risen out of the embers of the 1916 Rising. O'Brien, according to Hederman, was preoccupied with a different form of martyrdom; one that excluded him from the various but intertwined shades of Irishness that made up *The Crane Bag*. O'Brien had given a lecture on the Christian aesthetic philosopher Simone Weil that Hederman had attended:

While he was talking it became apparent to me that although his subject was Simone Weil, he was really using her to describe his own isolated position in Irish politics. Her unusual and highly personal philosophy which had led to her political martyrdom, was almost like a mirror image of his own. As events later unfolded, this comparison took on something of a prophetic quality. Before that year had ended Conor Cruise O'Brien had been rejected by his constituents and forced into exile in England, where he became an Editor-in-Chief of *The Observer*.[73]

O'Brien's sole contribution to *The Crane Bag*, an article entitled 'Nationalism and the Reconquest of Ireland', bluntly rebuked nationalist aspirations for the reunification of Ireland. O'Brien described a symbiosis between nationalist statesmen and the Provisional IRA that allowed the former to draw political sustenance from the lethal actions they deplore.[74] If a military theoretician might categorise the fighting in Northern Ireland as a 'low intensity operation' so too was Catholic nationalist politics a low intensity operation. Few Catholics, he argued, would do much to achieve a united Ireland. None the less the aspiration remained: 'diffuse, elusive, persistent, cryptic, lightly pervasive, a chronic mist'.[75] This mist prevented any practical engagement with the aspirations of both Catholics and Protestants.

In 1978 O'Brien, by then out of office and Editor-in-Chief of *The Observer*, gave four memorial lectures in memory of Christopher Ewart-Biggs the British ambassador who had been killed by the IRA in Dublin in 1978. These were published as *Neighbours* (1980). He argued that there were no conceivable changes that would ensure an end to violence or prevent its recurrence in the future. It was not possible to simultaneously appease and disarm those who wanted to break the connection with Great Britain and those who passionately opposed that aim. The unpalatable truth was that no halfway compromise would work. There was the inevitable allusion to Yeats:

> It is not here Yeats's case of the best lacking all conviction whilst the worst are full of passionate intensity. The worse are up to specification all right, but with the best it is now a case of losing, through compassion, the power to think, and in consequence, acquiring convictions of an irrational character, either irrelevant or damaging to those whom they seek to help, nor is this tendency confined to us Irish. Indeed Englishmen of goodwill, wishing to think about Ireland in a positive way, are particularly susceptible to this disease.[76]

O'Brien, by way of example, criticised proposals by Ewart-Biggs's predecessor Sir John Peck for an Anglo-Irish Council as well-meaning but foolish. Such initiatives would hardly mollify the IRA and would alarm Unionists. He believed that direct rule was the only viable option:

> The chances of any agreement at all in the near future seem very slim. But if we assume, as I do, that direct rule will be there for a long time, then the important thing in the present and near future, is to avoid actions and language which would prejudice a slow *rapprochement* and possible

agreement at a later date. If that does not happen, then either direct rule continues indefinitely or we or our children will have to face the *dire consequences of British withdrawal in the continuing absence of any agreement* between the Northern Ireland communities. Those consequences would profoundly affect all Ireland, and these islands generally. To recognise that now, and to observe the prudence its recognition dictates, is the only means we can hope to avoid such an eventual disaster.[77]

O'Brien made much of attitudinal data in *Neighbours*. Some 68 per cent of Catholics in the Republic of Ireland favoured a united Ireland. However, just 39 per cent of Northern Catholics thought likewise. British public opinion and Irish America were listening to the wrong Catholics. The majority of Northern Catholics had, he argued, a much clearer idea where pressure for unity could lead and of what would follow a British withdrawal than people had in the Republic.[78]

States of siege

In 1986 O'Brien participated in the filming of a documentary in Belfast. The filmmakers were approached by a group of children who asked who he was. He told them to go home and tell their fathers that they had just met Conor Cruise O'Brien, and added under his breath 'and they'll probably beat the life out of you'.[79] Much of what he published in and around 1986 explored commonalities between the political predicaments and belligerence of three besieged peoples: Zionists, Afrikaners and Ulster Protestants. He had travelled to Israel a number of times whilst writing for *The Observer* and had been feted. He responded in kind, identifying strongly with Zionism and hardly at all with Palestinians in *The Siege: The Saga of Israel and Zionism* (1986).[80] When preparing the book he refused to meet Yasser Arafat and only a small fraction of the sources he drew on (20 entries in a bibliography of 296 items) were Arab.[81]

The Siege drew some comparisons between how British troops behaved in Tel Aviv in 1947 and how the Black and Tans did in Ireland between 1919 and 1921.[82] O'Brien argued that unlike Israel the Republic of Ireland had no enemies that wished to destroy the Irish state. He argued that valid comparisons could be drawn between the Catholics of Northern Ireland and the Palestinian Arabs. The Plantation of Ulster had displaced Catholics from their homelands. But the 'natives' remained in the area, mainly as tenants on the poorer land and in unskilled employment. The settlers developed the better land and built up industry. Although the material position of Catholics had improved, the relationship between Catholics and Protestant, native and settler, had 'lost nothing of its pristine animosity'.[83] In the general election of 1983 almost one-third of Catholics voted for a party that declared 'its unambiguous support for the armed struggle'. That is to say they voted for the IRA, which 'for years has been systematically murdering their Protestant neighbours'. And those who voted for them, he emphasised, were *not* the older people, clinging to ancient grievances. They were mainly the young, hoping to win what their ancestors had lost three and a half centuries previously. The Irish case he concluded did not offer much encouragement to hopes of an early settlement embracing both Jews and Palestinian Arabs.[84]

In 1986, in addition to *The Siege*, he published a lengthy piece of reportage on white South African perspectives on apartheid. 'What Can Become of South Africa?' drew on interviews and accounts of with those who felt under siege and the nuanced criticisms of white critics of apartheid such as the writer J. K. Coetzee. He argued that outsider critics would be unlikely to behave differently if they were put in the same position:

> Afrikaners are neither the uniquely virtuous *volk* of their own rhetoric ... nor the moral monsters depicted by outside rhetoric. They are ordinary human beings, with the normal quotas of greed, arrogance and so forth, operating within a unique predicament, which they have inherited and are now thrashing around in. I suspect that some of the righteous who denounce them from afar might have behaved quite like them if they were caught in a similar unique predicament – if, for example, there had been a black majority in America in the 1950s.[85]

O'Brien described an all-white rally of P. W. Botha's National Party composed of stolid, undemonstrative people, similar to an Orange Rally in Northern Ireland – at least when no Catholics were present. But physical encounters with Catholics could evoke latent hysteria and violence. He imagined participants of the National Party rally would have been similarly exercised were black people to turn up.[86]

O'Brien had for decades opposed apartheid but got into trouble with anti-apartheid campaigners in Ireland and in South Africa when in 1986 he accepted an offer to give a lecture course in the desegregated University of Cape Town on siege societies following his research visit for 'What Can Become of South Africa?' In that essay he had highlighted what he saw as growing opposition by whites to apartheid. He believed that economic sanctions worked to encourage such opposition but that intellectual isolation did the opposite. He highlighted the 'crowning irony' that whilst the regime censored journalists, some of the dottier anti-apartheid activists, 'know-nothings' who hated liberalism (amongst whom he numbered 'Sean McBride, the Nobel and Lenin International Prize of Peace-winning former Director of Amnesty International') tried to inflict similar damage on South Africa's academic community.[87]

The equivalences between Northern Ireland, Israel and South Africa identified by O'Brien played out something like this. All three were dominated by communities under siege that had come to be unhelpfully demonised and dehumanised in international debates. In all three cases much of the international sympathy lay with their supposed victims and exacerbated the states of siege experienced by Unionists, Zionists and Afrikaners. O'Brien argued that the experiences of Catholics in Ireland were now nothing like apartheid but he showed little or no sympathy for the plight of displaced Palestinians. He lumped the PLO together with Sinn Fein and the IRA as the bearers of unreasonable causes by unacceptable means. O'Brien was not alone emphasising such equivalences. On the ground in Northern Ireland some nationalist enclaves took to flying the Palestinian flag, Unionists the Israeli flag in theirs.

In yet another 1986 piece in *The New York Review of Books*, a dismissive review of a biography of Bobby Sands, the first IRA hunger striker to die in 1981, he argued that both the Republic of Ireland and the British State had miscalculated the level of Unionist opposition to any proposed settlement. Unless both governments backed off there was a danger of 'Holy War': the escalation from smouldering conflict to full conflagration. O'Brien used the review as a platform to argue against the 1985 Anglo-Irish agreement which he argued was doomed to fail. O'Brien warned of a potential apocalypse:

> Readers may ask what solution to the problem I envisage? None. I think the language of 'problem' and 'solution' is inappropriate to the case. What we have here is a *conflict*, which is likely to continue as long as the island of Ireland contains both a large Ulster Protestant community, and a significant and determined minority of Irish Republicans, with a hold on the Catholic community. This looks like being quite a long time. No tinkering will reconcile those irreconcilables and the effort to reconcile them often serves only to inflame the conflict, by arousing conflicting hopes and fears. On the other hand, if the Governments in London and Dublin learn, from unhappy experience of this Agreement that it is better to stop tinkering with ambitious 'solutions', and to return to quiet co-operation in security matters, then the level of violence involved in the conflict of irreconcilable wills could in time be reduced. It would also help if future Dublin Governments and their American backers could desist from their well-meant efforts to bring about progress towards a united Ireland; efforts whose unintended effects help on the Holy War.[88]

This pessimism was the focus of *Godland: Reflections on Religion and Nationalism* (1987), a collection of Harvard University lectures that was part of the same suite of writings. He used the term nationalism in a wider sense than it was generally used by political scientists who saw it as a modern phenomenon. O'Brien emphasised commonalities between modern nationalisms and older primordial forms of collective identity. He saw these as deeply rooted in human nature and unlikely to go away.[89] *Godland* argued that nationalism had an essentially religious character in all times and places. Even the secular French Republic was built on an edifice of state worship, the nation idolising itself. O'Brien emphasised three kinds of nationalism based, 'in ascending order of arrogance and destructiveness' on the notion of 'chosen people', the 'holy nation' (the chosen people with tenure) and, worst of all, the 'deified nation' that basked in God's permanent favour.[90] He emphasised underlying commonalities between Zionism, the invocation of God in American nationalism (his examples included declarations of manifest destiny, the Battle Hymn of the Republic and national prayer breakfasts), Covenants with God as declared by Northern Irish Protestants and by Protestant Afrikaners and Patrick Pearse's attempt to sanctify the Irish nation through a self-styled Christ-like sacrifice. Bobby Sands' 'self-immolation', O'Brien argued in *The New York Review of Books*, was self-consciously in this Pearsean tradition. Both alluded to Christ-like patriotic sacrifice in their writings.

In his 1986 *New York Review of Books* essay he also argued that there co-existed a hard version and a soft version of the demand for a united Ireland. The hard version was kept going by American money for the IRA, the soft version by Irish American politicians like Senators Edward Kennedy and Daniel Moynihan who condemned the IRA but still claimed to support a united Ireland 'by consent'. But how, O'Brien asked, was consent possible when nearly a million Ulster Protestants did not consent? The subtext, O'Brien argued, was an inference that by refusing to compromise they had nobody but themselves to blame if the IRA kept attacking them. Whenever he put this to exponents of the soft version they just shrugged. The soft version, he argued, abetted the hard version.

The 1985 Anglo-Irish agreement, he explained to his American readers, had infuriated Ulster Protestants who saw it as a betrayal by Britain, at the instigation of its Catholic enemies. In their support for this agreement Northern Catholics, he claimed, had consciously provoked the Protestant population:

> (Catholic) acceptance is not based on any perception of a potential for reconciliation in the Agreement, but on a very clear perception, and keen enjoyment, of the Agreement's power to infuriate the Protestant enemy. 'I like hearing Paisley squeal', as one Catholic put it. So far from reconciling, this Agreement adds new fuel to a communal animosity now nearly four centuries old.[91]

In essence, he argued that constitutional nationalists and the British and Irish governments that took their side were as much part of the siege as the IRA.

The man and the echo

In 1954, an English Jesuit being guided by O'Brien around Belfast asked how many Catholic Unionists there were. The group of Northern Catholics with them scratched their heads and managed to identify just one, but he had been snubbed by one side and boycotted by the other.[92] By the early 1990s O'Brien had decided to walk in this man's shoes. In response to the 1994 IRA ceasefire – part of a settlement that he believed ignored the views of and sold out the interests of Unionists – he formally became a Unionist. He explained his decision to join the small UKUP in his *Memoir* in the following terms: 'I didn't feel myself so much to be a Friend of the Union as a friend of the unionist people of Northern Ireland and a person determined to associate with them in support of their determination not to be pushed in a direction that they did not want to go.'[93] In 1996 he represented the UKUP in the Northern Ireland Forum, a consultative body on the future of Northern Ireland where Unionists were in the majority, but, in his view, nevertheless ignored. O'Brien's analysis was that the proposed settlement being put forward by the British government, and backed by the Republic of Ireland and the United States, was one aimed at appeasing Northern nationalists. When Sinn Fein were admitted to the talks without the IRA having relinquished its weapons the UKUP along with Ian Paisley's Democratic Unionist Party (DUP) pulled out.

O'Brien believed that the Peace Process replayed the dynamics of previous efforts by the British and Irish governments to resolve the Northern crisis without the consent of the Protestant Unionist majority. Back in 1957 Donal Barrington had criticised the expectation amongst Irish nationalists that the international community should make the British agree to a united Ireland. Frank Aiken, MacBride's successor as Minister of External Affairs called this brandishing the sore thumb. O'Brien's analysis of various efforts to arrive at a peaceful solution to the post-1969 conflict emphasised how Northern constitutional nationalists and the Republic used their influence to get the Americans to put pressure on the United Kingdom to, in effect, impose a solution on Unionists. O'Brien's analysis that the Unionists had very little political influence within the United Kingdom led him to argue in the last chapter of his 1998 memoir that to protect themselves the Unionists should propose to leave the Union and join a United Ireland where they would have significant political influence and might, O'Brien argued, marginalise Sinn Fein and end the IRA by removing its *raison d'étre*. O'Brien went from being that rarity, a Catholic Unionist, to being *reduction ad absurdum* Ireland's only anti-nationalist Unionist anti-partitionist.[94]

The context was one he described as a British betrayal of Unionists both by the British Prime Minister Tony Blair and the leader of the Ulster Unionist Party David Trimble for their apparent willingness to go into government with Sinn Fein, a party that still possessed a private army that had not given up its weapons. Over time O'Brien was proved wrong. The IRA effectively disbanded, the DUP under Ian Paisley as First Minister formed a coalition with Sinn Fein. Martin McGuinness, one-time leader of the IRA, became Deputy First Minister. Both men worked remarkably well together. Sinn Fein had entered government alongside the DUP in the North years before

Sinn Fein participation in a Southern government could even be contemplated by other political parties there. None of this was what O'Brien forecast.

A much-cited 1977 interview in *The Crane Bag* with Seamus Heaney addressed O'Brien's unique position in Irish politics, the difficulties he presented to Catholic nationalist intellectuals and what turned out to be an important contribution to ending the post-1969 Northern conflict. Do you not think, the interviewer Seamus Deane asked Heaney, that the kind of humanism which Conor Cruise O'Brien sponsors, though welcome from a rational point of view, 'renders much of what he says either irrelevant or wrong'. The obstinate voice of rationalist humanism, Heaney retorted, was important for if that was lost everything was lost. He argued that O'Brien did an utterly necessary job in rebuking all easy thought about the Protestant community in the North: 'It is to be seen in this way: 7 or 8 years ago there was tremendous sentiment for Catholics in the North, amongst intellectuals, politicians and ordinary people in the South. Because of his statements O'Brien is still reviled by people who held these sentiments; yet now these people harbour sentiments which mirror O'Brien's thinking, and still they do not cede to the clarity or the validity of his position.'[95] But surely, Deane objected, O'Brien's 'bourgeois form of humanism' imposed a rational clarity upon the Northern position that was untrue to the reality. Heaney replied that O'Brien's real force was in the South rather than the North; 'it is not enough for people to simply say "ah, they're all Irishmen" when some Northerners actually spit at the word Irishman'. O'Brien's contribution was an obstinate insistence on facing up to this kind of reality.[96]

CHAPTER THIRTEEN

Fintan O'Toole's second republic

For more than a quarter of century Ireland's leading public intellectual Fintan O'Toole (born 1958) has railed against corruption in Irish public life. For more than two decades he has been a star contributor to *The Irish Times* and has been variously its deputy editor, literary editor and theatre critic and international correspondent. On any given Saturday *The Irish Times* might contain several articles by him. Major current affairs features sit alongside theatre reviews and, whilst I was writing this book, the latest weekly instalment of a hundred-part series on objects that have shaped Irish society. Then there are the articles he publishes on weekdays and occasional pieces for international periodicals explaining Ireland's social, political and moral failings to the world.

The focus of this chapter is upon his attempts to address these as developed in several books and collections of essays published over the last two decades. His seminal 1995 book *Meanwhile Back at the Ranch: The Politics of Irish Beef* became the template for a whole genre of Irish books that have dissected Ireland's political and financial corruption.[1] In 2003, in *After the Ball*, written for a left-of-centre think tank, he offered an unheeded civics lesson on the need for responsible taxation and social policy. He argued that the fruits of prosperity were being squandered in the absence of a mature and responsible political culture.[2] A 2005 co-authored book *Post Washington: Why America Can't Rule the World* was published by the same think tank.[3] By the time of his 2009 book *Ship of Fools: How Stupidity and Corruption Sank the Celtic Tiger* his critique of the condition of Ireland had become the dominant analysis.[4] The following year, in *Enough is Enough: How to Build a New Republic*, he proposed fifty reforms that would, he hoped, nudge the Irish people and their politicians towards responsible citizenship.[5] In his series on a history of Ireland in one hundred objects one of his selections was a handwritten document listing names of members of the Irish parliament and the rewards they received for voting for the Act of Union, including peerages, army commissions and financial payments.[6] This had obvious resonance in a twenty-first-century Ireland that had produced its own lists of payments received by corrupt politicians and had experienced, partly as a result of such corruption, a loss of sovereignty under the terms of the 2010 International Monetary Fund (IMF) and European Central Bank (ECB) bailout deal.

O'Toole grew up in what was then the western edge of Dublin and he was a Christian Brothers' boy. At ten years of age, under duress, he bought *Our Boys*, a periodical that the Brothers had run since 1914 (on its masthead: 'To God and Eire true') when he would have preferred comics such as *X-Men*. In the late 1960s and early 1970s it was still full of second-hand versions of English *Boy's Own* stories from the 1920s, sometimes with Irish names superimposed on their stock characters – Murphy instead of Billy Bunter or cowboys called O'Leary.

Wild West metaphors reoccur in many of O'Toole's early essays. His first collection of these was called *A Mass for Jesse James*.[7] The Christian Brothers, he recalled in a 1997 essay, stood for Catholic faith, strict discipline, social mobility and nationalism, and out of these things they did much to shape modern Ireland and its sense of place in the world:

> As every catechism told us, God made the world. But there were times when it seemed that the Christian Brothers had been his main subcontractors. On the back of all my brick-coloured and red-margined copybooks, full of compound interest, irregular verbs and days at the seaside, was a map of the world. At the centre of this world was Ireland, and arising out of Ireland like shooting stars were lines leading to Australia, North America, Argentina, Africa – the contours of a spiritual conquest that had begun in 1802 when Edmund Ignatius Rice founded the Christian Brothers in Waterford. Shining over it all was the five-pointed radiant star of the Brothers' logo. It was our Empire, our own answer to the British maps of the world in which its colonial possessions glowed scarlet in every continent.[8]

The ideal Brothers boy, O'Toole recalled, recollecting that he had wanted to be one, held himself 'as straight as an exclamation mark!' His tie was 'as straight as a plumbline, pointing to the centre of his moral gravity – his unbreakable, unquestioning faith'. But *Our Boys* could not compete with television, rock music or *X-Men*. Their boys went on to create a materialist Ireland, profoundly different from the one the Brothers had in mind. But they also produced in Fintan O'Toole the straight-backed opposite to a literary outlaw determined to face down the black-hatted outlaws of Irish politics, their buddies the cowboy builders and corrupt ranchers, whilst Ireland's not-so-law-abiding citizens kept their shutters down.

Much of his invocation of pop culture does not hold up well compared to his serious literary criticism. 'Going West: The Country Versus the City in Irish Writing', published in *The Crane Bag* in 1985, was at once a deft survey of the role of theatre in the modernisation of Ireland and something of a personal intellectual manifesto. It cited Karl Marx's *The Eighteenth Brumaire of Louis Napoleon* on the distinction between revolutions that drew their poetry from the past and those that stripped away all superstitions and drew poetry from the future.[9] O'Toole endorsed something close to the latter – the need to do away with the rural imaginary that had long dominated Irish theatre at the expense of representations of urban realities.

In 1990, in the post-modernist *A Mass for Jesse James*, he explained that a thatched cottage on the stage of a new Irish play would inevitably be seen by its audience as something that was there to be immediately contradicted and subverted, and that readers of literature were well used to – and even expected – unreliable narrators. In many of his early essays metaphors and pop-culture allusions played a role that came to be replaced in later critiques of the condition of Ireland by facts and figures. A 1984 essay republished in *A Mass for Jesse James*, 'Bright with Cosy Homesteads', derided the aesthetics of rural modernisation and piled on stereotypes and exaggeration for effect:

> Many of the biggest new houses in places like Leitrim, Roscommon and Mayo belong to cattle dealers, the new aristocracy of the west, and the mythology of the big ranchers is strong. The cattle dealers built houses like 'The High Chaparral' in County Mayo, with white picket fences and Mexican verandas and wagon-train wheel cartwheels decorating the walls, and a horned bull's skull over the driveway entrance, houses that can only have been conceived in the midst of a cowboy fantasy.[10]

But in his 1995 book *Meanwhile Back at the Ranch*, he turned from such cartoons to facts and figures and to linear narratives that readers could have faith in. O'Toole's writings on politics and society came to emphasise the importance of being earnest in a political context where there were all too many unreliable narrators. Cultural analysis, he reflected in an afterword to a 2003 anthology of his theatre criticism, tends to be solipsistic. As a critic he was accountable to nobody. Not so when it came to his interventions in social and political affairs:

> If I write that Politician C took a bribe from Businessman B. I have to prove it objectively with documents, witnesses or other evidence. Other people can establish whether or not I'm telling lies. But if I claim that my correspondent's 'stylistically and thematically heterogeneous play' actually struck me as a bit of a mess, no one can tell whether I'm giving a truthful account of how I felt when I came out of the theatre or pursuing some stupid ideological or personal agenda. . . . As someone who spends many of his waking hours as a journalist demanding accountability of people who occupy positions of public power, I cannot be unaware of the irony of occupying a position of minor but essentially unaccountable power myself. If a politician accused of bad faith were to say 'Trust me', I would be the first to attack.[11]

Vignettes about hacienda-style bungalows and about the priest who said Mass once a year for the repose of the soul of Jesse James glided uncomprehendingly over the surface of a middle-Ireland he never quite came to grips with. His theatre criticism continued to follow hermeneutic trails from one play to the next – the lines of continuity between the peasant plays of the Abbey theatre and later plays set in urban tenements – but none of this should be confused with ethnographies of real rural or urban communities. His journalism on the other hand has focused on what could be categorically stated and measured – who, what, where, when and how much? The problem was why? For all his attention to arts and culture, facts and figures, and later to the ideal of an Irish Republic, he has never seemed anthropologically fascinated by what Flann O'Brien called the plain people of Ireland. Instead he has drawn on standard sociological and political science critiques of Irish political culture, secularisation, underdevelopment and globalisation. These have been helpful only up to a point in explaining why the majority who ought to have been as angered as he has been about the condition of Ireland have been part of the problem.

Two key themes stand out in his multitudinous writings on the crises of accountability, political corruption and institutional failure that have been revealed in recent decades. Firstly he has been preoccupied with the vacuum created by the decline of the twin pillars of authority upon which the Irish State was founded, institutional Catholicism and populist nationalism. Secondly he has focused on the causes and consequences of an impoverished public domain – the apparent inability, as he sees it, of the Irish to govern themselves both individually and collectively. Ireland's problems, as he has depicted them, have been ones of individual and collective moral failure.

But his finest book to date is arguably his 1997 biography of Richard Brinsley Sheridan, *A Traitor's Kiss*. Sheridan was a fellow-Irishman and Whig-turned-republican contemporary of Edmund Burke's in the House of Commons, a hugely successful theatre impresario and the playwright who wrote *School for Scandal* and *The Rivals*.[12] Sheridan's father, Thomas, an actor and teacher of rhetoric who had been mentored for a time by Jonathan Swift, fervently believed that public virtue could be upheld by public eloquence. In this, O'Toole argued, he was vindicated by the extraordinary ability of his son to wield it as a weapon in the fight for human decency.[13] O'Toole, as a journalist and polemist, placed his considerable gifts to similar use. He could applaud Sheridan for surviving a political setback 'by exploiting with extraordinary presence of mind the gap between appearance and reality, between performance and intention', whilst excoriating Charles Haughey and Bertie Ahern for using similar sleights of hand to exploit, what Ahern called in one of his finest malapropisms, the 'smoke and daggers' of Irish politics. O'Toole, for his part, insisted that grimy realities be held up against the light of what ought to be.

The wild west

In a 1987 pamphlet, *The Southern Question*, O'Toole staked out ground upon which he would fight for civic republican virtue over the next quarter century.[14] It recalled his childhood memories of the 1966 fiftieth anniversary commemoration of the 1916 Rising. That year for a week the West Dublin children in Crumlin stopped playing Cowboys and Indians and instead recreated the house-to-house fighting that devastated Dublin in 1916 as reconstructed by Hugh Leonard's *Insurrection* on Ireland's five-year-old television station. Children in new working class suburbs – places without history but given a kind of one by streets named for ancient dioceses and the patriot dead – were schooled in the 1916 Proclamation, ballads of the war of independence and were made to act pageants of patriotic martyrdom. O'Toole recalled standing on stage at the age of eight in starched white shirt, tri-coloured tie, green short trousers and green socks reciting a monologue on the death of a young Irish solider at the hands of the Black and Tans whilst other children acted out the story. What should have been serious and solemn became a glorious farce. The adult audience became helpless and hysterical with laughter as the on-stage pallbearers dragged the dead martyr to the wings, the tricolour bunching around the child's neck, his head bumping off the rough boards to the side of the stage.

Much of O'Toole's subsequent theatre criticism emphasised the power of the theatre to revel in the contradictions of Irish society. But his 2011 RTE television documentary *Fintan O'Toole: Power Plays* worried whether Irish theatre had the capacity to artistically address the post-Celtic Tiger crisis facing Irish society to the same extent that Sean O'Casey and other great dramatists had done in the past. Irish theatre, he argued, had responded powerfully to the cultural shift that took place during his own childhood. Playwrights like Brian Friel, Tom Murphy and John B. Keane created vivid moral dramas about a society torn between past and future.

But there had been, he lamented, no equivalent coherent response to more recent crises because there was no longer a single driving narrative to latch onto. The old straightforward conflicts between tradition and modernity with their binary shifts from rural and urban and religious and secular were now part of history. The choices thrown up in the Celtic Tiger appeared rather less heroic. Deciding whether or not to buy a holiday home in Bulgaria or Florida was not the same stuff of drama as agonising about whether or not to emigrate from rural Donegal to urban America, the subject of Brian Friel's much-produced play *Philadelphia Here We Come*. The old stock narratives, whether these were deployed in theatre or politics, no longer served Ireland well.

In *The Southern Question* his main theme was the cynical manipulation of nationalist iconography by Charles Haughey to mask much that was rotten in the politics of late twentieth-century Ireland. The rhetoric of

Irish politics had evolved out of nineteenth-century romanticism, post-independence ideals of rural frugality of a united Ireland. Haughey became the new maestro of such rhetoric, inserting into the old teetering narratives of national destiny whilst simultaneously becoming mysteriously and conspicuously wealthy. O'Toole's concern in 1987 was not that Haughey was a crook; that came fully into the public domain a few years later. It was that Haughey personified the spirit of Fianna Fáil, the party that dominated the politics of Southern Irish identity, which could vanquish any meaningful consideration of social issues by invoking the rhetoric of a united Ireland. Haughey was all too adept at the posture politics of faith and fatherland and made it work for him in a context where faith was in decline and old-style nationalism should have meant a lot less than it did.

From Haughey's speeches O'Toole diagnosed the symptoms (as distinct from root causes) of many problems besetting late twentieth-century Ireland. Trailing what would become his big theme, *The Southern Question* described an Ireland that had experienced economic modernisation without being able to construct 'an economic polis'. It had gone from being a pre-urban society to a post-urban one without coherent, transparent and accountable planning systems. The underlying problem, he argued, was a political culture that blocked the emergence of a strong public realm. In *The Southern Question* he blamed this failure, as had many of Ireland's political scientists, on the dominance of clientalist politics.[15] Clientalism, whereby a highly personalised nature of social relationships leads to a belief that the authorities can be approached only through the intercessions of patrons or brokers with 'pull', was, in O'Toole's summary, a form of peasant politics that had persisted in a post-peasant society. It turned politics into a private arrangement between voter and politician within which corruption could flourish.

A decade after the publication of *The Southern Question* Ireland was in the midst of an era of unprecedented economic growth and the nationalist rhetoric that once appeared hegemonic became apparently consigned to the dustbin of history. A peaceful settlement had been found to the Northern question. In the introduction to a 1997 collection of essays *The Ex-Isle of Ireland* O'Toole suggested that economic prosperity had undermined such nationalist chauvinism and its equivalent amongst Northern Unionists:

> The fact is that both unionists and nationalists had a vested interest in the image of the Free State as a decrepit, underdeveloped, impoverished backwater. For nationalists, that image supplied the necessary sense of grievance – look at what the Brits have done to us, and if only we were free we would be the happiest, most prosperous people on God's earth. For unionists it provided a warning – look what we would be like if the boggy mediocrity of the South were allowed to seep across the border.
>
> For nationalists, Ireland being a Third World country was a source of pride, lending the glamour of international anti-imperialism to a squalid ethnic conflict in an obscure corner of the First World. For unionists, the

Republic being a Third World country allowed the rather comic illusion that Northern Ireland itself is a beleaguered outpost of threatened modernity. But either as an excuse for failure or dire warning to stick to nurse for fear of something worse, the rich Republic of the mid-1990s, rolling in dollars and ECUS, is of little use to either nationalists or unionists.[16]

A substantial 1997 essay on the CEO of Heinz, press baron and former Irish rugby star Tony O'Reilly, explored the impact of global capitalism and the chasm between what the modern Ireland nationalist politicians believed they were forging and the neo-liberal 'Ireland PLC' that came to pass. O'Rielly became 'an icon a changing Ireland' and a 'folk hero of capitalism', one by no means incompatible with the other. In 1962, when he was just twenty-six, he was appointed general manager of Bord Bainne (the Milk Marketing Board) by the Taoiseach Sean Lemass, who had also advanced the political career of his son-in-law Charles Haughey. Lemass, a member of the 1916 gerontocracy that had dominated Irish politics since independence, had urged a generational shift. In a speech quoted by O'Toole he urged older company directors to stand aside for a younger generation.[17]

In 1962 agriculture still employed nearly a third of the Irish workforce. O'Rielly's first big success was the creation of the Kerrygold brand to market Irish butter internationally. The government appointed him to head up an even larger State enterprise, the Irish Sugar Company, and its subsidiary Erin Foods, which had been set up to sell the produce of Irish agricultural co-operatives and state-owned factories to the urban Irish and British markets. O'Reilly entered Erin Foods into a partnership with the huge international brand Heinz and in 1969 went to work for Heinz, rose up its food chain and became its chief executive. In 1990 he discontinued the Erin brand.

Had O'Reilly turned down the offer from Heinz he could have had a cabinet post in Jack Lynch's government as Minister of Agriculture with a good chance of later becoming Taoiseach. But O'Reilly explained that a career in Irish politics could not compare to one as a multinational company executive. In O'Toole's summary:

Given the choice between running a multinational company and running a small European country, he chose the former. He had seen that once Ireland opened itself up to American multinationals, the idea of national sovreignity, of state control, had become untenable. Years later, when idealistic nationalists came to power in Africa, first Robert Mugabe in Zimbabwe, then Nelson Mandela in South Africa, he would point out that they could not run their own economies, that economic nationalism was dead, that they would have to come to terms with the power of scarce and demanding capital.[18]

When O'Reilly took over Waterford Crystal he commissioned market research in the United States asking whether customers knew if Waterford was in Ireland. If they did the workers at the Waterford plant might have some power against the mobility of global capital. But since they did not the crystal may as well have been manufactured in Czechoslovakia where it could be made more cheaply, which was what then happened.

As recounted by O'Toole, O'Reilly's story was a parable of rapacious globalisation and one of disconnection from the patriotic aspirations of the previous generation. O'Reilly claimed that he had 'practically been raised' by a friend's uncle Peadar O'Donnell, the republican socialist. But cautionary tales about global capitalism were overshadowed by the malign home-grown variety that was the subject of much of O'Toole's journalism.

His 1995 book *Meanwhile Back at the Ranch* forensically peeled back layer after layer of corruption in Ireland's indigenous beef industry, the history of which he traced back to William Petty's plans to turn Ireland into a depopulated ranch. The dominant company Goodman International had an annual turnover of about £500 million during the 1980s and this accounted for about 4 per cent of Ireland's GDP. Larry Goodman sold 1.3 million head of cattle a year and 'one pound in every twenty generated in the country passed through this man's hands'.[19] Yet, his company paid only £80,000 corporation tax between 1986 and 1989 whilst drawing large subsidies from the exchequer.[20]

In September 1987 Haughey's government agreed to indemnify Goodman International exports of Irish beef to Iraq to the tune of $134.5 million. Goodman's deal with Iraq depended on the Irish government providing credit insurance. But Goodman International was simultaneously under investigation for various kinds of fraud. In 1983 a Cork customs officer discovered South African customs stamps en route to an Irish printer that had been ordered by one of Goodman's subsidiaries. Much of Ireland's beef was sold to the EU beef mountain at subsidised rates. Further EU subsidies applied to beef sold outside Europe. Beef stamped as sold outside the EU was worth £150 million to the Irish economy. Some of this was clearly the subject of fraudulent claims. The Department of Agriculture called in the Fraud Squad and this led to a three-year investigation of Goodman International. There was much money to be made by surreptitiously re-labelling the nature, origins and destinations of produce. Investigations revealed practices of over declaring weights of shipments in order to increase the amount of export refunds from the EU, substituting ineligible trimmings and cheap cuts for the more expensive cuts declared on shipping cartons.[21]

Needless to say most of the beef sent to Iraq was not halal, as the contract had specified. Similar tricks were used to avoid paying taxes to the Irish state. Goodman International also made cash payments to non-existent companies so that employees could be paid off the books. 'Anybody', as Larry Goodman's counsel told the beef tribunal, 'who thinks that the meat industry is conducted according to the same principle as the activities of mother Teresa of Calcutta would be mistaken'.[22] The eventual loss covered by the Irish State was around 83 million euros.[23]

The previous government had refused to provide credit insurance partly because of the poor reputation Iraq had acquired for making payments and partly because of the Iran–Iraq war. Iraq had acquired the reputation for only servicing debts when ever-increasing amounts of credit were forthcoming. From 1983 the Department of Industry and Commerce had recommended limiting credit exposure to Iraq, and in March 1987 Michael Noonan the then-Minister of Finance submitted a memorandum to Cabinet confirming that no cover was being granted for Iraq and that this would remain the case until there was an identifiable improvement in Iraq's repayment record.[24] But within days after Fianna Fáil returned to power in 1987 this policy was reversed by Noonan's successor Albert Reynolds, without a Cabinet decision and without input from government officials. An initial approval of £35 million credit insurance was soon increased by many multiples.

Meanwhile Back at the Ranch found no smoking gun of political corruption. Instead O'Toole emphasised Fianna Fáil's betrayal of is own ideals. The party represented a nationalism rooted amongst small landowners that could be traced back to the nineteenth century. But its small farmer rhetoric could not be squared with the economic importance of the beef industry:

In 1937–8 cattle and beef exports accounted for just over half of all Irish agricultural exports. By 1960–1 they accounted for over 70 per cent. In the meantime emigration, mostly to Britain, reached levels of 50,000 a year. William Petty's colonial vision of Ireland as a giant cattle ranch with the bulk of its population resettled in England was being realised.[25]

Not only had the beef industry depopulated Fianna Fáil's then-rural heartland, it had come to 'limit the development of the kind of coherent, confident civil and political society which could control that industry and integrate it into a working notion of the common good'.[26] In claiming this O'Toole drew a contrast with rural development in Denmark. The Danes had come to develop a highly cooperative society. They managed to keep the people on the land and develop agriculture as an industry at the same time. Cattle exports without the kinds of cooperative enterprise that had emerged in Denmark did little to build a stable rural society. Irish cattle exports coincided with emigration and rural depopulation and concentrated wealth in the hands of a rural minority.

Goodman had made donations to Fianna Fáil and as a major economic player had access to Fianna Fáil's inner circle. The widely used expression 'golden circles' was coined during a motion of no confidence in Charles Haughey in November 1991 to describe the belief than an elite had access to insider information which was making them very rich.[27] Such access and a very forceful personality enabled Goodman to bypass the proper channels by which applications for credit insurance, subsidies and other considerations would ordinarily be processed by government departments. Reynolds was cut from the same cloth as Goodman. He owed his wealth to a chain of rural dancehalls and later moved into the meat industry, specialising in the export of pet food as distinct from beef. As described by O'Toole, both were part of a new bonanza culture.

Revelations about state favouritism towards Goodman International led to the establishment of the Beef Tribunal, which sat for more than three years (1991–4) and cost about £320 million. Subsequent tribunals lasted for years and cost hundreds of millions more, creating a new class of millionaire barristers but also a drip feed of revelations to journalists like O'Toole. For example, the McCracken Tribunal (1997) and Moriarty Tribunal (2002–10) revealed that offshore accounts were used to evade tax and launder payments to politicians including Haughey.[28] The Flood/Mahon Tribunal's (1997–2012) investigation of payments to politicians by developers and land rezoning corruption triggered the resignation of the then-Taoiseach Bertie Ahern in 2008.

The boomtown rats

The paradox of Irish political culture, O'Toole argued in his 2009 polemic *Ship of Fools: How Stupidity and Corruption Sank the Celtic Tiger*, was that such revelations of corruption made things worse. In the 1980s and 1990s, 'when anyone with a sense of smell could get a ripe hum of rottenness of figures like Haughey', glimpses of whose dubious financial dealings occasionally emerged through the fog of Ireland's heavily restrictive libel laws, it was possible to believe that if incontrovertible proof emerged that the system would be shaken to its core. O'Toole was perhaps recalling his motivation for writing *Meanwhile Back at the Ranch*:

> The assumption was that some kind of rough morality actually operated, and that wrongdoing, once revealed, would be punished. The old culture would not survive, and if Fianna Fáil itself were to do so, it would have to be thoroughly reformed.
>
> What actually happened, however, was something much stranger and ultimately more damaging. From the mid-1990s onwards, it became ever more undeniable that corruption was deeply embedded, both at the top and at the bottom of Irish public life .... Sleazy as these crimes were, they were not unique to Irish politics. What was peculiar to Ireland, however, was what happened next – virtually nothing.[29]

Despite all the revelations there had been no meaningful change in the political culture.[30] The problem was not just one of corrupt politicians but of a fragile civic morality. The Irish political system had remained tribal, local and clientalist. There was a strong impulse to vote for candidates who would successfully manipulate the system on behalf of constituents individually and the constituency as a whole. It was not unusual for politicians to top polls after evidence of corruption had come to light. A big problem was the failure of the various tribunals and inquiries that had lasted for years to effectively punish wrongdoers:

> Because knowledge did not lead to action and the same system remained in place, the ultimate impact of the certainty that there was deep corruption in Irish politics was cynicism about politics itself. Voters got to watch their leaders developing unfortunate memory loss in sworn inquires. They saw the operation of *omerta*, as big political players were protected and defended by their colleagues while the small fry were abandoned to their fate. They witnessed the ruthlessness with which loyalties were abandoned or restored, as a figure like Haughey went from paragon to pariah to patriot, as the Party's needs dictated. Instead of raising standards, the revelations inadvertently lowered them. The broad public response to the stripping away of the illusions of patriotism and public service was that all politics are corrupt.[31]

The 1995–2001 'Celtic Tiger' economic boom had resulted from genuine increases in productivity and exports. But this had been superseded by a State-sanctioned property and speculation-led boom that threw up an army of property developers more, if anything, ruthlessly indifferent to State rules and regulation than Larry Goodman. The Fianna Fáil and Progressive Democrat government elected in 1997 promised and delivered light touch regulation of business which levered further foreign investment but also allowed the cancers in the body politic identified by O'Toole in *Meanwhile Back at the Ranch* to metastasise:

> In general, the government did not just tolerate low standards in public life and business by doing little to challenge them. It preserved the attitudes that kept them in place. In doing so, it failed to alter the well-established climate of financial adventurism, in which recklessness was encouraged by impunity. An atmosphere of insider intimacy in which cronyism thrives continued to hang over boomtime Ireland. On their own, either political stupidity or a tolerance for sleaze would have threatened the sustainability of the Irish economic miracle. Together, they ensured its demise.[32]

Subsequent revelations of a business culture where companies expected to be tapped for funds for Haughey or his successor Ahern coincided with large-scale tax avoidance in which the banks were complicit. Banks were legally required to withhold tax from interest paid to borrowers on deposit accounts but the use of bogus non-resident accounts by persons who were in fact living in Ireland turned out to be widespread. Between £300 million and £400 million was salted away in 1991 alone depriving the state of about £100 million in taxation. Revelation followed revelation without any real focus on responsibility or regulation:

> Although two large criminal conspiracies had been uncovered, there were no prosecutions .... Not only was there no legal accountability there was no managerial responsibility either. There was no clear-out of senior bank management. The blue chip accountancy firms whose audits had somehow missed the fact that their clients were colluding in large-scale fraud remained in business. The banking culture in which everyone raced towards the bottom of the ethical barrel for fear of losing business to a more unscrupulous rival remained entirely intact.[33]

Ship of Fools went on to detail many aspects of the ethical and political climate that inflated the property bubble that, when it burst, brought down the pyramid schemes of a corrupt and irresponsible banking system. O'Toole's emphasis was the underlying pathologies as he saw them, the prevalence of moral ambiguity, hypocrisy and double standards in public life but also in Irish society more generally. Irish society had an extraordinary capacity to both know and not know what was going on. Irish people, he argued, knew well about physical abuse in Church-run industrial schools but were genuinely shocked when this became officially revealed during the 1990s. Long before Donald Rumsfeld drew the distinction between 'known unknowns' and 'knowns' Irish people simultaneously knew and did not know about widespread political and financial corruption.

O'Toole's explanation was that when Catholicism declined there was no deep-rooted civic morality to take its place, nor had there been one in the first place. The Irish had been taught for generations to identify morality with religion and the kind most emphasised by the Irish Church was sexual morality:

> Morality was what happened in bedrooms, not in boardrooms. It was about the body, not the body politic. Masturbation was a much more serious sin than tax evasion. In a mindset where homosexuality was much worse than cooking the books, it was okay to be bent as long as you were straight. This nineteenth-century ethic was not pushed aside by the creation of a coherent and deeply rooted civic, democratic and social morality. It mostly collapsed under its own weight of hypocrisy.[34]

In 2006 Ahern presided over a State funeral for Haughey that paid 'tribal homage' to 'the Boss' and the political culture he exemplified. Unlike Shakespeare's Mark Antony at Caesar's funeral, Ahern had come to give praise. 'Haughey', Ahern asserted, 'was a patriot to his fingertips. When the shadows have faded the light of his achievements will remain'. The shadows were cast, O'Toole retorted, by the towers of money that Haughey had accumulated whilst holding high political office: 'the equivalent in 2006 of about €45 million, or 171 times his lifetime's salary as a full-time politician'.[35]

During the Celtic Tiger years the Fianna Fáil-led government introduced a plethora of tax relief schemes worth €8.4 billion in 2004 or nearly one-quarter of the tax take at the time, many of which benefited those who were making fortunes out of what was now a property speculation boom. A study by the Revenue Commissioners of the 400 richest taxpayers found that six had an effective tax rate of zero per cent, forty-three paid less than 5 per cent and most paid less than 15 per cent. At that time the top rate for ordinary taxpayers was 42 per cent.[36]

However, the problem was not just one of delinquent elites. In *After the Ball* he argued that the ambivalence of the Irish people to taxation ran deep. Except for those caught in the Pay As You Earn (PAYE) net the available statistics suggested that tax dodging was endemic. In 2000 235,000 self-employed people including farmers earned almost €10 billion and paid just €1.9 billion in tax, an effective rate of less than 20 per cent.[37] A 1984 European Value Systems Study showed that the Irish believed that homosexuality, divorce, prostitution or having an affair were significantly worse sins than cheating on your taxes. On ambivalence to tax evasion the Irish came top of the European league.[38]

Missing from this analysis was a focus on the media. O'Toole's diagnosis of Ireland's ills sidestepped the extent to which even *The Irish Times* of which he was the deputy editor had a stake in stoking the boom. *The Irish Times*' weekly property supplement was where Ireland's real and imagined rich found their urban haciendas and holiday villas and where those on lower incomes were exhorted to take out 35-year mortgages on inconveniently located future ghost estates built as tax shelters by those who creamed it during the boom.

The dead republic

In the aftermath of Ireland's 2010 economic collapse O'Toole's critique of the dominant political culture become the prevailing one. As put by Elaine Byrne in *Political Corruption in Ireland 1922–2010*:

> Ultimately, the exercise of corruption is intrinsically undemocratic because it seeks to bestow unfair and unjust advantage to the few which is contrary to the belief in liberty, equality and fraternity. It undermines and delegitimises the principle of democratic action. The relationship between power and citizenship is dependent on a voluntary contract of trust. In the September 2009 Eurobarometer poll, Ireland had virtually the lowest level of public-trust in government across the twenty-seven

European countries surveyed.[39]

Nor was he alone in his prescription for improving the condition of Ireland. Again as put by Byrne:

> Ireland's loss of economic sovereignty in 2010, due to a perception of political failure and the unorthodox influence of vested interests, may yet motivate Irish public life to engage in state-building and reimagine Irish society with an emphasis on the moral duties of citizenship.[40]

Enough is Enough: How to Build a New Republic (2010) opened with an allegorical tale of a young officer who successfully leads his men off a mountain in a blizzard with what turns out to be the wrong map.[41] O'Toole's point was that any map was better than none. Mapping Ireland's future was particularly difficult because the twin towers of Southern Irish identity – Catholicism and nationalism – were already teetering before the great boom began in 1995. The foundations of institutional Catholicism had been shaken by secularisation, the sexual revolution and its own scandals. Nationalism, affected by the vicious conflict in Northern Ireland, the venality of 'patriotic' politicians, membership of the European Union and by cultural globalisation, offered few easy answers.

That was why, he believed, that the Celtic Tiger had been embraced with such fervour. It offered a substitute identity at a time when Catholicism and nationalism, the old cornerstones of Irish identity, no longer worked. On one hand it brought mad consumerism, arrogance towards the rest of the world and a wilful sundering of the ties to history and tradition. But the Celtic Tiger had also engendered optimism, a new openness and an absence of fear. It had 'banished the underlying Irish sense of doom, the bitter spectre of self-contempt that was always whispering in our ears that we would screw it all up'. No wonder then that the Celtic Tiger had been embraced with such fervour and why its sudden demise was such a psychic shock. The shock was all the worse because the economic and social benefits of prosperity had been so badly squandered:

> And then we screwed it all up. Given unimaginable bounty – a durable peace settlement, overflowing state coffers, a generation born into the expectation of limitless possibilities – we managed not just to squander it but to end up in some respects worse off than we were before. The question that nags at us now is if we couldn't make a go of it in the longest boom in our history, how can we make a go of it with a vast burden of debt, a continuing global crisis and a landscape scarred with half-built houses whose increasingly decrepit emptiness mocks our delusions of grandeur?[42]

By 2010 Ireland had experienced a banking crisis, a crisis in the public finances, an economic crisis, a social crisis caused by mass unemployment and a reputational crisis. But the biggest crisis, O'Toole insisted, was the one in Irish political culture.[43] The focus of the Irish State was mostly on the first two and least upon what was rotten about the state of Ireland. O'Toole insisted that without political transformation there could be no solutions to economic and fiscal problems:

> To get itself out of the hole it's in, Ireland will have to become an extremely well-run and deeply engaged society. It will have to have a set of common goals that can animate a sense of collective purpose. It will need a map – even if it does not match the contours of a rough terrain – that gives it the courage to find its way home. None of these things is remotely on offer in the current political system. None is likely to be created by a mere change in government, from one led by a clapped-out populist right-of-centre party to one led by a fresher, hungrier right-of-centre party.
>
> Most current political debate in the Western world is organised around a clash between the left's argument for a strong state and the right's argument for a strongly engaged society. In the depths of its despair, Ireland badly needs both. And I believe that these ideas can be fused in what is a rather old concept – that of the republic. A republic can and should be a state that draws its strength from the active and independent engagement of its citizens.[44]

His precedent was the first Dáil of January 1919 which had adopted a Democratic Programme that was republican in what it proposed to do. In less than 600 words the Democratic Programme set out principles of liberty, equality and justice that were subsequently abandoned: the right of every citizen to an 'adequate share of the produce of the Nation's labour', 'the duty to make provision for the physical, mental and spiritual well-being of the children' and to provide for the aged by 'abolishing the present odious, degrading and foreign Poor Law System, substituting therefore a sympathetic native scheme for the care of the Nation's aged and infirm.'

What instead prevailed was the rule of private property, the coercion of children in the care of the state in a system of industrial schools, a political system that sidelined cooperative movements and local government and which fostered a political culture in which clientalism and jobbery prevailed. There were commonalities, he argued, to all the crises thrown up over the previous two decades that revealed corruption as a vivid pattern in Irish public life.[45] In its complicity with such corruption the state had failed to act in the interests of Irish citizens. *Enough is Enough* made the case for an ethical austerity. What Ireland needed was not cuts in public spending but a moral seriousness in public life. There was, he insisted, no need for vapid pieties. Irish society mostly needed to just impose some concrete rules and stick to them:

Ireland doesn't need to go into self flagellation to expunge its sins of self indulgence and self delusion. But it does need to develop a republican ethic of citizenship in which excess is not worshipped, rules are agreed to and kept and responsibility is taken – for ourselves and society.[46]

How hard could that be? A whole new mindset was needed – a new intolerance of greed, cynicism and of the pursuit of private gain over public good. But how likely was that to come about? A new form of individualism was needed – not the cowboy ethic of doing whatever you could get away with, but the idea of taking personal responsibility for the public realm. And how might this be realised short of cloning Fintan O'Toole a couple of million times? There had to be, he insisted, a new form of collectivism – not the tribal and parochial loyalties that had shaped the political culture but a wider sense of mutual obligation.[47]

O'Toole's fifty-point plan included the total reform of local government by strengthening its powers, giving it power over public services run by unelected bodies and shoring up local accountability whilst preventing the kinds of people who often dominated local politics – auctioneers, property developers or planning consultants – from holding office. He advocated changing the proportional representation system for electing members of parliament (TDs) that, Irish political scientists explained, was also a driver of clientalist politics.[48] Given the intense competition for votes in multi-seat constituencies Irish politicians had to promise support for all manner of things. He gave the example of one TD who, in a fourteen-year period, had made 220,000 mostly useless written representations on behalf of constituents. Each of these would have to be processed by civil and public service bureaucrats. He extrapolated that about 49,800 such demands for action were directed at the civil service every working day. The culture of 'imaginary patronage' was that politicians rarely refused to endorse a client's request for patronage. Politicians met their constituents not as citizens with rights but as clients in clinics. Such constituency work took up much of the time of cabinet ministers. O'Toole gave several examples of politicians making written pleas on behalf of paedophiles whose families had votes in their constituency.[49]

Electoral reforms were needed that would depersonalise the relationship between politicians and voters. But how might the Irish people be persuaded to take such medicine given that their ambivalence was part of the problem? His hope was that given the mood of anger and despair leading up to the 2011 election they might be willing to do more than just punish Fianna Fáil at the polls. *Enough is Enough* and *Ship of Fools* were number one bestsellers but O'Toole's idea for a second republic sparked little or no debate.[50] As recalled by the novelist Keith Ridgeway in the aftermath of the 2011 election:

Having been attacked and derided and ridiculed by the political, business and media gobshites who were the fluffers of the bogus boom, you'd think O'Toole would be in a fairly good position now to have an eager audience not only for his diagnosis of the problems of the failed state but for his suggested remedies as well. And you'd be right – he does have an audience, and a lot of (late but deserved) respect. But the audience remains largely passive, placid, afraid, and there has been little sign in the recent election or in the discourse since . . . that anyone has really heard what he said.[51]

Before the election, together with another of Ireland's best known public intellectuals, the journalist and economist David McWilliams, O'Toole tried to put together a new political movement comprising well-known public figures, 'people with some kind of reputation' as he put it in an RTE radio interview, that were not aligned to any of the existing political parties who would stand on the platform he had set out in *Enough is Enough*.

O'Toole's aim was to stand Democracy Now candidates for election in each parliamentary constituency. The hope was that twenty or so would be elected, enough to hold the balance of power and be in a position to lever reform of the Irish political system. Those who were approached to stand included a few well-known media celebrities, a gay hurling star, a football pundit and a disability campaigner. The plan collapsed when the election was called before Democracy Now could be set up.[52] On 30 January 2011 he cancelled the revolution on Twitter: 'Apologies to everyone who was hoping for an electoral initiative. I've never worked harder or been more disappointed. Nearly worked too.' This claim was hardly convincing. As put by Keith Ridgeway:

> The reason for not running was, in the end, so undramatically prosaic and dull that no one I've talked to believes a word of it, and yet can't quite rouse themselves into thinking up a reasonable conspiracy theory either. It's just too boring. According to O'Toole there was simply not enough time. The election had come too soon. They couldn't 'do it properly'. Never mind that independents all over the country seemed to be able to manage it. The O'Toole people had jobs, families, *these things are difficult, the upheaval* . . . and it petered out into a sort of mumble of *the-dog-ate-my-homework-sir*. It looked and sounded pathetic.[53]

Nobody was willing to be inconvenienced for, let alone die for, a new republic. Just one of the figures linked to Democracy Now, Shane Ross, a financial journalist who had a reputation for exposing financial corruption (he had co-written a book on the banking industry in the style of *Meanwhile Back at the Ranch*) was elected as an independent TD.[54] While Fianna Fáil lost all but 20 of their 78 seats the mould of Irish politics was by no means shattered. A Fine Gael and Labour Party coalition was formed and a loose group of independent TDs was established that included a few socialists, as well as Shane Ross, but also Mick Wallace, a former property developer who in 2012 faced considerable criticism for tax avoidance. Other independents included Michael Lowry, who had topped the poll in several elections after having being the focus of a tribunal investigating payments to politicians.

In a November 2011 article O'Toole ruefully reflected that the Irish were not even capable of having a proper crisis. Crisis, he explained, was a term rooted in Greek tragedy that meant 'a decisive moment or turning point in a dramatic action'. A crisis was a moment of suffering and confusion when everything that seemed fixed suddenly becomes unstable. The value of a crisis in a Greek tragedy was that it called forth a catharsis – a feeling of profound purification and redemption, a feeling of newborn hope and liberation. An old adage suggested that it was a shame to waste a good crisis. But it seemed that the Irish did not do catharsis.[55]

And yet! In a 1995 theatre review he considered what made for a good polemical play. Its purpose was to induce shame, not to be an aesthetic creation of enduring majesty. If the play did last it would be because it had failed, because it did not make the world it described a barbarous anachronism. There was a strong tendency to patronise such writing but polemical plays could be good or bad. A bad play about genocide was also bad morality. If it was trivial, tedious or patronising it made a bad situation worse, by discrediting the moral outrage is sought to evoke. O'Toole listed the attributes of good agitprop theatre: it could be didactic but not preachy, passionate and deadly serious but not po-faced. Even his greatest admirers found him preachy and po-faced at times. Pointing the finger of blame, he acknowledged, might not be the most elegant gesture that can be performed on stage, but if it were done well it would always be a powerful one.[56] By such criteria O'Toole sometimes came up trumps. The best of his work is likely to last because of its serious moral purpose and because what it rails against has endured.

CHAPTER FOURTEEN

Ghosts of futures past

Overall the twelve figures considered in my previous chapters fit within three broad intellectual traditions that competed to shape Ireland's future. Firstly, a number could be described as conservatives. Under this heading I group not just Catholic conservatives but also nationalist anti-modernists and those otherwise influenced by the Counter-Reformation and the Counter-Enlightenment. Cultural nationalists no less than Catholic conservatives have argued that ideologies of progress have served Ireland poorly. Such arguments are never far from the surface of Irish intellectual debates. Secondly, a number could be described as liberals. Classical liberalism advocated individual freedoms and limited government. In economics this translated into laissez-faire, in politics into an ideal of individual liberty and in social policy it emphasised how education might improve character and enable individuals to contribute to the greater good as economic actors. Poverty was portrayed as a moral problem of individual failure. Liberal reformers generally opposed anything more than a minimal distribution of resources. But they also opposed laws and rules that apparently hampered the capabilities of individuals to improve themselves. Thirdly, a number could be described as Republicans. For all that Irish Republicanism has often seemed as just another name for ethnic nationalism, republicanism espouses principles of universalism that distinguish it from cultural nationalism and from the liberal economic nation-building project that has predominated for the last several decades.

Conservative legacies

Irish conservatisms have been variously defined in opposition to the Reformation, against what William Petty called political economy – the new science of Francis Bacon as applied to social engineering and colonisation – in opposition to the Enlightenment and against the economic liberalism espoused by nineteenth-century political economists such as Richard Whately and Thomas Malthus. Edmund Burke is now claimed as the intellectual father of British Conservatism although he was, in his own day, a Whig reformist opposed to despotic government. Catholic conservatives like Jeremiah Newman have emphasised that Burke's political philosophy had much in common with Catholic thought (in particular, according to Newman, 'with the Catholic conviction that liberty must be ordered').[1] Mitchel professed an iconoclastic anti-modernism rooted in the writings of Thomas Carlyle. Catholics during the late nineteenth century developed a distinctive school of European anti-modernist thought inspired by Thomas Aquinas that stood opposed to socialism as well as liberalism. Like Carlyle, Catholic conservatives idealised the fixed social hierarchies of the Middle Ages as an alternative to liberalism. Irish cultural nationalists found some common cause with such conservatism in championing a cultural restoration that might somehow turn back the clock of Irish history to a time before the Reformation and to reinstate the Gaelic civilisation that was apparently swept aside by Petty and his ilk.

Nicholas Canny in *Making Ireland British 1580–1650*, a history of the decades before Petty's arrival, emphasises that much of what Petty advocated had been part of Crown policy long before he was born.[2] Institutionally, this began with the Plantation of Munster in the 1580s and had been significantly underway by the time of Cromwell's arrival in 1649. Many Catholic landlords were displaced by Protestants. But a class of Catholic sub-tenants survived into the eighteenth century as an underground gentry. These held intergenerational leases to lands their families once owned and exercised hereditary authority.[3] Daniel O'Connell came from such a background. The Catholic Irish never shipped to England and to the colonies in sufficient numbers to change the underlying political arithmetic. Understood in terms of William Petty's calculus – the ratio of Protestants to Catholics – the Reformation was at best a partial success. Yet, a definite rupture with the pre-seventeenth-century social and political order has since been emphasised by most Irish historians. Well into the twentieth century some conservative Catholic intellectuals sought a purging of post-Reformation ideas and mindsets. Cultural nationalists sought the restoration of the Catholic Gaelic Irish civilisation they believed was usurped during the seventeenth century. They had to advocate for this in English, the language through which most Irish people expressed themselves. With such audiences in mind James Connolly in *Labour and Irish History* declared the pre-capitalist century Gaelic social order to be an inspiration for an Irish socialist future.[4]

More characteristically Daniel Corkery's *The Hidden Ireland* argued that Munster's eighteenth-century peasant poets were the lineal descendants of a vibrant Gaelic culture. Corkery evoked an Ireland that was hidden not just from the twentieth century but from earlier colonial elites. In doing so he wished to challenge the 'slave mind' legacies of what he termed 'the Ascendancy's creed': its belief that the native Irish were a lesser breed and anything of theirs ('except their land and their gold!') was of little value: 'If they have had a language and a literature it cannot have been anything but a *patois* used by the hillmen amongst themselves; and as for their literature, the less said the better.'[5] *The Hidden Ireland* endorsed a post-colonial nation-building project supported by censorship and isolationism as well as the revival of the Gaelic language. Corkery insisted that no Ascendancy writer had ever been authentically Irish ('The life of Ireland, which is the life that counts, the national life, is not for them; it is as deeply hidden from them as the life of India is from the English Ascendancy there').[6]

William Butler Yeats retorted that 'everything great' in Ireland could be traced to Protestant patriotism.[7] His 1934 preface to *The Words Upon the Window Pane*, a one-act play in which the ghost of Jonathan Swift is contacted at a séance, sought to reincarnate Molyneux's *Case for Ireland Restated*:

> The battle of the Boyne overwhelmed a civilisation full of religion and myth, and bought in its place intelligible laws planned out upon a great blackboard, a capacity for horizontal lines, for rigid shapes, for buildings, for attitudes of mind that could be multiplied like an expanding bookcase: the modern world, and something that appeared and perished in its dawn, an instinct for Roman rhetoric, Roman elegance. It established a Protestant aristocracy, some of whom neither called themselves English nor looked with contempt or dread upon conquered Ireland. Indeed the battle was scarcely over when Molyneux, speaking their name, affirmed the sovereignty of the Irish parliament. No one had the right to make our laws but the King, Lords and Commons of Ireland.[8]

A 1938 article by Michael Tierney argued for a Catholic cultural 'restoration' that would turn back the clock on nineteenth-century utilitarianism and liberalism and on other 'great heresies' of the last three hundred years.[9] Tierney was a leading Fine Gael intellectual and Professor of Greek at University College Dublin (UCD). He subsequently became the UCD president who oversaw the building of a huge modernist campus in the Dublin suburbs. His article was a response to a book by Sean O'Faoláin, *King of the Beggars* (1938), about Daniel O'Connell.[10] The prevailing view of O'Connell amongst cultural nationalists was one dictated by John Mitchel some seven decades previously – that O'Connell was much to blame for the liberal utilitarian conquest of Ireland. According to Tierney, the main vehicle for 'utilitarian anti-culture' had been the English language. Middle-class liberalism, universal suffrage and the Land Acts between them had created an Ireland 'as different as anything could be' from the Ireland that collapsed after the battle of Kinsale and the Treaty of Limerick.[11] The spirit of Corkery continues to be channelled. For example, as put by Kevin Whelan in a 2010 essay about Brian Friel's canonical play *Translations* in *The Field Day Review*:

> Colonialism is never just a political and economic condition but also a psychic one … colonialism presented the acquisition of English as a

liberation, the golden bridge that carried the native beyond localism, rescuing him from provincialism by awarding him full participation in British civic life. The toll was the relinquishment of the native language, disavowal of the native language, severance from native culture.[12]

The Field Day Review exemplifies the widespread use in recent decades of post-colonial theory by Irish intellectuals to make such arguments. *Translations* is a play (in English) about replacement of Gaelic place names with English ones. Such Anglicisation served, as Whelan put it, to strip the Irish landscape of meaning and narrative that began with William Petty's Down Survey. Petty, according to Whelan, 'advocated genocide as a necessary prelude to a new beginning in Ireland. Maps did not only record, they also obliterated'.[13] Whelan, like many earlier cultural nationalists, saw advocates of progress as the handmaidens of colonialism and, like Corkery, blamed liberalism, utilitarianism and Daniel O'Connell for the destruction of the old Gaelic culture. As put by O'Connell and cited by Whelan:

> Therefore, although the Irish language is connected with many recollections that twine around the hearts of Irishmen, yet the superiority utility of the English tongue, as the medium of all modern communication is so great, that I can witness without a sigh the gradual disuse of the Irish.[14]

It may seem mischievous to locate post-colonial literary critics within an Irish conservative tradition. But the echoes of earlier conservatisms are explicit. For all that nineteenth-century Irish nationalism was a product of modernity – made possible, for example, by mass literacy and mass media – it came to develop an influential anti-modernist strand. Intellectually, critiques of Irish colonisation explicitly overlap with those of Catholic conservatives of modernity. Catholic conservatives like Jeremiah Newman, Irish post-colonial theorists of recent decades and cultural nationalists at all points in between shared an antipathy to the imposition, as Declan Kiberd put it, 'of an Enlightenment model of the state upon peoples whose traditions are very different'.[15] In Ireland, as elsewhere, the Reformation met with a Counter-Reformation. The Enlightenment met with a Counter-Enlightenment and Romantic nationalism. Newman, for his part, sought intellectual allies amongst postmodernist and poststructuralist theorists. Irish cultural nationalists from Corkery to Kiberd have similarly challenged Enlightenment conceptions of knowledge and truth or otherwise opposed, as put by Seamus Heaney in a 1983 article in praise of Corkery's *The Hidden Ireland*, the imposition of an official British culture upon the local anthropological one.[16]

Irish Catholic conservatives dated the rupture they would repair to the Reformation. Corkery emphasised the displacement of Medieval culture by the Renaissance as the moment of great damage to Gaelic culture. In the wider European context the fault line between tradition and modernity was the 1789 French Revolution that birthed the French Republic and hopes for an Irish Republic. The stakes Edmund Burke identified in the French Revolution played out also in the Ireland of the 1790s even though *Reflections on the Revolution in France* was written for an English audience. By this I mean not just the specific dangers of revolution but his defences of historical tradition and *ancien régime* as the bedrock of social cohesion. The reasons why Ireland could not build its future on such conservatism were clear to Burke. Molyneux's appeal for the legitimacy of a Protestant Parliament was one that professed neither solidarity with nor duties to the Catholic majority. In Kevin Whelan's succinct summary of Burke's analysis: 'Catholic traditions, beliefs, and habits were so ingrained in the fabric of Irish culture that a political system that failed to recognise them would inevitably lack the crucial bonding force that gave political systems their endurance – the affections of the people who lived under them.'[17]

Burke was adamant that what had become the Protestant gentry possessed no such legitimacy. It could not provide adequate foundations for an Irish political conservatism. Some Catholics turned to Jacobinism as Burke feared they would and when this failed in 1798 others, led by Daniel O'Connell, allied themselves with Liberal opponents of the *ancien régime* in England. O'Connell's Whig constitutional reformism was in turn superseded by the romantic cultural nationalism of Young Ireland. The kind of reformism advocated by Burke was once again cast aside. It was resurrected again by the Irish Parliamentary Party only to be discarded by Sinn Fein from 1912. In the twenty-six county Free State it came to be ingrained within the political system. In lieu of an *ancien régime* the Catholic Church became the institutional focus of conservatism. Its pageantry – most vividly expressed through the 1932 Eucharistic Congress – provided the kind of binding symbolism that in England was delivered by the Monarchy. What Jeremiah Newman called a Catholic public morality prevailed for a number of decades. In the North, until the peace process, the Burkean option for Catholics seemed as unlikely as it had been under the Ascendancy parliament. It is no wonder that many of the most prominent post-colonial intellectuals who applied Edmund Said's *Orientalism* to the Irish case were Northern Catholics.[18]

It was also no wonder that imposition of Catholic public morality in the Free State unnerved the Protestant minority. In a 1925 Senate speech Yeats railed against legislation prohibiting divorce. It was at once hypocritical – Daniel O'Connell and Charles Stuart Parnell were well-known as adulterers – and, he argued, an expression of anti-Protestant sectarianism:

I think it is tragic that within three years of this country gaining its independence we should be discussing a measure which a minority of this nation considers to be grossly oppressive. I am proud to consider myself a typical man of that minority. We against whom you have done this thing are no petty people. We are one of the great stocks of Europe. We are the people of Burke; we are the people of Grattan; we are the people of Swift, the people of Emmet, the people of Parnell. We have created the most of the modern literature of this country. We have created the best of its political intelligence.[19]

Yeats situated himself as the poet laureate of Irish anti-modernism. Frank O'Connor described him as a 'rabid Tory' who saw world crises in the dammed liberalism he hated, a lover of tradition, hater of reason, popular education and mechanical logic, who had much more of the Catholic in him than Church of Ireland.[20] In his preface to *The Words Upon the Window Pane*, Yeats wrote that 'Decartes, Locke and Newton took away the world and gave us its excrement instead'.[21] His 1939 poem 'Statues' declared that the Irish had been thrown upon a 'filthy modern tide'. All this might have resonated with post-independence Catholic conservatives and cultural nationalists but not his case for a full place for Protestants in an independent Ireland.[22]

Liberal orthodoxies

When John Mitchel railed against the last conquest of Ireland he meant variously the influence of utilitarian liberalism on Irish constitutional nationalism, liberal capitalism as a system of economic exploitation and, by implication, liberalism as an ideology of progress. The liberalism that Mitchel opposed had 'incorporated a variety of heterogeneous political languages, and evolved piecemeal over a long period of social change. Intellectual sources as diverse as natural rights doctrines, Whiggism, classical political economy, utilitarianism, evangelical Christianity, idealism, and evolutionary biology all played a part in liberal ideology, modifying its understanding of and emphasis on, the market mechanism and property ownership.'[23] Some decades before Max Weber identified the Protestant ethic as the spirit of capitalism Gladstone promoted liberalism using the language of theology. He depicted a Manichean struggle between the allure of the lower pleasures and improving higher ones. Liberal political economists exhorted the poor to improve their standard of living through self-restraint, to improve themselves by learning the middle-class values of their betters.[24] Liberalism found expression in social norms as well as in economic behaviour, notably in the representation of poverty as a moral problem of individual improvidence or as a crisis of character. Friedrich Engels was not impervious to such orthodoxies in his depiction of the Irish poor as 'dissolute, unsteady, drunken' and as having a 'strong degrading influence on their English companions in toil'.[25]

Political economy claimed ideological neutrality and the universal validity of its laws. It claimed to offer incontrovertible value-free knowledge. Utilitarianism attempted to reduce morality to a descriptive, scientific calculation of utility. The greater good was to be achieved by principle of laissez-faire, whereby individuals pursued their own self-interests and their interests pleasingly coincided in the operation of the market system. During the Famine and during the decade that followed almost all Irish political economists defended laissez-faire.[26] Thomas Malthus had argued that the condition of the rural Catholic poor could never be improved while laws against Catholics were in force. Liberalism stood for unfettered market forces but also for Catholic emancipation and the emancipation of slaves. But the Famine occurred notwithstanding Catholic emancipation. In a December 1847 paper, W. N. Hancock, who held the Whately Chair in Political Economy at Trinity College Dublin, gave the first of several papers advocating a laissez-faire response to the Famine.[27] In another paper the following year Hancock declared that laissez-faire and private enterprise would only yield the best results if 'emancipated from the restrictions which the ignorance and folly of past generations have allowed to become sanctioned by law'.[28] During the Famine several papers delivered at the Dublin Statistical Society sneered at John Mitchel's 1847 pamphlet, *Irish Political Economy* – mostly made up extracts from Swift and Berkeley – without condescending to name him.[29] Hancock declared Berkeley to be 'in error' for not comprehending the principles of laissez-faire.[30] Mitchel understood well enough that the laissez-faire principle in Ireland took the form of landlord capitalism.

In an unpublished article in 1848, John Stuart Mill wrote that the disaffection of millions of Irishmen could hardly be blamed on Mitchel. The social condition of Ireland was an abomination that warranted the kind of revolution that had occurred in France in 1789. England no longer tyrannised Ireland by means of religious persecution or economic protectionism. It did so through the system of land tenure it imposed on Ireland to the sole benefit of a 'handful of persons who neither by their labour nor skill contributed in any way to its productiveness'. The so-called laziness, recklessness or improvident multiplication of the Irish population was the result of an evil system. Amongst the peasantry competition for land and rents were such that:

> no industry, temperance, or prudence can make the peasant better off; the landlord takes all. If here and there a peasant saves anything, he takes care that his farm shall see no traces of it; he invests it in a distant savings bank, or hides it in the thatch of his cabin. On the other hand, no indolence, or improvident increase of numbers, makes him poorer: he and all his family are sure of potatoes while they are on the farm, and if there is nothing left, it is the landlord's loss, not his.[31]

The diagnosis was the one put forward by Malthus in *The Edinburgh Review* forty years earlier. The remedy that Mill was inching towards (and unwilling to publically advocate) was a radical change in land tenure. In the wake of the 1867 Fenian Rising, in a House of Commons speech that again cited Mitchel, he declared it complacent for gentlemen 'to soothe themselves with statistics, flattering themselves with the idea that Ireland is improving'. The thirty-nine years since Catholic emancipation had seen some material progress. However, the rulers of Ireland had allowed 'what was once indignation against particular wrongs to harden into a passionate determination to be no longer ruled on any terms by those to whom they ascribe all these evils'.[32] In an influential pamphlet, *England and Ireland* (1868), he advocated a system of peasant proprietorship, a remedy he had been pussyfooting around for more than twenty years. The time had passed for any amicable settlement of the Irish land question through gradual reform. Land needed to become the permanent holding of existing tenants purchasable by means of land annuities to the state who would then recompense former landlords.[33]

It took the Land War to bring much of this about. But the Encumbered Estates Act (1849) had facilitated the sale of debt-ridden estates to what became a Catholic rancher class. Subsequently much of what was left of a peasantry hugely reduced by famine and emigration became landowners. During the 1880s ownership of some 14–15 million acres of the total 17 million acres of agricultural land was transferred from some 19,000 proprietors to about 440,000 smallholders thus making small independent farmers the largest class in the Irish social structure by the time of independence.[34] Constitutional nationalist politics under Charles Stewart Parnell (a Protestant landowner), as under O'Connell, took the form of an alliance with the Liberal Party and would do so again under John Redmond a generation later. Notwithstanding Fenian agitation the ideology that Mitchel called the last conquest of Ireland became integral to Irish political nationalism. Following his 1932 visit to Dublin John Maynard Keynes described the outgoing leader of the Free State, W. T. Cosgrave, as very much the nineteenth-century liberal.[35] Nineteenth-century liberal orthodoxies held sway in the management of the Free State economy. The 1932 Fianna Fáil government was elected on a platform of economic isolationism. Eamon de Valera, the dominant political figure for the next two decades, promoted a doctrine of economic self-sufficiency. But economic decolonisation could not be made to work.

The 1950s saw the displacement of cultural nation-building aimed at reproducing Catholicism and Gaelic culture from one generation to the next by an economic nation-building project of modernisation that has held sway ever since. Accounts of twentieth-century modernisation such as Tom Garvin's *Preventing the Future: Why Was Ireland So Poor for So Long?* (2005) and Joseph Lee's *Ireland 1912–1986: Politics and Society* (1989) focus on the emergence of a new developmental consensus led by T. K. Whitaker, a civil servant, and Sean Lemass who replaced de Valera as Taoiseach.[36] In Lee's account a liberal project of modernisation with accompanying beliefs in meritocracy and individual agency challenged a longstanding post-Famine antipathy to progress. Lee's panacea against what he called a prosperity-blocking fatalism was a liberal mindset adept at enterprise.[37] The challenge was what it had been for Malthus: how might the Irish be improved? The answer was a derivation of the one proposed by Whately: educate them in political economy. School them in self-restraint. Teach them to be provident.

In 1860 the Victorian novelist Charles Kingsley, in a letter to his wife, described being haunted by the human chimpanzees he saw along a hundred miles of Irish country.[38] Whatley first encountered the Irish as migrant workers willing to live on straw and potatoes begging their way back to Ireland, who kept what money they had earned under wraps for their families. According to prevailing liberal political economy orthodoxies to which Whately subscribed, such Irish were improvident for bringing children into the world they could not feed and were not to be encouraged to do so by a generous Poor Law. Engels, like Whately, gave expression to clichés of the dissolute Irish. During the 1840s he depicted Irish peasants in England as a *lumpenproletariat* standing in the way of historical progress, part of a people potentially on the wrong side of history. The success of Irish cultural and political nationalism would subsequently change his mind about the crisis of Irish character. His inference was that the Irish found a future because they had modernised culturally and politically. In time Manchester's Irishtown disappeared, its inhabitants subsumed into a more ordered urban working class. Sociologists and historians have emphasised how the Catholic Church from the mid-nineteenth century brought order, moral discipline and education to emigrant Irish communities and the Irish at home.[39]

A hundred years after Kingsley's letter the *Commission on Itinerancy* was established by Charles Haughey to assimilate the last holdouts of such improvident Irishness. Many 'tinkers' or 'travellers' had been migratory agricultural workers much like those encountered by Magistrate Whately. Since they lost their toehold in the rural economy during the 1950s they have come to be routinely denigrated as enemies of Irish modernity.[40] This tendency might be dated to the 1907 premiere of J. M. Sygne's now-classic *The Playboy of the Western World* which met with a riot by cultural nationalists appalled by its slur on Irish character. *The Playboy*, like Sygne's *The Tinker's Wedding* (1908), depicted rural Irish ways of life that apparently had no more place in a modern Irish nation than in a modern political economy. An Irish Traveller in a 1998 memoir eloquently described his people as ghosts of an earlier form of existence.[41] The real Irish past had become a foreign country and some of those who most resembled its inhabitants had no viable Irish future.

The elusive Republic

The banking crisis that succeeded the Celtic Tiger brought about a political crisis that resulted in a change of government but in very little meaningful reform of the Irish State. On one hand there was a legitimacy crisis, on the other hand political leaders admonished those who talked Ireland down and in doing so supposedly undermined confidence in the Irish economy. The management of Ireland's economy passed to a 'troika' of representatives of the International Monetary Fund, the European Commission and the European Central Bank. Enda Kenny's government promised a return of Irish sovereignty – meaning economic sovereignty – before the centenary of the 1916 Proclamation that Ireland was a Republic.

What the signatories of the 1916 Proclamation meant by a Republic was less than crystal clear. In a 1906 essay Patrick Pearse imagined that Ireland in 2006 would be a constitutional monarchy.[42] Ten year later in the GPO, in a discussion overheard by Garret FitzGerald's father Desmond FitzGerald, Pearse discussed with Joseph Mary Plunkett the possibility that Ireland freed from British rule by a German victory in the Great War, would inevitably become a monarchy with, most likely, the Kaiser's sixth son Prince Joachim as the king.[43] Pearse and others ignored an early declaration that Ireland was a Republic by the Irish Republican Brotherhood.[44] Arthur Griffith, who served as President of the Irish Republic from the election of the Second Dáil in January 1922 until his death six months later, had been a monarchist. Those who described themselves as republicans during the civil war fought for the principle of Irish self-determination understood as an all-Ireland state and as not having to take oaths of allegiance to the British Sovereign. The civil war was won by Free Staters who took the oath (but professed not take it seriously) and who settled for a twenty-six county polity.

The 1916 Proclamation declared a Republic that would guarantee religious and civil liberty, equal rights and equal opportunities to all its citizens, and resolved 'to pursue the happiness and prosperity of the whole nation and of all its parts, cherishing all the children of the nation equally'. The 1919 Democratic Programme of the First Dáil, another short document, declared 'in the name of the Republic' 'the right of every citizen to an adequate share of the produce of the nation'. It stated that the first duty of the Government of the Republic would be to make provision for the physical, mental and spiritual well-being of all children. It promised to replace 'the present odious, degrading and foreign Poor Law System' with a sympathetic native scheme for the care of the nation's old and infirm. It also promised to develop Irish industries along co-operative lines.[45] The 1922 Constitution declared the new state a co-equal member of the British Commonwealth rather than a republic. It prohibited religious discrimination (Article 8) and guaranteed freedom of speech, assembly and association subject to 'public morality' (Article 9). It guaranteed free elementary education to all citizens (Article 10) but made no reference to redistribution or to co-operative industry. Kevin O'Higgins was only stating the obvious in claiming that Ireland's surviving victorious revolutionaries were the most conservative in the world. He also dismissed the 1919 Democratic Programme as 'mostly poetry'.[46] The institutions and politics of the Free State reflected an admixture of Catholicism and economic liberalism. Catholicism defined public morality and institutionally crowded out civil society. Economic liberalism like Catholicism advocated a minimalist state. In de Valera's 1937 Constitution there was no reference at all to a republic. Although a Republic of Ireland was declared in 1947 republicanism stood on very weak institutional foundations.[47]

Since the time of Connolly republican ideals have found expression on the political margins. For example, Sheehy Skeffington advocated a Republic that conferred equal citizenship upon women. In Fintan O'Toole's summary, in an edited volume *Up the Republic!: Towards a New Ireland* (2012), republicanism has three basic elements. There is a conception of individual freedom that goes beyond liberal or neo-liberal kinds – a freedom from what O'Toole termed unaccountable forms of domination. This necessitates radical state interference aimed, for example, at preventing banks from imposing crushing debts on citizens. A strong state willing and able to interfere with markets is presumed. The second pillar of republicanism, according to O'Toole, concerns the accountability of the state to its citizens.[48] The third requires active and even obstreperous citizens working individually and collectively to keep the state on its toes. Various contributors to this edited collection elaborated on these themes. *Up the Republic!* quoted President Michael D. Higgins from his book *Renewing the Republic* (2011) on the need for an ideal of citizenship based on radical inclusion as distinct from radical individualisation ('This citizenship should be based on equality and respect – a citizenship floor – below which no one should be allowed to fall').[49] In the final chapter of *Up the Republic!* the poet Theo Dorgan concluded that previous efforts to constitute a republic failed because Irish people were not minded to want one:

> Ireland's tragedy is that, having broken the law to seize power, we immediately reinstated that very law we had overthrown . . .
>
> The revolution that we never had is that interior revolution. Because we did not change in our spirits, nothing of any substance was ever displaced by the arrival of a new set of facts. We failed, if I might put it very simply indeed, to change our minds . . .
>
> I believe that our present crisis stems from a double failure: the failure of the revolutionary generation to establish a true republic, and our inevitable consequent failure to imagine a new state from inside the facts and language of the present state.[50]

And Dorgan's conclusion? '[I]f we are to imagine a new republic, we are constrained to do so from outside the walls of the state'.[51] To this Burke might reply, as he argued in *Reflections on the Revolution in France*, that it is more prudent to rebuild existing institutions than build again from scratch. But in truth there may be no twenty-first-century revolution in

Ireland to reflect on. Nothing of the scale of groundwork that preceded earlier nation-building projects has been envisaged. To put this in context, the revolution that led to Irish independence was built on a sixty-year-long programme of cultural nationalism (if we date this from Thomas Davis and *The Nation*) and a far longer history of mass politics (if we date this from O'Connell's decision in 1824 to reduce membership rates for the Catholic Association from a guinea to a penny per month). Advocates of a new republic emphasise the need to build civil society from the bottom. During the nineteenth century the Catholic Church built up a parish system that remains the communal unit of organisation in many parts of twenty-first-century Ireland. Twenty-first-century Irish republicanisms, like those of the early twentieth century, are mostly likely to develop in uneasy symbiosis with other Irish political and intellectual traditions. It is just as well then that republicanism does not hold the monopoly on aspirations for justice, reform, accountability, citizenship, community and social cohesion.

The history of the Irish future that perhaps now most needs to be written is one that envisages the place of Ireland's now-large immigrant communities within the Irish nation state and in Northern Ireland. Irish openness to immigration is apparently a consequence of the dominance of economic rules of belonging over cultural ones. The Irish state actively encouraged large-scale immigration during the boom years but there has been little or no political backlash against immigrants during the post-Celtic Tiger economic crisis. Yet there has been considerable resistance to thinking of immigrants as potentially Irish.[52] In a 2004 citizenship referendum 80 per cent of voters asserted that the Irish-born children of immigrants should have no birthright to Irish citizenship. However, more than a century after the Gaelic revival English remains the language of integration into Irish society and Polish has become the second most commonly spoken language. How this future will play out is of course unknown but how it is now debated will come to be seen from some future vantage point to shed some light on our own time.

NOTES

Chapter One

1   For an essay on Pearse written alongside this book see Bryan Fanning, 'Patrick Pearse Predicts the Future', *Dublin Review of Books*, 2013, 39, http://www.drb.ie. On Pearse's political writings and speeches see Bryan Fanning and Tom Garvin, *The Books that Define Ireland* (Dublin: Merrion, 2014).

2   On intellectual intersections between Catholicism and liberalism see Bryan Fanning, *The Quest for Modern Ireland: The Battle of Ideas 1912–1986* (Dublin: Irish Academic Press, 2008).

3   Jonathan Swift, *A Modest Proposal For Preventing the Children of poor People in Ireland from being a Burden to their Parents or Country, and for making them beneficial to the Public* (Dublin, 1729).

4   Alan D. Chambers, *Jonathan Swift and the Burden of the Future* (Newark: University of Delaware Press, 1995), p.15.

5   Patrick Reilly, *Jonathan Swift: The Brave Disponder* (Carbondale: Southern Illinois University Press, 1982), p.95.

6   Jonathan Swift, *A Proposal For the Universal Use of Irish Manufacture in Cloaths and Furniture and Houses, &c. Utterly Rejecting and Renouncing every Thing wearable that comes from England* (Dublin, 1720).

7   Jonathan Swift, *A Proposal that all the Ladies and Women of Ireland should appear constantly in Irish Manufactures* (Dublin, 1729).

Chapter Two

1   Letter from Petty to Robert Southwell, 14 July 1686, cited in Edmond Fitzmaurice, *The Life of Sir William Petty 1623–1687* (London: John Murray, 1895), p.3.

2   Fitzmaurice, *Life of Sir William Petty*, p.7.

3   Murray N. Rothbard, *Economic Thought before Adam Smith* (Alabama: Edward Elgar, 1995), p.300.

4   Emil Strauss, *Sir William Petty: Portrait of a Genius* (London: Bodley Head, 1954), p.26.

5   William Petty, *Advice of Mr W.P. to Mr. Hartlib for the advancement of some particular parts of learning* (London, 1655).

6   Strauss, *Sir William Petty*, p.53.

7   T. C. Barnard, 'Planters and Policies in Cromwellian Ireland', *Past and Present*, 1973, 61, 31–69, p.32.

8   Fitzmaurice, *Life of Sir William Petty*, p.24.

9   Thomas Bartlett, *Ireland: A History* (Oxford: Oxford University Press, 2010), p.1130.

10   T. C. Barnard, 'William Petty', *Oxford Dictionary of National Biography*, vol.43.

11   Raymond Gillespie, *Seventeenth Century Ireland* (Dublin: Gill and Macmillan, 2006), p.200.

12   I. Mascon and A. J. Young, 'Sir William Petty F.R.S.', *News and Notes of the Royal Society* (1960), 79–90.

13   Gillespie, *Seventeenth Century Ireland*, p.190.

14   T. C. Barnard, 'Sir William Petty as Kerry Ironmaster', *Proceedings of the Royal Irish Academy. Section C: Archaeology, Celtic Studies, History, Linguistics, Literature*, 1982, 82c, 1–32, p.4.

15   Thomas E. Jordan, *A Copper Farthing: Sir William Petty and his Times* (Sunderland: University of Sunderland Press, 2007), p.99.

16   William Petty, *The Political Anatomy of Ireland*, (Shannon: Irish University Press, 1970).

17   Petty cited in Alessandro Roccaglia, *Petty: The Origins of Political Economy* (Cardiff: University College of Cardiff Press, 1985), p.97.

18   Roccaglia, *Petty: The Origins of Political Economy*, p.21.

19   Letter from Petty to Robert Southwell, 3 November 1687, cited in Edmond Fitzmaurice, *The Life of Sir William Petty 1623–1687* (London: John Murray, 1895).

20   C. H. Hull, *Economic Writings of Sir William Petty*, vol.2 (Cornell, 1899), p.60.

21   Author's preface, Petty, *The Political Anatomy of Ireland*.

22   C. H. Hull, 'Note on "A Treatise on Ireland" ', *Economic Writings of Sir William Petty*, vol.2 (Cornell, 1899), p.547.

23   Gillespie, *Seventeenth Century Ireland*, p.241.

24   William Petty, 'A Treatise of Ireland', C. H. Hull (ed.) *Economic Writings of Sir William Petty*, vol.2 (Cornell, 1899), Chap 1.5.

25   William Petty, *A Treatise of Ireland*, Chap 1.5.

26   Fitzmaurice, *Sir William Petty*, p.32.

27   T. C. Barnard, 'Lord Broghill, Vincent Gookin and the Cork Elections of 1659', *The English Historical Review*, 1973, 88.347, 352–65, p.356.

28   Barnard, *Lord Broghill, Vincent Gookin and the Cork Elections of 1659*, pp.356–8.

29   Originally published in 1655. Vincent Gookin, *The Great Case of Transplantation in Ireland Discussed* (London: John Cook, 1955).

30 Tory meaning 'an outlaw', specially 'a robber' from the Irish *toruighe* 'plunderer', originally pursuer, searcher, from the Irish: e.g. *toirghim*, I pursue.

31 Aidan Clarke, 'The Colonisation of Ulster and the Rebellion of 1641', in T. W. Moody and F. X. Martin (eds) *The Course of Irish History* (Dublin: Mercier Press, 1967), p.203.

32 Petty, *The Political Anatomy of Ireland*, pp.30–1.

33 Petty, *The Political Anatomy of Ireland*, p.34.

34 Petty, *The Political Anatomy of Ireland*, p.27.

35 Petty, *Treatise on Ireland*, Chap 3.1.

36 Petty, *Treatise on Ireland*, Appendix of Objections, 6.2.

37 Petty, *Treatise on Ireland*, Appendix of Objections, 6.2.

38 Petty, *The Political Anatomy of Ireland*, p.26.

39 Petty, *Treatise on Ireland*, Appendix: Another View of the Same Matters By Way of Dialogue Between A and B.

40 Bartlett, *Ireland: A History*, p.127.

41 William Petty, 'No. 21; Of Reconciling the English and Irish and Reforming Both Nations', in Edmond Fitzmaurice (ed.) *The Petty Papers*, vol.2 (London: Routledge, 1997).

42 See Ted McCormick, 'Transmutation, Inclusion and Exclusion: Political Arithmetic from Charles II to William III', *Journal of Historical Sociology*, 2007, 20.3, 255–78.

43 Thomas E. Jordan, *Sir William Petty, 1623–1687: The Genius Entrepreneur of Seventeenth-Century Ireland* (New York: Edwin Mellon, 2007), p.53.

44 Strauss, *Sir William Petty*, p.133.

45 Thomas E. Jordan, *Sir William Petty: 1623–1687: The Genius Entrepreneur of Seventeenth-Century Ireland* (New York: Edwin Mellon, 2007), pp.57–64.

46 Barnard, *Petty as Kerry Iron Master*, p.2.

47 Fitzmaurice, *Sir William Petty*, pp.291–2.

48 Fitzmaurice, *Sir William Petty*, pp.310–11.

Chapter Three

1 A. M. Foster, 'The Molyneux Family', *Dublin Historical Record*, 1960, 16.1, pp.9–15.

2 John Locke, *An Essay Concerning Human Understanding*, ed. P. H. Nidditch (Oxford: Oxford University Press, 1975), II.9.1.

3 William Molyneux, *The Case of Ireland's being Bound by Acts of Parliament in England, Stated* (facsimile, Online Library of Liberty, 1698).

4 Gerard O'Brien, 'The Grattan Mystique', *Eighteenth Century Ireland*, 1986, 1, 177–94, pp.192–4.

5   John Dunn, *Political Obligation in its Historical Context* (Cambridge: Cambridge University Press, 1980), p.68.

6   Jacqueline Hill, 'Ireland without Union: Molyneux and His Legacy', in John Robertson (ed.) *A Union for Empire: Political Thought and the British Union of 1707* (Cambridge: Cambridge University Press, 1995), p.274.

7   J. Locke, W. Molyneux and T. Molyneux, *Some Familiar Letters Between Mr Locke and Several of his Friends* (London: A. and J. Churchill, 1708).

8   Thomas Duddy, *A History of Irish Thought* (London: Routledge, 2002), pp.74–6.

9   John Locke, *An Essay on Human Understanding*, II.23.

10   John Locke, *Second Treatise of Government*, ed. C.B. McPherson (Indianapolis and Cambridge: Hackett Publishing Company, 1980).

11   Jules Steinberg, *Locke, Rousseau and the Idea of Consent: An Inquiry into the Liberal-Democratic Theory of Political Obligation* (London: Greenwood, 1978), pp.133–6.

12   Bryan Fanning, *Evil, God, the Greater Good and Rights: The Philosophical Origins of Social Problems* (New York: Edwin Mellon, 2007), pp.143–5.

13   A .J. Simmons, *The Lockean Theory of Rights* (Princeton: Princeton University Press, 1994), pp.16–37.

14   Locke, *Two Treatises*, II.4.

15   Simmons, *Lockean Theory of Rights*, p.84.

16   Dunn, *Political Obligation in its Historical Context*, p.51.

17   Capel Molyneux, *An Account of the Family and Descendants of Thomas Molyneux* (Evesham, 1820), p.74.

18   This claim refers to the *Magna Charta Hiberniae* (Great Charter of Ireland).

19   The only known copy of the *Magna Charta Hiberniae* was destroyed when the Four Courts were burnt in 1922. This was a fourteenth-century manuscript contained in the *Red Book of the Dublin Exchequer*. Reproduced in E. Curtis and R. B. McDowell, *Irish Historical Documents* (London: Methuen, 1943).

20   Locke, *Two Treatises*, II.4.

21   Locke, *Two Treatises*, II.85.

22   Wayne Glausser, 'Three Approaches to Locke and the Slave Trade', *Journal of the History of Ideas*, 1990, 51.2, 199–216, p.199.

23   Locke, *Second Treatise of Government*.

24   Simmons, *Lockean Theory of Rights*, p.176.

25   Glausser, *Locke and the Slave Trade*, p.205.

26   Ian McBride, *Eighteenth Century Ireland* (Dublin: Gill and McMillan, 2009), p.278.

27   Dunn, *Political Obligation in its Historical Context*, p.69.

28   Anonymous, *The alarm, or the Irish spy. In a series of letters on the present state of affairs in Ireland, to a lord high in the opposition. Written by an*

ex-Jesuit, employed by his lordship for the purpose (Dublin, 1779), 58 cited from Kelly, *Perceptions of Locke*, p.27.

29 For example, Burke's *A Theory of Moral Sentiments*, Berkeley's *The Querist*, Hutchenson's *System of Moral Philosophy*. See David Berman, 'Enlightenment and Counter-Enlightenment in Irish philosophy', *Archiv fur Geschiche der Philosophie*, 1982, pp.257–9.

30 Jonathan Swift, *The Drapier's Letters and Other Works, 1714–1725 (The Works of Jonathan Swift, vol. X) I*, ed. H. Davies (Oxford, 1966), p.88.

31 Dunn, *Political Obligation in its Historical Contexts*, p.63.

32 M. P. Thompson, 'The Reception of Locke's Two Treatises of Government 1690–1705', *Political Studies*, 1976, 34.2, 184–91, p.184.

33 Charles Leslie, *Considerations of importance to Ireland in a letter to a member of parliament thereupon the occasion of Mr Molyneux's later book* (Early English Books Online, facsimile of 1698 edition).

34 In Hume's essay 'Of the Original Social Contract'. C. W. Hendel (ed.) *David Hume's Political Essays* (New York, 1953), p.43.

35 Patrick Kelly, 'Perceptions of Locke in Eighteenth-Century Ireland', *Proceedings of the Royal Irish Academy*, 1989, 89c, 17–35, p.19.

36 Kelly, *Perceptions of Locke*, p.27.

37 Patrick Kelly, 'Molyneux and the Spirit of Liberty in Eighteenth-Century Ireland', *Eighteenth-Century Ireland*, 1988, 3, 136–40.

38 Patrick Kelly, 'Molyneux and the Spirit of Liberty in Eighteenth-Century Ireland'.

Chapter Four

1 A letter to Richard Burke Esq (uncompleted), 1794. Unless otherwise indicated citations are from Edmund Burke, *Letters, Speeches and Tracts on Irish Affairs*, ed. Matthew Arnold (London: McMillan, 1881).

2 Letter to Dr Laurence, 5 June 1797.

3 Letter to the Right Hon. William Windham, 30 March 1796.

4 A letter to William Smith Esquire, 29 January 1795.

5 Letter to Windham.

6 F. P. Lock, *Edmund Burke: Volume I, 1730–1784* (Oxford: Clarendon Press, 2008), pp.14, 48.

7 Lock, *Edmund Burke: Volume I, 1730–1784*, p.15.

8 Conor Cruise O'Brien, 'Introduction', to Edmund Burke, *Reflections on the Revolution in France* (London: Penguin, 1968), p.30.

9 Sir George Eliot, 2 May 1793, Countess de Minto, *Life and Letters of Sir G. Eliot* (London, 1874), p.136.

10 Luke Gibbons, *Edmund Burke and Ireland: Aesthetics, Politics and the Colonial Sublime* (Cambridge: Cambridge University Press, 2003).

11 Theobald Wolfe Tone, Journal, 1–3 March 1797, *Life of Theobold Wolfe Tone*, ed. Tom Bartlett (Dublin: The Lilliput Press, 1998), p.734.

12 Burke, *Reflections*, p.156.

13 Burke, *Reflections*, p.124.

14 Herbert A. Deane, *The Political and Social Ideas of St. Augustine* (New York: Columbia University Press, 1966), pp.152–3.

15 Augustine, *The City of God* (New York: Denton, 1947), v.17.

16 Gibbons, *Edmund Burke and Ireland*, pp.7–8.

17 Gibbons, *Edmund Burke and Ireland*, p.24.

18 Lock, *Edmund Burke: Vol. 1*, p.44.

19 David Merman, 'David Hume on the 1691 Rebellion in Ireland', *Studies*, 1976, 65.258, 101–12.

20 Ian McBride, *Eighteenth-Century Ireland* (Dublin: Gill and Macmillan, 2009), p.95.

21 Herbert Butterfield, *The Whig Interpretation of History* (London: Bell, 1931).

22 Edward Valence, *The Glorious Revolution: 1688 Britain's Fight for Liberty* (London: Abacus, 2007), pp.13–20.

23 Burke, *Letter to Richard Burke*.

24 Edmund Burke, *Speech on Conciliation with America* (1775).

25 Burke, *Speech on Conciliation with America* (1775).

26 Burke, *Tracts on the Popery Laws* (unpublished 1760–5).

27 Burke, *Tracts on the Popery Laws*.

28 Burke, *A Letter to Sir Hercules Langrishe, Bart, M.P., on the subject of the Roman Catholics of Ireland, and the Propriety of Admitting them to the Elective Franchise, Consistently With The Principles Of The Constitution As Established in 1792*, 3 January 1792.

29 Burke, *Letter to Langrishe*.

30 Burke, *Letter to Langrishe*.

31 Burke, *Letter to Langrishe*.

32 Burke, *Letter to Langrishe*.

33 Burke, *Letter to Langrishe*.

34 Burke, *Reflections on the Revolution in France*, p.119.

35 Burke, *Letter to Langrishe*.

36 Burke, *Letter to Langrishe*.

37 Burke, *Letter to Langrishe*.

38 Burke, *A second Letter to Sir Hercules Langrishe*, 26 May 1795.

39 Burke, *Reflections*, p.122.

40 Burke, *Letter to Richard Burke*.

41 Burke, *Letter to William Smith Esq.* (1795).

42 Burke, *Letter to William Smith Esq.*

43   Denis Gywnn, 'Dr Hussey and Mr Burke', *Studies*, 1928, 17.68, 529–68.

44   Conor Cruise O'Brien, *The Great Melody; A Thematic Biography of Edmund Burke* (London: Sinclair Stevenson, 1992), pp.551–5.

45   Burke, *Letter to Rev. Dr. Hussey* (1796).

46   Burke, *Letter to Rev. Dr. Hussey*.

47   Marcus Tanner, *Ireland's Holy War: The Struggle for a Nation's Soul 1500–2000* (New Haven: Yale University Press, 2001), p.193.

Chapter Five

1   William Hazlitt, *A Reply to the Essay on Population By the Rev. T. R. Malthus in A Series of Letters to Which is Added Extracts from the Essay With Notes* (London: Longman, Hurst, Rees and Orme, 1807), p.4.

2   T. R. Malthus, *An Essay on the Principle of Population as it Affects the Future Improvement of Society with Remarks on the Speculations of Mr. Goodwin, M. Condorcet and Other Writers* (London: J. Johnson, 1798).

3   William Otter, 'Memoir of Robert Malthus', in Thomas Robert Malthus, *Principles of Political Economy: 2nd Edition* (New York: Augustus M. Kelly, 1968), p.xxi.

4   Malthus, *Principle of Population*, p.2.

5   John Avery, *Progress, Poverty and Population: Re-reading Condorcet, Godwin and Malthus* (London: Frank Cass, 1997), p.77.

6   Malthus, *Principle of Population*, p.5.

7   See Hazlitt, *Reply to the Essay*, p.48.

8   Malthus, *Principle of Population*, p.56.

9   Malthus, *Principle of Population*, p.6.

10   Hazlitt, *Reply to Malthus*, p.63.

11   William Godwin, *Enquiry concerning Political Justice and its influence on General Virtue and Happiness, Vol. II* (London, 1793), p.538.

12   Malthus, *Principle of Population*, p.80.

13   Malthus, *Principle of Population*, p.82.

14   Hazlitt, *Reply to Malthus*, p.127.

15   Hazlitt, *Reply to Malthus*, p.21.

16   T. R. Malthus, *An Essay on the Principle of Population Or A View of Its Past And Present Effects on Human Happiness With An Inquiry into Our Prospects Respecting The Future Removal Or Mitigation Of The Evils Which It Occasions*, vol.1, (Everyman edition, 1803), pp.227–8.

17   William Richardson, *Simple Measures by Which the Recurrence of Famines may be prevented* . . . Printed in the *Pamphleteer*, 1816, vol. VII, p.160 and cited in Patricia James, *Population Malthus: His Life and Times* (London: Routledge and Kegan Paul, 1979), p.147.

18   James, *Population Malthus*, p.146.

19   James, *Population Malthus*, p.20.

20   James, *Population Malthus*, p.20.

21   James, *Population Malthus*, p.21.

22   James, *Population Malthus*, p.22.

23   James, *Population Malthus*, p.66.

24   James, *Population Malthus*, p.66.

25   James, *Population Malthus*, p.66.

26   James, *Population Malthus*, p.67.

27   T. R. Malthus, *The Crisis: A View of the Present Interesting State of Great Britain by a Friend to the Constitution* (1796, unpublished), cited by Otter, *Memoir of Robert Malthus*, p.xxxvi.

28   Malthus, *The Crisis*, p.134.

29   Malthus, *The Crisis*, p.24.

30   Malthus, *The Crisis*, p.24.

31   Malthus, *The Crisis*, p.26.

32   Malthus, *The Crisis*, p.16.

33   Malthus, *The Crisis*, p.67.

34   Malthus, *The Crisis*, p.31.

35   James, *Population Malthus*, p.82.

36   Malthus, *Principle of Population*, p.30.

37   T. R. Malthus, *Principles of Political Economy: Second Edition* (New York: Augustus M. Kelly, 1968), p.161.

38   Malthus, *Principles of Political Economy*, p.311.

39   T. R. Malthus, 'Newenham and Others on the State of Ireland' (April 1808), in Bernard Semmel (ed.) *Occasional Papers of TR Malthus on Ireland, Population and Political Economy* (New York: Burt Franklin, 1963).

40   T. R Malthus, 'Newenham and the State of Ireland' (July 1809), in Bernard Semmel (ed.) *Occasional Papers of TR Malthus on Ireland, Population and Political Economy* (New York: Burt Franklin, 1963).

41   T. R Malthus, 'Newenham and the State of Ireland', p.34.

42   T. R Malthus, 'Newenham and the State of Ireland', p.37.

43   Malthus, *Principles of Political Economy*, p.221.

44   Malthus, *Principles of Political Economy*, p.42.

45   Malthus, *Principles of Political Economy*, p.40.

46   Malthus, *Principles of Political Economy*, p.35.

47   Malthus, *Principles of Political Economy*, p.228.

48   Malthus, *Principles of Political Economy*, p.46.

49   Malthus, *Principles of Political Economy*, p.46.

50   Malthus, *Principles of Political Economy*, p.46.

51 Malthus, *Principles of Political Economy*, p.47.

52 Malthus, *Principles of Political Economy*, p.48.

53 Rev H. Dudley, *A Short Address to the Most Reverend and Honourable William, Lord Primate of Ireland, recommending some Commutation or Modification of the tithes of that Country: with a few remarks on the present state of the Irish Church* (London, 1808).

54 Dudley, *A Short Address*, p.48.

55 T. R. Malthus, 'Newenham and Others on the State of Ireland', p.69.

56 Malthus, 'Newenham and the State of Ireland', p.51.

57 Malthus, 'Newenham and the State of Ireland', p.51.

58 Malthus, 'Newenham and the State of Ireland', p.49.

59 Malthus, 'Newenham and the State of Ireland', p.49.

60 Malthus, 'Newenham and the State of Ireland', p.50.

61 Malthus, 'Newenham and the State of Ireland', p.50.

62 Malthus, 'Newenham and the State of Ireland', p.66.

63 Malthus, *Principles of Political Economy*, p.259.

64 Malthus, *Principles of Political Economy*, p.228.

65 Malthus, *Principles of Political Economy*, p.212.

66 Malthus, *Principles of Political Economy*, p.346.

67 Malthus, *Principles of Political Economy*, p.347.

68 Malthus, *Principles of Political Economy*, p.349.

69 Malthus, *Principles of Political Economy*, p.349.

70 Malthus, *Principles of Political Economy*, p.350.

71 Malthus, 'Newenham and the State of Ireland'.

72 T. R. Malthus, *A Letter to Samuel Whitbread Esq., MP on his Proposed Bill for the Amendment of the Poor Law* (London: Johnson and Hatchard, 1807).

73 Edmond Cox, 'Malthusian Population in a War-Based Economy', in Michael Turner, *Malthus and His Time* (London: Macmillan, 1986), p.233.

74 Malthus, *Principles of Political Economy*, p.226.

75 Malthus, *Principles of Political Economy*, p.226.

76 Malthus, *Principles of Political Economy*, p.227.

Chapter Six

1 William John Fitzpatrick, *Memoirs of Archbishop Whately with a Glance at his Contemporaries and Times*, vol.1 (London: Chard Bentley, 1864), p.73.

2 E. Jane Whately, *Life and Correspondence of Richard Whately, D.D. Late Archbishop of Dublin*, vol.2 (London: Longmans, Green and Co, 1866), p.112.

3   David de Giustino, 'Finding an Archbishop: The Whigs and Richard Whately in 1831', *Church History*, 1995, 64.2, 218–36, p.220.

4   Richard Brest, 'Richard Whately', *Oxford Dictionary of National Biography*, vol. 58 (2004) p.396; also see Jane Whately, *Life and Correspondence*, vol.1, p.110.

5   Brest, 'Richard Whately', p.1.

6   Fitzpatrick, *Memoirs of Archbishop Whately*, vol.1, p.60.

7   Fitzpatrick, *Memoirs of Archbishop Whately*, vol.1, p.65.

8   Initially in an anonymously written pamphlet, *Letters on the Church, by an Episcopalian* (1826). See de Giustino, *Richard Whately's Ideas in the 1830s*, p.54.

9   Letter to Lord Grey, 10 May 1832, cited in Jane Whately, *Life and Correspondence*, vol.1, p.152.

10   De Giustino, *Finding an Archbishop*, p.219.

11   Jane Whately, *Life and Correspondence*, p.65.

12   Jane Whately, *Life and Correspondence*, p.67.

13   Richard Whately, *On Lord Melbourne as a Statesman*, Appendix V. Jane Whately, *Life and Correspondence*, vol.2, p.452.

14   Letter to the Secretary of the Howard Society 15 February 1833, cited in Whately, *Life and Correspondence*, vol.2, p.182.

15   Richard Whately, *Thoughts on Secondary Punishments in a Letter to Earl Grey* (London: B. Fellows, 1832), p.4.

16   Richard Whately, *Proposal for the gradual Abolition of Slavery*, 24 October 1830, cited in *Life and Correspondence*, p.85.

17   Third Report of the Commission for Inquiry into the Conditions of the Poorer classes in Ireland (Dublin, 1836), p.8.

18   Letter to Senior, 8 July 1832, cited in Jane Whately, *Letters and Correspondence*, vol.1, p.163.

19   Letter to Senior (undated) August 1834, cited in Jane Whately, *Letters and Correspondence*, vol.1, p.95.

20   Jane Whately, *Letters and Correspondence*, vol.2, p.114.

21   Undated letter to Senior, 1835, cited in Jane Whately, vol.1, p.301.

22   Peter Grey, *The Making of the Irish Poor Law, 1815–43* (Manchester: Manchester University Press, 2009), p.49.

23   Peter Grey, *The Making of the Irish Poor Law*, p.65.

24   Correspondence cited in Peter Grey, *The Making of the Irish Poor Law*, p.88.

25   Correspondence cited in Peter Grey, *The Making of the Irish Poor Law*, p.88.

26   See Jane Whately, *Letters and Correspondence*, vol.1, p.200.

27   *Third Report of the Commission into the Conditions of the Poorer Classes*, p.5.

28   Letter to Senior 1837 in Jane Whately, *Letters and Correspondence*, vol.1, p.402.

29 Letter to Senior, 2 October 1836, in Jane Whately, *Letters and Correspondence*, vol.1, p.300.

30 Richard Whately, *The Past and Future of Ireland as Indicated By Its Educational System* (London: Ward, 1850), p.135.

31 James Lydon, *The Making of Ireland* (London: Routledge, 1997), p.288.

32 Richard Whately, *On the Protestant Church in Ireland*, Appendix VIII Jane Whately, *Letters and Correspondence*, vol.2, p.458.

33 Fitzpatrick, *Memoirs of Archbishop Whately*, vol.1, p.169.

34 Fitzpatrick, *Memoirs of Archbishop Whately*, vol.1, p.83.

35 Cited in Fitzpatrick, *Memoirs of Archbishop Whately*, vol.1, p.152.

36 Marcus Tanner, *Ireland's Holy Wars: The Struggle for a Nation's Soul 1500–2000* (New Haven: Yale University Press, 2001), p.208.

37 Fitzpatrick, *Memoirs of Archbishop Whately*, vol.1, p.149.

38 Fitzpatrick, *Memoirs of Archbishop Whately*, vol.1, p.190.

39 Fitzpatrick, *Memoirs of Archbishop Whately*, vol.1, p.158.

40 Patrick O'Donoghue, 'Causes of the Opposition to Tithes, 1830–38', *Studia Hibernica*, 1965, no. 5, 7–28, p.11.

41 Evidence by John Dunn in the Second report of the Select Committee of the House of Commons on Tithes, 1831–32 XXI 245, minutes of evidence, Q. 2793. See O'Donoghue, *Causes of Opposition*, pp.11–12.

42 Fitzpatrick, *Memoirs of Archbishop Whately*, vol.1, p.79.

43 Fitzpatrick, *Memoirs of Archbishop Whately*, vol.1, p.149.

44 Letter to the Lord-Lieutenant, 14 January 1832, cited in Jane Whately, *Letters and Correspondence*, vol.1, p.125.

45 Letter to the Bishop of Llandaff, 19 January 1832, cited in Jane Whately, *Letters and Correspondence*, vol.1, p.127.

46 Letter to the Bishop of Llandaff, 19 January 1832, cited in Jane Whately, *Letters and Correspondence*, vol.1, p.128.

47 Letter to the Bishop of Llandaff, 30 June 1832, cited in Jane Whately, *Letters and Correspondence*, vol.1, p.166.

48 Letter to the Bishop of Llandaff, 19 January 1832, cited in Jane Whately, *Letters and Correspondence*, vol.1, p.128.

49 Fitzpatrick, *Memoirs of Archbishop Whately*, vol.1, p.159.

50 Letter to Dr Pusey, early 1832, cited in Jane Whately, *Letters and Correspondence*, vol.1, p.134.

51 Fitzpatrick, *Memoir of Archbishop Whately*, vol.1, pp.274–304.

52 Richard Whately, 'On the Protestant Church in Ireland', in Jane Whately, *Letters and Correspondence*, vol.2, Appendix VIII, p.458.

53 Letter to Lord Melbourne, 4 May 1835, cited in Jane Whately, *Letters and Correspondence*, vol.1, p.303.

54 Letter to Lord Melbourne, 4 May 1835, in Jane Whately, *Letters and Correspondence*, vol.1, p.305.

55 Letter to Lord Melbourne, 4 May 1835, in Jane Whately, *Letters and Correspondence*, vol.1, p.307.

56 Lydon, *The Making of Ireland*, p.294.

57 Jane Whately, *Letters and Correspondence*, vol.2, p.114.

58 Cited in Aine Hyland and Kenneth Milne (eds), *Irish Educational Documents Vol. 1* (Dublin: Church of Ireland Education, 1987), p.90.

59 Whately, *Past and Future of Ireland*, pp.74–6.

60 Whately, *Past and Future of Ireland*, pp.76–7.

61 Whately, *Past and Future of Ireland*, p.106.

62 Rev. Martin Brennan, *Schools of Kildare and Leighlin* (Dublin: Gill and Son, 1935), p.39.

63 'Resolutions Drawn Up at a Meeting of the Archbishops and Bishops of the Roman Catholic Church in Ireland, held in Dublin, on the 21st January 1826', cited in *Notes on Education Reform in Ireland During the First Half of the 19th Century Compiled from Speeches, letters, &c., contained in The Unpublished Memoirs of the Rt. Hon. Sir Thomas Wyse, K.C.B., by his Niece Winifred M. Wyse* (Waterford: Redmond and Co., 1901), p.7.

64 'Resolutions Drawn Up at a Meeting of the Archbishops and Bishops', p.26.

65 'Resolutions Drawn Up at a Meeting of the Archbishops and Bishops', p.10.

66 Graham Balfour, *The Educational Systems of Great Britain and Ireland* (Oxford: Clarendon, 1898), p.87.

67 Fitzpatrick, *Memoir of Archbishop Whately*, vol.1, p.337.

68 Excerpts reproduced in Jane Whately, *Letters and Correspondence*, vol.2, pp.235–49.

69 Balfour, *The Educational Systems of Great Britain and Ireland*, p.102.

70 Peadar Mac Suibhne, *Paul Cullen and His Contemporaries*, vol.4 (Kildare: Leinster Leader, 1974), p.8.

71 Fitzpatrick, *Memoir of Archbishop Whately*, vol.1, pp.348–50.

72 Tanner, *Ireland's Holy Wars*, p.247.

73 Letters to the Lord Lieutenant, 5 July 1853, 21 July 1853 and 24 July 1853 cited in Jane Whately, *Letters and Correspondence*, vol.2, pp.268–91.

74 Mac Suibhne, *Paul Cullen and His Contemporaries*, vol.2, p.180. Also see Tanner, *Ireland's Holy Wars*, p.247.

75 Foreword to Mac Suibhne, *Paul Cullen and His Contemporaries*, vol.5.

76 Letter to William J. Fitzpatrick, 15 December 1860, in Mac Suibhne, *Paul Cullen and His Contemporaries*, vol.3, p.331.

77 Letter to Kirby, 21 June 1863, in Mac Suibhne, *Paul Cullen and His Contemporaries*, vol.4, p.147.

78 Cited in Mac Suibhne, *Paul Cullen and his Contemporaries*, vol.3, pp.372–3.

79 Letter to Kirby cited in Mac Suibhne, *Paul Cullen and His Contemporaries*, vol.4, p.155.

80　Emmet Larkin, 'The Devotional Revolution in Ireland, 1850–75', *The American Historical Review*, 1977, 77.3, 625–52, p.640.

81　Mark Tierney, 'Catalogue of Letters Relating to the Queen's Colleges, Ireland, 1845–50', in the papers of Archbishop Michael Slattery of Tuam, *Franciscan Province of Ireland: Collectanea Hibernia*, No.9 (1966), pp.83–120.

82　Correspondence dated 8 June 1848, in the papers of Archbishop Michael Slattery of Tuam, p.107.

83　Whately, *Past and Future of Ireland*, p.191.

84　Richard Whately, 'On Popular Imagination', in Jane Whately, *Letters and Correspondence*, vol.2, Appendix III, p.450.

85　Whately, *Past and Future of Ireland*, p.1.

86　Whately, *Past and Future of Ireland*, pp.15–16.

87　Whately, *Past and Future of Ireland*, p.16.

88　Whately, *Past and Future of Ireland*, p.28.

89　Whately, *Past and Future of Ireland*, p.35.

90　Whately, *Past and Future of Ireland*, pp.42–4.

Chapter Seven

1　*The Condition of the Working Class in England* was first published in German in 1845; a second German edition did not appear until 1892. By then two English-language editions had been published, one in New York in 1887, a second in London in 1892. Engels provided forewords to and, as such, endorsed both. All references and quotations here are taken from the London edition.

2　Thomas Carlyle, *Chartism* (Boston: Charles Little and James Brown, 1940), p.1.

3　Amy E. Martin, 'Blood Transfusions: Constructions of Racial Difference, the English Working Class, and Revolutionary Possibility in the Work of Carlyle and Engels', *Victorian Literature and Culture* (2004), 32.1, 83–102, p.86.

4　Tristam Hunt, *The Frock-Coated Communist: The Revolutionary Life of Friedrich Engels* (London: Allen Lane, 2009).

5　Jerold Seigel, *Marx's Fate: The Shape of a Life* (Pennsylvania: State University Press, 1978), pp.147–9.

6　Grace Carlton, *Friedrich Engels: The Shadow Prophet* (London: Pall Mall Press, 1965), p.15.

7　Grace Carlton, *Friedrich Engels*, p.37.

8　Grace Carlton, *Friedrich Engels*, pp.37–8.

9　Written under the pen name of Friedrich Oswald, *Telegraph für Deutschland* Nos.2–5, January 1841, *MECW*. All references to Marx and Engels' journalism and correspondence cited from *Karl Marx and Frederick Engels Collected Works* (London: Lawrence and Wishart).

10 F. Engels, *Telegraph für Deutschland* Nos.2–5, January 1841, *MECW*.

11 F. Engels, 'The Magyar Struggle', in *Neue Rheinische Zeitung* No.194, 13 January 1849 *MECW*. On the wider context see Mike Rapport, *1848: Year of Revolution* (London; Abacus, 2008), p.181.

12 F. Engels, *The Magyar Struggle*, p.181.

13 G. Hegel, 'The English Reform Bill', in *Hegel's Political Writings*, ed. ZA Pelgczynski, trans. T. M. Knox (Oxford : Oxford University Press, 1964), p.308.

14 Hunt, *Frock-Coated Communist*, p.100.

15 Hunt, *Frock-Coated Communist*, p.100.

16 Engels, 'A Review of *Past and Present* by Thomas Carlyle, London 1843', *Deutsch-Franzosische Jahrbucher* (1844) *MECW*.

17 James Anthony Froude, *Life of Carlyle* (abridged into a single volume from three original ones) ed. John Clubbe (London: John Murray, 1979), p.380.

18 Carlyle cited in Engels, *Review of Past and Present*.

19 Engels, *Condition of the Working Class*, p.101.

20 K. Marx and F. Engels, *The Communist Manifesto*, p.1.

21 Engels, *Condition of the Working Class*, p.67.

22 Engels, *Condition of the Working Class*, p.91.

23 Engels, *Condition of the Working Class*, pp.94–5.

24 Engels, *Condition of the Working Class*, p.95.

25 Carlyle, *Chartism*, pp.31–2.

26 Engels, Schweizerischer Republikaner No. 51, 27 June 1843.

27 Engels, Schweizerischer Republikaner No. 51, 27 June 1843.

28 Engels, Schweizerischer Republikaner No. 51, 27 June 1843.

29 Engels, *Condition of the Working Class*, p.119.

30 Engels, *Condition of the Working Class*, p.146.

31 Engels, *Condition of the Working Class*, pp.105–6.

32 Engels, *Condition of the Working Class*, p.116.

33 Carlyle, *Chartism*, pp.31–2.

34 Engels, *Condition of the Working Class*, p.92.

35 Engels, *Condition of the Working Class*, p.93.

36 Engels, *Condition of the Working Class*, p.27.

37 Engels, *Condition of the Working Class*, p.27.

38 Letter from Engels to Marx, 23 May 1856.

39 Letter from Engels to Marx, 29 November 1867.

40 F. Engels, *Notes for a History of Ireland* (Moscow: Progress Publishers, 1974).

41 Engels, *Notes for a History of Ireland*.

42 Letter from Engels to Jenny Longuet.

43 Engels, Letter to Karl Kautsky, 7 February 1882.

44 Engels, Letter to Eduard Bernsten, 26 June 1882.

45 Interview with Engels in the *New Yorker Volkszeitung*, 20 September 1888.

46 See M. A. Busteed and R. I. Hodgson, 'Irish Responses to Urban Life in Early Nineteenth-Century Manchester', *The Geographical Journal*, 1996, 162.2, 139–53, p.141.

47 K. O'Rourke, 'Emigration and Living Standards in Ireland since the Famine', *Journal of Population Economics*, 1995, 8.4, 407–21, p.408.

Chapter Eight

1 John Mitchel, *The Last Conquest of Ireland (Perhaps)* (Dublin: UCD Press, 1873/2005).

2 John Mitchel, *The Irish Citizen*, 14 January 1854.

3 Thomas Davis, *The Nation*, 9 September 1943.

4 John Mitchel, 'The People's Food', *The Nation*, 25 October 1845.

5 James Lydon, *The Making of Ireland* (Routledge: London, 1998), p.297.

6 John Mitchel, 'Threats of Coercion', *The Nation*, 22 November 1845.

7 Mitchel, *Last Conquest*, pp.11–12.

8 Mitchel, *Last Conquest*, p.30.

9 An unspecified newspaper report cited by Mitchel, *Last Conquest*, pp.30–1.

10 An unspecified newspaper report cited by Mitchel, *Last Conquest*, p.61.

11 Louis J. Walsh, *John Mitchel* (Dublin: Talbot Press, 1934), p.109.

12 Mitchel, *Last Conquest*, p.31.

13 Mitchel, *Last Conquest*, p.75.

14 Mitchel, *Last Conquest*, p.135.

15 Mitchel, *Last Conquest*, p.136.

16 James Quinn, *John Mitchel* (Dublin: University College Dublin Press, 2008), pp.26–8.

17 Mitchel, *Jail Journal*, p.357.

18 Mitchel, *Jail Journal*, p.376.

19 Patrick Maume, 'Introduction', to John Mitchel, *The Last Conquest of Ireland (perhaps)*, p.xi.

20 Quinn, *John Mitchel*, pp.12–13.

21 John Mitchel, *Jail Journal* (Dublin: Gill and Son, 1913), p.204.

22 John Morrow, 'Thomas Carlyle, Young Ireland and The "Condition of Ireland Question"', *The Historical Journal*, 2008, 51.3, 643–67, p.662.

23 Charles Gavan Duffy, *Conversations with Carlyle* (London: Sampson, Low Marston and Company, 1892), pp.4–7.

24 Letter from Carlyle to Duffy, *Conversations with Carlyle*, 19 January 1846.

25 Carlyle to Duffy, *Conversations with Carlyle*, 1 March 1847.

26 Morrow, *Thomas Carlyle*, p.661.

27 Duffy, 'Wanted a Few Workmen', first published in *The Nation* in 1849, republished in *Conversations with Carlyle*, pp.135–45.

28 Carlyle, 'Trees of Liberty, Workmen Needed', first published in *The Nation* in 1849, republished in *Conversations with Carlyle*, pp.147–9.

29 Quinn, *John Mitchel*, p.44.

30 Thomas Carlyle, 'Occasional Discourse on the Nigger Question', *Fraser's Magazine*, December 1849. On the term 'dismal science', see Peter Groenewegen, 'Thomas Carlyle, "The Dismal Science", and the Contemporary Political Economy of Slavery', *History of Economics Review*, 2001, 75–94, p.74.

31 Carlyle, *The Nigger Question*.

32 Niamh Lynch, 'Defining Irish Nationalist Anti-Imperialism: Thomas Davis and John Mitchel', *Éire-Ireland*, 2007, 42.1 and 2, 82–107, p.95.

33 James Quinn, 'John Mitchel and the Rejection of the Nineteenth Century', *Éire-Ireland*, I, 2003, 38.3–4, 98–108.

34 Mitchel, *Jail Journal*, p.375.

35 Mitchel, *Jail Journal*, p.393.

36 John Mitchel, *The Citizen*, 23 September 1854.

37 Rebecca O'Connor, *Jenny Mitchel: Young Irelander* (Arizona: The O'Connor Trust, 1985), p.227.

38 Mitchel, *Last Conquest*, p.207.

39 Mitchel, *Last Conquest*, p.209.

40 Quinn, *John Mitchel*, p.21.

41 Letter from Daniel O'Connell to P. V. Fitzpatrick, 14 May 1839. It is cited by Sean Ó Faoláin in the front materials of his *King of the Beggars: A Life of Daniel O'Connell, the Irish Liberator, in a Study of the Rise of the Modern Irish Democracy 1775–1847* (Dublin: Cahill Printers, 1938).

42 Mitchel, *Last Conquest*, p.72.

43 Mitchel, *Last Conquest*, p.219.

44 Mitchel, *Last Conquest*, p.30.

45 Mitchel, *Last Conquest*, p.82.

46 Mitchel, *Last Conquest*, p.129.

47 Mitchel, *Last Conquest*, p.212.

48 Mitchel, *Last Conquest*, p.120.

49 Mitchel, *Last Conquest*, p.83.

50 Mitchel, *Last Conquest*, p.219.

51 Mitchel, *Last Conquest*, p.115.

52 Mitchel, *Last Conquest*, p.212.

53 Mitchel, *Last Conquest*, p.12.

54 Mitchel, *Last Conquest*, p.127.

55 Mitchel, *Last Conquest*, p.124.

56 Mitchel, *Last Conquest*, p.12.

57 O'Connor, *Jenny Mitchel*, p.35.

58 O'Connor, *Jenny Mitchel*, p.48.

59 Mitchel, *Last Conquest*, p.214.

60 Mitchel, *Last Conquest*, p.210.

61 Mitchel, *Last Conquest*, p.17.

62 Mitchel, *Last Conquest*, p.219.

63 Cited in P. S. O'Hegarty, *John Mitchel* (Dublin: Maunsel and Company, 1912), pp.122–3.

64 Douglas Hyde, *The Necessity for De-Anglicising Ireland*, delivered to the Irish National Literary Society in Dublin, 25 November 1892.

65 Cited in Dominic Daly, *The Young Douglas Hyde* (Dublin: Irish Academic Press, 1974), p.xvii.

66 Douglas Hyde cited in Janet Egleston Dunleavy and Gareth W. Dunleavy, *Douglas Hyde; A Maker of Modern Ireland* (Berkeley: University of California, 1991), p.311.

67 Arthur Griffith, 'Preface to John Michel', *Jail Journal* (M. H. Gill and Son, 1913), p.xiv.

68 Fredrick Nietzsche, *The Gay Science; Second Edition 1887*, trans. Josefine Nauckhoff, ed. Bernard Williams (Cambridge: Cambridge University Press, 2001) book three, 117.

69 Griffith, Preface to *Jail Journal*, pp.ix–x.

70 Patrick Pearse, 'From a Hermitage' in *Collected Works of Padraig H. Pearse; Political Writings and Speeches* (Dublin: Phoenix, 1917), p.168.

71 Roy Foster, *W. B. Yeats: A Life*, vol.1, *The Apprentice Mage* (Oxford: Oxford University Press, 1997), p.524.

72 W. B. Yeats, *Last Poems (1936–9)* (Dublin: Cuala Press, 1939).

Chapter Nine

1 Donal Nevin, *James Connolly: A Full Life* (Dublin: Gill and Macmillan, 2005), p.58.

2 James Connolly, *Erin's Hope: The End and the Means* (Dublin, 1897); James Connolly, *Selected Political Writings* (ed.) Owen Dudley Edwards and Bernard Ransom (New York: Grove, 1974), pp.187–8.

3 James D. Young, 'A Very English Socialism and the Celtic Fringe', *History Workshop*, 1993, 35.1, 135–52, p.149.

4 Nevin, *James Connolly*, p.268.

5 James Connolly, *The Re-Conquest of Ireland* (Dublin, 1915). All citations from James Connolly, *Collected Works*, vol.1 (Dublin: New Books, 1987), p.184.

6   James Connolly, *The Re-Conquest of Ireland*, p.184.

7   James Connolly, *Socialism Made Easy* (Chicago: Charles H. Kerr, 1909).

8   Nelson Ó Ceallaigh Ritschel, 'Under Which Flag, 1916', *New Hibernia Review*, 1998, 2.4, 54–68, p.64.

9   Sean O'Casey/Sean Ó'Cathasaigh, *The Story of the Irish Citizen Army* (London: Maunsel and Co., 1919).

10 Letter to John Carstairs Matheson, 30 January 1908. All letters cited from Donal Nevin (ed.) *Between Comrades: James Connolly Letters and Correspondence 1889–1916* (Dublin: Gill and Macmillan, 2007).

11 Letter to Lillie Reynolds, 6 April 1890.

12 Nevin, *James Connolly*, p.688.

13 Connolly, *The Harp*, January 1909.

14 Douglas Hyde, *The Necessity of De-Anglicising Ireland* (Dublin, 1892); D. P. Moran, *The Philosophy of Irish-Ireland* (Dublin, 1905).

15 James Connolly, *Labour in Irish History* (Dublin, 1912). All citations from James Connolly, *Collected Works*, vol.1 (Dublin: New Books, 1987).

16 Connolly, *Erin's Hope*.

17 Gregory Dobbins, 'Wherever Green is Red: James Connolly and Postcolonial Theory', *Nepantla: Views from the South*, 2000, 1.3, 605–48, p.633.

18 William Thompson, *An Inquiry into the principles of the distribution of Wealth most conducive to Human Happiness as applied to the newly-proposed System of the Voluntary Equality of Wealth* (London: Longman, Hust Rees, Orne, Brown and Green, 1824).

19 William Thompson, *Labour Rewarded, the Claims of Labour and Capital Conciliated; or, How to Secure to Labour the Whole Product of its Exertions* (London: Hunt and Clarke, 1827).

20 William Thompson, *Practical Directions for the Speedy and Economical Establishment of Communities on Principles of Mutual Co-operation, United Possession's and Equality of Exertions and the Means of Enjoyments* (London, Strange and E. Wilson, 1830).

21 Cited in Nevin, *James Connolly*, p.136.

22 Connolly, *Worker's Republic*, 5 August 1899.

23 Connolly, *Worker's Republic*, 13 August 1898.

24 Connolly, 'Socialism and Nationalism', *Shan Van Vocht*, 8 January 1897.

25 Connolly, 'Patriotism and Labour', *Shan Van Vocht*, 8 August 1897.

26 Connolly, *Worker's Republic*, 22 July 1899.

27 Letter from Connolly to William O'Brien, August 1903.

28 In the single-volume history of Ireland that gives most weight to Connolly. F. L. S. Lyons, *Ireland Since the Famine* (Glasgow: Fontana, 1973), p.275.

29 Letter from Connolly to Thomas Brady, 23 May 1903.

30 From Connolly to Jack Mulray, June 1905.

31 Nevin, *James Connolly*, p.279.

32 Letter to O'Brien, 24 May 1909.

33 Connolly to William O'Brien, 18 December 1909.

34 Socialist Party of Ireland leaflet advertising meetings addressed by Connolly, July and August 1909.

35 Nevin, *James Connolly*, p.385.

36 Letter to William O'Brien, 29 July 1913.

37 Connolly, 'North-East Ulster', *Forward*, 2 August 1913.

38 Connolly, *Forward*, July 1913 cited in Levin, *James Connolly*, p.411.

39 Nevin, *James Connolly*, p.432.

40 Lyons, *Ireland Since the Famine*, pp.28–5.

41 Nevin, *James Connolly*, p.554.

42 Connolly, *Irish Worker*, 8 August 1914.

43 Various articles in *The Irish Worker*, August–December 1914.

44 Connolly, *Irish Worker*, 21 November 1914.

45 Donal Nevin, 'Introduction', *Between Comrades: Letters and Correspondence 1889–1916* (Dublin: Gill and Macmillan, 2007), p.63.

46 Connolly, 'Why the Citizen Army Honours Rossa', in Desmond Ryan (ed.), *James Connolly, Labour and Easter Week 1916* (Dublin: Sign of the Three Candles, 1949), pp.69–70; Nevin, *James Connolly*, p.600.

47 Connolly, *Worker's Republic*, 2 October 1915.

48 Connolly, *Worker's Republic*, 22 January 1916.

49 Nevin, *James Connolly*, p.630.

50 C. Desmond Greaves, *The Irish Transport and General Worker's Union: The Formative Years 1909–1923* (Dublin: Gill and Macmillan, 1982), p.162.

51 Cited in Nevin, *James Connolly*, p.632. Also see Desmond Ryan, *James Connolly* (Dublin: Talbot Press, 1924), pp.101–4.

52 Connolly, *Worker's Republic*, 12 February 1916.

53 Connolly, *Worker's Republic*, 11 March 1916.

54 Connolly, 'Sinn Fein, Socialism and the Nation', *Irish Nation*, 23 January 1909.

55 Patrick Pearse, 'From a Hermitage', in *Collected Works of Padraic Pearse; Political Writings and Speeches* (Dublin: Phoenix, 1917).

56 Patrick Pearse, 'The Sovereign People', *Collected Works*.

57 Peter Berrisford-Ellis, *A History of The Irish Working Class* (London Victor: Gollancz, 1972), p.205.

58 Berrisford-Ellis, *History of the Irish Working Class*, p.245.

59 Richard English, 'Socialism and Republican Schism in Ireland: The Emergence of the Republican Congress in 1934', *Irish Historical Studies*, col. xxvii, no. 105 (May 1990), 48–65, pp.49–56.

60 Connolly, *The Worker's Republic*, 29 January 1916. Also see Nevin, *James Connolly*, p.613.

61 Peter Finlay S. J., 'Socialism and Catholic Teaching', *Studies*, 1919, 8, 352–66.

62 Lambert McKenna, S. J., *The Social Teachings of James Connolly* (Dublin: Catholic Truth Society, 1921).

63 Lambert McKenna S.J., 'The Bolsheviks', *Studies*, 1921, 10, 218–39.

64 Peter Somerville, 'A Catholic Labour College', *Studies*, 1921, 10, 391–400.

Chapter Ten

1 Margaret Ward, *Hanna Sheehy Skeffington: A Life* (Cork: Attic Press, 1997), p.4.

2 Diarmuid Ferriter, *The Transformation of Ireland* (London: Profile, 2004), p.132.

3 Ferriter, *The Transformation of Ireland*, p.xii.

4 Ferriter, *The Transformation of Ireland*, p.xii.

5 Carl Latham, 'Feminine Rebel of Eire Here On Tour of Nation', *The San Francisco Chronicle*, 13 March 1938.

6 Rosemary Cullen Owens, *Smashing Times: A History of the Irish Women's Suffrage Movement 1889–1922* (Dublin: Attic Press, 1984), p.20.

7 Cullen Owens, *Smashing Times*, p.25.

8 Maria Luddy, 'Isabella M. S. Tod', in Mary Cullen and Maria Luddy (eds) *Women, Power and Consciousness in 19th Century Ireland* (Dublin: Attic Press, 1995).

9 Isabella M. S. Tod, 'Advanced Education for Girls of the Upper and Middle Classes', *Transactions of the National Association for the Promotion of Social Science* (London, 1874).

10 Isabella M.S Tod, *On the Education of Girls of the Middle Class* (London, 1874).

11 Luddy, *Isabella M. S. Tod*, p.219.

12 Isabella M.S. Tod, Letter to the *Northern Whig*, 18 June 1886.

13 Jane Cote and Dana Herne, 'Anna Parnell', in Mary Cullen and Maria Luddy (eds) *Women, Power and Consciousness in 19th Century Ireland* (Dublin: Attic Press, 1995).

14 Michael Davitt, *The Fall of Feudalism in Ireland* (New York: Harper, 1904), p.299.

15 Anne Parnell, *The Tale of a Great Sham* (Dublin, 1986), p.90.

16 Margaret Ward, *Hanna Sheehy Skeffington* (Dublin: Attic Press, 1997), pp.9–11.

17 Andrée Sheehy Skeffington, 'James Joyce and "Cupid's Confidante" ', *James Joyce Quarterly*, 1984, 21.3, pp.205¬14.

18 Richard Ellman, *James Joyce* (Oxford: Oxford University Press, 1966), p.63.

19 Andrée Sheehy Skeffington, *Skeff: A Life of Owen Sheehy Skeffington 1909–1970* (Dublin: Lilliput Press, 1991), p.5.

20 Leah Levenson, *With Wooden Sword: A Portrait of Francis Sheehy Skeffington Militant Pacifist* (Boston: Northeastern University Press), p.43.

21 Francis Sheehy Skeffington, *In Dark and Evil Days* (Dublin: James Duffy & Co., 1936).

22 HSS, 'Reminiscences of an Irish Suffragette', in Andrée Sheehy Skeffington and Rosemary Owens (eds) *Votes for Women, Irish Women's Struggle for the Vote* (Dublin, 1975), p.12.

23 Luddy, *Hannah Sheehy Skeffington*, p.16.

24 Advertisement in *The Irish Citizen*, 6 December 1913.

25 E. A. Browning, 'Women's Work and Wages in Dublin', *The Irish Citizen*, 2 August 1913.

26 'The Suffragists' Catechism', *The Irish Citizen*, 17 May 1913.

27 HSS, *Reminiscences*, p.18.

28 HSS, *Reminiscences*, p.12.

29 HSS, 'Mass Meeting of Irish Women: An Impression From The Platform', *The Irish Citizen*, 8 June 1912.

30 HSS, *Reminiscences*, p.20.

31 Reproduced in Cullen Owens, *Smashing Times: A History of the Irish Women's Suffrage Movement*, p.33.

32 Owens, *Smashing Times*, p.64.

33 HSS, *Reminiscences*, p.20.

34 HSS, *Reminiscences*, p.14.

35 HSS, 'Votes For Women In The West', *The Irish Citizen*, 14 March 1914.

36 HSS, 'The Woman's Movement: Ireland', *The Irish Review*, 1912, 2.17, pp.225–7.

37 HSS, *Reminiscences*, p.22.

38 Luddy, *Hanna Sheehy Skeffington*, p.23.

39 Louise Ryan, *Irish Feminism and the Vote*, p.18.

40 Louise Ryan, *Irish Feminism and the Vote*, p.83.

41 Louise Ryan, *Irish Feminism and the Vote*, p.43.

42 Marcus Tanner, *Ireland's Holy Wars: The Struggle for a Nation's Soul 1500–2000* (New Haven: Yale University Press, 2001), p.275.

43 Diane Urquhart, *Women in Ulster Politics 1890–1940*, p.25.

44 Owens, *Smashing Times: A History of the Irish Women's Suffrage Movement*, pp.109–10.

45 HSS, 'Rolling Up the Map of Suffrage', *The Irish Citizen*, 8 August 1914.

46 FSS, 'Editorial: The Writing On The Wall', *The Irish Citizen*, 9 August 1914.

47 Ward, *Hanna Sheehy Skeffington*, p.133.

48 Mary McSwiney, Untitled, *The Irish Citizen*, 21 November 1914. Also see Cliona Murphy, *The Women's Suffrage Movement and Irish Society in the Early Twentieth Century* (New York: Harvester Wheatsheaf, 1989), p.79.

49 HSS, 'The Duty Of Suffragists', *The Irish Citizen*, 15 August 1914.

50 HSS, *The Irish Citizen*, September 1916.

51 HSS, *British Militarism As I Have Known It* (New York, 1917).

52 HSS, 'Easter Week in Ireland', 13 May 1922.

53 HSS, 'Ireland's Joan of Arc', *Saoirse Na H'Eireann*, March 1928.

54 HSS, *The Irish Citizen*, February 1920.

55 P. S. O'Hegarty, *The Victory of Sinn Fein* (Dublin: Talbot Press, 1924), p.10.

56 P. S. O'Hegarty, *The Victory of Sinn Fein*, p.57.

57 P. S. O'Hegarty, *The Victory of Sinn Fein*, p.102.

58 John P. McCarthy, *Kevin O'Higgins; Builder of the Irish State* (Dublin: Irish Academic Press, 2006), p.72.

59 HSS, 'Record of Current Irish Events', *The Irish World*, 20 May 1922.

60 Dail Eireann debate, 2 March 1922.

61 HSS, 'Easter Week in Ireland', *The Irish World*, 13 May 1922.

62 HSS, 'Coalition Policy an Ominous One', *The Irish World*, 10 June 1922.

63 HSS, 'Horrors of the Belfast Pogroms', *The Irish World*, 29 April 1922.

64 HSS, 'Seeking Common Grounds for Agreement', *The Irish World*, 27 May 1922.

65 HSS, 'Coalition Policy an Ominous One'.

66 HSS, 'Ireland's Military Dictatorship', *The Irish World*, 5 August 1922.

67 HSS 'Camouflaged Black and Tanism', *The Irish World*, 12 August 1922.

68 HSS, 'Alphabet', (undated) National Archives MS 33,618 (12).

69 HSS, 'Horrors of the Belfast Pogroms', 29 April 1922. On trade union anti-Semitism see Bryan Fanning, *Racism and Social Change in the Republic of Ireland* (Manchester: Manchester University Press, 2012), p.45.

70 HSS, 'Easter Week in Ireland', 13 May 1922.

71 Dail Eireann, 15 February 1927.

72 McCarthy, *Kevin O'Higgins*, p.267.

73 'Editorial: Is The Law an Ass – Or Worse?', *The Irish Citizen*, 10 August 1912.

74 M. E. Duggan, 'In The Courts', *The Irish Citizen*, 11 July 1914.

75 M. E. Duggan, 'The Woman Lawyer – Her Work For Peace', *The Irish Citizen*, 24 April 1915.

76 Mrs E. Sanderson, 'Watching The Courts', *The Irish Citizen*, 19 June 1915.

77 HSS, 'Letter to the Editor', *Voice of Labour*, 12 March 1927.

78 Anonymous, 'A "Light" Offence?', *The Irish Citizen*, May 1919.

79 L. A. M. Priestley-McCracken, 'Wife Beating', *The Irish Citizen*, September 1919.

80 Maryann Gialanella Valiulis, 'Power, Gender and Identity in the Irish Free State', *Journal of Women's History*, 1995, 6.1, 117–35, p.123.

81 HSS, July 1937, cited in Ward, *Hanna Sheehy Skeffington*, p.326.

82 Dermot Keogh, 'The Jesuits and the 1937 Constitution', in Bryan Fanning (ed.), *An Irish Century: Studies 1912–2012* (Dublin: UCD Press, 2012).

83 HSS, July 1937, cited in Ward, *Hanna Sheehy Skeffington*, p.326.

84 Mary E. Daly, 'Women in the Irish Free State 1922–39: The Interaction between Economics and Ideology', *Journal of Women's History*, 1995, 6.4, 99–116, pp.103–10.

85 Daly, *Women in the Irish Free State*, p.103.

86 HSS, 'The Position of Women in Ireland: Some grievances and a Moral', *The Vote*, 11 January 1929.

87 HSS, *An Phoblacht*, 16 July 1932.

88 Hanna Sheehy Skeffington's 1943 Election Manifesto, cited in Luddy, *Hanna Sheehy Skeffington*, p.50.

89 HSS, 'Women in Politics', *The Bell*, 1943, 7.2, 143–8.

Chapter Eleven

1 Liam Irwin, 'Jeremiah Newman', *Dictionary of Irish Biography* (Cambridge: Cambridge University Press, 2009).

2 'Cardinal Insists that Bishop Was a Happy Man.', *Limerick Leader*, 10 April 1995.

3 Olivia O'Leary, 'The Mullah of Limerick', *Magill*, 21 March 1985, pp.24–33.

4 Irwin, *Jeremiah Newman*, DIB.

5 Newman, *The Postmodern Church* (Dublin; Four Courts Press, 1990), p.17.

6 Fiona Buckley, 'Limerick's Modern and Moderate Prelate', *Limerick Leader*, 26 October 1974.

7 Conversation with author, 16 April 2012.

8 Conversation with author, 10 April 2012.

9 Newman, *Conscience Versus Law: Reflections of the Evolution of Natural Law* (Dublin: Talbot Press, 1971), p.143.

10 Newman, *Race, Migration and Integration* (London: Burns and Oates, 1968).

11 O'Leary, *The Mullah of Limerick*, p.33.

12 Newman, *Puppets of Utopia: Can Irish Democracy Be Taken For Granted?* (Dublin: Four Court Press, 1987).

13 Newman, 'On Church–State Relations', *Christus Rex*, 1955, xi.1, 76–85.

14 Newman, *Studies in Political Morality* (Dublin: Scepter, 1962), p.199.

15 Paul Blanshard, *American Freedom and Catholic Power* (Boston, 1949); Blanshard, *The Irish and Catholic Power* (Boston, 1953).

16 Newman, *Studies in Political Morality*, p.207.

17 Newman, *Studies in Political Morality*, p.331; Paul Blanshard, *The Irish and Catholic Power* (Boston, 1953).

18 Newman, *Studies in Political Morality*, p.240.

19 Newman, *Studies in Political Morality*, p.265.

20 Newman, *Studies in Political Morality*, p.52.

21 Newman, *Studies in Political Morality*, p.89.

22 Newman, *Studies in Political Morality*, p.97.

23 Newman, Review of Joseph H. Fischer, *Sociology* (University of Chicago Press, 1958) *Christus Rex*, 1959, xiii.3, pp.220–1.

24 Newman, Review of Eva J Ross, *Basic Sociology* (Milwaukee: Bruce Publishing Company, 1960), *Christus Rex*, 1961, xv.1, 73–7, p.75.

25 For an analysis of *Christus Rex* see Bryan Fanning, *The Quest for Modern Ireland: The Battle of Ideas 1912–86* (Dublin: Irish Academic Press, 2008).

26 David Thornley, 'Ireland: The End of an Era', *Studies*, 1964, 52.1–17, p.2.

27 Newman, 'Report on Limerick Rural Survey', *Christus Rex*, 1961, xv.1, pp.20–2.

28 Newman, *Report on Limerick Rural Survey*, p.19.

29 Newman, 'Vocations in Ireland: 1966', *Christus Rex*, 1967, xxi.2, pp.105–22.

30 Newman, 'The Laity and the Mission of the Church', in Jeremiah Newman (ed.) *Vatican II: The Christian Layman* (Dublin: Sceptre, 1966), p.49.

31 Newman, 'The Laity and the Mission of the Church', p.61.

32 Newman, 'Progress and Planning', *Christus Rex*, 1970, xxiii.3, pp.173–86.

33 Newman, *Conscience Versus Law*, p.159.

34 Newman, *Conscience Versus Law*, p.157.

35 Newman, *Conscience Versus Law*, pp.150–2.

36 Newman, *Conscience Versus Law*, p.178.

37 Newman, 'Socio-Political Aspects of Divorce', *Christus Rex*, 1969, xxiii.1, pp.5–15.

38 Newman, *Conscience Versus Law*, p.182.

39 Newman, *Conscience Versus Law*, p.181.

40 Newman, *Conscience Versus Law*, p.186.

41 H. L. A. Hart, *Law, Liberty and Morality*, (Oxford: Oxford University Press, 1962), p.26.

42 Hart, *Law, Liberty and Morality*, pp.9–10.

43 Hart cited (Lord) Patrick Devlin, *The Enforcement of Morals* (Oxford: Oxford University Press), 1961, pp.13–14.

44 Newman, *The State of Ireland* (Dublin: Four Courts Press, 1977), p.12.

45 Newman, *The State of Ireland*, p.25.

46 Newman, *The State of Ireland*, p.39.

47 Newman, *The State of Ireland*, p.55.

48 Garret FitzGerald, *Towards a New Ireland* (London: Charles Knight, 1972), pp.100–1.

49 Newman, *Ireland Must Choose* (Dublin: Four Courts Press), p.14.

50 Newman, *Ireland Must Choose*, p.68.

51 Newman, *Puppets of Utopia*, p.13.

52 Newman, *Puppets of Utopia*, p.75.

53 Newman, *Puppets of Utopia*, p.108.

54 Newman, *The Post Modern Church*, pp.33–4.

55 Newman, *The Post Modern Church*, pp.140–1.

56 Newman, *The Post Modern Church*, p.147.

57 Newman, *The Post Modern Church*, p.125.

58 Tom Inglis, *Moral Monopoly; The Rise and Fall of the Catholic Church in Modern Ireland* (Dublin: UCD Press, 1998).

59 'Man Who Kept Fighting Battles of Long Ago', *Irish Times*, 4 April 1995.

60 Newman, *Conscience Versus Law*, p.279.

61 Cited in *Irish Times*, 1 March 1994.

62 'Man Who Kept Fighting Battles of Long Ago', *Irish Times*, 4 April 1995.

63 Marie Keenan, *Child Sexual Abuse and the Catholic Church: Gender, Power and Organizational Culture* (Oxford: New York, 2012), p.23.

Chapter Twelve

1 The former by Roy Foster, 'The Cruiser', *Standpoint*, 1 February 2009, the latter in an obituary by Brian Fallon in *The Guardian*, 19 December 2008.

2 D. K. Akenson, *Conor: A Biography of Conor Cruise O'Brien* (New York: Cornell University Press, 1994), p.444.

3 *Sunday Independent*, 28 October 2007.

4 Conor Cruise O'Brien, *Parnell and His Party 1880–90* (Oxford: Clarendon Press, 1957), p.17.

5 Maurice Goldring, *Pleasant the Scholar's Life: Irish Intellectuals and the Construction of the Nation State*, (London: Serif, 1993), p.14.

6 CCO'B, *States of Ireland* (London: Panther 1974, originally published 1972), p.104.

7 O'Brien drew attention to this in an account of the social milieu from which he sprung, States of Ireland, p.63.

8 CCO'B, *The Great Melody: A Thematic Biography of Edmund Burke* (London: Sinclair Stevenson, 1992), pp.53–4.

9 CCO'B, *States of Ireland*, p.20.

10 Donat O'Donnell, 'Horizon', *The Bell*, 1945, 1030–8, p.1033.

11 Sean O'Faolain, 'For the Future', *The Bell*, 1940, 1.2, 5–6.

12   Tom Garvin, 'Imaginary Cassandra? Conor Cruise O'Brien as Public
     Intellectual in Ireland', *Irish University Review*, 2007, 37.2, 430–40.

13   CCO'B, *To Katanga and Back: A UN Case History* (London: Hutchinson,
     1962).

14   Fintan O'Toole, 'The Life and Times of Conor Cruise O'Brien: Part Two: A
     Liberal in Chaos', *Magill*, 1 May 1986, p.26.

15   Diarmuid Whelan, *Conor Cruise O'Brien: Violent Notions* (Dublin: Irish
     Academic Press, 2009), p.67.

16   CCO'B, *Camus* (London: Fontana 1982, originally published 1970).

17   W. J. McCormack, 'The Historian as Writer or Critic? Conor Cruise
     O'Brien and His Biographers', *Irish Historical Studies*, 1996, 30.117,
     111–19, p.112.

18   CCO'B, 'A Vindication of Edmund Burke', *National Review*, 17 December
     1990.

19   CCO'B, 'A Vindication of Edmund Burke'.

20   In 1908, Cardinal Mercier, the primate of Belgium, publicly denounced George
     Tyrell, an Irish Jesuit priest, as a leader of the modernist heresy. Tyrell drew a
     fundamental distinction between faith on one hand and the changing human
     synthesis of reason, science and theology on the other hand. Tyrell was
     subsequently excommunicated. See Bryan Fanning, 'George Tyrell, Jacques
     Maritain and the Challenge of Modernity', *Studies*, 2012, 101.403, 291–9.

21   Fanning, 'George Tyrell, Jacques Maritain and the Challenge of Modernity',
     Studies, 2012, 101.403.

22   Conor Cruise O' Brien, *Memoir: My Life and Themes* (London: Profile, 1998),
     p.160.

23   Akenson, *Conor*, pp.129–30.

24   CCO'B, *Memoir*, pp.145–6.

25   Sean McBride, *That Day's Struggle: A Memoir 1904–1951* (Dublin: Curragh
     Press, 2005), pp.181–2.

26   Sean McBride, *That Day's Struggle: A Memoir 1904–1951*, pp.181–2.

27   'L'Unité de L'Irelande et les Irlandais d'Amérique', in the *Revue Général Belge*
     57 in July 1950, pp.1–9.

28   Akenson, *Conor*, pp.144–6.

29   Akenson, *Conor*, p.568.

30   Akenson, *Conor*, 1945, pp.144–6.

31   Akenson, *Conor*, p.142.

32   CCO'B, *Parnell and His Party*, p.191.

33   CCO'B, *Parnell and His Party*, p.349.

34   CCO'B, *Parnell and His Party*, p.189.

35   CC0'B, 'Parnell and His Party Reconsidered', Spring 1981, republished in
     D. H. Akenson (ed.) *Conor: A Biography of Conor Cruise O'Brien: Anthology*
     (Belfast: McGill-Queens University Press, 1994), pp.248–50.

36 Donal Barrington, 'United Ireland', *Studies*, 1957, 46, pp.379–402.

37 Donal Barrington, 'United Ireland', pp.381–2.

38 Donal Barrington, 'United Ireland', p.387.

39 Donal Barrington, 'United Ireland', p.390.

40 Donal Barrington, 'United Ireland', p.395.

41 CCO'B, 'A Sample of Loyalties', *Studies*, 1957, 46, 403–10, p.403.

42 CCO'B, 'A Sample of Loyalties', p.402.

43 CCO'B, 'A Sample of Loyalties', p.404.

44 CCO'B, 'A Sample of Loyalties', pp.406–8.

45 CCO'B, 'The Embers of Easter', *Irish Times*, 7 April 1966.

46 CCO'B, *Murderous Angels: A Political Tragedy and Comedy in Black and White* (London: Hutchinson, 1969).

47 CCO'B, 'Burke, Marx and History', in Donald Harman Akenson (ed.), *Anthology: A Biography of Conor Cruise O'Brien Volume II* (Belfast; McGill-Queens University Press, 1994).

48 CCO'B, *Suspecting Glance*, pp.38–9.

49 CCO'B, *Suspecting Glance*, p.47.

50 CCO'B, *Suspecting Glance*, p.48.

51 CCO'B, *Suspecting Glance*, p.49.

52 CCO'B, *Passion and Cunning and Other Essays* (London: Weidenfield and Nicolson, 1988), p.40.

53 CCO'B, *Passion and Cunning and Other Essays*, p.2.

54 Frank O'Connor, 'The Old Age of A Poet', *The Bell*, Feb 1941, 1.5, pp.7–9.

55 CCO'B, *Passion and Cunning*, pp.41–54.

56 CCO'B, *Suspecting Glance*, p.52.

57 CCO'B, *Suspecting Glance*, p.73.

58 CCO'B, *Suspecting Glance*, p.69.

59 CCO'B, *Passion and Cunning*, p.8.

60 CCO'B, 'An Exalted Nationalism', (London) *Times*, 28 January 1989.

61 CCO'B, *States of Ireland*, p.16.

62 CCO'B, *States of Ireland*, p.19.

63 CCO'B, *States of Ireland*, p.152.

64 Maire and Conor Cruise O'Brien, *Concise History of Ireland* (London: Thames and Hudson, 1972), p.172.

65 Maire and Conor Cruise O'Brien, *Concise History of Ireland*, p.48.

66 CCO'B, *The Siege: The Saga of Israel and Zionism* (London: Paladin, 1986), p.21; CCO'B, 'What Can Become of South Africa?', *Atlantic Monthly*, March 1986.

67 CCO'B, *States of Ireland*, p.65.

68 CCO'B, *What Can Become of South Africa?*.

69   CCO'B, *States of Ireland*, p.310.

70   CCO'B, *States of Ireland*, p.311.

71   CCO'B, *States of Ireland*, pp.312–13.

72   CCO'B, *States of Ireland*, p.315.

73   Mark Patrick Hederman, 'The Crane Bag and the North', *The Crane Bag*, 1980, vol.4.1, 94–103, p.98.

74   CCO'B, 'Nationalism and the Reconquest of Ireland', *The Crane Bag*, 1977, 1.2, p.98.

75   CCO'B, 'Nationalism and the Reconquest of Ireland', 1.2, p.99.

76   CCO'B, *Neighbours*, p.48.

77   CCO'B, *Neighbours*, p.56.

78   CCO'B, *Neighbours*, pp.84–5.

79   Akenson, *Conor*, p.460.

80   Akenson, *Conor*, p.461.

81   Akenson, *Conor*, p.463.

82   CCO'B, *The Siege*, pp.330–1.

83   CCO'B, *The Siege*, p.332.

84   CCO'B, *The Siege*, p.332.

85   CCO'B, *What Can Become of South Africa?*, p.154.

86   CCO'B, *What Can Become of South Africa?*, p.124.

87   CCO'B, *What Can Become of South Africa?*, p.132.

88   CCO'B, 'Bobby Sands: Mutations of Nationalism', in *Passion and Cunning* (originally published in *The New York Review of Books* 21 April 1886), p.211.

89   See also CCO'B, 'The Wrath of Ages; Nationalism's Primordial Roots', *Foreign Affairs*, November/December 1993, pp.142–9.

90   CCO'B, *Godland: Reflections on Religion and Nationalism* (Cambridge Mass: Harvard University Press, 1987), pp.40–2.

91   CCO'B, *Godland: Reflections on Religion and Nationalism*, p.206.

92   Akenson, *Conor*, p.146.

93   CCO'B, *Memoir*, p.426.

94   CCO'B, *Memoir*, pp.448–57.

95   Seamus Deane, 'Unhappy at Home', *The Crane Bag*, 1977, 1.2, 62–4.

96   Seamus Deane, 'Unhappy at Home', *The Crane Bag*, 1977, 1.2, 69.

Chapter Thirteen

1   Fintan O'Toole, *Meanwhile Back at the Ranch: The Politics of Irish Beef* (London: Vintage, 1995).

2   Fintan O'Toole, *After the Ball* (Dublin: TASC/New Island, 2003), p.169.

3   Tony Kinsella and Fintan O'Toole, *Post Washington: Why America Can't Rule the World* (Dublin: TASC/New Island, 2005).

4   Fintan O'Toole, *Ship of Fools: How Stupidity and Corruption Sank the Celtic Tiger* (London: Faber and Faber, 2009).

5   Fintan O'Toole, *Enough is Enough: How to Build a New Republic* (London: Faber and Faber, 2010).

6   Fintan O'Toole, 'A History of Ireland in 100 Objects: Act of Union Blacklist, Early 19th century', *Irish Times*, 14 July 2012.

7   Fintan O'Toole, *A Mass for Jesse James: A Journey through 1980's Ireland* (Dublin: Raven Press, 1990).

8   Fintan O'Toole, 'Our Boys', in *The Ex-Isle of Erin* (Dublin: New Island, 1997), p.74.

9   Fintan O'Toole, 'Going West: The Country Versus the City Irish Writing', *The Crane Bag*, 1985, 9.2, 111–16.

10   O'Toole, *Going West*, p.111.

11   Fintan O'Toole, 'Afterword', to Julia Furay and Redmond O'Hanlon (eds), *Critical Moments: Fintan O'Toole on Irish Theatre* (Dublin: Carysfort Press, 2003), p.382.

12   Fintan O'Toole, *A Traitor's Kiss: The Life of Richard Brinsley Sheridan* (London: Granta, 1997).

13   O'Toole, *A Traitor's Kiss*, p.230.

14   Republished as Fintan O'Toole, 'The Southern Question', Dermot Bolger (ed.) *Letters from the New Ireland* (Dublin: Raven Arts Press, 1991).

15   Basil Chubb, 'Going about Persecuting Civil Servants: The Role of the Irish Parliamentary Representative', *Political Studies*, 1963, 10.3, 272–86.

16   Fintan O'Toole, *The Ex-Isle of Ireland* (Dublin: Island Books, 1997), p.19.

17   O'Toole, *The Ex-Isle of Ireland*, p.47.

18   O'Toole, *The Ex-Isle of Ireland*, p.52.

19   O'Toole, *Meanwhile Back at the Ranch*, p.35.

20   O'Toole, *Meanwhile Back at the Ranch*, p.93.

21   O'Toole, *Meanwhile Back at the Ranch*, p.64.

22   O'Toole, *Meanwhile Back at the Ranch*, p.25.

23   Elaine A. Byrne, *Political Corruption in Ireland 1922–2010* (Manchester: Manchester University Press, 2012), p.125.

24   O'Toole, *Meanwhile Back at the Ranch*, p.93.

25   O'Toole, *Meanwhile Back at the Ranch*, p.18.

26   O'Toole, *Meanwhile Back at the Ranch*, p.21.

27   Byrne, *Political Corruption in Ireland*, p.106.

28   Byrne, *Political Corruption in Ireland*, p.180.

29   O'Toole, *Ship of Fools*, p.31.

30   O'Toole, *Ship of Fools*, p.33.

31   O'Toole, *Ship of Fools*, p.38.

32   O'Toole, *Meanwhile Back at the Ranch*, p.25.

33   O'Toole, *Meanwhile Back at the Ranch*, p.68.

34   O'Toole, *Ship of Fools*, p.183.

35   O'Toole, *Ship of Fools*, p.27.

36   O'Toole, *Ship of Fools*, p.88.

37   O'Toole, *After the Ball*, p.133.

38   O'Toole, *Enough is Enough*, p.216.

39   Byrne, *Political Corruption in Ireland*, p.238.

40   Byrne, *Political Corruption in Ireland*, p.238.

41   O'Toole, *Enough is Enough*, p.2.

42   O'Toole, *Enough is Enough*, p.5.

43   O'Toole, *Enough is Enough*, p.17.

44   O'Toole, *Enough is Enough*, p.17.

45   O'Toole, *Enough is Enough*, p.32.

46   O'Toole, *Enough is Enough*, p.216.

47   O'Toole, *Enough is Enough*, p.237.

48   Lee Komito, 'Irish Clientelism: A Reappraisal', *The Economic and Social Review*, 1984, 15.3, 173–94.

49   O'Toole, *Enough is Enough*, p.42.

50   Except amongst like-minded academics. See Peadar Kirby and Mary Murphy, *Towards a Second Republic: Irish Politic after the Celtic Tiger* (London: Pluto Press, 2011).

51   Keith Ridgeway, *Fintan O'Toole*, http://keithridgeway.com/2011/03/05.

52   Podcast of Marian Finucane Show, 21 January 2011. Available from http://www.rte.ie.

53   Podcast of Marian Finucane Show.

54   Niamh Moore and Sean Ross, *The Banksters* (Dublin: Penguin Ireland, 2009).

55   Fintan O'Toole, 'Ireland Isn't Even Capable of Having a Proper Crisis', *Irish Times*, 19 November 2011.

56   Fintan O'Toole, 'Review of *The Business of Blood* by Donal O'Kelly and Kenneth Glenaan', *Irish Times*, 26 September 1995.

Chapter Fourteen

1   Jeremiah Newman, *Studies in Political Morality* (London: Scepter, 1962), p.688.

2   Nicholas Canny, *Making Ireland British: 1580–1650* (Oxford: Oxford University Press, 2001), p.553.

3   Kevin Whelan, 'An Underground Gentry? Catholic Middlemen in Eighteenth-Century Ireland', in James S. Donnolly and Kerby A. Miller (eds), *Irish Popular Culture: 1650–1850* (Dublin: Irish Academic Press, 1998), p.121.

4   James Connolly, *Labour in Irish History* (Dublin, 1912).

5   Daniel Corkery, *The Hidden Ireland: A study of Gaelic Minster in the Eighteenth Century* (Dublin: Gill and Macmillan, 1970, originally published 1924).

6   Daniel Corkery, *Synge and Anglo-Irish Literature* (Dublin: Longmans, 1931) pp.38–9.

7   Roy Foster, *Yeats: A Life: II The Arch Poet* (Oxford: Oxford University Press, 2003), p.411.

8   W. B. Yeats, 'Preface', to *The Words Upon the Window Pane* (Dublin: Cuala Press, 1934).

9   Michael Tierney, 'Daniel O'Connell and the Gaelic Past', *Studies*, 1938, 27.107, 353–80.

10 Sean O'Faoláin, *King of the Beggars* (Dublin: Cahill Printers, 1938).

11 Tierney, *O'Connell and the Gaelic Past*, pp.136–9.

12 Kevin Whelan, 'Between: The Politics of Culture in Friel's *Translations*', *Field Day Review* 6, 2010, 7–27, p.8.

13 Kevin Whelan, 'Between: The Politics of Culture in Friel's *Translations*', p.13.

14 Daniel O'Connell (1833) cited in Whelan, p.13.

15 Declan Kiberd, 'Strangers in their Own Country', in Edna Longley and Declan Kiberd, *Multi-Culturalism: The View From The Two Irelands* (Armagh, Centre for Cross Border Studies, 2001), p.67.

16 Seamus Heaney, 'Forked Tongues, Ceilís and Incubators', *Fortnight*, 1983, 197.

17 Whelan, *Politics of Culture*, pp.161–2.

18 Edward Said, *Orientalism* (New York: Pantheon, 1978).

19 Donald R. Pearce (ed.) *The Senate Speeches of W. B. Yeats* (London: Prenderville, 2001), p.99.

20 Frank O'Connor, 'The Old Age of the Poet', *The Bell*, 1941, 1.5, 7–9.

21 W. B. Yeats, 'Introduction', *The Words Upon the Window Pane* (Dublin: Cuala Press, 1934).

22 F. L. S. Lyons, 'Yeats and the Anglo-Irish Twilight', in Oliver MacDonagh, W. F. Mandle and Pauric Travers (eds.), *Irish Culture and Nationalism: 1750–1950* (London: Macmillan, 1983), p.230.

23 Richard Bellamy, *Victorian Liberalism: Nineteenth Century Political Thought and Practice* (London: Routledge, 1990), p.2.

24 Bellamy, *Victorian Liberalism*, p.7.

25 Freidrich Engels, *The Condition of the Working Class in England* (London, 1892), p.122.

26 Thomas A. Boylan and Timothy P. Foley, *Political Economy and Colonial Ireland* (London: Routledge, 1992), p.117.

27 W. N. Hancock, 'On the Use of the Doctrine of Laissez-Faire in Investigating the Economic Resources of Ireland', *Transactions of the Dublin Statistical Society*, 1847, 1, 9.

28 W. N. Hancock, 'On the Economic Causes of the Present State of Agriculture in Ireland, Part 1', *Transactions of the Dublin Statistical Society*, 1848a, 1, 6.

29 Boylan and Foley, *Political Economy and Colonial Economy*, p.4.

30 Hancock, *On the Use of the Doctrine of Laissez-Faire*, p.16.

31 J. S. Mill, 'What Has To Be Done With Ireland?' (1948), in John A. Robson (ed.), *Essays on England, Ireland and the Empire by John Stuart Mill: Collected Works Volume VI* (London: Routledge, 1996), p.502.

32 J. S. Mill, *Hansard (Parliamentary Debates)*, 12 March 1868, cols. 1517–18.

33 J. S. Mill, *England and Ireland* (London: Longman, Green, Reader and Dyer, 1868), p.36.

34 Tony Fahey, 'The Family Economy in the Development of Welfare Regimes: A Case Study', *European Sociological Review*, 2011, 18.1, 51–64.

35 Robert Skidelsky, *John Maynard Keynes: The Economist as Saviour 1920–1937* (London: Macmillan, 1992), p.479.

36 Tom Garvin, *Preventing the Future: Why Was Ireland So Poor for So long?* (Dublin: Gill and Macmillan, 2005).

37 J. J. Lee, *Ireland 1912–1985: Politics and Society* (Cambridge: Cambridge University Press, 1989), p.647.

38 Charles Kingsley in an 1860 letter to his wife cited from L. P. Curtis, *Anglo-Saxons and Celts, A Study of Anti-Irish Prejudice in Victorian England* (New York: New York University Press, 1968), p.84.

39 Aron I. Abell, 'The Catholic Factor in Urban Welfare in the Early Period: 1850–1880', *The Review of Politics*, 1952, 14.3, 289–324, p.301; Margaret Preston, 'Race, Class and the Language of Charity in Nineteenth Century Dublin', in Tadhg Foley and Sean Ryder, *Ideology in Ireland in the Nineteenth-Century* (Dublin: Four Courts, 1998), p.101.

40 Bryan Fanning, 'From Developmental Ireland to Migration Nation: Immigration and Shifting Rules of Belonging in the Republic of Ireland', *The Economic and Social Review*, 2010, 41.3, 295–412, pp.403–4.

41 Sean Maher, *The Road to God Knows Where: A Memoir of a Travelling Boyhood* (Dublin: Veritas, 1998), p.164.

42 Patrick Pearse, *An Claidheamh Soluis*, 4 August 1906.

43 Garret Fitzgerald, 'Civic and Irish Republicanism', in Iseult Honohan (ed.), *Republicanism in Ireland* (Manchester: Manchester University Press, 2008), p.165.

44 Margaret O'Callaghan, 'Reconsidering the Republican Tradition in Nineteenth-Century Ireland', in Honohan, *Republicanism in Ireland*, p.38.

45 Dáil Éireann, *Volume 1*, 21 January 1919.

46 Fintan O'Toole, 'Do You Know What a Republic Is?', in O'Toole (ed.) *Up the Republic!: Towards a New Ireland* (London: Faber and Faber, 2012), p.14.

47 Tom Garvin, 'An Irish Republican Tradition', in Honohan (ed.), *Republicanism in Ireland*, pp.23–4.

48 O'Toole, 'Do You Know What a Republic Is?', in O'Toole (ed.), *Up the Republic!*, pp.18–20.

49 Michael D. Higgins, *Renewing the Republic* (Dublin: Liberties Press, 2011), p.21.

50 Theo Dorgan, 'Law Poetry and the Republic', in O'Toole (ed.), *Up the Republic!*, pp.200–2.

51 Dorgan, 'Law, Poetry and the Republic', in O'Toole (ed.), *Up the Republic!*, p.204.

52 Bryan Fanning, *New Guests of the Irish Nation* (Dublin: Irish Academic Press, 2009), p.2.

SELECT BIBLIOGRAPHY

Newspaper articles, correspondence and archival material are cited in the Notes section.

Abell, Aron, 'The Catholic Factor in Urban Welfare in the Early Period: 1850–1880', *The Review of Politics*, 1952, 14.3, 289–324.

Akenson, Donald Harman (ed.), *Anthology: A Biography of Conor Cruise O'Brien Volume II* (Belfast: McGill-Queens University Press, 1994).

—— *Conor: A Biography of Conor Cruise O'Brien* (New York: Cornell University Press, 1994).

Augustine, *The City of God* (New York: Denton, 1947).

Avery, John, *Progress, Poverty and Population: Re-reading Condorcet, Godwin and Malthus* (London: Frank Cass, 1997).

Balfour, Graham, *The Educational Systems of Great Britain and Ireland* (Oxford: Clarendon, 1898).

Barnard, T. C., 'Planters and Policies in Cromwellian Ireland', *Past and Present*, 1973, 61, 31–69, p.32.

—— 'Lord Broghill, Vincent Gookin and the Cork Elections of 1659', *The English Historical Review*, 1973, 88.347, 352–65.

—— 'Sir William Petty as Kerry Ironmaster', *Proceedings of the Royal Irish Academy. Section C: Archaeology, Celtic Studies, History, Linguistics, Literature*, 1982, 82C, 1–32.

—— 'William Petty', *Oxford Dictionary of National Biography*, 43.

Barrington, Donal, 'United Ireland', *Studies*, 1957, 46, 379–402.

Bartlett, Thomas, *Ireland: A History* (Oxford: Oxford University Press, 2010).

Bellamy, Richard, *Victorian Liberalism: Nineteenth Century Political Thought and Practice* (London: Routledge, 1990).

Berman, David, 'Enlightenment and Counter-Enlightenment in Irish Philosophy', *Archiv fur Geschiche der Philosophie*, band 64 (1982), shelf 2, 148–65, 257–9.

Berrisford-Ellis, Peter, *A History of the Irish Working Class* (London: Victor Gollancz, 1972).

Blanshard, Paul, *American Freedom and Catholic Power* (Boston, 1949).

—— *The Irish and Catholic Power* (Boston, 1953).

Bolger, Dermot (ed.) *Letters from the New Ireland* (Dublin: Raven Arts Press, 1991).

Boylan, Thomas A. and Foley, Timothy P., *Political Economy and Colonial Ireland* (London: Routledge, 1992).

Brennan, Martin, *Schools of Kildare and Leighlin* (Dublin: Gill and Son, 1935).

Brest, Richard, 'Richard Whately', *Oxford Dictionary of National Biography*, 2004, 58, 396.

Burke, Edmund, *Reflections on the Revolution in France* (London: Penguin, 1968).

—— *Letters, Speeches and Tracts on Irish Affairs* (ed.) Matthew Arnold (London: McMillan, 1881).

Busteed, M. A. and Hodgson, R. I., 'Irish Responses to Urban Life in Early Nineteenth-Century Manchester', *The Geographical Journal*, 162.2, 139–53.

Butterfield, Herbert, *The Whig Interpretation of History* (London: Bell, 1931).

Byrne, Elaine A., *Political Corruption in Ireland 1922–2010* (Manchester: Manchester University Press, 2012).

Canny, Nicholas, *Making Ireland British: 1580–1650* (Oxford: Oxford University Press, 2001).

Carlton, Grace, *Friedrich Engels: The Shadow Prophet* (London: Pall Mall Press, 1965).

Carlyle, Thomas, *Chartism* (Boston: Charles Little and James Brown, 1940).

—— 'Occasional Discourse on the Nigger Question', *Fraser's Magazine*, December 1849.

Chambers, Alan D., *Jonathan Swift and the Burden of the Future* (Newark: University of Delaware Press, 1995).

Chubb, Basil, 'Going About Persecuting Civil Servants: The Role of the Irish Parliamentary Representative', *Political Studies*, 1963, 10.3, 272–86.

Connolly, James, *Erin's Hope: The End and the Means* (Dublin, 1897).

—— *Socialism Made Easy* (Chicago: Charles H. Kerr, 1909).

—— *Labour in Irish History* (Dublin, 1912).

—— *Selected Political Writings* (ed.) Owen Dudley Edwards and Bernard Ransom (New York: Grove, 1974).

—— *Collected Works: Volume One* (Dublin: New Books, 1987).

Corkery, Daniel, *The Hidden Ireland: A Study of Gaelic Minster in the Eighteenth Century* (Dublin: Gill and Macmillan, 1970).

—— *Synge and Anglo-Irish Literature* (Dublin: Longmans, 1931).

Cullen, Mary and Luddy, Maria (eds), *Women, Power and Consciousness in 19th Century Ireland* (Dublin: Attic Press, 1995).

Cullen Owens, Rosemary, *Smashing Times: A History of the Irish Women's Suffrage Movement 1889–1922* (Dublin: Attic Press, 1984).

Curtis, E. and McDowell, R. B., *Irish Historical Documents* (London: Metheun, 1943).

Curtis, L. P., *Anglo-Saxons and Celts: A Study of Anti-Irish Prejudice in Victorian England* (New York: New York University Press, 1968).

Daly, Dominic, *The Young Douglas Hyde* (Dublin: Irish Academic Press, 1974).

Daly, Mary E., 'Women in the Irish Free State 1922–39: The Interaction Between Economics and Ideology', *Journal of Women's History*, 1995, 6.4, 99–116.

Davitt, Michael, *The Fall of Feudalism in Ireland* (New York: Harper, 1904).

de Giustino, David, 'Finding an Archbishop: The Whigs and Richard Whately in 1831', in *Church History*, 1995, 64.2, 218–36.

—— 'Disconnecting Church and State: Richard Whately's Ideas in the 1830s', *Albion: A Quarterly Journal Connected with British Studies*, 2003, 35.1, 55–70.

Deane, Herbert A., *The Political and Social Ideas of St. Augustine* (New York: Columbia University Press, 1966).

Deane, Seamus, 'Unhappy at Home', *The Crane Bag*, 1977, 1.2, 62–4.

Dobbins, Gregory, 'Wherever Green is Red: James Connolly and Postcolonial Theory', *Nepantla: Views from the South*, 2000, 1.3, 605–48.

Donnolly, James S. and Miller Kerby, A. (eds), *Irish Popular Culture: 1650–1850* (Dublin: Irish Academic Press, 1998).

Duddy, Thomas, *A History of Irish Thought* (London: Routledge, 2002).

Dudley, Rev H., *A Short Address to the Most Reverend and Honourable William, Lord Primate of Ireland, recommending some Commutation or Modification of the tithes of that Country: with a few remarks on the present state of the Irish Church* (London, 1808).

Duffy, Charles Gavan, *Conversations with Carlyle* (London: Sampson, Low Marston and Company, 1892).

Dunleavy, Janet Egleston and Dunleavy, Gareth W., *Douglas Hyde: A Maker of Modern Ireland* (Berkeley: University of California, 1991).

Dunn, John, *Political Obligation in its Historical Context* (Cambridge: Cambridge University Press, 1980).

Ellman, Richard, *James Joyce* (Oxford: Oxford University Press, 1966).

Engels, Friedrich, *The Condition of the Working Class in England* (London, 1892).

English, Richard, 'Socialism and Republican Schism in Ireland: The Emergence of the Republican Congress in 1934', *Irish Historical Studies*, 1990, xxvii.105, 48–65.

Fahey, Tony, 'The Family Economy in the Development of Welfare Regimes: A Case Study', *European Sociological Review*, 2002, 18.1, 51–64.

Fanning, Bryan, *Evil, God, the Greater Good and Rights: the Philosophical Origins of Social Problems* (New York: Edwin Mellon, 2007).

—— *The Quest for Modern Ireland: The Battle of Ideas 1912–86* (Dublin: Irish Academic Press, 2008).

—— *New Guests of the Irish Nation* (Dublin: Irish Academic Press, 2009).

—— 'From Developmental Ireland to Migration Nation: Immigration and Shifting Rules of Belonging in the Republic of Ireland', *The Economic and Social Review'*, 2010, 41.3, 295–412.

—— *Racism and Social Change in the Republic of Ireland* (Manchester: Manchester University Press, 2012).

—— (ed.) *An Irish Century: Studies 1912–2012* (Dublin: UCD Press, 2012).

—— 'George Tyrell, Jacques Maritain and the Challenge of Modernity', *Studies*, 2012, 101.403, 291–9.

Fanning, Bryan and Garvin, Tom, *The Books that Define Ireland* (Dublin: Merrion, 2014).

Ferriter, Diarmuid, *The Transformation of Ireland* (London: Profile, 2004).

Finlay S. J., Peter, 'Socialism and Catholic Teaching', *Studies*, 1919, 8, 352–66.

FitzGerald, Garrett, *Towards a New Ireland* (London: Charles Knight, 1972).

Fitzmaurice, Edmond, *The Life of Sir William Petty 1623–1687* (London: John Murray, 1895).

—— (ed.) *The Petty Papers: Volume II* (London: Routledge, 1997).

Fitzpatrick, William John, *Memoirs of Archbishop Whately with a Glance at his Contemporaries and Times: Volume 1* (London: Chard Bentley, 1864).

Foley, Tadhg and Ryder, Sean (eds), *Ideology in Ireland in the Nineteenth-Century* (Dublin: Four Courts, 1998).

Foster, A. M., 'The Molyneux Family', *Dublin Historical Record*, 1960, 16.1, 9–15.

Foster, Roy, *W. B. Yeats: A Life vol. 1, The Apprentice Mage* (Oxford: Oxford University Press, 1997).

—— *W. B. Yeats: A Life: II The Arch Poet* (Oxford: Oxford University Press, 2003).

Froude, James Anthony, *Life of Carlyle* (abridged) (London: John Murray, 1979).

Furay, Julia and O'Hanlon, Redmond (eds), *Critical Moments: Fintan O'Toole on Irish Theatre* (Dublin: Carysfort Press, 2003).

Gibbons, Luke, *Edmund Burke and Ireland: Aesthetics, Politics and the Colonial Sublime* (Cambridge: Cambridge University Press, 2004).

Garvin, Tom, *Preventing the Future: Why Was Ireland So Poor for So Long?* (Dublin: Gill and Macmillan, 2005).

—— 'Imaginary Cassandra? Conor Cruise O'Brien as Public Intellectual in Ireland', *Irish University Review*, Autumn–Winter 2007, 37.2, 430–40.

Gillespie, Raymond, *Seventeenth Century Ireland* (Dublin: Gill and Macmillan, 2006).

Glausser, Wayne, 'Three Approaches to Locke and the Slave Trade', *Journal of the History of Ideas*, 1990, 51.2, 199–216.

Godwin, William, *Enquiry Concerning Political Justice and its Influence on General Virtue and Happiness, Vol II* (London, 1793).

Goldring, Maurice, *Pleasant the Scholar's Life: Irish Intellectuals and the Construction of the Nation State* (London: Serif, 1993).

Gookin, Vincent, *The Great Case of Transplantation in Ireland Discussed* (London: John Cook, 1955).

Greaves, C. Desmond, *The Irish Transport and General Worker's Union: The Formative Years 1909–1923* (Dublin: Gill and Macmillan, 1982).

Grey, Peter, *The Making of the Irish Poor Law, 1815–43* (Manchester: Manchester University Press, 2009).

Groenewegen, Peter, 'Thomas Carlyle, "The Dismal Science", and the Contemporary Political Economy of Slavery', *History of Economics Review*, 2001, 75–94.

Gywnn, Denis, 'Dr Hussey and Mr Burke', *Studies*, 1928, 17.68, 529–68.

Hancock, W. N., 'On the Use of the Doctrine of Laissez-Faire in Investigating the Economic Resources of Ireland, *Transactions of the Dublin Statistical Society*, 1847, 1, 9.

—— 'On the Economic Causes of the Present State of Agriculture in Ireland, Part 1', *Transactions of the Dublin Statistical Society*, 1848, 1, 6.

Hart, H. L. A., *Law, Liberty and Morality* (Oxford: Oxford University Press, 1962).

Hazlitt, William, *A Reply to the Essay on Population By the Rev. TR. Malthus in A Series of Letters to Which is Added Extracts from the Essay With Notes* (London: Longman, Hurst, Rees and Orme, 1807).

Heaney, Seamus, 'Forked Tongues, Ceilís and Incubators', *Fortnight*, 1983, 197.

Hederman, Mark Patrick, 'The Crane Bag and the North', *The Crane Bag*, 1980, 4.1, 94–103, p.98.

Hegel, Georg, *Hegel's Political Writings*, ed. ZA Pelgczynski, trans. T. M. Knox (Oxford: Oxford University Press, 1964).

Higgins, Michael D., *Renewing the Republic* (Dublin: Liberties Press, 2011).

Honohan, Iseult (ed.) *Republicanism in Ireland* (Manchester: Manchester University Press, 2008).

Hill, Jacqueline, 'Ireland without Union: Molyneux and His Legacy', in John Robertson (ed.) *A Union for Empire: Political Thought and the British Union of 1707* (Cambridge: Cambridge University Press, 1995).

Hull, C. H., *Economic Writings of Sir William Petty: Vol. I* (New York: Augustus Kelly, 1964).

—— *Economic Writings of Sir William Petty: Vol. II* (New York: Augustus Kelly, 1964).

Hume, David, *David Hume's Political Essays*, ed. C. W. Hendel (New York, 1953).

Hunt, Tristam, *The Frock-Coated Communist: The Revolutionary Life of Friedrich Engels* (London: Allen Lane, 2009).

Hyde, Douglas, *The Necessity of De-Anglicising Ireland* (Dublin, 1892).

Hyland, Aine and Milne, Kenneth (eds), *Irish Educational Documents Vol. 1* (Dublin: Church of Ireland Education, 1987).

Inglis, Tom, *Moral Monopoly: The Rise and Fall of the Catholic Church in Modern Ireland* (Dublin: UCD Press, 1998).

Irwin, Liam, 'Jeremiah Newman', *Dictionary of Irish Biography* (Cambridge: Cambridge University Press, 2009).

James, Patricia, *Population Malthus: His Life and Times* (London: Routledge and Kegan Paul, 1979).

Jordan, Thomas E., *A Copper Farthing: Sir William Petty and his Times* (Sunderland: University of Sunderland Press, 2007).

—— *Sir William Petty, 1623–1687: The Genius Entrepreneur of Seventeenth-Century Ireland* (New York: Edwin Mellon, 2007).

Keogh, Dermot, 'The Jesuits and the 1937 Constitution', in Bryan Fanning (ed.) *An Irish Century: Studies 1912–2012* (Dublin: UCD Press, 2012).

Keenan, Marie, *Child Sexual Abuse and the Catholic Church: Gender, Power and Organizational Culture* (Oxford: New York, 2012).

Kelly, Patrick, 'Molyneux and the Spirit of Liberty in Eighteenth-Century Ireland', *Eighteenth-Century Ireland*, 1988, 3, 136–40.

—— 'Perceptions of Locke in Eighteenth-Century Ireland', *Proceedings of the Royal Irish Academy*, 1989, 89c, 17–35.

Kinsella, Tony and O'Toole, Fintan, *Post Washington: Why America Can't Rule the World* (Dublin: TASC/New Island, 2005).

Kirby, Peadar and Murphy, Mary, *Towards a Second Republic: Irish Politic after the Celtic Tiger* (London: Pluto Press, 2011).

Komito, Lee, 'Irish Clientelism: A Reappraisal', *The Economic and Social Review* 1984, 15.3, 173–94.

Larkin, Emmet, 'The Devotional Revolution in Ireland, 1850–75', *The American, Historical Review* 1977, 77.3, 625–52.

Lee, J. J., *Ireland 1912–1985: Politics and Society* (Cambridge: Cambridge University Press, 1989).

Leslie, Charles, *Considerations of importance to Ireland in a letter to a member of parliament thereupon the occasion of Mr Molyneux's later book* (Early English Books Online, facsimile of 1698 edition).

Levenson, Leah, *With Wooden Sword: A Portrait of Francis Sheehy Skeffington Militant Pacifist* (Boston: Northeastern University Press).

Lock, F. P., *Edmund Burke: Volume I, 1730–1784* (Oxford: Clarendon Press, 2008).

Locke, John, *An Essay Concerning Human Understanding*, ed. P. H. Nidditch (Oxford: Oxford University Press, 1975).

—— *Second Treatise of Government*, ed. C. B. McPherson (Indianapolis and Cambridge: Hackett Publishing Company, 1980).

Locke J., Molyneux, W. and Molyneux T., *Some Familiar Letters Between Mr Locke and Several of his Friends* (London: A. and J Churchill, 1708).

Longley, Edna and Kiberd, Declan, *Multi-Culturalism: The View from the Two Irelands* (Armagh: Centre for Cross Border Studies, 2001).

Lydon, James, *The Making of Ireland* (Routledge: London, 1998).

Lynch, Niamh, 'Defining Irish Nationalist Anti-Imperialism: Thomas Davis and John Mitchel', *Éire-Ireland*, 2007, 42.1 and 2, 82–107.

Lyons, F. L. S., *Ireland Since the Famine* (Glasgow: Fontana, 1973).

McBride, Ian, *Eighteenth Century Ireland* (Dublin: Gill and McMillan, 2009).

McBride, Sean, *That Day's Struggle: A Memoir 1904–1951* (Dublin: Curragh Press, 2005).

McCarthy, John P., *Kevin O'Higgins: Builder of the Irish State* (Dublin: Irish Academic Press, 2006).

McCormack, W. J., 'The Historian as Writer or Critic? Conor Cruise O'Brien and His Biographers', *Irish Historical Studies*, 1996, 30.117, 111–19.

McCormick, Ted, 'Transmutation, Inclusion and Exclusion: Political Arithmetic from Charles II to William III', *Journal of Historical Sociology*, 2007, 20.3, 255–78.

MacDonagh, Oliver, Mandle, W. F. and Travers, Pauric (eds), *Irish Culture and Nationalism: 1750–1950* (London: Macmillan, 1983).

McKenna, S.J. Lambert, *The Social Teachings of James Connolly* (Dublin: Catholic Truth Society, 1921).

—— 'The Bolsheviks', *Studies*, 1921, 10, 218–39.

Mac Suibhne, Peadar, *Paul Cullen and His Contemporaries, vol.3* (Kildare: Leinster Leader, 1963).

—— *Paul Cullen and His Contemporaries, vol. 4* (Kildare: Leinster Leader, 1974).

—— *Paul Cullen and His Contemporaries, vol. 5* (Kildare: Leinster Leader, 1977).

Maher, Sean, *The Road to God Knows Where: A Memoir of a Travelling Boyhood* (Dublin: Veritas, 1998).

Malthus, T. R., *An Essay on the Principle of Population as it Affects the Future Improvement of Society with Remarks on the Speculations of Mr. Goodwin, M. Condorcet and Other Writers* (London: J. Johnson, 1798).

—— *A Letter to Samuel Whitbread Esq., MP on his Proposed Bill for the Amendment of the Poor Laws* (London: Johnson and Hatchard, 1807).

—— *An Essay on the Principle of Population Or A View of Its Past And Present Effects on Human Happiness With An Inquiry into Our Prospects Respecting The Future Removal Or Mitigation Of The Evils Which It Occasions,* (Everyman edition, 1803).

—— *Occasional Papers of TR Malthus on Ireland, Population and Political Economy*, ed. Bernard Semmel (New York: Burt Franklin, 1963).

—— *Principles of Political Economy: 2nd Edition* (New York: Augustus M. Kelly, 1968).

Martin, Amy E., 'Blood Transfusions: Constructions of Racial Difference, the English Working Class, and Revolutionary Possibility in the Work of Carlyle and Engels', *Victorian Literature and Culture*, 2004, 32.1, 83–102.

Mascon, I. and Young, A. J., 'Sir William Petty F.R.S.', *News and Notes of the Royal Society*, 1960, 79–90.

Merman, David, 'David Hume on the 1961 Rebellion in Ireland', *Studies*, 1976, 65.258, 101–12.

Mill, John Stuart, *England and Ireland* (London: Longman, Green, Reader and Dyer, 1868).
—— *Hansard (Parliamentary Debates)*, 12 March 1868, cols. 1517–18.
Mitchel, John, *Jail Journal* (Dublin: Gill and Son, 1913).
—— *The Last Conquest of Ireland (perhaps)* (Dublin: UCD Press, 2005).
Moore, Niamh and Ross, Sean, *The Banksters* (Dublin: Penguin Ireland, 2009).
Morrow, John, Carlyle, Thomas, 'Young Ireland and The "Condition of Ireland Question" ', *The Historical Journal*, 2008, 51.3, 643–67.
Molyneux, Capel, *An Account of the Family and Descendents of Thomas Molyneux* (Evesham, 1820).
Molyneux, William, *The Case of Ireland's being Bound by Acts of Parliament in England, Stated* (facsimile, Online Library of Liberty, 1698).
Moody, T. W. and Martin, F. X. (eds), *The Course of Irish History* (Dublin: Mercier Press, 1967).
Moran, D. P., *The Philosophy of Irish-Ireland* (Dublin, 1905).
Murphy, Cliona, *The Women's Suffrage Movement and Irish Society in the Early Twentieth Century* (New York: Harvester Wheatsheaf, 1989).
Murphy, David and Devlin, Martina, *The Banksters: How a Powerful Elite Squandered Ireland's Wealth* (Dublin: Penguin Ireland, 2009).
Nevin, Donal, *James Connolly: A Full Life* (Dublin: Gill and Macmillan, 2005).
—— (ed.) *Between Comrades: James Connolly, Letters and Correspondence 1889–1916* (Dublin: Gill and Macmillan, 2007).
Newman, Jeremiah, 'On Church-State Relations', *Christus Rex*, January 1955, xi.1, 76–85.
—— 'Report on Limerick Rural Survey', *Christus Rex*, 1961, xv.1, 20–2.
—— *Studies in Political Morality* (Dublin: Scepter, 1962).
—— (ed.) *Vatican II: The Christian Layman* (Dublin: Scepter, 1966).
—— 'Vocations in Ireland: 1966', *Christus Rex*, 1967, xxi.2,105–22.
—— *Race, Migration and Integration* (London: Burns and Oates, 1968).
—— 'Socio-Political Aspects of Divorce', *Christus Rex*, 1969 xxiii.1, 5–15.
—— 'Progress and Planning', *Christus Rex*, 1970, xxiii.3, 173–86.
—— *Conscience Versus Law: Reflections of the Evolution of Natural Law* (Dublin: Talbot Press, 1971).
—— *The State of Ireland* (Dublin: Four Courts Press, 1977).
—— *Ireland Must Choose* (Dublin: Four Courts Press, 1983).
—— *Puppets of Utopia: Can Irish Democracy Be Taken for Granted?* (Dublin: Four Court Press, 1987).
—— *The Postmodern Church* (Dublin: Four Courts Press, 1990).
Nietzsche, Friedrich, *The Gay Science, Second Edition*, 1887, trans. Josefine Nauckhoff, ed. Bernard Williams (Cambridge: Cambridge University Press, 2001).
O'Brien, Conor Cruise, 'A Sample of Loyalties', *Studies*, 1957, 46, 403–10.
—— *Parnell and His Party 1880–90* (Oxford: Clarendon Press, 1957).
—— *To Katanga and Back: A UN Case History* (London: Hutchinson, 1962).
—— *Murderous Angels: A Political Tragedy and Comedy in Black and White* (London: Hutchinson, 1969).
—— *States of Ireland* (London: Panther 1974, originally published 1972).
—— 'Nationalism and the Reconquest of Ireland', *The Crane Bag*, 1977, 1.2.
—— *Camus* (London: Fontana 1982, originally published 1970).

—— *The Siege: The Saga of Israel and Zionism* (London: Paladin, 1986).

—— *Godland: Reflections on Religion and Nationalism* (Cambridge, Mass: Harvard University Press, 1987).

—— *Passion and Cunning and Other Essays* (London: Weidenfield and Nicolson, 1988).

—— *The Great Melody: A Thematic Biography of Edmund Burke* (London: Sinclair Stevenson, 1992).

—— 'The Wrath of Ages: Nationalism's Primordial Roots', *Foreign Affairs*, November/December 1993, 142–9.

—— *Memoir: My Life and Themes* (London: Profile, 1998).

O'Brien, Gerard, 'The Grattan Mystique', *Eighteenth Century Ireland*, 1986, 1, 177–94.

O'Brien, Marie and O'Brien, Conor Cruise, *Concise History of Ireland* (London: Thames and Hudson, 1972).

O'Casey, Sean, *The Story of the Irish Citizen Army* (London: Maunsel and Co, 1919).

Ó Ceallaigh Ritschel, Nelson, 'Under Which Flag, 1916', *New Hibernia Review*, 1998, 2.4, 54–68.

O'Connor, Frank, 'The Old Age of the Poet', *The Bell*, 1941, 1.5, 7–9.

O'Connor, Rebecca, *Jenny Mitchel: Young Irelander* (Arizona: The O'Connor Trust, 1985).

O'Donnell, Donat, 'Horizon', *The Bell*, March 1945, 1030–8.

O'Donoghue, Patrick, 'Causes of the Opposition to Tithes, 1830–38', *Studia Hibernica*, No. 5, 1965, 7–28.

Ó Faoláin, Sean, *King of the Beggars: A Life of Daniel O'Connell, the Irish Liberator, in a Study of the Rise of the Modern Irish Democracy 1775–1847* (Dublin: Cahill Printers, 1938).

—— 'For the Future', *The Bell*, 1940, 1.2, 5–6.

O'Hegarty, P. S., *John Mitchel* (Dublin: Maunsel and Company, 1912).

—— *The Victory of Sinn Fein* (Dublin: Talbot Press, 1924).

O'Leary, Olivia, 'The Mullah of Limerick', *Magill*, 21 March 1985, 24–33.

O'Rourke, Kevin, 'Emigration and Living Standards in Ireland since the Famine', *Journal of Population Economics*, 1995, 8.4, 407–21.

O'Toole, Fintan, 'Going West: The Country Versus the City Irish Writing', *The Crane Bag*, 1985, 9.2, 111–16.

—— *A Mass for Jesse James: A Journey through 1980's Ireland* (Dublin: Raven Press, 1990).

—— *Meanwhile Back at the Ranch: The Politics of Irish Beef* (London: Vintage, 1995).

—— *A Traitor's Kiss: The Life of Richard Brinsley Sheridan* (London: Granta, 1997).

—— *The Ex-Isle of Erin* (Dublin: New Island, 1997).

—— *The Ex-Isle of Ireland* (Dublin: Island books, 1997).

—— *After the Ball* (Dublin: TASC/New Island, 2003).

—— *Ship of Fools: How Stupidity and Corruption Sank the Celtic Tiger* (London: Faber and Faber, 2009).

—— *Enough is Enough: How to Build a New Republic* (London: Faber and Faber, 2010).

—— *A History of Ireland in 100 Objects* (Dublin: Royal Irish Academy, 2013).

—— (ed.) *Up the Republic!: Towards a New Ireland* (London: Faber and Faber, 2012).

Parnell, Anne, *The Tale of a Great Sham* (Dublin, 1986).

Pearce, Donald R. (ed.), *The Senate Speeches of W. B. Yeats* (London: Prenderville, 2001).

Pearse, Patrick, *From a Hermitage* (Dublin: Irish Freedom Press, 1915).

—— *From a Hermitage*, 13 October 1913, *Collected Works of Padraic Pearse* (Dublin: Phoenix, 1917).

Petty, William, *Advice of Mr W. P. to Mr. Hartlib for the advancement of some particular parts of learning* (London, 1655).

—— *The Political Anatomy of Ireland* (Shannon: Irish University Press, 1970).

Quinn, James, 'John Mitchel and the Rejection of the Nineteenth Century', *Éire-Ireland*, I, 2003, 38.3–4, 98–108.

—— *John Mitchel* (Dublin: University College Dublin Press, 2008).

Rapport, Mick, *1848: Year of Revolution* (London: Abacus, 2008).

Reilly, Patrick, *Jonathan Swift: The Brave Disponder* (Carbondale: Southern Illinois University Press, 1982).

Robertson, John (ed.), *A Union for Empire: Political Thought and the British Union of 1707* (Cambridge: Cambridge University Press, 1995).

Robson, John A. (ed.), *Essays on England, Ireland and the Empire by John Stuart Mill: Collected Works Volume VI* (London: Routledge, 1996).

Roccaglia, Alessandro, *Petty: The Origins of Political Economy* (Cardiff: University College of Cardiff Press, 1985).

Ross, Shane, *The Bankers: How the Banks Bought Ireland to its Knees* (Dublin: Penguin Ireland, 2009).

Rothbard, Murray N., *Economic Thought before Adam Smith* (Alabama: Edward Elgar, 1995).

Ryan, Desmond, *James Connolly* (Dublin: Talbot Press, 1924).

—— (ed.) *James Connolly, Labour and Easter Week 1916* (Dublin: Sign of the Three Candles, 1949).

Said, Edward, *Orientalism* (New York: Pantheon, 1978).

Seigel, Jerold, *Marx's Fate: The Shape of a Life* (Pennsylvania: State University Press, 1978).

Sheehy Skeffington, Andrée, 'James Joyce and "Cupid's Confidante" ', *James Joyce Quarterly*, 1984, 21.3, 205–14.

—— *Skeff: A Life of Owen Sheehy Skeffington 1909–1970* (Dublin: Lilliput Press, 1991).

—— *The Ex-Isle of Erin* (Dublin: New Island, 1997), p.74.

Sheehy Skeffington, Andrée and Owens, Rosemary (eds), *Votes for Women, Irish Women's Struggle for the Vote* (Dublin, 1975).

Sheehy Skeffington, Francis, *In Dark and Evil Days* (Dublin: James Duffy & Co., 1936).

Sheehy Skeffington, Hanna, *British Militarism As I Have Known It* (New York, 1917).

—— 'Women in Politics', *The Bell*, 1943, 7.2, 143–8.

Simmons, A. J., *The Lockean Theory of Rights* (Princeton: Princeton University Press, 1994).

Skidelsky, Robert, *John Maynard Keynes: The Economist as Saviour 1920–1937* (London: Macmillan, 1992).

Somerville, Peter, 'A Catholic Labour College', *Studies*, 1921, 10, 391–400.

Steinberg, Jules, *Locke, Rousseau and the Idea of Consent: An Inquiry into the Liberal-Democratic Theory of Political Obligation* (London: Greenwood, 1978).

Strauss, Emil, *Sir William Petty: Portrait of a Genius* (London: Bodley Head, 1954).

Swift, Jonathan, *A Proposal For the Universal Use of Irish Manufacture in Clothes and Furniture and Houses, &c. Utterly Rejecting and Renouncing every Thing wearable that comes from England* (Dublin, 1720).

—— *A Modest Proposal For Preventing the Children of poor People in Ireland from being a Burden to their Parents or Country, and for making them beneficial to the Public* (Dublin, 1729).

—— *A Proposal that all the Ladies and Women of Ireland should appear constantly in Irish Manufactures* (Dublin, 1729).

—— *The Drapier's Letters and Other Works, 1714–1725 (The Works of Jonathan Swift, vol. X) I*, ed. H. Davies (Oxford, 1966).

Tanner, Marcus, *Ireland's Holy Wars: The Struggle for a Nation's Soul 1500–2000* (New Haven: Yale University Press, 2001).

Thompson, M. P., 'The Reception of Locke's Two Treatises of Government 1690–1705', *Political Studies*, 1976, 34.2, 184–91.

Thompson, William, *An Inquiry into the principles of the distribution of Wealth most conducive to Human Happiness as applied to the newly-proposed System of the Voluntary Equality of Wealth* (London: Longman, Hust Rees, Orne, Brown and Green, 1824).

—— *Labour Rewarded, the Claims of Labour and Capital Conciliated; or, How to Secure to Labour the Whole Product of its Exertions* (London: Hunt and Clarke, 1827).

—— *Practical Directions for the Speedy and Economical Establishment of Communities on Principles of Mutual Co-operation, United Possession's and Equality of Exertions and the Means of Enjoyments* (London, Strange and E. Wilson, 1830).

Thornley, David, 'Ireland: The End of an Era', *Studies*, 1964, 52, 1–17.

Tierney, Michael, 'Daniel O'Connell and the Gaelic Past', *Studies*, 1938, 27.107, 353–80.

Tod, Isabella M. S., 'Advanced Education for Girls of the Upper and Middle Classes', *Transactions of the National Association for the Promotion of Social Science* (London, 1874).

—— *On the Education of Girls of the Middle Class* (London, 1874).

Tone, Theobald Wolfe, *Life of Theobald Wolfe Tone*, ed. Tom Bartlett (Dublin: The Lilliput Press, 1998).

Turner, Michael, *Malthus and His Time* (London: Macmillan, 1986).

Urquhart, Diane, *Women in Ulster Politics 1890–1940* (Dublin: Irish Academic Press, 2000).

Valence, Edward, *The Glorious Revolution: 1688 Britain's Fight for Liberty* (London: Abacus, 2007).

Valiulis, Maryann Gialanella, 'Power, Gender and Identity in the Irish Free State', *Journal of Women's History*, 1995, 6.1, 117–35.

Walsh, Louis J., *John Mitchel* (Dublin: Talbot Press, 1934).

Ward, Margaret, *Hanna Sheehy Skeffington: A Life* (Cork: Attic Press, 1997).

Whately, E. Jane, *Life and Correspondence of Richard Whately, D.D. Late Archbishop of Dublin: Vol. 2* (London: Longmans, Green and Co, 1866).

Whately, Richard, *Thoughts on Secondary Punishments in a Letter to Earl Grey* (London: B. Fellows, 1832).

—— *The Past and Future of Ireland as Indicated By Its Educational System* (London: Ward, 1850).

Whelan, Diarmuid, *Conor Cruise O'Brien: Violent Notions* (Dublin: Irish Academic Press, 2009).

Whelan, Kevin, 'Between: The Politics of Culture in Friel's *Translations*', *Field Day Review*, 2010, 6, 7–27.

Yeats, W. B., *The Words Upon the Window Pane* (Dublin: Cuala Press, 1934).

—— *Last Poems (1936–9)* (Dublin: Cuala Press, 1939).

—— *The Senate Speeches of W. B. Yeats*, ed. Donald R. Pearce (London: Prenderville, 2001).

Young, James D., 'A Very English Socialism and the Celtic Fringe', *History Workshop*, 1993, 35.1, 135–52.

INDEX